Global Information So

Global Information Society Watch
2008

Steering committee

Karen Banks (APC)
Roberto Bissio (ITeM)
Anriette Esterhuysen (APC)
Paul Maassen (Hivos)
Loe Schout (Hivos)
Magela Sigillito (ITeM)

Coordination committee

Pablo Accuosto (ITeM)
Inés Campanella (ITeM)
Monique Doppert (Hivos)
Karen Higgs (APC)
Natasha Primo (APC)

Editor

Alan Finlay

Assistant editor

Lori Nordstrom

Publication production

Karen Higgs

Graphic design

MONOCROMO
Myriam Bustos, Leticia da Fonte, Pablo Uribe
info@monocromo.com.uy
Phone: +598 (2) 400 1685

Cover illustration

Matias Bervejillo

Proofreading

Lori Nordstrom
Lisa Cyr

Website

www.GISWatch.org
Andrea Antelo
Ximena Pucciarelli
Monocromo

Printed by

CinnamonTeal Print and Publishing

Printed in India

Global Information Society Watch 2008
Published by APC, Hivos and ITeM
2008

ISBN: 92-95049-65-9
APC 200812 CIPP R EN P 0050

Table of contents

Preface

This year's thematic focus for Global Information Society Watch (GISWatch) is "access to infrastructure". The Geneva Plan of Action that emerged from the first phase of the World Summit on the Information Society (WSIS) declared information and communications technology (ICT) infrastructure an "essential foundation for the Information Society" and identified it as one of six main action lines.

In spite of this attention, it is beginning to be considered of less importance by some development funders and practitioners, including civil society and communication and information activists.

One of the consequences of this is the development of a conventional wisdom that leaves the domain of infrastructure development to the market; to operators and investors who do not always see the broader social value of communications in society; to governments that lack capacity and often clear strategy; and to international institutions that tend to approach it in a limited and "technocratic" way.

Access to infrastructure is important in its own right. It constitutes the layer that enables communication, and is interlinked with other access challenges such as the capacity to use ICTs, access to content and knowledge, as well as access to public participation and citizenship. In this sense, the overall theme of access to infrastructure links to GISWatch 2007's focus on access to participation, and is a bridge to GISWatch 2009's theme of access to knowledge.

GISWatch is both a publication and a process. While producing an annual report which is published in print and online, it also aims to build networking and advocacy capacity among civil society organisations who work for a just and inclusive information society. The number of participating organisations is growing: 38 country reports are published here – 16 more than in our previous edition – analysing the status of access in countries as diverse as the Democratic Republic of Congo, Mexico, Switzerland and Kazakhstan.

Besides thematic reports dealing with key issues affecting access, such as net neutrality, open standards, spectrum management, trends in technology and access to content, for the first time GISWatch includes regional overviews for North America, Latin America and the Caribbean, Africa, the countries of the former Soviet Union, South-East Asia, and the Pacific.

While focusing on ICTs, GISWatch aims to make a critical contribution to building a people-centred information society. Its purpose is to stimulate a collaborative approach to policy advocacy, and to create a common platform where disparate experiences can be shared, and progress – or lack of progress – assessed. Ultimately, it hopes to impact on policy development processes in countries, regions, and at a global level.

We hope you find GISWatch 2008 thought-provoking and challenging. ■

Roberto Bissio
Third World Institute (ITeM)

Anriette Esterhuysen
Association for Progressive Communications (APC)

Loe Schout
Humanist Institute for Cooperation
with Developing Countries (Hivos)

Box 1: **Extract from WSIS Plan of Action: ICT infrastructure**

C2. Information and communication infrastructure: An essential foundation for the Information Society

9. Infrastructure is central in achieving the goal of digital inclusion, enabling universal, sustainable, ubiquitous and affordable access to ICTs by all, taking into account relevant solutions already in place in developing countries and countries with economies in transition, to provide sustainable connectivity and access to remote and marginalized areas at national and regional levels.

a. Governments should take action, in the framework of national development policies, in order to support an enabling and competitive environment for the necessary investment in ICT infrastructure and for the development of new services.

b. In the context of national e-strategies, devise appropriate universal access policies and strategies, and their means of implementation, in line with the indicative targets, and develop ICT connectivity indicators.

c. In the context of national e-strategies, provide and improve ICT connectivity for all schools, universities, health institutions, libraries, post offices, community centres, museums and other institutions accessible to the public, in line with the indicative targets.

d. Develop and strengthen national, regional and international broadband network infrastructure, including delivery by satellite and other systems, to help in providing the capacity to match the needs of countries and their citizens and for the delivery of new ICT-based services. Support technical, regulatory and operational studies by the International Telecommunication Union (ITU) and, as appropriate, other relevant international organizations in order to:

    i. broaden access to orbital resources, global frequency harmonization and global systems standardization;

    ii. encourage public/private partnership;

    iii. promote the provision of global high-speed satellite services for underserved areas such as remote and sparsely populated areas;

    iv. explore other systems that can provide high-speed connectivity.

e. In the context of national e-strategies, address the special requirements of older people, persons with disabilities, children, especially marginalized children and other disadvantaged and vulnerable groups, including by appropriate educational administrative and legislative measures to ensure their full inclusion in the Information Society.

f. Encourage the design and production of ICT equipment and services so that everyone, has easy and affordable access to them including older people, persons with disabilities, children, especially marginalized children, and other disadvantaged and vulnerable groups, and promote the development of technologies, applications, and content suited to their needs, guided by the Universal Design Principle and further enhanced by the use of assistive technologies.

g. In order to alleviate the challenges of illiteracy, develop affordable technologies and non-text based computer interfaces to facilitate people's access to ICT.

h. Undertake international research and development efforts aimed at making available adequate and affordable ICT equipment for end users.

i. Encourage the use of unused wireless capacity, including satellite, in developed countries and in particular in developing countries, to provide access in remote areas, especially in developing countries and countries with economies in transition, and to improve low-cost connectivity in developing countries. Special concern should be given to the Least Developed Countries in their efforts in establishing telecommunication infrastructure.

j. Optimize connectivity among major information networks by encouraging the creation and development of regional ICT backbones and Internet exchange points, to reduce interconnection costs and broaden network access.

k. Develop strategies for increasing affordable global connectivity, thereby facilitating improved access. Commercially negotiated Internet transit and interconnection costs should be oriented towards objective, transparent and non-discriminatory parameters, taking into account ongoing work on this subject.

l. Encourage and promote joint use of traditional media and new technologies.

Source: **Geneva Plan of Action, 2003: www.itu.int/wsis/docs/geneva/official/poa.html**

Introduction: Access to infrastructure

Willie Currie
APC
www.apc.org

2008 was a year in which there was much focus on the issue of universal access to information and communications technologies (ICTs) and the internet. Many global institutions focused on access, resulting in initiatives such as the International Telecommunication Union (ITU) Global Symposium for Regulators on Open Access; an Organisation for Economic Co-operation and Development (OECD) publication called *Global Opportunities for Internet Access Developments*; the GSM Association's report *Universal Access: How mobile can bring communications for all*; the Global Alliance for ICT and Development (GAID) Global Forum on Access and Connectivity; and *info*Dev's publication on broadband in Africa, as well as the European Commission's call for universal broadband in Europe by 2010, and the Internet Governance Forum's (IGF) adoption of "Internet for All" as the overall theme for its third meeting in Hyderabad.

Within these institutions there is a broad recognition that while the digital divide, driven by the spread of mobile, has closed dramatically with regard to voice telephony, a new access gap is emerging with respect to broadband internet infrastructure and services. In this decade, the rapid increase in user-generated content and interactivity on the internet, sometimes known as Web 2.0,[1] has transformed the digital environment. This process was facilitated by the expansion of broadband internet access, and the eclipse of narrowband internet access through dial-up connectivity. In 2004, the number of broadband subscribers in the OECD surpassed the number of dial-up subscribers. At the end of 2003, there were 83 million broadband subscribers in the OECD. By June 2007, there were 221 million – an increase of 165% (OECD, 2008a, p. 23). In 2006, about 70% of broadband subscribers worldwide were located in OECD countries, which accounted for only 16% of the world's population. In contrast, 30% of broadband subscribers were found in developing countries, with 84% of the population. The situation in least developed countries (LDCs) is much worse – there were only 46,000 broadband subscribers in 22 out of 50 LDCs with broadband services in 2006 (ITU, 2007).

Why is access to broadband so important? The ITU says this:

> Ensuring the information society requires not only access and availability of ICT, but a high quality ICT experience. Broadband-enabled services have the potential to create economic and empowerment opportunities, and improve lives (ITU, 2007, p. 7-8).

European Union (EU) Telecoms Commissioner Viviane Reding:

> High speed internet is the passport to the Information Society and an essential condition for economic growth. That is why it is the Commission's policies to make broadband internet for all Europeans happen by 2010 (BBC, 2008).

And the OECD Council on Broadband Development:

> Broadband not only plays a critical role in the workings of the economy, it connects consumers, businesses, governments and facilitates social interaction (OECD, 2008a, p. 7).

When opinion-makers, policy think tanks and industry players in developed countries look at the issue of broadband in developing countries, they tend to say that broadband will be delivered by wireless networks. For example, the OECD says "all indications are that the majority of the next several billion users, mainly from developing countries, will connect to the internet principally via wireless networks. In some developing countries the number of wireless subscribers already outnumbers those for fixed networks by more than 20 to one" (OECD, 2008b, p. 4). While this kind of statement may be generally true, it tends to elide with the notion that these wireless networks will be those of the mobile phone operators and that the solution to the broadband divide will be simply left to the private sector in the form of the mobile operators to resolve. Global institutions representing the interests of mobile subscribers take this point up with alacrity and make claims that "mobile communication will deliver affordable voice, data and Internet services to more than five billion people by 2015" (GSMA, 2008, p. 1). Free market activist financial journals like *The Economist* champion the mobile web when they argue: "The developing world missed out on much of the excitement of the initial web revolution, the dotcom boom and Web 2.0, largely because it did not have an internet infrastructure. But developing countries may now be poised to leapfrog the industrialised world in the era of the mobile web" (Economist, 2008).

Among the hoary rhetorical notions that have exceeded their sell-by date, the idea that developing countries will somehow leapfrog over developed countries with regard to access to broadband infrastructure should really be abandoned. This is akin to the myth that there are more telephone subscribers in Manhattan than the whole of Africa, which was popular in the 1990s and continued to be trotted out even when it was demonstrably no longer true.

1 en.wikipedia.org/wiki/Web_2.0

With 70% of the population of OECD countries already connected to broadband internet infrastructure and universal broadband service on the horizon, there is nothing to leapfrog over.

Southern-based policy research centres have a more sober view on the matter. In its review of policy outcomes in Africa, Research ICT Africa! says the following:

> The excitement about the extension of telecommunications networks and services in countries across the continent over the last few years, particularly in the area of mobile telephony, should be tempered by the fact that these have not been optimal. While gains have clearly been made this review of the telecommunications sector performance in 16 African countries suggests that national policy objectives of pervasive and affordable ICT services are often undermined by many countries' own policies and practices, market structures and institutional arrangements. While Africa may have the highest growth rate in mobile telephony this is off a very low base. Large numbers of people do not have permanent access to basic telephony. The enhanced ICT services required for effective participation in the economy and society continue to elude the vast majority of the continent's people (Esselaar et al., 2007, p. 9).

It is likely that wireless networks, and not simply those of mobile operators, will play an important role in developing country access to broadband, particularly with regard to local access. But it is necessary to recognise the considerable complexity involved in building access to broadband in developing countries, which goes beyond the notion that mobile operators will simply supply it. At the IGF in Rio de Janeiro in 2007, African internet expert Mike Jensen (quoted in Jagun, 2008a) argued that reaching the goal of affordable universal access to broadband in developing countries requires the following combination of factors:

- More competition and innovation in the internet and telecom sector, with effective regulation.
- Much more national and international backbone fibre, with effective regulation of non-discriminatory access to bandwidth by operators and service providers.
- More effort to build demand, especially efforts by national governments to build useful local applications.
- Improved availability of electric power.
- Better indicators for measuring progress.

Speaking at an equitable access workshop before the Rio IGF, African telecommunications expert Lishan Adam identified the existing access gaps that are most stark in Africa, Latin America and Asia (Adam, 2008). Then, based on an analysis of the data and studies that have been made into why the policy programmes to stimulate access in developing countries have had such poor results, Adam posits a number of reasons for the failure by policy-makers and regulators to address these access gaps:

- Market-based approaches were not entirely effective in promoting equitable access – in particular, they failed to break fixed-line telecom monopolies and introduce effective competition in ICT networks and services.
- Regulatory institutions and frameworks remained rather weak. Roles and responsibilities between policy-makers and regulators were often confused, and regulators lacked the capacity to regulate effectively.
- Global regimes were not responsive to the need for equitable access. Developing countries lack the capacity to influence the shape of global ICT policy that cascades across regional and national domains.

After analysing three IGF workshops and the plenary session on access, APC identified a convergence of views on access as follows:

- First, there appeared to be agreement that the competitive (market) model[2] has been effective in increasing access in developing countries. There were therefore calls for policy coherence in the telecom sectors of developing nations and specifically for the principles of competition to be consistently and evenly applied to all areas of the telecom sector.
- Second, there was recognition of the applicability of collaborative models for providing access in areas where traditional market models seem to have failed. Such areas include rural and other underserved areas where the participation of diverse network operators and providers – including municipal government authorities, cooperatives, and community operators – has contributed to increasing access. There were therefore calls for the review of policy and regulation and the establishment of incentives to facilitate increased participation by this cadre of operators.

2 One in which consumers are able to select, from a range of providers, the product that best matches their needs at a price they feel is acceptable.

- Third, there continues to be conviction and consensus on the potential of ICTs as tools for development – particularly at the level of rural and local access. ICTs can be used in increasing accessibility to healthcare and education; they can help in decreasing vulnerabilities and improving citizen engagement with governments and their institutions. There was therefore a call for the promotion and adoption of a multi-sectoral approach in achieving universal, affordable and equitable access. Specifically, there was a recognised need for the integration of ICT regulation and policy with local development strategies, as well as the exploitation of complementarities between different types of development infrastructure (for example, transport networks, water pipes/canals, power/electrification, communication, etc.) (Jagun, 2008a).

However, there are apparent contradictions between some of these points. For example, there is (at least at face value) an inherent contradiction between acceptance of the "efficacy" of competitive models and their promotion in the telecom sector, and the call for increased participation of a more diverse range of network operators and providers, most of whom adopt non-market models to achieve wider access in rural areas. Will all stakeholders truly agree that in order to make universal access a reality, competitive models need to coexist with collaborative ones? One can see fault lines around the roll-out of municipal wireless networks running into opposition from private network operators in the United States (US).

This may not be a problem in developing countries where there is still considerable involvement of the public sector in ICT network provision and an increasing role in ICT services like e-government. In many developing countries the attempts to privatise public telecom operators had negative consequences for the introduction of competition and for reducing access gaps (Horwitz & Currie, 2007). It is unlikely that there will be a pure market approach in countries where the notion of the developmental state is prevalent. It is more likely that the primary modification of the telecom reform model will be that there is a role for public sector and community network provision within a predominantly competitive environment as long as it is transparent and non-discriminatory. Anyone can play, as the open access principle goes.

What is also needed is a modification of the mandates for universal access funds in developing countries to support the roll-out of community wireless networks in rural areas, as well as for capacity-building programmes and local content development to enable citizens to use ICTs effectively in local languages. Policy-makers and regulators need to support this roll-out with enabling regulations liberalising voice over internet protocol (VoIP), allowing community access to spectrum, and creating simple licensing and interconnection regimes for community-based networks.

Figure 1: **Concentric circles of monopolistic barriers**

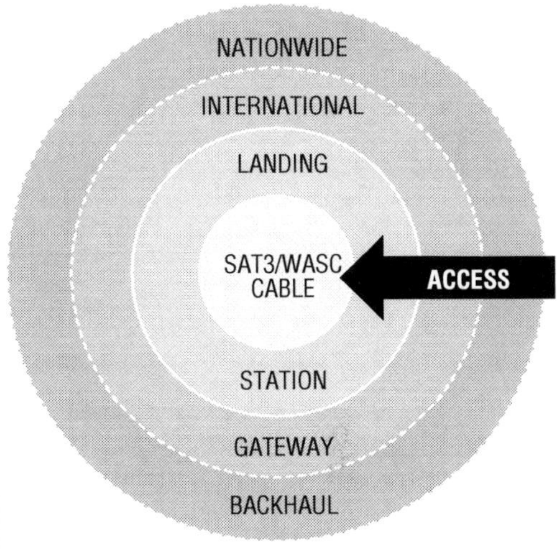

Access to fibre remains a problem for many developing countries. On the west coast of Africa, the problem has been compounded by the continued dominance of moribund monopolies propped up by rent-seeking patron-client networks in government. Research into the operations of the SAT-3/WASC[3] cable has identified what needs to be done to break these monopolies (Jagun, 2008b).

ICT for development analyst and researcher Abiodun Jagun illustrates what she calls the "reinforced monopolies" that inhibit the economic and developmental potential of the SAT-3/WASC cable from being realised in Figure 1. The diagram represents the varying kinds of monopolies of the cable that exist in many of its beneficiary countries in sub-Saharan African. It shows the monopolies operating at different levels, such as international gateway licences, landing stations, national backhaul network, etc. Those who want to "access" the bandwidth need to navigate these monopolies.

The solid lines represent pure monopolies. For instance, when the research was conducted, the SAT-3/WASC cable was the only fibre-optic cable offering connectivity to many countries in sub-Saharan Africa. In many cases the SAT-3/WASC landing station is also only restricted to one signatory.

3 South Atlantic 3/West Africa Submarine Cable.

Sorting out a policy and regulatory problem of this magnitude illustrates the complexity of what is at stake in building broadband in developing countries. And without resolving the problem of affordable access to international bandwidth, the promise of mobile operators to provide broadband internet access will be inhibited.

Nevertheless, sometimes a simple manoeuvre by a regulator can make a dramatic change in a seemingly hopeless state of affairs. One example is the case of Mauritius, where the regulator invited the monopoly operator into a price determination proceeding which enabled the issue of the high cost of international bandwidth to be discussed in public with full transparency. The outcome was that the regulator was able to get the operator to lower its prices for international bandwidth (Southwood, 2008). A problem, however, is the state of governance in developing countries. Developing country governments are often the worst enemies of their citizens. They lack the capability to get things done, lack responsiveness to their citizens' needs and rights, and are unaccountable for their actions. There may be all the consensus in the world as to what can be done to improve equitable access to ICTs, but it will be of little use if the state is dysfunctional. This is not to say that poor governance is limited to developing countries, but its impact is so much greater in countries that lack institutional capacity generally, and have to cope with poverty, conflict and lack of resources. This is a major challenge when it comes to equitable access.

Fortunately there is a growing awareness in most developing country governments of their shortcomings with regard to governance. The issue is on the agenda globally and nationally with international agencies developing indicators to measure good governance, such as the World Bank Institute's Governance and Anti-Corruption programme, which produces a set of governance indicators for each country reflecting:

- Voice and accountability
- Political stability
- Government effectiveness
- Rule of law
- Regulatory quality
- Control of corruption.

The indicators are a form of incentive to some developing countries to improve their standing, but they are also useful for civil society organisations to understand where the governance problems in a particular state lie and what space there is for effective advocacy on equitable access. The indicators on regulatory quality and government effectiveness are particularly important here.[4]

However, what is missing in the good governance methodology is sufficient recognition of the role of patron-client networks in developing country governance. The ITU-D (the telecommunications development sector of the ITU) never addresses this in its engagement with developing country governments and regulators. The various ITU policy documents are disseminated in what amounts to an apolitical state, suggesting there is a straight line between following their policy advice on communications policy reform and positive outcomes on the ground. This lacuna in communication policy reform – that it tries to address policy and regulatory shortcomings as a function of institutional failure and the incorrect application of incentives in the language of institutional economics – does not reach into the realities of client-patron relations and rent-seeking in the politics of developing countries (Khan, 2004). There is unlikely to be much improvement in communications policy reform until these political dynamics are addressed.

The critical success factor of working towards good governance is the extent to which developing countries take it seriously themselves, without the prompting of developed countries and international development institutions. Within Africa, the New Partnership for Africa's Development (NEPAD) has initiated a peer review process which examines:

- Democracy and good political governance
- Economic governance and management
- Corporate governance
- Socio-economic development.[5]

Such steps are important and help create a climate for good governance, which in turn may enable effective ICT regulators to emerge as greater awareness of the value of good governance grows. More effective government may lead to a situation such as in Kenya. There the government is driving the expansion of broadband access in the country and across the region by taking the initiative to lay a fibre-optic submarine cable, TEAMS,[6] and then applying the lessons for broadband delivery systematically and coherently with

4 World Bank Institute Governance and Anti-Corruption programme: web.worldbank.org/WBSITE/EXTERNAL/WBI/EXTWBIGOVANTCOR/0, contentMDK:20672500~menuPK:1740553~pagePK:64168445~piPK:64168309~theSitePK:1740530,00.html

5 African Peer Review Mechanism: www.nepad.org/aprm

6 www.engineeringnews.co.za/article.php?a_id=120703

the enthusiastic support of all stakeholders. If the Kenyan government can pull this off, it will provide a powerful example for other countries in Africa to follow.[7]

References

Adam, L. (2008) *Policies for equitable access.* London: APC. Available at: www.apc.org/en/pubs/research/openaccess/world/policies-equitable-access

African Peer Review Mechanism: www.nepad.org/aprm

BBC (2008) EC call for 'universal' broadband. *BBC News*, 26 September. Available at: news.bbc.co.uk/2/hi/technology/7637215.stm

Economist (2008) The meek shall inherit the web. *The Economist*, 4 September. Available at: www.economist.com/science/tq/displaystory.cfm?STORY_ID=11999307#top

Esselaar, S., Gillwald, A. and Stork, C. (2007) *Towards an African e-Index 2007: Telecommunications Sector Performance in 16 African Countries.* Research ICT Africa! Available at: www.researchictafrica.net/images/upload/Africa_comparativeCORRECTED.pdf

GSMA (GSM Association) (2008) *Universal Access: How mobile can bring communications for all.* Available at: www.gsmworld.com/universalaccess/index.shtml

ITU (International Telecommunication Union) (2007) *Trends in Telecommunication Reform 2007: The Road to Next-Generation Networks (NGN).* Geneva: ITU.

Horwitz, R. and Currie, W. (2007) Another instance where privatization trumped liberalization: The politics of telecommunications reform in South Africa – A ten-year retrospective. *Telecommunications Policy*, 31.

Jagun, A. (2008a) *Building consensus on internet access at the IGF.* Montevideo: APC. Available at: www.apc.org/en/pubs/issue/openaccess/all/building-consensus-internet-access-igf

Jagun, A. (2008b) *The Case for "Open Access" Communications Infrastructure in Africa: The SAT-3/WASC cable (Briefing).* Glasgow: APC. Available at: www.apc.org/en/node/6142

Khan, M. (2004) State Failure in Developing Countries and Strategies of Institutional Reform. In Tungodden, B., Stern, N. and Kolstad, I. (eds.), *Toward Pro-Poor Policies: Aid Institutions and Globalization.* Washington and New York: Oxford University Press and World Bank.

OECD (Organisation for Economic Co-operation and Development) (2008a) *Broadband Growth and Policies in OECD Countries.* Paris: OECD.

OECD (2008b) *Global Opportunities for Internet Access Developments.* Paris: OECD.

Southwood, R. (2008) *The Case for "Open Access" in Africa: Mauritius case study.* London: APC. Available at: www.apc.org/en/pubs/issue/openaccess/africa/case-open-access-africa-mauritius-case-study

World Bank Institute Governance and Anti-Corruption programme: web.worldbank.org/WBSITE/EXTERNAL/WBI/EXTWBIGOVANTCOR/0,,contentMDK:20672500~menuPK:1740553~pagePK:64168445~piPK:64168309~theSitePK:1740530,00.html

7 The Kenyan case is interesting in that the country scores quite well on accountability and regulatory quality indices, while doing poorly in other governance indicators. One dimension in Kenya is an awareness that political stability is fragile, which policy-makers like the permanent secretary in their ICT Ministry incorporates into planning as far as he can.

Thematic reports

Net neutrality

Peter Lange
Intelligent Networx
www.intelligent.net.au

The end of the internet as we know it?

Although the term was coined already in the early 2000s and the concept goes back much further, the discussion about "network neutrality", or net neutrality, has intensified in the past few years, with a particular focus on the internet. Activists warning of a doomsday when the internet as we know it will "die" are dismissed as conspiracy theorists by the CEOs of some of the biggest telecommunications companies in the world. However, industry regulators and governments are working to create legislation that would regulate net neutrality, and the issue was also a topic in the 2008 presidential elections in the United States (US).

So what is net neutrality, and why is it important?

Net neutrality, in its modern context, is the principle of letting all internet traffic flow equally and impartially, without discrimination. It allows internet users to access any web content or applications they choose, without restriction or limitation.

This principle is taken for granted by most of the billions of people who access the internet every day worldwide, even though users in quite a number of countries are affected by government-controlled censorship of the internet. However, the discussion about net neutrality is not limited to countries with restrictive governments exercising internet censorship – on the contrary, the debate is actually most intense in the US. And because global connectivity to the internet is maintained through a complicated set of interconnection arrangements, any restrictions or limitations applied in the US would affect the worldwide internet community and economy.

Those who fear that net neutrality may be compromised in the future claim that certain telecommunications companies – those who own and operate the transmission lines that carry telephone calls and internet traffic – are planning to introduce a scheme of charging extra for certain services on these lines, in this way making the internet more expensive and unaffordable to some. Premiums would be charged from content and application providers for services that would make their websites and servers more accessible than others (i.e., faster) while standard services could be slowed down. These extra costs could squeeze small content providers who cannot afford them out of the market; and the rest would have to pass the costs on to the end-users.

Worse yet, with many of the telecommunications carriers becoming content providers themselves, a particular concern is that internet content could become biased or even censored by them in order to gain competitive advantages. For example, if one of those carriers decided to launch its own search engine, it could prioritise its own service over, say, Google's, and derive commercial gains from this through things like advertising revenue.

Critics of the net neutrality debate – first and foremost the large telecommunications carriers – say that this cannot happen in a competitive market, and that competition rather than regulation should be the answer to ensuring net neutrality. However, the recent consolidation in the sector, especially in the US, is giving rise to exactly this concern: that the level of competition may be compromised to an extent that will not guarantee net neutrality in the future.

Pro

From its origins in the military, academic and research sectors, the internet has seen a transformation towards commercial applications since the late 1990s and developed into a vital communications system. At least in the developed world, it has joined the road and rail networks, the postal system and the global telephone network in the ranks of basic and essential infrastructure and services, without which many business processes and personal communication have become unthinkable. Developing countries, too, are benefiting from the convergence of the internet with conventional telecommunications and media, which are often underdeveloped due to the limited strength of the private sector. The tremendous growth of the internet can be attributed to its open architecture and the fact that it is largely unregulated, allowing individuals and businesses around the world to contribute and reach a global market.

It is not surprising then that the general public and the global business community are sensitive to the issue of net neutrality and generally in favour of anything that may ensure continued unrestricted access, low costs, and a free and unbiased content universe. At the same time, however, there is of course also broad support for measures to take offensive or criminal content off the net (e.g., child pornography) or to crack down on spam.

Small content and application providers in particular have to be worried about being squeezed out of the market by higher fees for premium connections of their servers to the internet. Net neutrality ensures that the best ideas are rewarded rather than the best-funded ideas. Yet even heavyweights such as Google, Yahoo, eBay and Amazon are among the supporters of net neutrality, because it is they who would pay the most in absolute terms should carriers introduce premium fees for premium services.

A wide array of other organisations support net neutrality, including consumer rights groups, free press and free speech advocates, as well as personalities counted among the founding fathers of the internet and the World Wide Web, such as Vint Cerf and Tim Berners-Lee.

On the political level in the US, during the 2008 elections campaign, Democratic presidential candidates spoke out for net neutrality. Both Barack Obama and Hillary Clinton were co-sponsors of the Internet Freedom Preservation Act, also referred to as the "Net Neutrality Bill". While Republican candidate John McCain, with his opposition to net neutrality regulation, was more successful in attracting campaign contributions from the leading US telecom companies, he trailed both Democratic candidates in terms of contributions from these companies' employees – which shows that the employees as individuals feel quite differently to their employers about the issue.

Contra

McCain has stated that net neutrality legislation could be counterproductive and actually harm the openness of the internet. He is supported in this view by the major telecom companies and internet service providers (ISPs), as well as leading internet inventors and network engineers, hardware manufacturers and other business groups.

At the heart of the opposition to net neutrality by major telcos and broadband service providers is the quality of service issue. They claim the internet was not designed to handle the bandwidth-intensive applications that are becoming commonplace these days, such as video-on-demand, peer-to-peer (P2P) networking or online games, and that they must be allowed to control their quality of service by offering differentiated (or tiered) services to their customers.

These opponents of net neutrality like to compare the present state of the internet to the telephone system some twenty years ago, when it started offering a "second tier" of service in the form of wireless mobile phones. The prices for mobile phone services were initially high, because the operating companies had to recoup their investment in the new infrastructure. Only wealthier people were able to afford the new service at first, but over time it became cheaper and better in an unregulated free market. In the view of net neutrality opponents, government regulation to prevent a tiered internet would remove the incentive to invest in network infrastructure and to develop improvements to it.

Internet inventors argue that in fact, the internet protocol (IP) by design contains parameters to request differentiated levels of service, and that even today the internet is not the level playing field that net neutrality proponents want to protect. Delay-sensitive applications such as voice and live video are given priority over data applications that do not require transmission in real-time. Calls via the internet to national emergency numbers may be given an even higher priority. The BitTorrent P2P application that is used to share large amounts of data is widely given reduced bandwidth or even blocked entirely. And in most countries it is normal for ISPs to offer tiered broadband packages with different amounts of bandwidth, where users exceeding their monthly limit are either throttled to dial-up speed or pay extra for additional bandwidth used.

If network operators cannot install infinite transmission capacity, they must rather develop the network infrastructure incrementally according to demand. In situations where they are unable or unwilling to develop the network quickly enough to satisfy the demand, they must control the demand by increasing prices and in this way maximising their profit. This is what some internet activists hold against them; but it is also the main obligation of a private company – to maximise the return to its shareholders.

A balanced view: Competition rather than regulation

The net neutrality debate has focused on whether or not to impose regulations to enforce neutrality. Many supporters of the principles of net neutrality actually do not support its regulation, believing that this could easily lead to over-regulation and set a precedent for even more intrusive regulation of the internet. However, many participants in the net neutrality debate confuse regulating the internet as such with regulating the telecommunications infrastructure that it uses.

The fear that the internet itself could be monopolised and require regulation is indeed unwarranted. All attempts in the past by various service providers to create their own "walled garden", a self-contained content and services sphere that charges a premium for full internet access, have miserably failed and are unlikely to be repeated. Customers simply voted with their feet and went to other service providers with fewer restrictions.

Regulation is only necessary where competition has failed or has not yet developed – and this is often the case with the telecommunications infrastructure that the internet uses. In virtually every country in the world, telecommunications has originally been the monopoly of a state-owned telecom entity, which has built up a national and international telecommunications network over many decades, funded by monopoly prices for services. Following the introduction of competition, it is usually not feasible for a new entrant into the market to replicate this infrastructure completely in a reasonable amount of time in order to compete head-on with the incumbent. As a result, the new competitors will negotiate to lease parts of the incumbent's infrastructure for providing their own services, until they have their own infrastructure in place, or even indefinitely.

However, as long as the incumbent telco is also a retail service provider, it will see the new market entrants as competitors rather than wholesale customers, and try everything possible to make life difficult for them. The answer to this problem is the structural separation of the incumbent telco. This means splitting it up into two independent entities: a retail service provider on the one hand, and on the other a separate entity that owns and operates the network infrastructure and provides wholesale services to other service providers, including the former incumbent's retail division.

Structural separation is resisted by most incumbent telcos, even though the few examples that exist to date (first and foremost British Telecom) tell impressive success stories. It is a complex business transformation process that takes time.

In the meantime, local loop unbundling (LLU or ULL) regulation can guarantee alternative service providers fair and open access to the incumbent's local network infrastructure. In countries with functioning LLU regulation (mostly in Western Europe), many alternative service providers have established themselves and co-located their own DSLAM (digital subscriber line access multiplexer) equipment at the incumbent's exchanges to provide their own DSL broadband services. Competition between these service providers automatically ensures net neutrality: if one of them decided to charge higher premium fees, customers would have no difficulty finding a competitor that does not, or that charges less.

In most developing countries, however, the competition situation is far worse, with the incumbent telco still monopolising international access and the national backbone network. In terms of neutrality towards content and applications, a particular concern has been the obstruction of competition by incumbent telcos to protect their traditional voice telephony business against new service providers using voice over internet protocol (VoIP). In several countries, even after VoIP had been legalised, the incumbents were using their monopolistic ownership of the national infrastructure and the international gateway to disadvantage VoIP offerings of competing service providers. In some cases, interconnection arrangements with such service providers were outright refused or delayed, and some incumbents have been accused of slowing down VoIP traffic from competing service providers to degrade the quality of service. The regulatory authorities in many developing countries are relatively weak and often fail to enforce existing regulations.

A particular situation exists in the US, which was hailed as an example for infrastructure-based competition between the traditional telcos and the cable TV companies, which kick-started the development of broadband in the late 1990s. The last few years have seen massive consolidation among the major telcos, with AT&T and Verizon now controlling approximately 80% of the DSL market and rapidly taking market share from the cable companies. The resulting degradation of competition, coupled with lacklustre LLU regulation, is the reason why net neutrality is much more fiercely discussed in the US than elsewhere.

Open standards

Sunil Abraham
Centre for Internet and Society, Bangalore
www.cis-india.org

Most computer users today remain "digitally colonised" (Bhattacharya, 2008) due to our unquestioning use of proprietary standards. As users of proprietary standards we usually forget that we lose the right to access our own files the moment the licence for the associated software expires. For example, if I were to store data, information or knowledge in .doc, .xls or .ppt format, my ability to read my own files expires the moment the licence for my copy of Microsoft Office expires.

Definition

Unlike the terms "free software" or "open source software", the term "open standard" does not have a universally accepted definition. The free and open source software (FOSS) community largely believes that an open standard is:

> [S]ubject to full public assessment and use without constraints [royalty-free] in a manner equally available to all parties; without any components or extensions that have dependencies on formats or protocols that do not meet the definition of an open standard themselves; free from legal or technical clauses that limit its utilisation by any party or in any business model; managed and further developed independently of any single vendor in a process open to the equal participation of competitors and third parties; available in multiple complete implementations by competing vendors, or as a complete implementation equally available to all parties (Greve, 2007).

The controversy

Proprietary software manufacturers, vendors and their lobbyists often provide a definition of open standards that is not in line with the above definition on two counts (Nah, 2006).

One, they do not think it is necessary for an open standard to be available on a royalty-free basis as long as it is available under a "reasonable and non-discriminatory" (RAND) licence. This means that there are some patents associated with the standard and the owners of the patents have agreed to license them under reasonable and non-discriminatory terms (W3C, 2002). One example is the audio format MP3, an ISO/IEC [International Organisation for Standardisation/International Electrotechnical Commission] standard where the associated patents are owned by Thomson Consumer Electronics and the Fraunhofer Society of Germany. A developer of a game with MP3 support would have to pay USD 2,500 as royalty for using the standard. While this may be reasonable in the United States (US), it is unthinkable for an entrepreneur from Bangladesh. Additionally, RAND licences are incompatible with most FOSS licensing requirements. Simon Phipps of Sun Microsystems says that FOSS "serves as the canary in the coalmine for the word 'open'. Standards are truly open when they can be implemented without fear as free software in an open source community" (Phipps, 2007). RAND licences also retard the growth of FOSS, since they are patented in a few countries. Despite the fact that software is not patentable in most parts of the world, the makers of various distributions of GNU/Linux do not include reverse-engineered drivers, codecs, etc., in the official builds for fear of being sued. Only the large corporation-backed distributions of GNU/Linux can afford to pay the royalties needed to include patented software in the official builds (in this way enabling an enhanced out-of-the-box experience). This has the effect of slowing the adoption of GNU/Linux, as less experienced users using community-backed distributions do not have access to the wide variety of drivers and codecs that users of other operating systems do (Disposable, 2004). This vicious circle effectively ensures negligible market presence of smaller community-driven projects by artificial reduction of competition.

Two, proprietary software promoters do not believe that open standards should be "managed and further developed independently of any single vendor," as the following examples will demonstrate. This is equally applicable to both new and existing standards.

Microsoft's Office Open XML (OOXML) is a relatively new standard which the FOSS community sees as a redundant alternative to the existing Open Document Format (ODF). During the OOXML process, delegates were unhappy with the fact that many components were specific to Microsoft technology, amongst other issues. By the end of a fast-track process at the ISO, Microsoft stands accused of committee stuffing: that is, using its corporate social responsibility wing to coax non-governmental organisations to send form letters to national standards committees, and haranguing those who opposed OOXML. Of the twelve new national board members that joined ISO after the OOXML process started, ten voted "yes" in the first ballot (Weir, 2007). The European Commission, which has already fined Microsoft USD 2.57 billion for anti-competitive behaviour, is currently investigating the allegations of committee stuffing (Calore, 2007). Microsoft was able to use its financial muscle and monopoly to fast-track the standard and get it approved. In this way it has managed to subvert the participatory nature of a standards-setting organisation. So even though Microsoft is ostensibly giving up control of its primary file format to the ISO, it still exerts enormous influence over the future of the standard.

HTML, on the other hand, is a relatively old standard which was initially promoted by the Internet Engineering Task Force (IETF), an international community of techies. However, in 2002, seven years after the birth of HTML 2.0, the US Department of Justice alleged that Microsoft used the strategy of "embrace, extend, and extinguish" (US DoJ, 1999) in an attempt to create a monopoly among web browsers. It said that Microsoft used its dominance in the desktop operating system market to achieve dominance in the web-authoring tool and browser market by introducing proprietary extensions to the HTML standard (Festa, 2002). In other words, financial and market muscle have been employed by proprietary software companies – in these instances, Microsoft – to hijack open standards.

The importance

There are many technical, social and ethical reasons for the adoption and use of open standards. Some of the reasons that should concern governments and other organisations utilising public money – such as multilaterals, bilaterals, civil society organisations, research organisations and educational institutions – are listed below.

- **Innovation/competitiveness:** Open standards are the bases of most technological innovations, the best example of which would be the internet itself (Raymond, 2000). The building blocks of the internet and associated services like the world wide web are based on open standards such as TCP/IP, HTTP, HTML, CSS, XML, POP3 and SMTP. Open standards create a level playing field that ensures greater competition between large and small, local and foreign, and new and old companies, resulting in innovative products and services. Instant messaging, voice over internet protocol (VoIP), wikis, blogging, file-sharing and many other applications with large-scale global adoption were invented by individuals and small and medium enterprises, and not by multinational corporations.

- **Greater interoperability:** Open standards ensure the ubiquity of the internet experience by allowing different devices to interoperate seamlessly. It is only due to open standards that consumers are able to use products and services from competing vendors interchangeably and simultaneously in a seamless fashion, without having to learn additional skills or acquire converters. For instance, the mail standard IMAP can be used from a variety of operating systems (Mac, Linux and Windows), mail clients (Evolution, Thunderbird, Outlook Express) and web-based mail clients. Email would be a completely different experience if we were not able to use our friends' computers, our mobile phones, or a cybercafé to check our mail.

- **Customer autonomy:** Open standards also empower consumers and transform them into co-creators or "prosumers" (Toffler, 1980). Open standards prevent vendor lock-in by ensuring that the customer is able to shift easily from one product or service provider to another without significant efforts or costs resulting from migration.

- **Reduced cost:** Open standards eliminate patent rents, resulting in a reduction of total cost of ownership. This helps civil society develop products and services for the poor.

- **Reduced obsolescence:** Software companies can leverage their clients' dependence on proprietary standards to engineer obsolescence into their products and force their clients to keep upgrading to newer versions of software. Open standards ensure that civil society, governments and others can continue to use old hardware and software, which can be quite handy for sectors that are strapped for financial resources.

- **Accessibility:** Operating system-level accessibility infrastructure such as magnifiers, screen readers and text-to-voice engines require compliance to open standards. Open standards therefore ensure greater access by people with disabilities, the elderly, and neo-literate and illiterate users. Examples include the US government's Section 508 standards, and the World Wide Web Consortium's (W3C) WAI-AA standards.

- **Free access to the state:** Open standards enable access without forcing citizens to purchase or pirate software in order to interact with the state. This is critical given the right to information and the freedom of information legislations being enacted and implemented in many countries these days.

- **Privacy/security:** Open standards enable the citizen to examine communications between personal and state-controlled devices and networks. For example, open standards allow users to see whether data from their media player and browser history are being transmitted along to government servers when they file their tax returns. Open standards also help prevent corporate surveillance.

- **Data longevity and archiving:** Open standards ensure that the expiry of software licences does not prevent the state from accessing its own information and data. They also ensure that knowledge that has been passed on to our generation, and the knowledge generated by our generation, is safely transmitted to all generations to come.

- **Media monitoring:** Open standards ensure that the voluntary sector, media monitoring services and public archives can keep track of the ever-increasing supply of text, audio, video and multimedia generated by the global news, entertainment and gaming industries.

In democracies, watchdogs should be permitted to reverse-engineer proprietary standards and archive critical ephemeral media in open standards.

Policy implications

Corporations have a right to sell products based on proprietary standards just as consumers have a right to choose between products that use open standards, proprietary standards, or even a combination of such standards. Governments, however, have a responsibility to use open standards, especially for interactions with the public and where the data handled has a direct impact on democratic values and quality of citizenship. In developing countries, governments have greater responsibility because most often they account for over 50% of the revenues of proprietary software vendors. Therefore, by opting for open standards, governments can correct an imbalanced market situation without needing any additional resources. Unfortunately, many governments lack the expertise to counter the campaigns of fear, uncertainty and doubt unleashed by proprietary standards lobbyists with unlimited expense accounts.

Most governments from the developing world do not participate in international standard-setting bodies. On the other hand, proprietary software lobbyists like the Business Software Alliance (BSA) and Comptia attend all national meetings on standards. This has forced many governments to shun these forums and exacerbate the situation by creating more (totally new) standards. Therefore, governments need the support of academic and civil society organisations in order to protect the interests of the citizen. For example, the Indian Institute of Technology in Kanpur (IIT-K) helped the government of India develop the open standard Smart Card Operating System for Transport Applications (SCOSTA) for smart card-based driving licences and vehicle registration documents. Proprietary vendors tried to jettison the move by saying that the standard was technically not feasible. IIT-K developed a reference implementation on FOSS to belie the vendor's claims. As a consequence, the government of India was able to increase the number of empanelled smart-card vendors from four to fifteen and reduce the price of a smart card by around USD 7 each (UNDP, 2007a). This will hopefully result in enormous savings during the implementation of a national multi-purpose identification card in India.

In some instances, proprietary standards are technically superior or more universally supported in comparison to open standards. In such cases the government may be forced to adopt proprietary and de facto standards in the short and medium term. But for long-term technical, financial and societal benefits, many governments across the world today are moving towards open standards. The most common policy instruments for implementation of open standards policy are government interoperability frameworks (GIFs). Governments that have published GIFs include the United Kingdom, Denmark, Brazil, Canada, the European Union, Hong Kong, Malaysia, New Zealand and Australia (UNDP, 2007b).

While challenges to the complete adoption of open standards in the public sector and civil society remain, one thing is certain: the global march towards openness, though slow, is irreversible and inevitable. ■

References

Bhattacharya, J. (2008) *Technology Standards: A Route to Digital Colonization. Open Source, Open Standards and Technological Sovereignty.* Available at: knowledge.oscc.org.my/practice-areas/government/oss-seminar-putrajaya-2008/technology-standards-a-route-to-digital/at_download/file

Calore, M. (2007) Microsoft Allegedly Bullies and Bribes to Make Office an International Standard. *Wired*, 31 August. Available at: www.wired.com/software/coolapps/news/2007/08/ooxml_vote

Disposable (2004) *Ubuntu multimedia HOWTO.* Available at: www.oldskoolphreak.com/tfiles/hack/ubuntu.txt

Festa, P. (2002) W3C members: Do as we say, not as we do. *CNET News*, 5 September. Available at: news.cnet.com/2100-1023-956778.html

Greve, G. (2007) *An emerging understanding of open standards.* Available at: www.fsfe.org/fellows/greve/freedom_bits/an_emerging_understanding_of_open_standards

Nah, S.H. (2006) *FOSS Open Standards Primer.* New Delhi: UNDP-APDIP. Available at: www.iosn.net/open-standards/foss-open-standards-primer/foss-openstds-withnocover.pdf

Phipps, S. (2007) *Roman Canaries.* Available at: blogs.sun.com/webmink/entry/roman_canaries

Raymond, E.S. (2000) *The Magic Cauldron.* Available at: www.catb.org/~esr/writings/cathedral-bazaar/magic-cauldron/index.html

Toffler, A. (1980) *The Third Wave.* New York: Bantam.

UNDP (United Nations Development Programme) (2007a) *e-Government Interoperability: A Review of Government Interoperability Frameworks in Selected Countries.* Available at: www.apdip.net/projects/gif/gifeprimer

UNDP (2007b) *e-Government Interoperability: Guide.* Available at: www.apdip.net/projects/gif/GIF-Guide.pdf

US DoJ (Department of Justice) (1999) *Proposed Findings of Fact – Revised.* Available at: www.usdoj.gov/atr/cases/f2600/v-a.pdf

W3C (World Wide Web Consortium) (2002) *Current patent practice.* Available at: www.w3.org/TR/patent-practice#def-RAND

Weir, R. (2007) *How to hack ISO.* Available at: www.robweir.com/blog/2007/09/how-to-hack-iso.html

Spectrum management

Ben Akoh
Open Society Initiative for West Africa (OSIWA)
www.osiwa.org

The "brick" – weighing down innovation in Ethiopia

In 1999, not so long after the Ethiopian Telecommunication Corporation (ETC) launched its mobile telephony service, Ethionet, it constrained users to a certain brand of Ericsson mobile phone commonly referred to as the "brick". The twin-line, green, monochrome display, blue-coloured cover and heavy battery packs were a status symbol, and Ethionet's de facto mobile communication device. Regulations restricted usage of other phone models irrespective of what advanced functionality they might have had. They were illegal. Although the country was far behind in the implementation of mobile communication compared to other African countries who were rapidly implementing mobile technology, the regime ensured it protected its cash cow from bleeding right from the onset. And it went on to lock access to all tiers of the industry. The internet, spectrum allocations, airwaves, value-added mobile services such as short message service (SMS), all, until recently, suffered under the heavy rule of the administration. Innovation was restricted and industry growth crippled.

In recent times, the global mobile telephony sector has seen an avalanche of innovation, with mobile manufacturers driving technology needs way ahead of network capabilities. It is not unusual to see highly advanced mobile devices, such as recently released third-generation (3G) phones, in use in lesser capable networks, say second-generation (2G) networks. The separation of control over access equipment, such as handsets, from transmission infrastructure, akin to the removal of control on wireline terminal equipment, has led to innovation in the mobile industry and across the entire spectrum of telecommunications. This has included remarkable growth and improvement in value-added services. SMS now contributes to a large percentage of the entire mobile revenue base, as do multimedia messaging service (MMS), general packet radio service (GPRS) and others.

African telecommunications have in recent times seen increasing growth driven by demand- and supply-side factors such as falling costs, regulatory reforms and technological innovations which have led to smaller, more efficient and affordable equipment (Gray, 2006). By 2004, Africa had added nearly 15 million mobile phone subscribers to its subscriber base, equivalent to the continent's total overall telephone subscribers (mobile and fixed) in 1996. Gray (2006) comments that mobile phone subscribers surpassed their fixed-line equivalent in 2004, with countries like Nigeria dramatically increasing their own telephone penetration rate from 0.5 to 8%.

Such penetration rates have raised certain arguments. For instance, some say that in the African context the mobile phone capitalises on the innate orality of African culture and society, perhaps explaining its rapid uptake. But, in the modern setting, it is an orality that has turned in on itself, because the cost of communication may have also eaten into the disposable income of the individual. A Europemedia report states that in 2003, global youth spending on mobile-related products and services stood at 13.5% of their disposable income, even affecting the sales of chocolate in the United Kingdom (UK) for the first time.[1] And the surge has continued amidst worldwide concerns over the economy.

A number of factors determine the cost of the mobile handset. These include design, high-tech appeal, quality, functionality and various consumer-specific requirements.[2] However, significant opportunity costs for manufacturers also contribute to handset costs; for example, where they consider an operational feature necessary, such as the need to incorporate extra frequency band in a handset for use in multiple and different network configurations (i.e., while roaming) (GSM Association, 2007). The increase in functionality from cramming things like multiband, Wi-Fi, GPRS, and wireless application protocol (WAP) into small form factors has a corresponding increase in the cost of a mobile device – and this translates into the need to stretch disposable income in order to afford devices.

A technical white paper released by the GSM Association (2007) concluded that there are significant economies of scale to be had in the production of terminals with internationally identified common frequency bands. It states that without the identification of common bands, handset costs could be set prohibitively high, and the effect will be a significant reduction in the uptake of mobile services. This would harm not only consumers and industry directly, but also the benefits that mobile offers to economies as a vital infrastructure. The white paper argues that chipset modification, handset integration and testing costs have multiplicative effects on the cost of mobile phone terminals, as manufacturers and operators squeeze multiple bands into "affordable" phones to make them network-ready across different networks, and sellable into different markets.

1 www.allbusiness.com
2 mic.iii.org.tw

Effectively, phones specifically manufactured for certain low-budget and heavily, negatively regulated spectrum markets may not be so economical. As the global mobile penetration rate increases, the supply of manufactured devices must increase to meet the associated demands, and so must operator services. Economies of scale should normally positively affect the cost of each unit, but certain policy issues may present hiccups to the downward price spiral of a mobile handset, or even the cost of services offered.

Why is spectrum a scarce resource?

Spectrum to the mobile or wireless operator could be likened to the race track to the race car driver – an essential resource for the transmission of data and voice from a transmitter to one or more receiving stations (Buigues & Ray, 2004). Certain factors determine the effective provisioning of services by the operator to consumers. A service provider must operate according to the requirements of and within the regulatory spectrum space (band) allocated to it, usually by its national regulatory agency who manages this resource (spectrum management). That space is finite and tends to become scarce as more operators "fit" their operations within the same spectrum band. Spectrum can be in short supply because there may be more potential users of particular frequencies than available spectrum. There is therefore a need for rationing its use and giving priority to more important applications.[3]

Spectrum is allocated to applications by several means, including a first-come, first-served basis, auctions, lotteries, discretionary decisions and beauty contests. Buigues and Rey (2004) very adequately explain these processes in their book *The Economics of Antitrust and Regulation in Telecommunications: Perspectives for the New European Regulatory Framework.* These methods have both their advantages and disadvantages and will not be discussed here. Most recently, the auction has become the preferred method for spectrum allocation because of its transparent nature, and, of course, because the bidding process tends to generate revenue for regulators.

Open or closed regimes: Market-based or commons approach?

In the United States (US), the Federal Communications Commission (FCC) has been managing and allocating spectrum since the 1920s. In 1993 it started spectrum auctions as a more efficient means to license – a recommendation favoured by economists such as Coase. Others argue in favour of an "open access" or commons approach to spectrum management, calling for the removal of exclusive use.

Ian Munro (2000), in a presentation to the International Telecommunication Union (ITU) Radiocommunication Bureau, observed: "With telecommunications markets being deregulated and opened to competition, it is crucial that spectrum assignment mechanisms be efficient, objective, timely and fair. Auctions possess clear advantages compared to other assignment mechanisms." Munro goes on to say that a large number of countries, including Australia, Germany, Canada and the UK, have gone on to implement advanced auctions (a market-based approach) following the success of the FCC.

Conversely, proponents of the commons approach tout innovation enjoyed in the unlicensed spectrum as the reason why a more liberal approach to spectrum management should be applied to current licensing regimes. The FCC's "Part 15" rule allowed for the development of innovative systems for spread spectrum technology, leading to developments in cordless phones, short-range wireless local area networks (LANs), and home networks such as Wi-Fi. If these Part 15 rules led to innovation, they should improve the rather disappointing innovation seen so far in the licensed band.

However, there is also an argument that a fully fledged commons approach leads to the "tragedy of the commons" (Heller, 1998), a situation that occurs when many parties have property-like rights for small slivers of spectrum, so that a party wanting to use a block of spectrum may find it costly and complicated to negotiate with many separate holders of spectrum usage rights. In such a case, the spectrum may go unused (hoarded) and become a wasted resource. Heller suggests the importance of introducing a hybrid or combined approach that takes into consideration the various strategies for effective spectrum management.

Glitches in the wheel: Anti-competitive behavior

A market-based approach may have yielded the FCC billions of dollars, the UK's Ofcom as much as 3% of gross domestic product (GDP),[4] and, indeed, constitutes a major revenue-generation scheme for most regulators, but the situation has led to anti-competitive behaviour. For instance, spectrum hoarding is not only a "tragedy of the commons". Here, a typical situation arises where "owners" of spectrum create scarcity of the valuable resource, making it difficult for potential buyers to access it. A recent case in point: in India, code division multiple access (CDMA) providers are alleged to be hoarding scarce underutilised spectrum, and thereby

3 For more information see the *info*Dev/ITU ICT Regulation Toolkit: www.ictregulationtoolkit.org.

4 www.ofcom.org.uk

keeping it from global system for mobile (GSM) operators.[5] The gravity of the situation is highlighted when one considers that Indian operators are allocated far lower spectrum than global averages (a third of global averages at 7.35 MHz compared to 22 MHz globally). Operators are required to optimise these allocations in the face of ever-increasing customer demands, putting them under dire pressure to deliver quality services.

The FCC's supposed "good practices" also do not come without glitches. Teletruth,[6] a group that claims to look after telecommunications customers' rights, filed a USD 8 billion complaint in June 2006, alleging anti-competitive practices by large companies such as Verizon, AT&T, Cingular (SBC, AT&T and BellSouth), T-Mobile and Sprint in spectrum auctions reserved for so-called "designated entities". These auctions allow individuals and businesses with limited assets and revenues to bid for licences.

In another example, Ofcom's recent announcement of the auctioning of its 2.6 GHz space has been met with criticism and, recently, litigation. This freed-up space, as a result of the switchover from analogue to digital (producing so-called "digital dividends"), sits in the ultra-high frequency band, and allows for the transmission of signals that effectively penetrate buildings and can be carried over large geographical spaces. It also supports ultra-fast wireless broadband, WiMAX, evolutions of 3G technology, mobile television, and additional digital terrestrial television channels. In criticising the auction announcement, analysts and WiMAX players have suggested that Ofcom should include "use or lose it" conditions and roll-out obligations to avoid spectrum hoarding by existing mobile operators who may want to restrict new WiMAX entrants.[7] Ongoing litigations by operators T-Mobile and O2 may result in the postponement of the auction to 2009.

Digital dividends: Creating space for access

On 5 May 2006, a public interest group, M2Z network,[8] filed an application to the FCC to lease a spectrum band in order for it to offer free nationwide wireless broadband access on spectrum that had been lying fallow for seven years. M2Z intended to roll out broadband to 95% of the US population in ten years. It also offered to serve federal, state, municipal and public safety organisations, while filtering indecent content to protect children. In exchange, 5% of its gross revenues would go to the US Treasury.

Digital dividends are particularly useful for the rapid deployment of wireless technologies in otherwise unreachable areas, especially remote rural African communities. However, this may not become a reality in the immediate future, as only some countries have started planning for digital migration to meet the ITU's 2015 deadline. In Africa, Kenya, Nigeria and South Africa are amongst the few who may have commenced talks by setting up committees to steer the migrations, with the latter at the most advanced stages, seeking to migrate in 2009 ahead of the 2010 FIFA World Cup.

These migrations do not come without implications for both operators, who need to consider the cost of converting their equipment to support digital broadcast signals, and consumers, who will need to pay for intelligent devices to receive these signals. Consequently, though it frees up certain frequency bands, digital migration does not automatically translate into immediately available spectrum space. It will take some time after signals have been migrated for regulators, especially those in Africa, to harness and facilitate the liberation of associated bands for other uses.

The need for regional harmonisation

Available spectrum itself may not be the challenge in Africa, but rather restrictive access to available spectrum, as a result of prohibitive entry costs and policy issues. Some of these could be better managed if spectrum administration is looked at from a regional perspective, rather than nationally.

The US and the European Union (EU) seem to present better spectrum management regimes, as they engage in consultative fora involving economists, activists and engineers to discuss the best form of administering these scarce resources. In a recent media release, the EU parliament announced certain measures to coordinate and harmonise radio spectrum use across the EU.[9] These measures propose the setup of a regional Body of European Regulators in Telecommunications (BERT), which will be composed of the 27 national regulatory authorities and involve a "co-regulation" procedure requiring national regulatory authorities to consult with BERT before regulatory decisions are taken – all in the interests of promoting investments in the next generation access networks. At the same time, the procedures would ensure that national regulators take measures requiring that a service supplied in a specific frequency band is justified by reference to general interest aims, such as ensuring safety of life, promoting social, regional or territorial cohesion, avoiding inefficient use of radio frequencies,

5 www.itvidya.com
6 www.teletruth.org
7 www.unstrung.com
8 www.m2znetworks.com

9 europa.eu/press_room

or promoting cultural and media aims such as cultural and linguistic diversity and media pluralism.

Similar measures may be required in Africa where there are already regional telecommunication regulatory assemblies. Discussions at these fora, especially with the West Africa Telecommunications Regulators Assembly (WATRA), have remained superficial, touching on the harmonisation of national telecommunication codes and affordable roaming services, but falling short of deeper issues such as regional spectrum management and administrative structures, and strategies for efficient harmonisation.

Conclusion

This report briefly touched on the intricacies of spectrum management, with a view to promoting better understanding and efficient administration of this seemingly "airborne" medium that defines important aspects of human existence and touches on day-to-day living. Telecommunications has evolved over the years, and has relevance to all aspects of development – from national security to individual empowerment; from regional or global governance structures to the local fish farmer.

While innovation may have pushed for the liberation of spectrum space, regulatory mechanisms may be slow in accelerating growth in the sector in developing regions. This is especially the case with the deployment of WiMAX and other potential services that could extend access to rural areas, and could possibly accelerate regional integration. Regulatory mechanisms must be instituted well ahead of innovation. The potential of WiMAX to reach largely unreachable places in Africa in the 2.5 GHz band should be encouraged, with licences awarded to service providers. Pro-people licensing regimes should be developed, such as unified licences with a specific focus on rural telephony, and mechanisms such as the FCC's designated entities should be put in place to allow smaller players to compete.

Access for all should be a driving force behind most telecommunication improvements, including the efficient management of spectrum. Regulators, equipment manufacturers, operators, regional economic commissions and governance structures all have a role to play, including those in Ethiopia. ■

References

All Business: www.allbusiness.com

Buigues, P. and Rey, P. (2004) *The Economics of Antitrust and Regulation in Telecommunications: Perspectives for the New European Regulatory Framework.* Cheltenham: Edward Elgar.

Europa Press Room: europa.eu/press_room

Gray, V. (2006) *The un-wired continent: Africa's mobile success story.* Geneva: ITU. Available at: www.itu.int/ITU-D/ict/statistics/at_glance/Africa_EE2006_e.pdf

GSM Association (2007) *The advantages of common frequency bands for mobile handset production.* Available at: www.gsmworld.com/using/spectrum/spectrum_papers.shtml

Heller, M. (1998) The Tragedy of the Anticommons: Property in the Transition from Marx to Markets. *Harvard Law Review*, 111(3), pp. 621-688.

*info*Dev/ITU (International Telecommunication Union) ICT Regulation Toolkit. Available at: www.ictregulationtoolkit.org

TVidya: www.itvidya.com

M2Z Networks: www.m2znetworks.com

Market Intelligence Center: mic.iii.org.tw

Munro, I. (2000) Auctions as a Spectrum Management Tool. Presentation to the ITU Radiocommunication Bureau Seminar, Geneva, Switzerland, 8 November. Available at: www.itu.int/ITU-R/conferences/seminars/geneva-2000/docs/00-20_ww9.doc

Ofcom (UK Office of Communications): www.ofcom.org.uk

Teletruth: www.teletruth.org

Unstrung News Analysis:www.unstrung.com

Trends in technology

Russell Southwood
Balancing Act
www.balancingact-africa.com

Bandwidth, the petrol of the new global economy

Put simply, bandwidth is what carries voice and data from one place to another. Bandwidth is the petrol of the new global economy; and cheap international bandwidth is essential for any developing country to remain competitive in a changing world.

Arguably, the use of bandwidth will increasingly substitute for tasks previously done by saying "send a driver" in many developing countries. In July 2008, the South Korean government, which is almost completely dependent on imports for its oil, issued an instruction that all government vehicles should only be used every other day to cut fuel costs. So there is an imperative to address the cost of things like information collection and delivery, meeting people and gathering opinions, which were previously reliant on conventional means of transport.

Cheap and accessible bandwidth encourages information, ideas and money to flow quickly within a country and between countries. Despite the best efforts of backward-looking governments, it allows a country's citizens to know what is happening in the world and what the world thinks about what is happening in their country. The world's tyrants may still be able to dominate their citizens, but they are that bit more vulnerable when faced with a freer flow of information about their deeds. Recent crises in places as diverse as Burma, Tibet and Zimbabwe attest to the power of information to influence those in power, even if it does not necessarily change who is in power.

There is a connection between the social and the economic. If it costs your country USD 7,000-10,000 per megabit per second (Mbps) per month – one of the units used to price bandwidth – to communicate with the rest of the world, you are likely to do less of it than another country where the same bandwidth sells for below USD 1,000 per Mbps per month. Those developing countries that have access to cheap bandwidth have some chance of staying ahead in the "dog eat dog" world of the new global economy. They can respond to new needs in the global economy and not simply rely on the changeable fortunes of selling agricultural produce, minerals and tourism.

Used strategically, bandwidth can create new "think work" industries like business process outsourcing (BPO) and call centres. For example, a single company in Ghana, ACS, employs 1,200 people doing data processing. The Indian Ocean island of Mauritius employs between 4,000 and 5,000 people in a combination of BPO and call centres. Over 10,000 people in the South African city of Cape Town work in these sectors.

If communications costs are not lowered, then the cost of financing trade and ultimately the price of the goods themselves will be higher than necessary for everyone. Many African countries rely on goods traded between themselves and nearby neighbours. The goods traded are not simply luxury goods, but also essential foodstuffs that make up the daily diet of all citizens. Cheap and accessible bandwidth encourages regional trade integration that helps reduce air miles: the product grown to meet local demand is not one that needs to be imported or exported half way round the world.

But perhaps the most crucial impact cheap bandwidth – taken together with competition – may have is on the cost of transferring money. There is considerable movement of people both between neighbouring countries and internationally. Take the example of West Africa. According to a report by the Organisation for Economic Co-operation and Development (OECD) Sahel and West Africa Club (SWAC),[1] there are three waves of population movement. Since the early 1960s, 80 million people have moved to the cities from rural areas. Populations also move from one country to another in West Africa, and this represents 90% of interregional migration. Finally, West Africans represent 3% of immigrants from non-OECD countries living in Europe.

Each of these people needs to be able to communicate with their family. The son who has gone overseas rings his mother back in West Africa. That same mother rings her grandmother in the village. Financial remittances flow all the way down this chain of communication and, according to the International Fund for Agricultural Development (IFAD), in 2006 these were worth USD 10 billion to West African countries. These remittances exceed the amount of money spent by international donors. But the cost of sending that money is around 12% of the total, whereas elsewhere in the world, such as Latin America, it has fallen to 6%. Cheaper communications and competition can bring cheaper transaction costs, and more of this money will arrive in developing countries.

The first wave of the communications revolution in Africa was the spread of mobile phones, which are now within reach of 60-70% of the continent's population. By contrast, the internet is only accessed by 12-15% of the population. Until recently, the experience of the internet in Africa has been like having to eat a three-course meal by sucking it through a straw: time-consuming, unreliable and expensive.

1 The OECD SWAC report defines West Africa as comprising fifteen ECOWAS member states as well as Mauritania, Chad and Cameroon.

While new mobile interfaces will increasingly allow mobile internet access, the second wave of the communications revolution will be the spread of relatively cheap internet use. For developing countries, particularly in Africa, the internet has been the poor cousin of much more widely distributed technologies like mobile phones and radio. However, despite the limitations of speed and cost, a surprisingly large number of people use it.

Based on national survey samples from a range of twelve African countries of different income levels,[2] between 2-15% of the population use the internet (except in the two poorest countries) and 1-8% use it on a daily basis (except for the four poorest countries). On this basis, there might easily be tens of thousands or hundreds of thousands of broadband subscribers depending on the size of the country. Literacy plays a part, but probably not as big a part as price.

There is a clear link between the price of international bandwidth and the retail price of voice and internet services to the consumer. However, this link is not just a result of the price of international bandwidth, but also a reflection of both its cost and availability within a country. Cheaper international bandwidth means that there should be cheaper national bandwidth. Indeed, without this occurring, anomalies are found, such as where it costs more to communicate between neighbouring countries or two cities within a country than it does to link the capital and a European or North American destination.

Except with widely distributed rural populations where satellite is more appropriate, the cheapest bandwidth can be delivered using fibre.

International bandwidth prices in Africa have come down for a number of reasons. There has been an extended discussion about how to ensure open and competitive access to new international fibre-optic cables currently being built.[3] As part of this process, national internet service provider (ISP) associations have lobbied the telecoms companies selling bandwidth and achieved price reductions. At the same time, the presence of two to three cable projects on either side of the continent ensures that each offers competitive pricing.

Through a combination of these factors, the price of bandwidth has gone from USD 7,000-10,000 per Mbps per month to USD 500-1,000 per Mbps per month due to two new cables (called SEACOM and TEAMS) that will be completed in mid-2009. These low international prices will put pressure on national operators to lower national prices, as it will be difficult to charge more for taking traffic between cities in an African country than for going all the way from that country to Europe.

Although market pressure has done a lot of the work in lowering prices, international organisations and African governments have also played their part. The World Bank's involvement in financing one of the cables (called EASSy) in a way that ensured open and fair access set the terms of the debate and also helped shape the market. In addition, the South African government declared a landing station for the SAT-3 cable, over which it has a monopoly, an "essential national facility". This has enabled the country's regulator to insist on co-location for a new competitor company, Neotel. The Mauritius regulator ICTA instituted a price determination against the monopoly fibre operator Mauritius Telecom that enabled much cheaper prices to be put in place.[4]

Once a fibre cable has reached the coast of a country, the key problem is then getting a truly national backbone in place. On the evidence so far, the private sector will only deliver national backbone capacity to a relatively small percentage of the population. Understandably, operators have to have a sufficient return to justify investing in relatively expensive capital projects like infrastructure. Except in the markets of larger countries or in the wealthier segments of national markets, there has been little incentive to invest. The effect of this is that traditionally there has only been one infrastructure operator, or "one and a half" infrastructure operators – the latter case being where competitors spring up in metro areas and on routes between main metro cities. So the issue is: how does one incentivise wider national roll-out without simply returning to the uncompetitive, monopoly position that was in place before liberalisation, and which resulted in high national rates?

While infrastructure competition does produce some level of price competition, its impact is limited. Two competitors on national backbone prices – even over busy national routes – rarely produce more than a 10-20% difference in price over the mid to long term. For example, in Uganda, where there are two infrastructure operators, the reduction in prices over three years has been 13%.

Africa's policy-makers and regulators have adopted a range of different approaches to creating infrastructure competition, not all of which are coherent, but will affect national backbone prices. The more liberal countries (such as Ghana, Nigeria, Kenya and Tanzania) have encouraged those who have built fibre for management purposes to sell their surplus. These entities include power utilities, railways, and oil pipeline and water companies. Alternative fibre operators have provided a competitive dynamic in some markets, but

2 EDGE Institute: www.the-edge.org.za
3 Fibre for Afrca: www.fibreforafrica.net

4 For case studies of countries on the SAT-3/SAFE cable, including Mauritius, see Jagun (2008).

Technologies that may have an impact on lowering prices and widening access in developing countries

VoIP
In its most immediate form (through things like Skype) it offers cheap international calling. This may become more widely available on mobiles in the not-too-distant future (see www.vyke.com).

Wireless technologies
Wi-Fi and WiMAX are offering alternative operators ways of offering cheaper internet access. They can also be used to create municipal networks that offer local authorities cheaper voice and data services. If regulators allow it a competitive space, the WiMAX mobile voice standard (802.16e) may yet offer newer mobile operators a way of cutting costs and offering better rates to customers.

Solar base stations
Indian start-up VNL is to manufacture a cheaper, solar-powered base station (see www.vnl.in). Given the absence of power supply and the cost of diesel for generators, this will have a clear impact on costs if its claims are verified in operational use.

Fibre slung from power lines
Fibre slung on power transmission towers is considerably cheaper to roll out compared to fibre that needs trenches in the ground. A recent example from Africa illustrates the potential (see www.balancingact-africa.com/news/back/balancing-act_416.html).

Mobile internet and short message service (SMS)
A significant percentage of people in developing regions use SMS on their mobile phones as their principal source of daily information. Newer handsets with intuitive graphic interfaces, like the iPhone, will extend this "mobile media" into the internet.

M-money services
For the un-banked who may carry the risk of losing their cash, m-money services like Safaricom's M-Pesa in Kenya (with 2.5 million users) will have an enormous impact. Remittances from diaspora communities are now more significant than aid flows in developing countries. New mobile-based services may help cut the cost of these transactions from around 12% to nearer 6%.

Low-cost handsets and computers
The high cost of handsets or computers is one of the primary barriers to greater access. A range of handset manufacturers are focused on trying to reduce the costs of a basic handset (for commentary, see our report on spectrum management in this edition of GISWatch). Based on the same logic, computer manufacturers (including AMD and Intel) have been drawn into the race to provide low-cost laptops by Nicholas Negroponte's One Laptop per Child initiative (see wiki.laptop.org).

have not really addressed issues like the need for wider geographic breadth of coverage.

The mobile companies have had to put up with high prices and indifferent service from many of the former incumbent telephone companies and, as a reaction, have almost all gone down the route of building all or part of their own backbone infrastructure. Where there are existing high national backbone prices, the financial incentive to build your own network is considerable: depending on the country, this may be as much as 50% cheaper.

A number of African governments have taken this insight and sought to create national fibre infrastructure companies: Ghana, Nigeria, Kenya, Rwanda, South Africa and Uganda are among their number. Often with the aid of government financing from Chinese vendor Huawei, the aim has been to create genuinely national networks as quickly as possible. This has raised a number of difficult issues.

In the first instance, a number of these countries have chosen the former incumbent (now usually privatised) to manage the resulting network. This is not something that creates trust among potential users that things will be any different from what went before. In addition, many operators have either already built some infrastructure or are about to do so. Unless the national infraco focuses on the more marginal areas, its impact will be to drive out potential investors.

But whether the policy route taken is to create a national fibre network or simply "in-fill" those places the market will not reach, these different approaches may all go some significant way to extending cheap bandwidth to nearly all of a developing country's citizens.

The final piece in the jigsaw has been to find a technological solution that will deliver voice and data services into the most marginal "bottom-of the-pyramid" communities, in a way that will create a business that will not require a constant drip-feed of donor aid. The larger and more centralised solutions have been offered by organisations like Grameen and the mobile companies. For example, Celtel Nigeria (shortly to become Zain) has offered entrepreneurs in Nigeria the opportunity to run the base station that delivers their voice service, as well as act as local agents for mobile phones. In other words, the entrepreneur remains in effect a franchisee of the larger company.

A more innovative and less centralised solution has been developed in South Africa by Dabba.[5] The idea was to create a microtelco operation from technology that could be supplied "out of the box", for use without specialist knowledge. Dabba has partners who want to expand into the townships of Alexandra and Soweto in the greater Johannesburg area, and Khayelitsha in Cape Town.

The business is focused on working financially with only 1,000 subscribers. The user would get a cheap voice over internet protocol (VoIP) wireless handset from someone like UT Starcom. A "super node" will deliver a coverage area of two kilometres, but the phone's range is only 100 metres. The alternatives are that there would have to be a greater density of wireless access points, or, as with the precursors to mobile phones, the access points might be physically marked and people could stand near them. The former would make sense for a large village; the latter might work in a smaller settlement.

Dabba is already interconnecting with South Africa's four main voice carriers, but reactions are mixed. One of the larger mobile carriers has been very helpful, while a couple have been blocking calls. Dabba's plan is to become an intermediary for the much smaller microtelcos, allowing them to aggregate traffic before entering the telco world, and providing much needed support. It will also enable the microtelcos to offer cheap calling to other microtelcos that work with Dabba.

For the mobile operator, it allows others to take the financial and control risks in areas of marginal business. And if it succeeds, it may offer valuable lessons in how to strip back capital expenditure to meet market demand in increasingly marginal areas. This will not prevent the more pig-headed mobile companies from trying to strangle it at birth.

It offers local entrepreneurs the opportunity to build a business. For the unspent millions in universal service funds all over Africa, it offers a new market-driven element that could energise the drive to reach the last 30-50% of Africans – and those in developing countries elsewhere across the world – who do not yet currently have access to voice or internet. ■

References

Balancing Act: www.balancingact-africa.com/news/back/balancing-act_416.html

EDGE Institute: www.the-edge.org.za

Fibre for Africa: www.fibreforafrica.net

Jagun, A. (2008) *The Case for "Open Access" Communications Infrastructure in Africa: The SAT-3/WASC cable (Briefing).* Glasgow: APC. Available at: www.apc.org/en/node/6142

Song, S. Village Telco Workshop. *Many Possibilities.* Available at: manypossibilities.net/2008/07/village-telco-workshop

VNL: www.vnl.in

Vyke: www.vyke.com

5 For more details see: manypossibilities.net/2008/07/village-telco-workshop

Accessing content

Daniel Pimienta
Networks and Development Foundation (FUNREDES)
www.funredes.org

The world wide web is, effectively, the largest public domain of information. But while it maintains its exponential growth in content, search engines are losing their capacity to index a significant part of it; and advertising directly and more perversely extends its reach, influencing users' behaviour when accessing content. At the same time, issues such as open content and the right to access this public domain of knowledge remain important, and some progress in this regard is being made. The demography of the net is finally evolving towards greater cultural and linguistic diversity, announcing the end of an initial and transitory phase of English dominance, which was a consequence of its historic development.

This chapter alerts us to the growing risk of bias from online search services: on the one hand, a bias that is culturally sensitive, and indirectly caused by a reduction in coverage or capacity; on the other, a bias that is the direct result of the influence of advertisers, who deliberately affect search results.

The extent of the challenge facing us is clear when we consider that a legitimate objective is for people to have access to online content in their own language, and sense that the digital divide is much deeper in terms of content than in terms of access to technology. And as new users get online, fewer and fewer of them appear to be content producers, emphasising the importance of digital literacy in the struggle against the digital divide.

Nurturing a wide public domain of information, especially in the sciences, is crucial for the future of our knowledge societies, and is important to the global development divide between the North and the South. It is commonplace that cyberspace must embrace and reflect the linguistic and cultural diversity of the world. The key, however, is how quickly this happens.

Content topology

What are the characteristics of what we commonly refer to as online "content"? Consider these figures: the number of internet hosts crossed the 500-million mark in 2008,[1] while the number of internet users is estimated around 1.4 billion,[2] the number of websites around 100 million or more, and the number of visible web pages[3] at least 140 billion.[4]

1 www.isc.org/index.pl
2 www.internetworldstats.com

Table 1: Worldwide internet statistics

Internet users	1.4 billion
Registered domains	140 million
Websites	100 million-170 million*
Web pages	140 billion-one trillion
Indexed web pages	20 billion-40 billion

* Differences in figures may be due to virtual sites which are hosted on servers. See news.netcraft.com/archives/web_server_survey.html

An idea of the topology of the "content universe" is obtained by constructing the following ratios:

- Three users per internet host
- One domain name for every ten users
- One website for every fourteen users
- 1,000 web pages per user, 150 of which are indexed by search engines.

These ratios have probably kept relatively stable over the years, except the last one. In recent years the percentage of indexed pages has been shrinking to less than 15% of the total, potentially making users much more vulnerable to the various biases which condition their access to content, besides being more malleable to targeted advertising strategies[5] launched on search services.

Bias in access to content

Powerful applications like Google have for years been able to keep track of our web navigation behaviour, posing a threat to our online privacy. Empirical evidence suggests that the order of presentation of search results is not only decided by the ranking algorithm which has made Google so successful, but that it feeds off our personal history of searches in order to target us with sponsored links. Furthermore, keywords are being sold to commercial interests, questioning the whole idea of "objective information retrieval". Add to this the fact that 85% of the visible web now escapes the attention of web

3 The invisible web (also called "deep web") is the sum of dynamic pages produced by databases or other programmed mechanisms that produce dynamic pages. Some authors estimate it could be 100 to 500 times larger than the visible web. See Bergman (2001).
4 Today it is impossible to find data for the total number of visible web pages. This figure has been extrapolated by the author from previous years' figures.
5 Advertising is so far the main driver of the content economy.

crawlers,[6] and the situation begins to feel like a subtle form of censorship.[7] Some voices are starting to complain[8] and citizens should follow carefully the evolution which makes a company like Google an ally for open access, as in their Google Scholar initiative,[9] but also a commercially biased operator that uses its basic search interface to make money.

Content diversity

While the average figures quoted above hold interesting meaning to understand the content universe, as always with averages, they hide the diversity factor.

The split of global internet users between regions[10] shows Africa with 4% and an internet penetration rate of only 5%, while Europe accounts for 27% of internet users and a penetration rate of 48%. The split of users per language shows English at 30%, followed by Chinese (17%), Spanish (9%), Japanese (7%), French (5%) and German (5%). As for the split of content on the web by language, there is no single source, and there are divergent figures for English.[11]

Indeed, the digital divide is not only a question of access: it is also, and even more, a question of content. FUNREDES studies[12] have shown that, for instance, more web pages are being produced in French by the United Kingdom (0.4% of the total) and Germany (0.5%) than the whole of Africa (0.3%), and that France is producing more English pages (0.7% of the total) than the whole of Africa (0.3%; 80% of them from South Africa). Furthermore, the trends observed show absolutely no improvement in the last five years. Language Observatory Project (LOP)[13] studies in Asia and Africa demonstrated than local languages accounted for a percentage of web pages in the order of 1%, 0.1% or 0.01% compared to cross-border languages (English, French, Russian or Arabic).

The depth of the digital divide as it is reflected through the lens of content appears much greater than the access gap: 4% of internet users are in Africa, while African languages account for less than 0.4% of all content, and less-spoken African languages for less than 0.04%!

And this is based on the 5% of the world's languages that have a digital existence – meaning that there is a codification scheme to transcribe their alphabets in digital form. Human beings have created some 40,000 different languages throughout history, of which some 7,000 are still used. Of these, only about 350 have a digital existence.

For the internet to be a resource for everyone, it will take much more than connecting everybody. It will mean allowing everyone to relate to the net in his/her mother tongue; which implies, obviously, the balanced existence of content in everyone's language.

The so-called pragmatics who believe this goal is unreachable – and therefore that it is acceptable to force people to work online in a non-native language and/or that English is the natural lingua franca of cyberspace – should consider the following: UNESCO studies[14] have shown that not being educated in a mother tongue is a significant handicap for children. And Wikipedia linguistic statistics[15] show the presence of articles in 264 languages, offering a reason to believe another world of content is possible...

The Internet Governance Forum (IGF)[16] in November 2007 started to take note of linguistic and cultural issues, as witnessed by a roundtable chaired by Gilberto Gil, the Brazilian minister of culture at the time, with the president of the World Network for Linguistic Diversity (MAAYA),[17] Adama Samassekou, invited as one of the speakers. Yet these efforts are focusing on the tip of the iceberg: while the internationalized domain name (IDN)[18] system will certainly mean progress when it allows users to navigate the web with links written in other character sets, this still falls short of confronting the challenges of cyberspace reflecting the genuine cultural and linguistic diversity of our planet.

At the time of writing this report, China has just passed the United States in terms of internet users (258 vs. 220 million)[19] – just one sign of the acceleration in the pace of change in internet demographics. What happens is a simple question of inflexion in curves getting closer to saturation when the penetration into a segment gets very high (the US has an internet penetration rate above 70%, and the figure for English speakers connected to the internet is above 50%).

6 At the time of writing, a new service, cuil.com, has been released. It claims to not retain the user search history, which is a good move, and also to index close to the whole web (122 billion pages). Unfortunately, the results so far are contradicting these claims.

7 FUNREDES studies have shown in particular that English content is over-represented in the search engines' indexes. See Observatory of Linguistic and Cultural Diversity on the Internet: funredes.org/lc

8 See in particular www.iicm.tugraz.at/iicm_papers/dangers_google.pdf

9 scholar.google.com

10 www.internetworldstats.com/stats.htm

11 Some sources claim that the percentage of web pages in English has been above 70% over the last ten years, in spite of the drastic change in user demographics, while others, such as FUNREDES, quote figures of less than 50% (funredes.org/lc). See UNESCO (2005).

12 See the above-mentioned studies at funredes.org/lc

13 www.language-observatory.org

14 portal.unesco.org/education/en/ev.php-URL_ID=21260&URL_DO=DO_TOPIC&URL_SECTION=201.html

15 en.wikipedia.org/wiki/Wikipedia:Multilingual_statistics

16 See www.intgovforum.org and in particular www.intgovforum.org/Rio_Meeting/IGF2-Diversity-13NOV07.txt

17 The World Network for Linguistic Diversity, like the IGF, was also a product of the World Summit on the Information Society (WSIS) process. See www.maaya.org

18 en.wikipedia.org/wiki/Internationalized_domain_name

19 See Barboza (2008). Note that the latest figures from Internet World Stats are different (May 2008: US=220, China=210). This serves to remind us that apart from the number of hosts the figures are not 100% reliable.

The above-mentioned FUNREDES studies have shown that initially there was a link between the growth of users and content in a given language. However, over time less content is produced proportionally to the number of users signing on: new users behave more like consumers than producers. The missing link is probably digital literacy, which includes sensitising users to the importance of content production.

Open content, the main global issue

The ultimate goal for universal access to telecommunication services is to allow citizens to communicate and access information and knowledge. The empowerment of all citizens through knowledge is indeed the essence of the information society, and the largest public domain of information shall be then considered a basic human right, and linked to social cohesion and economic development.

The Creative Commons[20] initiative offers a range of possibilities for legally protecting content in such a way that it becomes open content in the public domain, and it poses a significant challenge to traditional copyright protection. The point is to try to reverse a tendency of people overprotecting their content, and encouraging a more open approach, benefiting the general interest without causing harm to any particular interest.

Public domain information, also known as the "information commons", refers to freely accessing intellectual work, or the media on which this is stored, the use of which does not infringe on any intellectual property right, or breach any other communal right (such as indigenous rights) or any obligation of confidentiality.[21] The knowledge society must be built on the widest public domain to achieve its ambition.

Open access to content: An emblematic theme showing progress

Open access refers to scientific publications being placed in the public domain instead of being held by editors or publications. The current status quo is essentially the following: public money funds researchers, but the product of those researchers ends up being privately owned by publishers who legally take the intellectual property from the researcher, and indirectly from public administration and from the taxpayer. This is done in order to finance the editing and publishing system, which includes a peer-review system. The latter secures the prestige of a publication, on which researchers depend for academic recognition and credits. This suggests something of the challenge at stake in aiming to change a copyright regime – there are many interests involved!

20 creativecommons.org
21 unesdoc.unesco.org/images/0012/001297/129725e.pdf

It would be an extraordinary effort in worldwide collaboration, and a boost to research in a developing world which can hardly afford the high price of scientific publications, to see this wealth of scientific knowledge freely accessible at a click. Unfortunately, the complex resistance ingrained in a system created for the age of print prevents this from happening.

It is not that the scientific world has not tried to push the issue, as witnessed by the Berlin Declaration on Open Access to Knowledge in the Sciences and Humanities[22] in 2003 and initiatives such as the Public Library of Science (PLoS),[23] which are offering concrete solutions. The Scholarly Publishing and Academic Resources Coalition (SPARC)[24] is developing advocacy strategies in support of public policies on open access, and is reporting progress.

Again, the subject of linguistic and cultural diversity is not neutral to the struggle for open access, as the dominant system has played an important role in making English the language for scientific communication in most instances. ■

References

Barboza, D. (2008) China Surpasses U.S. in Number of Internet Users. *The New York Times*, 26 July. Available at: www.nytimes.com/2008/07/26/business/worldbusiness/26internet.html?_r=1&oref=slogin

Bergman, M. (2001) *The Deep Web: Surfacing Hidden Value.* Ann Arbor: Scholarly Publishing Office, University of Michigan Library. Available at: quod.lib.umich.edu/cgi/t/text/text-idx?c=jep;view=text;rgn=main;idno=3336451.0007.104

Berlin Declaration on Open Access to Knowledge in the Sciences and Humanities: oa.mpg.de/openaccess-berlin/berlindeclaration.html

Creative Commons: creativecommons.org

FUNREDES Observatory of Linguistic and Cultural Diversity on the Internet: funredes.org/lc

Internet Governance Forum: www.intgovforum.org

Internet Systems Consortium: www.isc.org/index.pl

Internet World Stats: www.internetworldstats.com

Netcraft (2008) September 2008 Web Server Survey. Available at: news.netcraft.com/archives/web_server_survey.html

Public Library of Science (PLoS): www.plos.org

Scholarly Publishing and Academic Resources Coalition (SPARC): www.arl.org/sparc

UNESCO (2005) *Measuring Linguistic Diversity on the Internet.* Available at: portal.unesco.org/ci/en/ev.php-URL_ID=20804&URL_DO=DO_TOPIC&URL_SECTION=201.html

World Network for Linguistic Diversity: www.maaya.org

22 oa.mpg.de/openaccess-berlin/berlindeclaration.html
23 www.plos.org
24 www.arl.org/sparc

Institutional overview

Institutional overview

David Souter
ict Development Associates *ltd*
www.ictdevelopment.co.uk

This overview chapter is concerned with ways in which global institutions have addressed access to infrastructure since the World Summit on the Information Society (WSIS), particularly during the last year (2007-2008). The policies and practice of global institutions usually change gradually rather than dramatically. The chapter therefore seeks to put their role in context. Its first section reviews key issues in recent debate about access to infrastructure. The second section considers recent developments in institutional policy and future access challenges.

The access debate

The starting point for this discussion is an understanding of access and the relationship between infrastructure and the access challenge. This section reviews the WSIS access objectives and then considers institutional approaches to three issues: the relationship between supply- and demand-side aspects of access; types and levels of service provision; and types and levels of infrastructure.

WSIS access objectives

The WSIS outcome documents stress perceived benefits of access to information and communications technologies (ICTs) and the desirability of universal access to high-quality (fast, cheap and reliable) ICT services and equipment. The Geneva Plan of Action, dating from November 2003 but largely agreed in earlier preparatory WSIS meetings, sought to define what access meant here through a list of targets, modelled on the Millennium Development Goals (the internationally agreed objectives in mainstream development areas such as health and education). These targets are set out in Box 1.

The targets present two analytical challenges:

- Firstly, they are imprecise. It is unclear what level of access/connectivity is intended (from a single telephone per village to widespread broadband deployment). This leaves them, effectively, non-measurable.
- Secondly, they are of their time. The pace of change in ICT technology and usage is such that targets need regular revision to retain contemporary meaning. Recent mobile telephone access targets, for example, have been rapidly exceeded and required revision everywhere.

The institutional framework established by WSIS to monitor progress towards its targets has also been weak:

- Action line meetings to review WSIS outcomes are held in Geneva each May. One session, coordinated by the International Telecommunication Union (ITU), is concerned with "information and communication infrastructure: an essential foundation for an inclusive information society". However, in practice, this enables information exchange rather than coordination of policy or implementation plans.
- Overall review of WSIS implementation is undertaken by the United Nations Commission on Science and Technology for Development (CSTD). This also lacks any strategic role on infrastructure plans.
- "Access" is a key theme of the annual Internet Governance Forum (IGF), established on the recommendation of WSIS. This meets annually, most recently in Rio de Janeiro in November 2007. It provides a forum for multistakeholder discussion about internet issues, including access, but has no decision-making powers.
- The WSIS follow-up framework, in short, merely provides discussion fora. Global institutional activity in relation to access and connectivity is largely developed, as before WSIS, within individual institutions rather than in global fora, though there has been some increased coordination (see examples below).

Supply- and demand-side approaches to access

Much literature about access to ICTs, particularly from development banks and international financial institutions (IFIs), focuses on the supply side – especially the supply of large-scale infrastructure. This top-down approach reflects approaches in other infrastructure sectors such as power, transport and water. IFIs particularly emphasise the value of infrastructure in enabling economic growth at a macroeconomic level.

Infrastructure is essential for access: without it, people cannot use the services that networks make available. However, meaningful access – at community or individual level – requires more than infrastructure. People also need the funds to afford access, the skills required to make use of services and equipment, and the availability of content which is of value to them. Broader understandings of access – more commonly found in literature from development agencies such as the United Nations Development Programme (UNDP) and the Canadian International Development Research Centre (IDRC) – stress demand-side factors which focus on enabling communities and empowering citizens.

The enabling policy and regulatory framework for communications is of concern to both IFIs and social development institutions. Strategies concerned with liberalisation and interconnection, for example, affect both the pace and nature of infrastructure deployment and the price and quality of services to end-users. Meaningful analysis of access therefore needs to consider both supply- and demand-side factors *and* the enabling framework which is created by governments and business. Since the 1980s, global institutions have emphasised this enabling framework while leaving financial investment largely to the private sector.

Service provision

There is ongoing debate amongst global institutions about the relative importance of access to basic telephony and internet/broadband services in developing countries. The context for this debate has shifted significantly this past year, because of technological and market change.

The availability of voice telephony has been transformed during the last decade by the advent of mass mobile cellular markets. Until the late 1990s, there was a large and growing gap in access to voice telephony between industrial and developing countries. Fixed-line teledensity in highly industrial countries had reached over 90% of households, while in least developed countries (LDCs) it languished below 1%. Most telephone companies believed they could not recover fixed-network deployment costs in low-income communities, particularly in rural areas, and so networks were concentrated on urban areas and inter-urban routes.

The advent of mobile networks has changed the economics of communications infrastructure. Wireless networks are cheaper to deploy and have a lower proportion of fixed costs – making it possible to recover investment costs more quickly. Mobile voice networks have therefore been widely deployed in low-income countries, through private investment. Teledensities in much of Africa have now reached 25% or more. The GSM Association (GSMA) – the leading association of cellular mobile companies – believes mobile networks can cover 95% of the global population on commercial terms. The World Bank, too, expects 90% of Africans to be provided with telephony by commercial networks. The "digital divide" in voice telephony is therefore narrowing rapidly, with little financial involvement by IFIs or development agencies.

Global institutions disagree about the sufficiency of this rapid growth in voice telephony. Some have argued that rapid growth in access to telephony – which requires few skills for use and delivers rapid benefits to all – should be prioritised, and that internet access will develop organically from this. Others argue that the important "digital divide" between societies and communities depends on access to the internet and broadband networks, which offer greater economic and empowerment value and which should therefore be prioritised.

This institutional debate is important because it affects decisions about the need for financial investment, particularly the use of public or IFI/development agency funds, and the need for fixed as well as wireless access networks. The debate is also changing as technology and markets evolve:

- On the supply side, past assumptions that expensive fixed networks are required to provide broadband access are being challenged by new wireless technologies like Wi-Fi and WiMAX.
- On the demand side, the prevalence of mobile phone access vis-à-vis fixed broadband networks suggests that most users in LDCs will gain internet experience through upgraded (third generation) mobile devices rather than fixed lines.

ICT businesses have responded more quickly to these technological and market changes than global institutions. Many businesses are now planning on the assumption that mass access to broadband in low-income countries will develop first through wireless, not fixed infrastructure. Global institutions are beginning to follow, but there is a need for sharper dialogue between ICT, funding agency and development professionals.

Infrastructure tiers

There are many ways of illustrating layers of ICT supply. Many readers will be familiar with the distinction commonly made between transport, services, terminal and content layers. Here, we are concerned with tiers within the transport (transmission or infrastructure) layer, of which three are particularly significant:

- International infrastructure
- Regional or national infrastructure
- The local access network.

All three tiers are required for access to global telephony or internet to be available in a community.

- The *quality* of access, in particular its bandwidth, will be primarily determined by the lowest quality amongst these tiers. For example, a high-bandwidth local access network which accesses the internet through low-bandwidth international infrastructure will provide low-bandwidth access to end-users.
- The *cost* of access, meanwhile, will depend on cumulative costs incurred. High-quality, affordable internet access will only be available to end-users if cheap, high-

Box 1: Geneva Plan of Action connectivity targets

- To connect villages with ICTs and establish community access points
- To connect universities, colleges, secondary schools and primary schools with ICTs
- To connect scientific and research centres with ICTs
- To connect public libraries, cultural centres, museums, post offices and archives with ICTs
- To connect health centres and hospitals with ICTs
- To connect all local and central government departments and establish websites and e-mail addresses
- To adapt all primary and secondary school curricula to meet the challenges of the information society, taking into account national circumstances
- To ensure that all of the world's population have access to television and radio services
- To encourage the development of content and to put in place technical conditions in order to facilitate the presence and use of all world languages on the internet
- To ensure that more than half the world's inhabitants have access to ICTs within their reach.

Source: **WSIS Geneva Plan of Action, para. 6: www.itu.int/wsis/docs/geneva/official/poa.html**

quality infrastructure is available in all three tiers. Data from 2006, for example, suggest that the average retail price for (generally lower quality) broadband access in sub-Saharan Africa was USD 366 per month, compared with between USD 6 and USD 44 for (generally higher quality) access in India (Williams, 2008).

Each tier poses different access and infrastructure challenges to policy-makers in governments and global institutions. Some of the key issues are as follows:

- The availability of international infrastructure varies greatly by geography. Very high traffic volumes can be conveyed by highly competitive submarine cable networks linking North America, Europe and the Pacific Rim, resulting in very low transit costs. Where submarine cables are non-competitive or non-existent (as in West and East Africa respectively), they offer much more limited (and so much slower) connectivity at much higher prices. Landlocked countries are also affected by the additional cost of cross-border connectivity to reach international cables, or the high cost and low capacity of satellite infrastructure.
- The availability, cost and quality of regional and national "backbones" – high-capacity infrastructure between local access and international networks – also varies substantially. In industrial countries, there is typically competition between backbones owned by fixed and mobile service providers and other carriers selling wholesale network capacity. These backbones usually rely on fibre-optic cable, which offers high capacity, but whose deployment involves significant fixed costs which can only be recovered rapidly where there is high demand. In low-income countries, there is usually much less competition, resulting in higher costs to users. In some areas, especially Africa, lower-capacity microwave links provide much backbone infrastructure. In addition, regulations often require other service providers to use the incumbent operator's backbone network or restrict the resale of capacity on mobile operators' backbone networks.
- In the past, telephone companies in developing countries assumed that demand in rural areas was insufficient to make (fixed) local access networks viable without subsidy. Recent private investment in (mobile cellular) networks suggests that only the remotest rural areas are commercially unviable, and universal access subsidies are now rarely needed for basic voice telephony. The economics of broadband networks are more challenging. There is therefore discussion in institutions about whether subsidies are required to facilitate higher-capacity fixed networks, and about the implications of possible broadband network monopolies.

The response of global institutions

The issues above raise questions for global institutions in two main areas:

- The technology and financing of infrastructure deployment, which primarily determine the *availability* of access.
- The regulation of infrastructure and markets, which primarily determine the *affordability* of access.

Since the early 1980s, global institutions have considered a willing private sector the primary source of investment for communications infrastructure, releasing IFI funds for more difficult infrastructure funding challenges like transport, power and water. This approach has seemed increasingly appropriate to them as wireless networks have been deployed, reaching much larger geographic areas and populations. Institutions have therefore focused on influencing policy and regulatory frameworks in order to encourage private investment and promote competition – in particular through liberalisation, the opening of markets to foreign investment and the removal of restrictions on the use of infrastructure and technology.

The scale of investment in ICT infrastructure in recent years is impressive. Between 1996 and 2006, some USD 23 billion was invested in telecommunications infrastructure in sub-Saharan Africa alone, the large majority by private sector telecommunications businesses. The geographic reach of telephone networks (in terms of the proportion of citizens enjoying access, public or private) has risen to 75% or more in many countries. The comparable 2006 figure for electric power – which has seen much greater public investment by IFIs and development agencies – was 40% or less.[1] Even higher levels of private investment are anticipated for the future. At the ITU's Connect Africa conference (Rwanda, October 2007), the GSMA "committed" its members to investing a further USD 50 billion between 2007 and 2012, entirely on commercial terms (ITU, 2007).

IFIs will not normally invest where private investment is available. However, as noted above, recent years have seen debate about the relative economics and developmental value of basic telephony and internet/broadband services and networks. Two issues have been prominent:

- While voice telephony may be commercially viable in almost all contexts, there will be some remote rural areas and small islands where it is not and where access infrastructure will require public investment or subsidy.
- The range of areas in which internet/broadband access may not be commercially viable is likely to be higher than that for voice telephony, and will include many more low-income rural areas. This is especially so if fixed infrastructure is required for broadband.

This debate focused during WSIS on the work of a Task Force on Financial Mechanisms (TFFM). Key conclusions of the Task Force, which were adopted by WSIS, included agreement amongst global institutions that:

- Investment in ICTs should come primarily from the private sector. Regulatory reform – including the promotion of liberalisation and open communications markets – should continue to be the foundation for institutional engagement with the sector.
- Nevertheless, there was scope for more public-private partnerships and the creative use of short-term public funding for capital investment where commercial viability was uncertain or unlikely. This might include both remote rural areas *and* the more general deployment of higher-capacity networks.
- There might also be scope for public participation, alongside the private sector, in major infrastructure investments such as regional backbones.
- Existing institutional funding mechanisms were sufficient to enable this additional investment. No new mechanisms were required.

Recent developments

The approach set out by the TFFM continues to provide the framework in which global institutions address access infrastructure. Their primary focus is on policy and regulatory reform.

However, some institutions also provide investment support where private finance is not sufficiently forthcoming. Since WSIS, this has led to some loosening of constraints on financial support for major infrastructure investments – for example, the International Finance Corporation's support for the Eastern Africa Submarine Cable System (EASSy) and agreements between African nations and the European Union (EU) on future infrastructure investment. There has also been some cooperation between funding institutions. While institutional interventions are usually piecemeal and do not form part of a global strategy for access development or for the use of infrastructure in development, the following paragraphs briefly illustrate examples of current interventions.

The best-known instance concerns the deployment of fibre-optic cable along Africa's east coast, the last major stretch of coastline without submarine cable access. For years before 2008, proposals to lay the EASSy cable, linking East African countries with South Africa and the Middle East (and thereby global cable networks), were mired in controversy. Amongst other things, there were fears that without appropriate regulatory intervention, EASSy's owners (mostly state-owned fixed network operators) would charge monopoly prices for cable capacity to their competitors. The World Bank Group offered financial support for EASSy on condition that it adopted open access principles (see below). By the

1 The World Bank (2007) says that only 25% of African households have "access to modern energy".

time EASSy resolved structural and management disputes in 2008, at least two competing private-sector-led initiatives were underway to lay alternative cables linking East Africa to global networks. These reflected new assessments of commercial viability and suggested that competition rather than institutional investment would stimulate new infrastructure.

The New Partnership for Africa's Development (NEPAD) initially saw EASSy as part of an institutionally led ICT Broadband Infrastructure Network for Africa. NEPAD's e-Africa Commission has promoted this large-scale programme, which envisages undersea cables along the East African coast and beyond Africa as well as new cross-border regional backbone infrastructure designed to address capacity problems within the continent. Broadband infrastructure is treated as a "public good" in this proposal, with ownership of infrastructure separated from use and also subject to open access principles. NEPAD believes that a comprehensive approach like this will attract the best mix of institutional and private funding. However, the complex design, financial and management arrangements required have caused problems, including the loss of EASSy from the project.

Another poorly served region with a major infrastructure renewal plan is the Pacific, where small low-income populations are dispersed over very large areas of ocean. Here, a regionally agreed Pacific Plan Digital Strategy aims to address the access challenge by improving local access to ICTs, particularly in remote and rural areas; increasing international bandwidth; reducing costs; removing inappropriate regulation; and strengthening capacity to make use of ICTs (thereby increasing demand). The strategy includes both new international submarine infrastructure (to reduce international transit costs) and an Australian-funded satellite network to improve local access in remoter islands.

These examples involve institutional participation within mixed (public/private) funding structures. Although there has been some shift in international institutions' thinking about financial engagement with ICT infrastructure, their primary approach continues to emphasise policy and regulatory reform. An important example of new thinking in this area can be found in a paper concerned with regional and national backbones, which was published by the World Bank and the associated ICT for development agency *info*Dev in August (Williams, 2008).

Wireless networks, which have low fixed costs and are readily scalable, are generally cheaper in the short and medium term where demand is relatively low. Fixed networks, with higher fixed costs, are generally cheaper in the medium and longer term where demand is high. This is as true of backbone networks as it is of local access networks. In most countries, core backbones have been implemented by fixed network incumbents, which have predominantly installed fixed (cable) infrastructure. In Africa, however, fixed networks were much less pervasive before the "mobile revolution", and so most backbone capacity is owned by mobile operators rather than incumbents. Much of this mobile network backbone is made up of microwave rather than cable infrastructure.

The World Bank paper is consistent with established institutional thinking about access infrastructure in that its policy prescriptions rest on two complementary components: creating an enabling environment for competition, and stimulating roll-out in underserved areas. The Bank thinks it "likely" that some rural areas will continue to require public funding – through subsidies, shared infrastructure or incentives – but envisages most access challenges being addressed through measures to promote investment, stimulate downstream (service) competition, and reduce political and commercial risks.

The continued emphasis on policy and regulatory reform, and the relationship between ICTs and other infrastructure, are also well illustrated by the EU-Africa Infrastructure Trust Fund, agreed between the European and African Unions in 2007. This aims to support infrastructure development in energy, transport, water and communications. In the ICT context, it aims to "develop connections with continental and regional networks while opening up the telecommunications sector to competition for efficient and low-cost provision of ICT services." In its first year, the Fund allocated EUR 109 million to initiatives, but only 5% of this, concerned with regulatory reform, addressed communications.

A final word in this context about community networks. There is interest in some development agencies in the possibility of building access outwards from remote or marginal communities, rather than relying on established national networks to overcome the access challenge. A number of examples of community networks have emerged, in both urban and rural areas, sponsored by local authorities or development agencies. Some of these are using new technologies such as Wi-Fi. Many have leveraged other funding sources, such as development finance for other infrastructure and/or volunteer labour, to reduce costs and so enable cost-effectiveness. Further research is needed on these initiatives, but they may provide a way of facilitating higher-quality affordable access in remote communities before this is likely to be offered by the mainstream communications sector.

Regulatory issues

The influence of regulatory choice on infrastructure deployment is considerable and much debated within global institutions, including the World Bank and ITU. Rapid changes in technology and markets mean that regulatory choices are inherently obsolescent. International institutions are exploring the regulatory opportunities of new technologies and network types (notably Wi-Fi and WiMAX), and of changing market demand, as part of their overall thinking about the industry.

Open access is one regulatory approach which has been backed, amongst others, by both the World Bank and by APC. Open access requires infrastructure owners to make downstream access to their networks available to competitors on non-discriminatory terms. It is particularly relevant where there are only one or two available routes which downstream network and service providers can use to connect customers to global networks, and where there is therefore a risk that owners of "bottleneck" facilities will extract monopoly prices which raise the cost of access to end-users. It has been an important issue in the debates about African submarine cable infrastructure.

Another example of regulatory impact on access and access prices arises from restrictions which some governments place on the wholesale market for backbone infrastructure. Where fixed networks are limited in geographical extent, the majority of national backbone infrastructure is likely to belong to mobile cellular companies. Regulations designed to protect fixed network incumbents sometimes prevent mobile operators from reselling capacity on their backbones. There may be similar constraints on the communications infrastructure owned by other utilities, such as electricity or rail operators (co-called "alternative infrastructure providers"). This not only results in underutilisation of infrastructure, but also acts as a disincentive to new network investment. Companies that cannot sell surplus capacity will tend to install less in the first place.

On the whole, global institutions believe that they can have greater impact on access outcomes by addressing regulatory constraints like these, and otherwise enabling competition – so unlocking private investment – than they can by investing funds directly in new communications infrastructure.

New issues

It is worth drawing attention, finally, to three new issues which are beginning to emerge.

The first concerns the interaction between different tiers of infrastructure, and the relationship between infrastructure and other factors influencing "real access" (such as user incomes and capabilities). The large majority of interventions by global institutions address only specific tiers of infrastructure (e.g., international connectivity or local networks) or particular aspects of the access challenge (such as the problem of high international bandwidth costs). Assumptions are often made about the relationship between different tiers of infrastructure (e.g., that lower international bandwidth prices will enable greater and more equitable local access). Likewise, assumptions are often made about the relationship between communications access and development outcomes which pay too little attention to the non-communications constraints in development contexts. At present, there is little holistic thinking in institutions' approach to the communications market as a whole, or about the interactions between it and development.

The second issue concerns the integration of communications access with access to other infrastructure-based resources. Communities in developing countries which lack affordable communications access also typically lack affordable (or any) access to other network infrastructures (such as transport, clean water and electric power). Such communities are thereby multiply disadvantaged. Surprisingly, however, almost no country has structured its response to such infrastructural deficits by integrating different infrastructure deployments and so leveraging economies of scope and scale.[2] IFIs and other funders have been reluctant to take an integrated network approach, preferring to deal with funding proposals at a sectoral or programme, even project level. There is a growing sense among some observers that, here too, a lack of holistic thinking may be curtailing investment and costing synergies.

The third issue beginning to emerge in institutional thinking relates ICT access to climate change. This has two facets. On the one hand, the ITU and others argue that the use of ICTs – to manage productive processes, transport networks, etc. – will reduce greenhouse gas emissions (GHGs). These potential carbon savings, however, require large-scale deployments of high-level technology in strategic locations such as factories and power plants. They will result, if they are achieved at all, from decisions taken within energy and industrial sectors other than communications. Increased access to ICTs itself, meanwhile, will substantially increase ICTs' overall contribution to GHGs, from 0.83 gigatonnes per annum in 2007 to an estimated 1.43 gigatonnes per annum in 2020 – an increase of 6% a year – with emissions from developing countries rising from 0.38 to 0.80 gigatonnes per annum (GeSI, 2008). The environmental impact of increased ICT access was not significantly discussed before the 2007 Internet Governance Forum. Recent discussion – in publications by the ITU and the (industry-funded) Global e-Sustainability Initiative – is largely couched in terms of

2 Mauritania is one of the few countries that have introduced an integrated universal access agency (APAUS), which seeks to integrate ICT investment with other rural needs.

trade-offs between emissions due to increased access and carbon savings resulting from potential ICT use in other sectors. This seems likely to become a more important factor in global institutional thinking about ICTs as concern continues to mount about climate change.

Conclusion

Access to ICT services depends on a number of factors, including infrastructure, which are constrained in most developing countries. Global institutions continue to focus on policy and regulatory change, rather than direct investment, in addressing communications infrastructure deficits. Private sector investment remains high and is expected to continue to grow, with mobile communications businesses seeming increasingly likely to lead the provision of broadband access in low-income countries, as they previously led the provision of telephony.

There are important infrastructural challenges at international, national and local levels. Global institutions have shown somewhat more interest, since WSIS, in supporting and leveraging investment in areas which are difficult to serve (such as remote areas) or require high levels of capital investment (such as international cables and regional/national backbones), though their primary focus remains on policy and regulatory change. However, there is still relatively little thought given to the integration of different tiers of access infrastructure, to the integration of communications with other infrastructure, and to the relationship between infrastructure and development. More holistic understanding of access and more attention to the demand side of access supply – in particular, to usage requirements and experience – would help institutions play a more dynamic role in this area. ▪

References

GeSI (Global e-Sustainability Initiative) and The Climate Group (2008) *SMART 2020: Enabling the Low Carbon Economy in the Information Age.* Available at: www.gesi.org

ITU (International Telecommunication Union) (2003) *WSIS Plan of Action.* Available at: www.itu.int/wsis/docs/geneva/official/poa.html

ITU (2007) *Connect Africa Summit: Outcomes Report.* Available at: www.itu.int/ITU-D/connect/africa/2007/finalreport.pdf

Williams, M. (2008) *Broadband for Africa: Policy for Promoting the Development of Backbone Networks.* World Bank and *info*Dev. Available at: www.infodev.org/en/Publication.526.html

World Bank (2007) *Clean Energy for Development Investment Framework: The World Bank Group Action Plan.* Available at: siteresources.worldbank.org/DEVCOMMINT/Documentation/21289621/DC2007-0002(E)-CleanEnergy.pdf

Measuring progress

Towards better measures of global ICT adoption and use

Mike Jensen and Amy Mahan
ICT4D consultant; LIRNE.NET
www.suvabay.com; www.lirne.net

Introduction

Efforts to agree on the most appropriate indicators to use for measuring disparities in information and communications technology (ICT) adoption and progress toward information society goals have continued in 2008. However as yet global consensus has not been reached and debate continues over what indicators would best take into account the growing broadband divide, what constitutes "universal access", and how to accommodate local realities regarding data availability, especially in developing countries.

Current background and status of work on global ICT indicators

In the area of ICTs, constant technology and market change has meant that until recently there was little global agreement on an appropriate set of indicators or indices. As a result, a wide range of ICT-related data has been gathered by national statistical and regulatory agencies, and many regional and international agencies have developed their own measures of ICT uptake over the last fifteen years.[1]

By the beginning of the new century, more concrete and universal information society goals were being developed. These began to focus at a global level with the targets of the World Summit on the Information Society (WSIS) Action Plan and the ICT-related components of the Millennium Development Goals (MDGs), which provided further momentum for two important developments in ICT uptake measurement.

First, three indices aimed at measuring and ranking national progress towards becoming information societies were developed and published by the International Telecommunication Union (ITU): the Digital Accessibility Index (DAI), the ICT Opportunity Index (ICT-OI) and the Digital Opportunity Index (DOI).[2] Using a small set of mainly ICT infrastructure and human capacity-related indicators such as teledensity and education levels, none of them were directly based on measures of achievement of the WSIS targets. Although they provide interesting general measures of progress toward some information society goals, important aspects were left out, partly because the data are not seen as relevant, or because the data are simply not available for many countries, especially data requiring household surveys.

The ITU has now begun work on a single index which aims to combine the best features of the ICT-OI and the DOI. At the 6th World Telecommunication/ICT Indicators Meeting in December 2007, the options for a single index were discussed but agreement was not reached, and a working group was set up to finalise the index. One of the outstanding issues, which highlights the difficulty of coming up with simple, globally applicable indicators, was the proposed use of international bandwidth as an indicator. Advanced countries isolated by language, such as South Korea or Japan, would not feature highly on use of international bandwidth because most of their traffic would be local. The meeting also considered community access indicators and a number of measures were proposed, including tracking the percentage of localities (villages, towns, etc.) with a public internet access centre, and those that are connected to the public telephone network. In addition, new indicators in the area of mobile/wireless broadband measurement and computer virus infection levels were discussed.

Second, and perhaps of greater significance, has been the formation of the international multi-stakeholder Partnership on Measuring ICT for Development. Established during the 11th United Nations Conference on Trade and Development (UNCTAD) session in 2004, the partnership now comprises the ITU, Organisation for Economic Co-operation and Development (OECD), UNCTAD, United Nations Educational, Scientific and Cultural Organisation (UNESCO), Eurostat, the World Bank Group and the UN regional agencies.[3]

The partnership was set up for three key reasons: to achieve a common set of core ICT indicators, agreed upon internationally; to help build the capacities of national statistical offices in developing countries to collect the necessary data; and to develop a global database on ICT indicators and make it available on the internet. Its two main report outputs are: *Measuring ICT: The Global Status of ICT Indicators*,[4] and *Core ICT Indicators*.[5] The former is the report of a global stocktaking exercise on the availability of ICT indicators. The 47% national response rate to this concerted effort underlines the problems in establishing global indicators – especially with particularly low numbers of responses for Africa and the Asia Pacific countries.[6]

1 A good comparison of the most important of these can be found in Minges (2005).

2 The *World Information Society Report 2007: Beyond WSIS*, a joint publication by ITU and UNCTAD, details the use of these different indices.

3 These are the UN Economic Commission for Africa (UNECA), UN Economic Commission for Latin America and the Caribbean (ECLAC), UN Economic and Social Commission for Asia and the Pacific (UNESCAP), and UN Economic and Social Commission for Western Asia (UNESCWA).

4 www.itu.int/ITU-D/ict/partnership/material/05-42742%20GLOBAL%20ICT.pdf

5 www.itu.int/ITU-D/ict/partnership/material/CoreICTIndicators.pdf

6 Not to mention the absence of some major economies which did not respond to the survey, such as China, Nigeria and South Africa.

The second work, *Core ICT Indicators*, describes a set of 41 core indicators that were identified during the stocktaking exercise and subsequently endorsed by the UN Statistical Commission in 2007. The core indicators are divided into four groups as follows:

- ICT infrastructure and access (twelve indicators)
- Access to and use of ICT by households and individuals (thirteen indicators)
- Use of ICT by businesses (twelve indicators)
- The ICT sector and trade in ICT goods (four indicators).

The full list of 41 core indicators is described in Annex A at the end of the chapter.

Several developing countries have since integrated the core indicators into existing household and business surveys. While the UN endorsement, and the partnership capacity-building activities, should lead to improvements in the number of countries that collect ICT indicators, and in the comparability of the data, there may need to be a rethink about what indicators should be contained in the "core list". In this respect it should be noted that the partnership does not claim the list to be complete, and identifies the process as continuous and subject to periodic review.

In an ideal world, the core list as proposed by the partnership would certainly provide a useful picture of ICT uptake that covers a large part of the Real Access Framework (RAF) criteria suggested by Bridges.org to assess access to ICTs. (The RAF has been used loosely in the country reports in GISWatch 2008 to reflect access challenges at a national level.) However, lack of data availability from many countries remains a key problem – only a small proportion of countries are able to report on all 41 indicators. In 2005 the partnership found that only about 40 countries worldwide collected ten or more household ICT indicators.

To maximise the number of countries that can report on a common set of indicators, the total number of indicators may have to be reduced, especially those that require user surveys. The core list also has many measures for factors that mainly concern business and trade, which could be reduced relative to those that focus on the general public. Developing countries need indicators which help them formulate regulatory and policy decisions around how to best extend the network using constrained resources. Shared use, community networks, telecentres and so forth are strategies that are not yet fully reflected or measured in the legacy indicators agreed to by the partnership – although the intention to use household survey data does take some steps towards accuracy in this regard.

There are also a number of other important aspects of Real Access that the core list does not explicitly address, including gender disaggregation. These areas are covered in more detail in the following section.

Principles and considerations for selecting future indicators

The number and range of ICTs available today has never been greater, and the interrelationships between them and their indicators are many. In order to effectively evaluate the choice of indicators, it is essential to have a clear conceptual framework on which to base the evaluation. In considering options for choosing indicators, the key considerations and assumptions can be summarised as follows:

- The goal should be to provide universally accepted measures of ICT adoption at a national level that encompass as many nations as possible, using consistent data definitions and timing for data reporting.
- The selection of indicators should be based on a solid conceptual framework that aims to provide measures of actual uptake and use. The use of factors that attempt to ascribe the potential for access are likely to find less wide acceptance. Similarly, supply-side indicators also tend to reflect potential use rather than actual use.
- Given the framing of the WSIS and MDG goals, the focus should be on personal rather than business use (although ideally in future when more data are available, household use and other types of disaggregation would also be more explicitly included in the indicators).
- To maximise the validity period in the face of evolving technologies, new infrastructure and new services adoption, the indicators need to anticipate the future evolution of ICT infrastructure and services.[7]
- Indicator data used should be provided by credible organisations which issue them on a regular basis to allow for longitudinal studies (over time).

Due to the general lack of up-to-date data, the smallest number of indicators is likely to be the most inclusive and comparable across countries. Data freshness is another factor here. Even for the most commonly used data such as teledensity, while an increasing amount of year-end 2007 data is becoming available, overall, 2006 is still the most recent year for globally representative data. This highlights a key problem in selecting a meaningful set of core indicators and also means that for policy-makers there is at least a two-year lag in seeing the results of policy decisions. While more up-to-date information may be available for some indicators, if it is not available for all indicators, the overall value decreases substantially. Since the availability of indicators with broad representation across countries is so small, these considerations also underline a key tension in the construction of the core list: the playoff between accuracy and country representation.

7 In this respect it is expected that networks will steadily evolve away from a circuit-switched infrastructure to packet-switched/internet protocol-based networks, commonly known as next generation networks (NGNs), which will also increasingly comprise larger numbers of wireless internet users.

Measures of equipment uptake need careful consideration for inclusion in a core list of indicators because of lack of accurate data in developing countries, and also due to technology change. For example, in considering the use of computer penetration, the definition of what actually constitutes a personal computer (PC) is becoming increasingly blurred because of mobile/PC convergence and the embedding of computing devices in other household equipment such as fridges.

Television (TV) penetration also suffers from similar problems. Data for TV sales are not up to date in many countries, are likely to be inaccurate due to grey market importing, and are currently only available for 85 countries. TV penetration measures are also not future-proof, considering rapid moves toward internet protocol TV (IPTV) and mobile phone TV, so that using traditional TV measures would bias against those countries that have already adopted these technologies. Radio penetration data suffer from the same sort of problems as PC and TV data.

Fixed-line penetration measures may also be problematic, considering that little new cable is being laid and many nations (especially developing countries) are skipping the use of fixed-line infrastructure and moving directly to wireless technologies. As a result, including fixed-line measures would be likely to bias against most developing countries.

In contrast to fixed lines, mobile phone access is becoming the de facto measure of basic access, and this indicator is of particular concern to developing countries where growth is still rapid and has not come close to reaching saturation. In addition, mobile phones are now being used more for internet access than PCs in some countries.[8] Mobile subscribers are accurately monitored in 220 countries by Wireless Intelligence,[9] the partnership between the GSM [global system for mobile] Association and Ovum. Quarterly data are even available a few months after the end of the quarter[10] and the data span mobile network operators across most technologies, including GSM, wideband code division multiple access (W-CDMA), time division multiple access (TDMA), personal digital cellular (PDC), cdmaOne, CDMA2000 1x, CDMA2000 1xEV-DO, analogue and integrated digital enhanced network (iDEN).

Similarly, a measure of the total number of internet users is an important indicator, but there are some limitations to subscriber data, which are usually provided by operators. This is because there is no clear relationship between the number of internet subscribers (relatively easily obtained) and internet *users,* many of whom may share the subscriber's connection. As a result, much of the available data are based on estimates, for which the level of accuracy is unclear.

Since broadband users, and in particular, wireless and mobile internet users, are becoming an increasingly important component of the internet user base, it may also make sense to include measures of these users, especially as there is now a well-accepted understanding of the importance of broadband for full access to the information society. The need for affordable pervasive access to broadband therefore extends beyond access to information and into active participation, as people with shared interests or problems become significantly active on the web only when broadband is available.

In measuring usage (rather than availability), until more widespread national survey data are available, the use of proxy indicators such as telephone minutes or internet bandwidth will be necessary. The main deficiency with these indicators is a tendency to over-emphasise international usage. Ideally more measures of national usage would be included. However, there is very little national internet traffic data currently available, and although there is some national voice-traffic data, the level of country representation is poor.

Although traffic indicators would appear to only measure usage, they also provide some indication of production of data, although ideally this aspect would be augmented in future by other measures such as numbers of local websites and domain names. These measures are difficult to gather, however, due to the use of generic top-level domains (gTLDs) by many in-country website operators who choose not to use country code top-level domains (ccTLDs). Similarly, the number of secure internet servers has been commonly adopted as an indicator of the extent to which reliable digital transactions are made. However, this indicator does not reflect the fact that many of the most popular online services requiring secure servers are global brands and not specific to any particular country (Amazon, eBay, etc.).

International internet bandwidth per capita has become an increasingly well-recognised indicator following its use at the G8 Dot-Force meeting in Kananaskis in 2002. It is fairly easy to obtain because there are a relatively small number of international internet service providers. Because of the relatively high costs of international bandwidth, it is likely to reflect actual usage rather than being a supply-side indicator based on the size of the pipe. There are also other ways of measuring or cross-checking estimates of internet bandwidth. For example, bandwidth data are gathered by the Stanford University SLAC PingER project.[11] The PingER project calculates the bandwidth of internet links by measuring the time it takes to send packets of data to internet hosts around the world. This indicator confirms that international bandwidth reports to the ITU are broadly in line with measured performance, although there are a number of exceptions at a national level that would be worth examining.

Ideally, if total national and international internet bandwidth could be measured, this figure, combined with the total number of internet users, would give a reasonable composite measure of the extent of internet use. However, given the growing importance of networks based on internet protocols and the decreasing use of switched-voice circuits, it will be increasingly important to identify other measures

8 www.communities-dominate.blogs.com/brands/2007/01/putting_27_bill.html

9 www.wirelessintelligence.com

10 www.gsmworld.com/news/statistics/index.shtml.

11 www.slac.stanford.edu/xorg/icfa/icfa-net-paper-jan07

of internet use. IP host numbers have been used, as this is a superficially attractive measure because it is easily available for every country and is relatively up to date. However, due to the prevalent use of private IP numbers behind firewalls, and allocations of numbers not in actual use, this measure is quite misleading. In addition, the transition from IPV4 to IPV6 is changing the entire IP numbering system, and some countries are more advanced in this process. In the long term, however, this will ultimately improve IP host numbers as a measure by eliminating the need for network address translation (NAT) and host address masquerading.

In the interim, a more valid approach would be to use a metric based on autonomous system numbers (AS numbers or ASNs). Unique ASNs are allocated to internet network operators by the regional registries (RIRs) for use in multi-path (BGP) routing (the protocol used to ensure that there is more than one route to the internet provider's network). The use of ASNs as an indicator was pioneered by OECD researcher Tom Vest, and based on his work, the OECD's Committee for Information, Computer and Communications Policy (ICCP) has now proposed the use of ASNs for measuring internet uptake in their member countries.[12]

Raw ASN information is available on a daily basis via automated file transfer protocol (FTP) download and is therefore the most up-to-date ICT indicator available in the world. The data are hosted by the University of Oregon Route Views Project[13] where the daily updated data go back to 1997. In this respect a key advantage of the ASN metric is that it does not rely upon country reporting and therefore does not further burden developing country national statistical offices (or the national regulator) with further indicator collection responsibilities.

Indicators to measure the level of exclusion from ICTs amongst the public are of special importance. While this has not been the direct focus of the other ICT uptake measurement efforts, the DOI focused on the related concept of opportunity. Of note is that the World Bank's *World Development Report 2006* advocates taking equity into account when determining development priorities.

Given current technology trends and long-stated gender concerns, it is becoming increasingly essential to have a clear picture of how the internet and women's access to ICTs are evolving in developing countries, and indeed throughout the world. So measures of gender-disaggregated access should be included, although currently gender-disaggregated data availability is minimal; for example, only 39 countries feature on the ITU's STAT page for female internet users.[14] There is no doubt that as national-level information society policies prioritise women's and girls' access to and ability to use ICTs, there will be efforts to measure these in order to document progress towards policy goals. But this is only just beginning to happen, and it will be a long time before there is a critical mass of gendered ICT indicators available.

Aside from measures of gender equity, other equity indicators would include the dispersion of public access facilities (telecentres, cybercafés or public phones), mobile coverage areas, mobile and broadband affordability, and basic literacy levels. Measures of network coverage should include national broadband coverage and the proportion of population covered by mobile networks. Ideally, affordability indicators would measure the prices of broadband subscriptions calculated pro-rata for a certain agreed speed of connection per month, such as one megabit per second (Mbps). This would allow comparison of countries with different speeds available and could also be expressed as a percentage of average monthly household income.

Another expression of affordability could be the OECD-defined basket of costs for mobile usage. Because of the complexity and variety of available mobile tariff packages, and the lack of identical packages in different countries, it should be noted that there may be some inherent variation in the data that does not reflect actual costs. In addition, a case could be made for using the medium basket, rather than the low-end user basket, which was defined in the early 1990s when mobile usage was relatively low.

It should also be noted that while the ICT access costs aim to measure affordability, when compared against country wealth they may not correlate fully with use. The poor may spend a much higher proportion of their income on communication costs. Flat-rate subscriptions with monthly minute packages also tend to skew this assessment.

Adult literacy levels are an obvious and well-represented indicator for the degree to which the public can use ICTs, but the measure does suffer from some biases. Mobile phone users do not necessarily have to be literate to use this technology, and intermediaries are often used by the non-literate to obtain information from the internet or to send messages. ■

References

ITU and UNCTAD (2007) *World Information Society Report 2007: Beyond WSIS.* Available at: www.itu.int/osg/spu/publications/worldinformationsociety/2007

Minges, M. (2005) *Evaluation of e-Readiness Indices in Latin America and the Caribbean.* Santiago, Chile: ECLAC. Available at: www.eclac.org/socinfo/publicaciones/xml/8/24228/w73.pdf

Partnership on Measuring ICT for Development (2005) *Measuring ICT: The Global Status of ICT Indicators.* Available at: www.itu.int/ITU-D/ict/partnership/material/05-42742%20GLOBAL%20ICT.pdf

Partnership on Measuring ICT for Development (2005) *Core ICT Indicators.* Available at: www.itu.int/ITU-D/ict/partnership/material/CoreICTIndicators.pdf

World Bank (2006) *World Development Report 2006: Equity and Development.* Washington: World Bank.

12 www.oecd.org/dataoecd/25/54/36462170.pdf

13 archive.routeviews.org/oix-route-views

14 www.itu.int/ITU-D/ict/statistics/at_glance/f_inet.html

Annex 1: The Partnership on Measuring ICT for Development – Core Indicator List

	Infrastructure and access
A1	Fixed telephone lines per 100 inhabitants
A2	Mobile cellular subscribers per 100 inhabitants
A3	Computers per 100 inhabitants
A4	Internet subscribers per 100 inhabitants
A5	Broadband internet subscribers per 100 inhabitants
A6	International internet bandwidth per inhabitant
A7	Percentage of population covered by mobile cellular telephony
A8	Internet access tariffs (20 hours per month), in USD, and as a percentage of per capita income
A9	Mobile cellular tariffs (100 minutes of use per month), in USD, and as a percentage of per capita income
A10	Percentage of localities with public internet access centres (PIACs) by number of inhabitants (rural/urban)
A11	Radio sets per 100 inhabitants
A12	Television sets per 100 inhabitants
	Household use
HH1	Proportion of households with a radio
HH2	Proportion of households with a TV
HH3	Proportion of households with a fixed-line telephone
HH4	Proportion of households with a mobile cellular telephone
HH5	Proportion of households with a computer
HH6	Proportion of individuals who used a computer (from any location) in the last 12 months
HH7	Proportion of households with internet access at home
HH8	Proportion of individuals who used the internet (from any location) in the last 12 months
HH9	Location of individual use of the internet in the last 12 months: (a) at home; (b) at work; (c) place of education; (d) at another person's home; (e) community internet access facility (specific denomination depends on national practices); (f) commercial internet access facility (specific denomination depends on national practices); and (g) others
HH10	Internet activities undertaken by individuals in the last 12 months: • Getting information: (a) about goods or services; (b) related to health or health services; (c) from government organisations/public authorities via websites or email; and (d) other information or general web browsing • Communicating • Purchasing or ordering goods or services • Internet banking • Education or learning activities • Dealing with government organisations/public authorities • Leisure activities: (a) playing/downloading video or computer games; (b) downloading movies, music or software; (c) reading/downloading electronic books, newspapers or magazines; and (d) other leisure activities
HH11	Proportion of individuals with use of a mobile telephone
HH12	Proportion of households with access to the internet by type of access: categories should allow an aggregation to narrowband and broadband, where broadband excludes slower speed technologies, such as dial-up modem, ISDN and most 2G mobile phone access. Broadband will usually have an advertised download speed of at least 256 kbit/s.
HH13	Frequency of individual access to the internet in the last 12 months (from any location): (a) at least once a day; (b) at least once a week but not every day; (c) at least once a month but not every week; and (d) less than once a month.

	Business use
B1	Proportion of businesses using computers
B2	Proportion of employees using computers
B3	Proportion of businesses using the internet
B4	Proportion of employees using the internet
B5	Proportion of businesses with a web presence
B6	Proportion of businesses with an intranet
B7	Proportion of businesses receiving orders over the internet
B8	Proportion of businesses placing orders over the internet
B9	Proportion of businesses using the internet by type of access: categories should allow an aggregation to narrowband and broadband, where broadband excludes slower speed technologies, such as dial-up modem, ISDN and most 2G mobile phone access. Broadband will usually have an advertised download speed of at least 256 kbit/s.
B10	Proportion of businesses with a local area network (LAN)
B11	Proportion of businesses with an extranet
B12	Proportion of businesses using the internet by type of activity: • Sending and receiving email • Getting information: (a) about goods or services; (b) from government organisations/public authorities via websites or email; and (c) other information searches or research activities • Performing internet banking or accessing other financial services • Dealing with government organisations/public authorities • Providing customer services • Delivering products online
	ICT sector and trade in ICT goods
ICT1	Proportion of total business sector workforce involved in the ICT sector
ICT2	Value added in the ICT sector (as a percentage of total business sector value added)
ICT3	ICT goods imports as a percentage of total imports
ICT4	ICT goods exports as a percentage of total exports

Regional and country reports

Introduction

Alan Finlay

Making contact with the world: From forest tribes to silver surfers...

While 22 country reports were included in GISWatch 2007, this year's publication collects the experiences of 38 countries from across the globe – countries as diverse as the Democratic Republic of Congo, Brazil, Uzbekistan, Switzerland and Bangladesh. To complement them, we have also introduced six regional reports: from North America, Latin America and the Caribbean, Africa, the former Soviet Union (a convenient way to group several new member states of the European Union, as well as countries in the Caucasus and Central Asia), South-East Asia and the Pacific. The authors of these regional reports have approached their tasks in different ways, and faced different challenges: how do you deal with a region like the Pacific made up of tiny islands, some with populations of less than 1,500? The regional reports contextualise the country experiences of accessing ICT infrastructure that follow, and will be developed in future publications.

This year's country reports are loosely structured around the Real Access Framework developed by bridges.org. The framework looks holistically at the drivers or factors that impact on access to information and communications technologies (ICTs). These factors go beyond physical access to technology, or the legal and regulatory framework that shapes roll-out and take-up, to include things like political will, affordability, human capacities, local content, the integration of technology into daily routines, and trust in technology, amongst others. These are now common concerns in any developmental context considering people's access to ICT infrastructure.

The country reports did not apply the framework – which in some senses is more easily applied at the local rather than national level – but simply used some of the factors as starting points for discussion on access to infrastructure.

While many reports consider physical access to technology and legal and regulatory frameworks, others explore more indirect drivers of ICT take-up. KICTANet (Kenya), for example, highlights the significant issue of trust in technology, which includes things like the reliability and safety of technology (when that cell phone burns your ear, what does it really mean?) and the security of personal information – issues which will become more important as convergence incrementally increases our access options.

The inclusion of "developed" countries like Switzerland is crucial to us. By juxtaposing "developed" with "developing", we hope to foreground the sometimes radically different experiences of the information society, and the divergent challenges faced, sometimes literally worlds apart. These juxtapositions graphically highlight the assumptions we sometimes hold when we talk about the "information society" as if it were an achievable level playing field, or even a common concern, rather than an imagined sphere of activity – an ideal – that we are consciously trying to construct. Compare, for instance, this extract from the report by comunica-ch (Switzerland):

> The share of older adults aged 50 and over who use the internet on a regular basis – so-called "silver surfers" – is still remarkably low... The Swiss Council of Seniors describes this situation as a "ticking time bomb".

with this point made by Radio Viva (Paraguay):

> Not long ago, in March 2004, there was a meeting between members of an indigenous organisation and a family from the indigenous Totobiegosode forest tribe, who had come out of the wilderness to establish contact with the modern world for the first time.

Several similar contrasts stand out in these reports, some of which suggest a trend *away* from the ideal of a global information society based on equitable access.

The mobile divide

Yes, mobile is the "miracle" technology: but some regions of the world seem doomed to play catch-up. SANGONeT (South Africa) notes that the challenge around mobile telephony in Africa lies in how to convert the ubiquity of the technology into direct development benefits. Its possibilities include the ability to transcend geographic constraints, while offering the benefits of "immediacy", "efficiency" and "security". A similar challenge is identified by the Civil Initiative on Internet Policy (Kyrgyzstan), while Hopeton Dunn (Jamaica) finds that mobile phones are now being seen more as tools for economic survival in his country, rather than simply being used for "useless chatter". Yet the *potential* of mobile technology appears sharply contrasted by the actuality of take-up and advanced use of mobile phones in, for example, many South-East Asian countries. As Madanmohan Rao points out in his regional report, Thailand's five million users accessing the internet through their mobile phones account for a staggering 40% of the country's internet user base. Put differently, the five million mobile internet users are the equivalent of around 10% of Africa's entire internet user base!

Growing divides within countries and in regions

Many reports note the rural/urban divide that exists in countries, but is it the case that when it comes to ICTs, this divide is growing rather than narrowing, despite the proliferation of grassroots technologies like cell phones? As Communautique notes in its North American regional report, even there a regional digital divide is becoming apparent, and "[in Canada] one adult out of two does not have the necessary skills to access online information." At the very least, the rapidity of technological change is an ambivalent force when it comes to narrowing the access gap. At times it appears that as many people get "disconnected" by technological change, as are boosted by its new potential. For instance, CONDESAN (Peru) notes:

> [D]eveloping countries [are pushed] towards the adoption of new technologies in urban areas even when there is no service readily available for "older technologies" in underserved areas. This presents a risk as well as an opportunity: the risk of widening the gap between those who do and those who do not have access to these services, and the opportunity for the excluded populations to "leapfrog" stages of development.

The policy divide

The European Union shows how regional consensus at a regulatory and policy level has the power and authority to rapidly scale up ICT take-up – see, for instance, the reports from Pangea (Spain) or ZaMirNET (Croatia). Similar consensuses have not matured in a number of other regions.

The spending divide

A number of reports note the less than efficient spending of universal access funds, and question whether the funds are effective in achieving universal access targets. Typically these funds are the result of a percentage "tax" on operator revenue, and by most accounts the coffers are swelling. Yet while India has "liberalised" its rules on spending, and focused on boosting innovations to improve rural connectivity, in Brazil conflicting legislation has effectively frozen access funds since 2002. Similarly, despite taxing operators for five years in Peru, only one pilot project was actually funded between 2001 and 2006. (In Argentina, meanwhile, operators *owe* the government some USD 750 million.)

The training divide (or the "interactive citizen")

While most people in least developed countries lack basic skills to participate and compete effectively in the information society, a country like South Korea has trained some 27 million people in classrooms set up in social work institutions, educational facilities, agricultural agencies, at home and online. This includes basic computer literacy courses, as well as training in daily life skills, and online banking and shopping.

The learning divide

Somewhat astonishingly, the reports show that when it comes to ICTs for development, basic lessons learned are not always lessons learned. This is no more apparent than when it comes to implementing ICTs in the classroom. Several decades of learning somehow end up gathering dust in jaded folders in school stock rooms, as expensive e-education programmes in countries as diverse as Switzerland and Uruguay are sometimes rolled out without adequate teacher training, curricula or buy-in.

At times it is impossible to compare like with like – a point raised in the indicators chapter of GISWatch 2008. These reports cover countries like the Republic of Congo, where the installation of automated teller machines (ATMs) is celebrated, and Ethiopia, where internet users total 164,000 – a 0.2% penetration. This is a long way from Switzerland, Spain, Costa Rica, or even South Africa; far from the "cloud computing" of the North, or the possibilities of fibre piped directly into the home, as commonplace as electricity or gas.

Yet what is clear from all the country reports is that despite the plethora of these "divides", all of the countries appear to have recognised the importance of ICTs for socio-economic development, and in one way or another are taking action. As the Fantsuam Foundation (Nigeria) notes:

> The level of awareness within the Nigerian government of the role ICTs can play in national development has gone past the stage of debating ICTs versus other development challenges, such as combating disease and poverty or ensuring food security and potable water. There is now an appreciation that connectivity is essential for development... ■

REGIONAL REPORT

North America

Monique Chartrand and Nathalie Caccamo[1]
Communautique
www.communautique.qc.ca

Access to an open internet: A basic right for all?

North America[2] represents a culture with a high level of diversity, gathered around liberal economic values. While the internet was primarily developed for national defence and academic purposes, its public and commercial use has enabled it to become a global communications resource. Telecommunications services in the region are considered universally accessible.[3]

However, Digital America is a picture of contradictions and tensions. On the one hand, it is fertile ground for monopolies (e.g., Microsoft, Google) but, on the other hand, it has given rise to large and active social network user populations. While it has given birth to imbalanced copyright laws – such as the Digital Millennium Copyright Act (DMCA) – which work to the detriment of authors and users, it has also sparked the free software movement and the Creative Commons.

This report by Communautique, an organisation which promotes citizen participation in the development of the information society, presents salient perspectives about the current North American situation with regard to communications infrastructure. These are intended to serve as a contrast to the other regional reports in GISWatch 2008. The report is based on information from government sources and from various economic and social observers.

Still an access powerhouse…

North America accounts for approximately 5% of the world's population, and currently represents 19% of internet users, with an average North American internet penetration rate of 70% in 2007.[4] This can be compared to a world average internet penetration of 16.3%.

And the sector is generally robust…

Like the infrastructure, the institutional and non-governmental ICT environment in North America is robust. Network regulation, monitoring and deployment are governed, in particular, by standardisation institutions and authorities such as the Internet Engineering Task Force (IETF) and the International Telecommunication Union (ITU), and by governmental committees, independent organisations and ministries, such as the Canadian Radio-television and Telecommunications Commission (CRTC), Industry Canada, the US Federal Communications Commission (FCC), the National Telecommunications and Information Administration (NTIA), and the US Department of Commerce. Within the existing regulatory frameworks, these entities may work towards several social objectives, such as universal service and access, quality of service, emergency appeals, media pluralism, cultural diversity and consumer protection. Civil society organisations such as Telecommunities Canada and the Trans Atlantic Consumer Dialogue (TACD) ensure public interests are represented amongst decision-makers and political authorities.

But no longer the "access leader"

The status of the region as the "access leader" is being challenged. In 2002, North America had the highest level of high-speed home connectivity in the world, with a household internet penetration rate in Canada twice that of the US. Canada was then ranked third worldwide, and the US seventh (Macklin, 2002). In 2008, more than one in two adults had high-speed home access (Horrigan, 2008). However, development in this region has slowed down in comparison with other regions of the world. In 2008 Canada was ranked ninth worldwide, and the US fifteenth – statistics which have nevertheless been challenged by the US State Department, saying that the ranking did not count all users because it excluded wireless access, amongst other things. According to the most recent survey, conducted by the Oxford Saïd Business School in London and the Universidad de Oviedo in Spain, the quality of internet networks in Canada is well below the global broadband quality threshold and will not be sufficient to support future internet usage (Nowak, 2008). Meanwhile, FCC Commissioner Michael Copps has said that the US urgently needs a broadband strategy to address its access deficit.

Access not the cheapest, either…

Once the mythical benchmark for almost "free" access, access costs are now higher than some European and Asian nations. According to one report (Davies, 2008), users in

1 Antoine Beaupré of Réseau Koumbit, Jean-Claude Guedon, professor of Comparative Literature at the University of Montreal, and Hugo Gervais and Aude Leroux-Lévesque of Communautique also contributed to this report.

2 Here defined as Canada and the United States (US), where the official languages are English, French (in Canada) and Spanish (in certain US states). According to the United Nations Statistics Division, Mexico is a part of Central America, and will be considered as such in this report.

3 According to the Canadian Radio-television and Telecommunications Commission (2007), 98% of Canadian households are subscribed to fixed or wireless telephone services.

4 Internet World Stats: www.internetworldstats.com/stats14.htm#north

the US pay about USD 53 a month for a good-quality, fast service, compared to USD 32 in Germany and USD 33 in the United Kingdom.

Private sector dominates...

Unlike a number of other regions in the world, connectivity in North America is primarily controlled by the private sector: companies such as Cogent, Verizon, SAVVIS, AT&T, Qwest, Sprint, AOL, and Level 3 Communications (L3). These giants have interconnected backbones which redistribute capacity to smaller service providers, which are often the subsidiaries or subcontractors of a single group.[5] Specifically in Canada, the concentration of networks connecting all users to the internet is mainly made up of a mere five companies: Bell, Telus, Videotron, Rogers and Shaw (Beaupré, 2007).

But at a price

The trend in the commercial strategy of the operators consists of having thousands of ultra-powerful servers interconnected in a cloud (so called "cloud computing"), and offering online content and software services where the core information or service is permanently stored on the servers, and only temporarily accessed by the client. This is, for example, the Google model. It is also one that many fear will end up disempowering the consumer, who may not be able to own or freely access content and software when off-line. Cloud computing potentially gives operators more access to users for advertising, and can tighten their grip on users as a constant source of market data.

Emerging digital divide

Despite North America's high level of infrastructural development, a regional digital divide is increasingly apparent, and not only in the US. Almost 10% of the population in Canada requires assistive technology applications to use a workstation, and one adult out of two does not have the necessary skills to access online information (Barr-Telford et al., 2005).

For governments in both Canada and the US, the telecommunications sector obviously has an important role to play in the economic and social structure. However, telecommunications infrastructure owners are now faced with the substantial costs of upgrading redundant "last-mile" infrastructures that are already in existence but are outmoded or unsuitable for higher-speed access. Unable to get a return on investments in rural areas, these companies are reluctant to provide high-speed connections to these areas, and sometimes even attempt to hinder potential competition that might try out new business models.

Convergence and state sovereignty

In a changing social context, and one driven by convergence, media and telecommunications companies are creating powerful conglomerations with telecommunications, media, marketing and financial concerns. These large groups extend their network of influence in areas such as telecommunications, finance, geostrategy, ecology and marketing. Through these spheres of influence, they can exert a kind of quasi-hegemonic control, and pressurise governments. At the same time, governments are attempting to prevent the establishment of monopolies. But they themselves are sometimes contractually linked to private enterprises via the privatisation of some functions of the public administration. Because of this, the question arises of the sovereignty of countries and states in the face of evolving market forces (Wu, 2006).[6]

Net neutrality is under attack...

It is the premise of a free internet that architecture and network operations may not discriminate between applications (or people) using the networks. Attacks on network neutrality affect the foundation of the internet itself. Currently, private networks attempt to give priority to certain data streams, to the detriment of others considered less important or less convertible into cash. However, civil society is getting organised,[7] while governments are attempting to respond to this new challenge, including with legislation.

But regulation is lagging

The neutrality of the network is being called into question. On one hand, there are the telecommunications giants who are protecting their business models focused on physical infrastructure and, on the other hand, monopoly vendors focused on content control, such as Microsoft. With changes in user habits, such as the migration from cable television to online videos, those responsible for licensing and content are losing control, and must review their approach.

The power of content producers...

Despite the growing digital divide, most individuals in the region have access to bandwidth in excess of their requirements.

5 List of cable internet providers, Wikipedia: en.wikipedia.org/wiki/List_of_cable_internet_providers#North_America

6 See also the Wikipedia article on "Network neutrality": en.wikipedia.org/wiki/Network_neutrality

7 See for example the SaveTheInternet.com Coalition: www.savetheinternet.com

The proliferation of online publications, peer-to-peer sharing, videoconferencing and online video sharing should increase in the future with the development of high-speed access, despite the obstruction by some sectors, notably the music industry. Networked society gives individuals and groups the opportunity to express themselves, and to become producers rather than just consumers of content. The "webconsumer" who becomes a "webactor" takes part in strengthening the social structure by acting outside of the market sphere, and taking part in the production of information-related, often non-merchant goods, such as the exchange and sharing of knowledge and culture. The 2008 presidential elections in the US showed how rapidly citizen producers of content can respond to and comment on current affairs. This is a cause for hope.

But citizen power needs to respond to growing market domination

The power of the market can be overwhelming. According to Ignacio Ramonet, the director of the French monthly *Le Monde diplomatique,* we need to create a "fifth estate" which will allow us to organise a citizen civic force against the dominant market hegemony. The function of a fifth estate would be to challenge the "superpowers" made up of the media and global e-content providers, who are part and parcel of neoliberal globalisation. It is a global media which, in some circumstances, has not only stopped defending citizens, but has sometimes begun to act against the people as a whole (Ramonet, 2003).

Can North America be a global leader?

A fundamental question must be posed in the face of these North American contrasts and even contradictions: can this society be trusted to produce the type of open pluralism that is required by a globalised world to ensure universal access in its truest sense? For the time being, marked by the trauma of 11 September 2001, the region unfortunately shows the signs of favouring repressive measures and institutions over its own republican and democratic traditions.

References

Barr-Telford, L., Nault, F. and Pignal, J. (2005) *Building on Our Competencies: Canadian Results of the International Adult Literacy and Skills Survey.* Statistics Canada. Available at: www.statcan.ca/bsolc/english/bsolc?catno=89-617-X

Beaupré, A. (2007) La menace de l'internet à deux vitesses. *L'Anarnet,* 8 February. Available at: anarcat.koumbit.org/2007-02-08-la-menace-de-linternet-deux-vitesses

CRTC (Canadian Radio-television and Telecommunications Commission) (2007) *Update to the CRTC Telecommunications Monitoring Report – 24 September 2007.* Available at: www.crtc.gc.ca/frn/publications/reports/PolicyMonitoring/2007/tmr2007.htm

Davies, F. (2008) Broad coalition backs universal broadband. *MercuryNews.com,* 25 June. Available at: www.mercurynews.com/business/ci_9689148?nclick

Horrigan, J. (2008) Home Broadband 2008: Adoption stalls for low-income Americans even as many broadband users opt for premium services that give them more speed. *Pew Internet & American Life Project,* 2 July. Available at: www.pewinternet.org/PPF/r/257/report_display.asp

Internet World Stats (2007) Internet Usage and Population Statistics for North America, November 2007. Available at: www.internetworldstats.com/stats14.htm#north

Macklin, B. (2002) Broadband and Dial-up Access. *E-telligence for Business TM,* August, pp. 30-31.

Nowak, P. (2008) Canada's broadband networks not ready for future: report. *CBC News,* 15 September. Available at: www.cbc.ca/technology/story/2008/09/15/tech-broadband.html?ref=rss

Ramonet, I. (2003) Le cinquième pouvoir. *Le Monde diplomatique,* October. Available at: www.monde-diplomatique.fr/2003/10/RAMONET/10395

SaveTheInternet.com Coalition: www.savetheinternet.com

Wu, T. (2006) Network Neutrality: Competition, Innovation, and Nondiscriminatory Access. Testimony before the House Judiciary Committee, April 24. Available at: www.timwu.org/network_neutrality.html

REGIONAL REPORT

Latin America and the Caribbean

Roque Gagliano, with contributions from Valeria Betancourt and Pablo Accuosto

Latin American and Caribbean Internet Addresses Registry (LACNIC); APC; ITeM

www.lacnic.net; www.apc.org; www.item.org.uy

Introduction

The Latin American and Caribbean region is characterised by linguistic, cultural and economic diversity. Consequently, any generalisations will not apply to every country or even every area inside those countries. However, clear progress has taken place recently in access to infrastructure throughout the region.

Coastal areas, in particular, have enjoyed important progress thanks to their proximity to the landing stations of submarine systems, and the diversity of operators and technologies in their areas. Several new systems and landing stations either have been announced or have been connected in the last twelve months. The new international undersea capacity needs to be added to other important inland projects that are planned, which can contribute to bridging the divide between the coastal areas and the rest of the continent.

Data centre and switching capacities have increased dramatically through the creation of new facilities and the expansion of existing internet exchange points (IXPs). The last twelve months have also seen an increase in the deployment of broadband wireless technologies in the region. The new services running over these technologies are offering competitive services to rival digital subscriber line (DSL) and cable modems. Although companies are still focusing on big urban areas, broadband access is increasingly available in areas away from the main cities.

The region, nevertheless, faces political challenges that impact on the high prices of broadband access (TeleGeography, 2008a). And considering that network services are still primarily focused on highly populated urban areas, despite new developments, there are still limitations in terrestrial infrastructure. Other important challenges for the region are related to the regulatory area, either regarding the need for deregulation or for improving existing regulations in order to create the necessary enabling environment for the development of network infrastructure. There is also a need for the creation of policies that clearly establish social development goals.

Some of these issues are addressed by the Action Plan for the Information Society in Latin America and the Caribbean (eLAC2010),[1] adopted by Latin American and Caribbean governments in San Salvador in February 2008. The plan includes 83 goals in six areas, aimed at promoting the development of infrastructure in the region and providing reliable, "preferably high-capacity" network coverage for 70% of the population in urban areas and 60% of the population in rural areas by 2010.[2]

Backbone capacity in the region

Universal access to information and communications technologies (ICTs) demands establishing strategies at several levels and across several areas, with the involvement of all relevant stakeholders (from government, civil society and the private sector). At regional and national levels this means, among other things, developing strategies for the deployment and use of backbone infrastructure.

Building backbone capacity today requires the construction of fibre links inside urban areas and between cities, regions and countries. Long-distance fibre communications are normally carried over an undersea cable system.

The Latin American and Caribbean backbone infrastructure can be divided into three regions: the Meso-American region (Central American and northern South American countries), the Southern South American region, and the Caribbean region.

The Meso-American and Caribbean regions are located closer to the United States (US). In these two regions several submarine cable systems are available, particularly in the Caribbean Sea and the Atlantic Ocean. Consequently, most of the countries and territories here have access to more than one system (TeleGeography, 2008b). The reality on the Pacific coast is different, where only two or sometimes one system is available, and countries such as Colombia and El Salvador have no access to any system at all.

Several new projects were finished or announced during 2007 and 2008, including the new landing of the SAM1 cable system in Colombia;[3] the finalisation of the Caribbean Crossing cable system by Columbus Networks,[4] which will bring redundant capacity to the Eastern Caribbean Region; and the announcement of new systems that will serve the Dominican Republic and Netherlands Antilles.[5] A new cable system running all the way from southern Mexico to northern Colombia will run fibre on top of the electrical power cable system. This project is driven by different states as part of the Plan

1 eLAC2010 is contained within a document entitled the San Salvador Commitment: www.cepal.org/socinfo/noticias/noticias/3/32363/2008-2-TICs-San_Salvador_Commitment.pdf

2 See the San Salvador Commitment/eLAC 2010.

3 www.telefonica-wholesale.com/ingles/notasprensa/notas/03-11-08.html?pais=www.telefonica.es

4 www.columbusnetworks.com

5 www.lacnic.net/en/eventos/lacniccaribe

Puebla Panama[6] and will provide alternative access to all the Central American undersea cable systems.

The Southern South American region consists of the southern Andean countries and the Southern Common Market (Mercosur) countries. Three systems are relevant in this region: the abovementioned SAM1 (implemented by Telefonica), SAC (Global Crossing)[7] and GlobeNet (Brasil Telecom).[8] This region has important backbone capacity with a diversity of carriers operating along the coastal areas. However, inland countries have difficulty accessing the backbone capacity at affordable prices.

A number of projects are underway in the region that are important to mention. One is the first high-capacity Uruguay-Argentina undersea network system which is being built by the Uruguayan state-owned telecom operator ANTEL and Telecom Argentina.[9] Another involves the use of long-distance electricity power cable systems to carry fibre optics. Using this particular technology, the company INTERNEXA plans to connect Venezuela, Colombia, Peru, Ecuador, Bolivia and Brazil.[10] Broadband over power lines (BPL) technologies, or using the residential electricity grid to provide broadband access, is also being explored. For example, the company EEQ (Empresa Eléctrica de Quito) has announced a BPL project to be carried during 2008.[11]

Competition in backbone services contributes to a reduction of the cost in megabits per second (Mbps) of access to international capacity for service providers. For example, just the announcement of the landing of the Telefonica SAM1 system in Ecuador has caused the cost per Mbps to the US to be reduced by 40%. Through this project, Ecuador will have its own undersea cable and will not depend on landing stations in Colombia. This also helps to improve regional interconnections, as regional capacity becomes less expensive compared to international links.

Nevertheless, a decrease in the cost of international connectivity does not necessarily impact immediately on reduced access costs for end-users. In the Caribbean, for instance, despite a clear improvement in network coverage, international connectivity is still controlled by a few dominant operators, which poses an important obstacle for the development of a truly competitive market (Stern, 2006). In other countries, such as Ecuador, internet users sign a contract that sets access prices for one year in advance. This prevents changes in international costs having a direct impact on what the end-users pay. These examples show how regulatory issues and consumer policies can determine access costs.

Other infrastructure costs, such as those related to data centres, access devices, and interconnections, should also be considered. The data centre market in the region is quickly adopting international standards, and the number of available square metres is increasing rapidly. IXPs are common connection points for different organisations, including internet service providers (ISPs), carriers, content providers, etc. For the eLAC2007 Infrastructure Working Group report,[12] 21 IXPs were identified, and nine were located in Brazil. Since then, new projects have been concluded or have been announced in Brazil, Colombia, Curaçao, the Dominican Republic, Ecuador, El Salvador and Saint Martin.[13] In the case of Ecuador, the new IXP – part of the NAP.EC network built by AEPROVI[14] – will be located in the city of Cuenca (with a population of 280,000). This means that ISP traffic will no longer have to go through the metropolitan areas of Guayaquil and Quito.

"Last-mile" connectivity

DSL continues to be the preferred technology for "last-mile" connectivity, followed by cable modems and a variety of wireless technologies. Probably the most important change in the broadband market in the last twelve months is the deployment of third generation (3G) mobile networks.

The deployment of 3G mobile networks is bringing new players to the broadband market, even in regions with quasi-monopoly DSL provision. The deployment is currently focused on important metropolitan areas, but there are plans to expand the services to other areas over the next years. It is not uncommon in the Latin American and Caribbean region to find rural areas where the mobile system is the only available telecommunication service, and 3G has the potential to bring broadband services to those areas. Regulation related to costs of devices should be considered as a key issue if mobile technology is meant to have development purposes.

Regional priorities

On 20 August 2008, the Latin American and Caribbean Network Information Centre (LACNIC),[15] APC and the Information Network for the Third Sector (RITS) called a multi-stakeholder meeting in Montevideo, Uruguay. The

6 www.planpuebla-panama.org

7 www.globalcrossing.com

8 www.globenet.net

9 www.antel.com.uy

10 www.internexa.com

11 www.eeq.com.ec/htmlDocs/noticia.php?mn=6&n=54

12 www.cepal.org/socinfo/noticias/noticias/2/32222/GdT_eLAC_meta_1.pdf

13 www.lacnic.net/en/eventos/lacnicxi/napla.html

14 www.aeprovi.org.ec

15 www.lacnic.net

purpose of the meeting was to hold an open policy dialogue to identify relevant issues and priorities for Latin America and the Caribbean. These would input into the discussions and agenda of the third Internet Governance Forum (IGF). One of the panels ("How to reach the next billion users?") focused on the problem of internet access in the region. A diagnosis of asymmetries was presented (World Bank, 2008) which highlighted the fact that Latin America and the Caribbean have the least degree of fairness in terms of access to technological infrastructure, as well as in terms of education and income. For this reason, it was concluded that national and regional strategies should aim at reducing infrastructure asymmetries in practical ways and improving access to information. The panel also concluded that it is necessary to expand network coverage for broadband internet access in the region and, at the same time, make access relevant to the potential users' lives, which includes making content available that is consistent with the needs of different people.

The IGF process has shown consensus, among all stakeholders, about the inability of models based exclusively on market approaches to provide access to ICTs for all. More effective and solid regulatory frameworks need to be adopted in most of the countries in the region, and policies have to be harmonised at regional and sub-regional levels. This will make it possible for the coexistence of commercial and community or collaborative models for deploying and using infrastructure. Policy and regulatory coherence in the telecommunications sector is crucial to create an enabling environment for ICT access. The Latin American and Caribbean region needs to strengthen its capacity to participate effectively in shaping the global ICT policy agenda, which has an impact on the national and regional context. ■

References

AEPROVI: www.aeprovi.org.ec

ANTEL: www.antel.com.uy

Columbus Networks: www.columbusnetworks.com

EEQ: www.eeq.com.ec

eLAC: www.cepal.org/socinfo/elac/default.asp?idioma=IN

Global Crossing: www.globalcrossing.com

GlobeNet: www.globenet.net

INTERNEXA: www.internexa.com

LACNIC: www.lacnic.net

Plan Puebla-Panama: www.planpuebla-panama.org

San Salvador Commitment/eLAC2010: www.cepal.org/socinfo/noticias/noticias/3/32363/2008-2-TICs-San_Salvador_Commitment.pdf

Stern, P. (2006) *Assessment of the Telecommunication Services Sector in CARICOM: Convergence Issues at the Regional and International Level.* Kingston: Caribbean Regional Negotiating Machinery. Available at: www.crnm.org/documents/studies/Telecoms_Report_Oct_12_06.pdf

Telefónica International Wholesale Services: www.telefonica-wholesale.com

TeleGeography (2008a) Global Traffic Map 2008. Available at: www.telegeography.com/products/map_traffic/index.php

TeleGeography (2008b) Submarine Cable Map 2008. Available at: www.telegeography.com/products/map_cable/index.php

World Bank (2008) World Development Indicators 2008. Available at: www.worldbank.com/data

Africa

Abiodun Jagun
Department of Management Science, Strathclyde Business School
www.strath.ac.uk/mansci/staff/abijagun

Introduction

Communications in Africa have made significant gains in a relatively short space of time. For example, thanks largely to spectacular growth in mobile cellular communications, it is now no longer credible to compare the number of telephones on the continent to what pertains in a single city elsewhere in the world.[1]

Problems of accessibility still persist, however, and the financial cost of access in African countries ranks amongst the highest in the world. Various factors contribute to such high cost, including slow implementation of regulatory reform and inconsistent government policies and legislation, which impact on the level of investment in the sector and reduce the robustness of competition in the telecoms market. The level of development of related sectors, in particular the energy sector (electrification), also has a significant influence on the cost of access, as do socioeconomic conditions including political stability, human capital indicators like literacy and educational levels, and the economic well-being of the population.

However, the dominant contributor to low and expensive access to communications infrastructure in Africa remains the lack of adequate basic telecommunications infrastructure.

M-volution

The International Telecommunication Union (ITU) calls the period when a country moves from having a teledensity[2] of ten lines per 100 inhabitants to 30 per 100 the "teledensity transition" (ITU, 1998). This transition is significant because it is when teledensity is above 30 per 100 inhabitants that economic and developmental prospects are greatly improved.[3] In the past, teledensity was measured according to fixed lines,

1 As was once the case in the frequently cited statistic of the Maitland Report which compared the number of telephones in Tokyo to teledensity in Africa: "Tokyo has more telephones than the whole of the African continent, with its population of over 500 million people" (ITU, 1985, p.13).

2 Teledensity is measured as the number of phones per 100 inhabitants. It is taken as one of the key measures of a country's ICT infrastructure.

3 At this level of teledensity, the majority of households and virtually all businesses have access to telecoms.

Figure 1: **Approximate number of years to achieve "teledensity transition" for mobile cellular networks in selected countries**

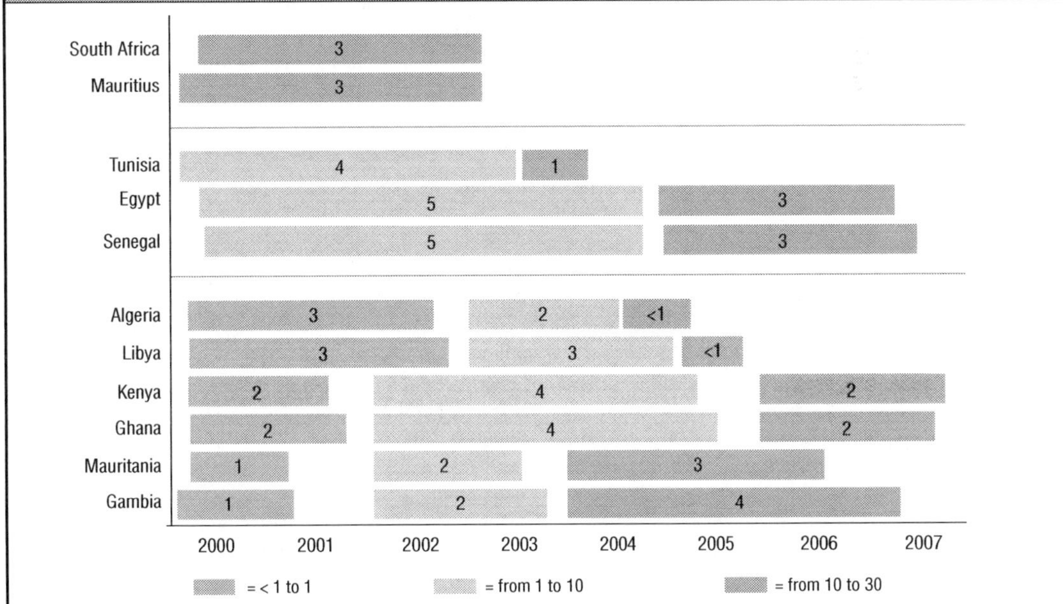

Source: **Constructed with data from the ITU ICT Statistics Database.**

and the time it took some developed countries to make the teledensity transition ranged from eight to 35 years (ITU, 1998).[4] This has changed with the introduction of mobile cellular networks, which are easier to deploy by operators and adopt by consumers. Figure 1 highlights this in a sample of African countries. It shows that in just seven years, six countries have been able to grow their number of mobile subscribers from less than one to over 30 subscribers per 100 inhabitants.

In fact, for Africa as a whole, "effective teledensity"[5] increased from 1.61 per 100 inhabitants to 28.11 in just under fourteen years (1993 to 2007) – i.e., from the "tipping point" to the "transition point" of teledensity. Such momentum and growth generates optimism and enthusiasm about what can be achieved in terms of communications and development in Africa.

Such optimism, however, takes for granted the existence of national backhaul and international communication infrastructure in Africa – specifically regarding reach and (bandwidth) capacities, as well as accessibility and affordability. Assumptions are also made about prerequisite supporting technologies and infrastructure (in particular energy) as well as "softer" issues such as the information needs of the continent's population, their patterns of knowledge creation, accumulation and sharing, and how these fit into global laws and policies that increasingly determine how information and knowledge are consumed.

How then does Africa build on the success of mobile cellular while maintaining a realistic and pragmatic approach to the significant gaps currently limiting the future of its application?

Acting on the convictions of policy dialogue

ọ̀nà kan ò wọ ọjà
More roads than one lead into the market.
Yoruba proverb

The manner in which telecom networks can be developed and reformed to deliver economic and social benefits has been the subject of numerous reports, committees, fora and summits. This has resulted in a high level of familiarity with issues regarding infrastructure development amongst relevant decision-makers and an appreciable amount of cross-national evidence and recommendations on how such issues can be resolved.

Perhaps the most familiar and accepted learning experience is the importance of liberalisation[6] – the success of mobile cellular is an example of how liberalisation, and the competitiveness that ensues, can be effective in increasing the availability of telecom services (OECD, 2008). African countries need to apply the principles of competition consistently and evenly in all areas of their telecom sectors. This would involve removing barriers that inhibit private sector participation in telecom sectors, and putting into effect regulations that on the one hand help ensure competition in the market while also addressing areas of market failure – that is, occasions where market mechanisms alone are insufficient in delivering desired policy outcomes (ITU, 2007a).

The point on *delivering desired policy outcomes* is worth expanding upon. Liberalisation is usually adopted based on the premise that it will ultimately create an environment in which consumers are able to select, from a range of providers, the product that best matches their needs at a price they feel is acceptable. It might still be early days, but experience of mobile cellular markets in Africa shows that affordability remains a key constraint for consumers. Research by LIRNE.NET conducted in a cross-section of developing regions indicates that the role mobile cellular plays amongst financially constrained groups remains limited (Samarajiva, 2006; Galperin & Mariscal, 2007; Gillwald, 2008). The emerging environment is therefore one of persisting (although lessening) divides – between income groups and geographic areas – even within a liberalised environment.

Desired policy outcomes are therefore not being achieved, and this has led to calls for the opening up of markets to not just multiple operators but also *diverse* types of players. African countries need to review policies and regulations that limit or place barriers on who can provide various types of telecom services, and establish incentives to facilitate a diversity of service providers – such as microtelcos, community operators, cooperatives, municipal governments, etc.

The Yoruba proverb, "More roads than one lead into the market," holds literal application where the liberalisation ethos is to be pursued. African countries should allow both operators and consumers to pursue the different routes into their communication markets. How does this differ from what currently occurs on the continent?

Facilitating diversity and choice in communications infrastructure

The first inch/last mile

Access to communications can be delivered via wired or wireless connections, and through a variety of devices: phones, televisions and personal computers. In Africa, growth in wired connections is progressing, but from a very low and almost non-existent base. In some cases, growth in fixed lines is reversing as incumbents, adopting a more profit-orientated approach, drop debtors, and customers abandon undependable fixed lines. Connectivity through fibre cables – fibre to the home (FTTH) – whether by telecommunications operators, cable television, or utility providers, is low to the extent of being practically non-existent in many African countries. Last-mile connectivity delivered via broadcasting channels such as satellite or cable television suffers from prohibitively high costs, and television penetration remains low on the continent (ITU, 2007b).

4 Figure refers to developed economies in Asia-Pacific.

5 Measured as "fixed lines or mobile users – whichever is higher – per 100 inhabitants" (Kelly, 2005).

6 Defined as the opening up of markets to multiple players.

However, low levels of wired connections pose little threat to connecting users given the capability to connect the last mile using wireless technologies. Other regions of the world (e.g., South Asia and South America) provide examples of how such technologies – notably code division multiple access (CDMA) – are being used to expand wired networks. But the extent to which these wireless technologies have developed in African countries, and the investment required in making them viable contributors to providing communication services (including the internet), are causes for concern.

CDMA Development Group estimates that only 26 African countries have commercial CDMA networks. In addition to the high cost of deployment and end-user devices, growth in wireless networks in Africa is also constrained by the dominance of the global system for mobile (GSM) standard. This calls for greater care in ensuring that regulatory frameworks remain flexible (especially in terms of spectrum allocation) and policies are technology-neutral (e.g., removing constraints that impact on the types of equipment that can be used for deploying networks). Efforts also need to be made at reducing the ambiguities over licensing faced by wireless operators – especially at the community or small-scale level (FMFI, 2008).

National backhaul networks

Advocating for last-mile wireless networks presupposes that a viable and extensive wired national backhaul network exists. Such wired networks – also referred to as backbone networks – facilitate the adoption of services requiring large bandwidth and speeds (such as the internet). Where they exist they are often the cheapest means by which such services can be delivered. Research by APC shows that service providers migrate from satellite (wireless) to fibre (wired) networks when they are available (Jagun, 2008).

However, few African countries, for various reasons – ranging from geographic topology to underinvestment to destruction during conflict – have extensive nationwide networks. Even with universal service obligations written into most GSM and (where applicable) second national operator (SNO) licences, profit-orientated models of network development have resulted in silos of urban infrastructure with operators looking to the incumbent to interconnect regions. So it is often the incumbent operator – operating as a monopoly and predominantly state-owned – that has the most extensive national network. Yet such networks suffer from underinvestment and threat from vandals, while at the same time having to service a broad range of operators and often bearing public service obligations themselves.

It is not surprising then that feasibility studies carried out by the ITU in 2005 concluded that Africa required as a minimum an additional 52,000 route kilometres of backbone infrastructure for intra- and inter-country connectivity (ITU, 2007c). Table 1 shows this breakdown per region.

Delivering this level of infrastructure improvement requires not only an upgrade of the incumbent's network, but also restructuring of the telecom sector to make it attractive for (private) investment so as to increase the number and types of players in this segment of the market. Licensing an SNO and encouraging participation by non-telco actors, in particular utility and transportation companies (electricity, road, rail, water, and where they exist, pipelines), holds the key for much-needed backbone infrastructure and competition. The result is likely to be a diverse mix of players and networks connecting nationwide through a variety of technologies – radio waves, microwaves, copper, and increasingly, fibre. Interconnection and interoperability will therefore remain key issues going into the future, and present critical areas in which the capacities of regulators should be improved upon.

Regional and international backbone infrastructure

Improving the reach and depth of last-mile access and nationwide networks will significantly increase connectivity within a country. However, communications also take place outside national boundaries, and the high cost yet poor quality of international communications is another area requiring the attention of African countries. Two key interrelated issues are worth emphasising here: the first is the availability of physical connections to international networks, and the second is the determination of who can legally build or gain direct access to such networks and what services they can legally provide.

In terms of physical infrastructure, compared with other regions of the world there is a dearth of international communications infrastructure in Africa. Although "every square inch of Africa is covered by satellite bandwidth" (IDRC, 2005) satellite markets in most countries remain under monopoly or duopoly control, and are subject to high licensing fees and restrictive operating conditions. In addition to satellite, Africa is also looking to submarine fibre-optic cables. These cable networks face similar challenges to those experienced by satellite, but also intersect with several national boundaries and must meet the operating conditions of each one. A lack of harmonisation in policies and regulations means that what is permissible in one country might be disallowed in another, and is a major disincentive to their development.

Table 1: Backbone infrastructure required (in route kilometres)

Central Africa	Northern Africa	Western Africa	Eastern and Southern Africa	Total
15,950	2,200	19,330	14,560	52,040

Source: ***Connectivity in Africa*** **(ITU, 2007c, p. 4)**

Figure 2: **Planned regional and international fibre projects in Africa**

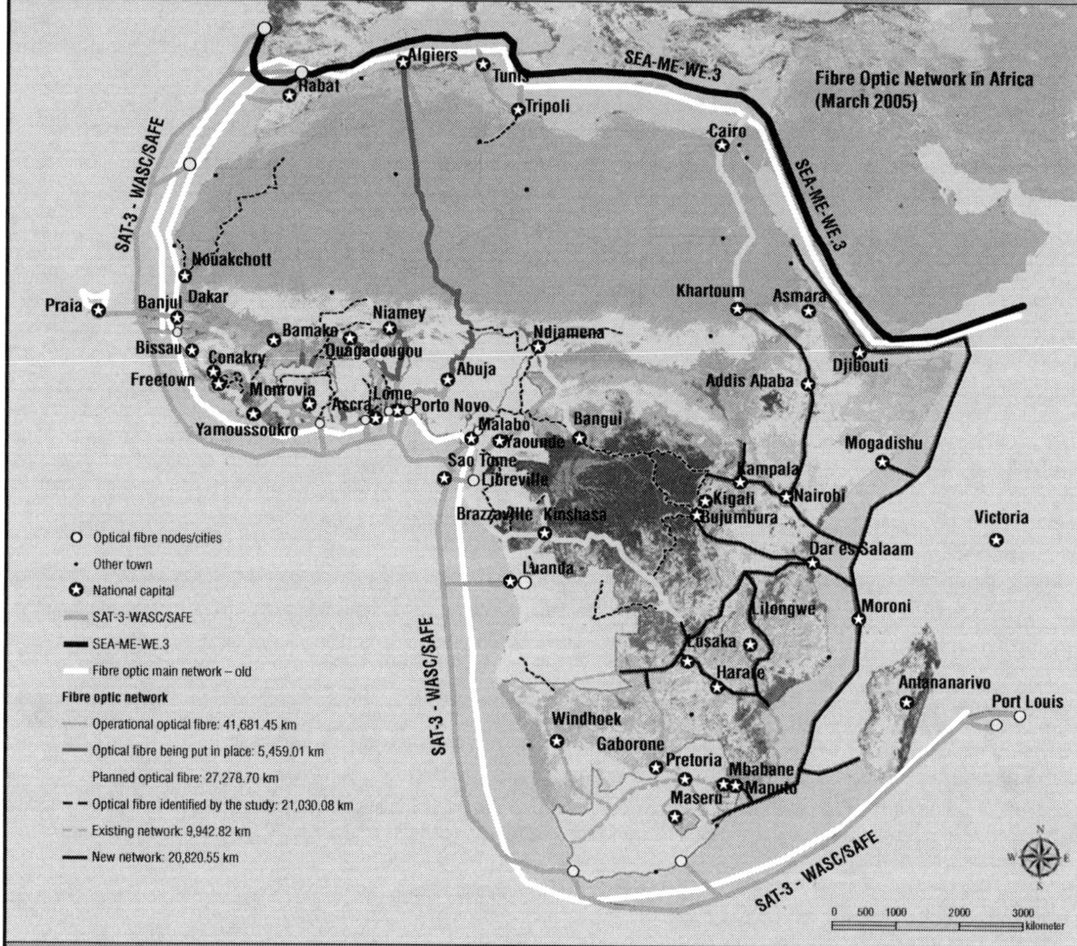

Source: ***Connectivity in Africa*** **(ITU, 2007c, p. 18)**

There is currently only one submarine cable providing international access in Africa: the much criticised[7] South Atlantic 3/West Africa Submarine Cable (SAT-3/WASC). However, more cable projects are planned (see Figure 2). The contributions these would make in alleviating Africa's connectivity problems will be hindered if recurring issues are not addressed, such as anti-competitive and monopolistic behaviour by operators, regulatory (particularly licensing) barriers that restrict participation in infrastructure projects, and a lack of harmony in laws and policies across countries.

There is much at stake in an increasingly information-driven global society. A review of the amount of international internet bandwidth available to African countries serves to illustrate the severity of the situation. In 2006, the availability of bandwidth to Africa as a total stood at 28,177 megabits per second (Mbps), less than one percent of the amount available globally. In comparison, in the same year, Norway had 43,019 Mbps bandwidth – approximately one and a half times more bandwidth than all of Africa (ITU, 2007b). Here is one scenario where the continent versus country comparison remains uncomfortably credible. ■

7 SAT-3 is criticised for being exploitative of the market and has been subject to legal and regulatory intervention in some countries in which it has a landing station.

References

Esselaar, S., Gillwald, A. and Stork, C. (2007) *Towards an African e-Index 2007: Telecommunications Sector Performance in 16 African Countries*. Research ICT Africa (RIA). Available at: www.researchictafrica.net/images/upload/Africa_comparativeCORRECTED.pdf

Galperin, H. and Mariscal, J. (2007) *Mobile Opportunities: Poverty and Mobile Telephony in Latin America and the Caribbean*. Diálogo Regional sobre Sociedad de la Información (DIRSI). Available at: www.dirsi.net/english/index.php?option=com_content&task=view&id=139&Itemid=69

FMFI (First Mile First Inch): www.fmfi.org.za

Gillwald, A. (2008) From Geneva to Tunis to Cairo: How far have we come? Presentation at ITU Telecom Africa, Cairo, Egypt, 12-15 May. Available at: www.researchictafrica.net/images/upload/Gillwald%20ITU_AfricaTelecom_2008v2.pdf

GSMA (GSM Association) (2008) *Mobile Investment Africa*. Available at: www.gsmworld.com/documents/digitaldivide/gsma_africa_magazine.pdf

IDRC (International Development Research Centre) (2005) *Acacia Atlas 2005: Mapping African ICT Growth*. Ottawa: IDRC. Available at: www.idrc.ca/uploads/user-S/11836495021Acacia_Atlas_2005.pdf

ITU (International Telecommunication Union) ICT Statistics Database. Available at: www.itu.int/ITU-D/ICTEYE/Indicators/Indicators.aspx

ITU (1985) *The Missing Link*. Geneva: ITU. Available at: www.itu.int/osg/spu/sfo/missinglink/The_Missing_Ling_A4-E.pdf

ITU (1998) *World Telecommunication Development Report: Universal Access*. Geneva: ITU. Available at: www.itu.int/ti/publications/WTDR_98/index.htm

ITU (2006) *World Information Society Report 2006*. Geneva: ITU. Available at: www.itu.int/osg/spu/publications/worldinformationsociety/2006/report.html

ITU (2007a) Creating an Enabling Environment for Investment. Background paper for Session Five, Connect Africa Summit, Kigali, Rwanda, 29-30 October. Available at: www.itu.int/ITU-D/connect/africa/2007/summit/pdf/s5-backgrounder.pdf

ITU (2007b) *Telecommunication/ICT Markets and Trends in Africa 2007*. Geneva: ITU. Available at: www.itu.int/ITU-D/ict/statistics/material/af_report07.pdf

ITU (2007c) Connectivity in Africa. Project proposal. Available at: www.itu.int/infrastructure/REM/project-proposal.doc

ITU (2007d) *World Information Society Report 2007*. Geneva: ITU. Available at: www.itu.int/osg/spu/publications/worldinformationsociety/2007/report.html

Jagun, A. (2008) *The Case for "Open Access" Communications Infrastructure in Africa: The SAT-3/WASC cable (Briefing)*. Glasgow: APC. Available at: www.apc.org/en/node/6142

Kelly, T. (2005) Changing ICT Rankings of African Nations. *The Southern African Journal of Information and Communication*, Issue 5. Available at: link.wits.ac.za/journal/j05-kelly-ict-rankings.pdf

OECD (Organisation for Economic Co-operation and Development) (2008) *Global Opportunities for Internet Access Developments*. Paris: OECD Directorate for Science, Technology and Industry and Development Co-operation Directorate. Available at: www.oecd.org/dataoecd/17/53/40596368.pdf

Samarajiva, R. (2006) Preconditions for Effective Deployment of Wireless Technologies for Development in the Asia-Pacific. *Information Technology and International Development*, 3(2), pp. 55-71.

REGIONAL REPORT

Former Soviet Union

Jeremy Druker
Transitions Online
www.tol.org

Introduction

The vast region of the former Soviet Union (FSU) – from the relatively prosperous new member states of the European Union (EU) to the impoverished countries in the Caucasus and Central Asia – is unsurprisingly home to extremely varied levels of information and communications technology (ICT) development. The small Baltic countries – Estonia, especially – have become leaders in e-government and e-participation not only among FSU states, but in Europe as a whole. In these countries, and to some extent in larger nations such as Russia and Ukraine, the digital divide has continued to close between the poorer and wealthier segments of society: the penetration of the internet and telecommunication services has risen uninterruptedly, and development has taken place with local and foreign investment and without overwhelming bureaucratic or regulatory hurdles.

At the other extreme are the countries of the Caucasus and Central Asia – the focus of this report, since access to infrastructure remains much more critical here than in the rest of the FSU. The impediments to access range far and wide. Similar to countries closer to the West, these nations still suffer mightily from the heritage of the Soviet Union, including a closed, often corrupt political elite short on transparency and good governance skills – let alone ICT knowledge. Simmering conflicts have sometimes soured neighbours on cooperation and made connecting parts of the region – already difficult because of rough terrain – an even greater challenge.

Telecom infrastructure is outdated and the small local markets continue to attract only a relatively small amount of capital, usually from Russian rather than West European investors. ICT skills are lacking, even in the industry.

All of this has added up to high costs of access for consumers, especially for broadband services, and especially for the majority of the local populations that are still struggling to survive in these transition economies.

Legislative reform is not enough

In perhaps the most in-depth study of ICT development in Central Asia in recent years, the director of the Telecoms Research Project at the University of Hong Kong, John Ure, notes that the problem in Central Asia no longer lies in non-existent or poor legislation that fails to enable ICT development. On the contrary, he says, well-meaning donors have funded programmes to overhaul the archaic post-Soviet legal system and support the passage of laws to promote e-government, e-commerce, and data protection, among other things. The main obstacle now is the lack of impetus from above to follow through and respect the letter and intention of the law – a direct heritage of decades of communist rule. "The reality in the Central Asian countries is that not even in the most 'independent' case, for example Mongolia, is the regulator given a genuinely free hand and the resources to do the job," Ure writes. He goes on:

> The reason is not a resource issue as such, but a governance issue. Transitional economies take time to change their legal structures, their cultures, their civil service management and career structures, and so on. It would therefore be far more productive to direct resources at the implementation level and allow regulators to gather more professional capacity and develop transparency than to focus in the short term on the ideal regulatory structures (Ure, 2005, p. 11).

Ure's thesis, though directed at Central Asia, could as well cover the Caucasus and parts of Eastern Europe, where the business and political elite have often been in cahoots to delay privatisation and preserve the monopolies of government-controlled telecoms industries – or, on the contrary, to award prized licences to politically connected firms that might not offer the best services (most of the FSU countries remain among the most corrupt countries in the world, as measured in surveys such as Transparency International's Corruption Perceptions Index).[1]

Skills deficit

Yet even with the right motivation on the part of the authorities, project management skills and ICT literacy remain deficits not only in the halls of government, but also in the private sector. At an *info*Dev workshop in 2005, ICT practitioners from Eastern Europe and Central Asia – most of them managers and staff of business incubators and other innovation and entrepreneurship organisations – noted a number of barriers to greater development. These included low ICT literacy among entrepreneurs, and even among specialists working in the field and at business incubators; inadequate protection of intellectual property; and problems in raising capital for small and medium enterprises (SMEs) (*info*Dev, 2005).

Part of the problem is that across Eastern Europe and the former Soviet Union, women have been severely underrepresented in ICT projects, according to a comprehensive report on the gender digital divide published by the United

1 www.transparency.org

Nations Development Fund for Women (UNIFEM) and United Nations Development Programme (UNDP) (Simerska and Fialova, 2004). Researchers found that at all levels of ICT initiatives, gender-specific issues had been poorly integrated or not considered at all in policy design. The region has largely been left out of global debates and international movements related to ICTs and gender, as donors have focused more on lesser developed countries in Africa and Asia. Overall, this has contributed to limited awareness of ICT policies and practices among women's groups, as well as a lack of advocacy to address gender in ICT debates, even from the ranks of activist groups working on women's issues.

Authoritarian practices

Another major obstacle in the region remains the authoritarian and semi-authoritarian practices of a number of the region's governments, which have stymied access to the internet and kept a heavy, Soviet-like hand on many levels of the economy, including the telecommunications sector. Combined fixed-line and mobile teledensity in Turkmenistan, for example, was estimated at just 16% in late 2007.[2] Only an estimated 1.4% of the population has internet access, partly as a result of the xenophobic authorities strictly controlling access (as well as blocking "unfriendly" sites, a widespread practice in Uzbekistan as well).[3] The Ministry of Education has promised to "fully computerise" schools throughout the country, but its recent purchase of 12,000 computers only amounts to one computer per 80 students (Mitas, 2008). Only a few of those apparently have internet access. As Stefan Mitas notes in a recent article, "Outside of the 20 schools connected by a United Nations Development Programme initiative, it is unclear how many schools have been connected, and whether they have any access to the wider internet outside a locally based and government-controlled education portal. Ministry of Education officials restrict access to schools by foreigners and researchers, making verification of their connectivity claims nearly impossible" (Mitas, 2008).

With the government still the dominant player in most countries, the private sector has been hard-pressed to come up with alternatives that would lower the high costs of access (roughly USD 80-90 per month for broadband access in Central Asia, for example). The domestic markets for ICT companies remain small, yet political tensions among neighbouring countries and a lack of free trade agreements (as well as a paucity of local capital and foreign direct investment) have hindered cross-border trade and expansion.

2 www.budde.com.au

3 www.itu.int

International support

International donors have stepped in to fill part of the gap, playing a major role in ICT development, with the World Bank and European Bank for Reconstruction and Development at the forefront. Numerous other multilateral organisations (especially UN agencies) and foreign governments, as well as private foundations and export-import banks, have also pitched in. Besides policy and legislative reform, their priorities have focused on capacity building in the state administration, including introducing e-government mechanisms; creating e-community portals on the local level; and spreading the use of computers and internet access in schools (Ure, 2005).

Still, even with such efforts, the countries of the Caucasus and Central Asia do not appear to be have been particularly active in terms of actions related to World Summit on the Information Society (WSIS) commitments, at least judging from the latest WSIS stocktaking report (ITU, 2008). In contrast to the Baltic countries, which submitted a wide range of impressive projects to the stockholding database, rare are the entries highlighted in the report from this part of the FSU. Among the few examples are the State Programme on Development of Communication and Information Technologies (2005-2008) of Azerbaijan, which focuses on the harmonisation of telecommunication, postal and information technologies with international standards to improve services; and Georgia's School Computerisation Programme (2005-2009), which envisions improving the computer-to-student ratio from the current 1:200 to 1:20 by providing computer rooms in 2,700 public schools, and boosting the ICT skills of teachers and students alike.

As a result, access to ICT infrastructure in Central Asia and the Caucasus remains far behind other FSU countries, such as Ukraine, Belarus, and Russia – let alone the Baltics or the formerly communist countries of Central Europe. Ure uses International Telecommunication Union (ITU) data on "effective" teledensity per capita (meaning the number of fixed or mobile lines, whichever is the greater, per 100 of the population) to posit geography as the main reason for the variance, since all the countries face similar post-Soviet realities such as state-run or controlled monopolies, increasing competition among providers of mobile and internet services, and the usual line-up of international donors. The landlocked Central Asian states, and to some extent the countries of the Southern Caucasus, however, remain relatively isolated from Western markets, capital, and ICT trends.

This has also certainly been true in the case of backbone infrastructure such as fibre, where the mountainous, difficult terrain of large parts of the region has complicated the creation of new networks – a situation which has been exacerbated by the simmering conflicts that have hampered the spread of technology. For example, ongoing disputes between Armenia and Azerbaijan, Armenia and Turkey, and Georgia and Russia have led to border closures and, correspondingly, hindered the spread of dark fibre links between countries in the South Caucasus (Sima, 2007). The recent war between Russia and Georgia could also affect the already expensive usage of the Black Sea fibre-optic cable that stretches between the port of Poti in Georgia to the city of Novorossiysk in Russia (most of Georgia's access to the internet flows through Russia and Turkey, though a new undersea cable leading to Bulgaria should be finished in the fall of 2008) (Markoff, 2008). Similar obstacles pertain to Central Asia, with the war in Afghanistan continuing uninterrupted next door and lingering border disputes among several of the Central Asian countries themselves, including some related to limited resources such as water.

These impediments – plus the relative unattractiveness of the small local markets for outside investors in infrastructure – slowed fibre development until recently, and led international donors to launch several satellite-based projects, in particular aimed at linking local researchers and academics to networks in the EU. The most prominent of these is the Silk Project (punning on the Silk Road or trade routes idea), which provides connectivity via satellite for National Research and Educational Networks (NRENs) in the countries of the Caucasus and Central Asia (including Afghanistan) to GÉANT2.[4] GÉANT2 is high-bandwidth internet connectivity serving Europe's research and education community, and already reaches the Baltic states and Russia (among the other countries of the FSU).

The Virtual Silk Highway, as the project is also known, has received most of its funding from the North Atlantic Treaty Organisation (NATO), but Cisco Systems donated USD 400,000 worth of equipment that was installed at eight NRENs, and Deutsches Elektronen-Synchroton, a German research institute, has provided in-kind management of the network. NATO has agreed to fund the project until at least late 2009. An accompanying project, called OCCASION,[5] manages SILK-2, the second generation of this research network, and provides assistance in the development of the region's NRENs, especially in the area of self-sustainability. Another goal is to monitor the region's advancement toward an international fibre network, which was also the subject of a major international feasibility study co-funded by the European Commission. The Porta Optica Study, which was completed in 2007, aimed to stimulate the "successful deployment" of a dark fibre-based network in Eastern Europe, the Baltic States and Southern Caucasus.

Several Japanese companies presented another fibre-based proposal, again playing on the Silk Road motif, at the Workshop on Broadband and ICT Development for Improved Communications in Central Asia in June 2007. Organised by several UN agencies and other organisations and governments, the conference was held in Uzbekistan and included representatives from both the public and private sectors. Speaking on behalf of the NTT West Corporation and InfoCom Research, respectively, Kiminori Sato and Yonosuke Harada called for a Silk Road Broadband Highway, a new fibre-optic backbone to increase reliability and escape an overdependence on submarine cables and the Trans-Asia-Europe (TAE) optical fibre cable network.[6] TAE stretches from Frankfurt to Shanghai – running through a large swath of the FSU – but, the presenters said, had limited potential because it was built for telecommunications rather than broadband and would not be able to meet future demand for broadband services (Sato & Harada, 2007).

Even if any of these ambitious plans takes off, ICT users in the Caucasus and Central Asia will probably end up using a mix of fibre, radio and satellite methods to access the internet and the high-speed networks of Europe and Asia. Even if new fibre networks appear and lower the cost of broadband, their reach will likely not extend far beyond major urban centres, mandating satellite access for the region's many rural areas and remote mountain regions.[7] While progress has been made, especially over the past five years, in deregulating the telecommunications markets throughout the FSU, state-controlled operators remain dominant and the need for capital investments to upgrade technology is urgent. Interest in accessing infrastructure, especially the internet, continues to rise unabatedly, but high costs that result from the many reasons described above could continue to damper demand for years to come. However, with the economy improving in parts of the region, especially in areas with rich gas and oil deposits, private companies may well become interested in investing in new networks if the region's governments can prove at least partially successful at implementing all those policies that look so good on paper. ■

4 www.geant2.net

5 www.ist-occasion.org

6 taeint.net/en

7 www.silkproject.org/project.htm

References

Budde.Comm: www.budde.com.au

Enomoto, M. (2007) United Nations Initiatives for the Promotion of Regional Cooperation in Central Asia on ICT for Development. Presentation at the Workshop on Broadband and ICT Development for Improved Communications in Central Asia, Tashkent, Uzbekistan, 21-22 June. Available at: www.unescap.org/icstd/events/RW_JUNE2007/ENOMOTO.pdf

GÉANT2: www.geant2.net

*info*Dev (2005) *Promoting Innovation and Entrepreneurship in Eastern Europe & Central Asia: Strategies and Partnerships.* Available at: http://www-wds.worldbank.org/servlet/main?menuPK=64187510&pagePK=64193027&piPK=64187937&theSitePK=523679&entityID=000310607_20061101143849

ITU (International Telecommunication Union) (2008) *Report on the World Summit on the Information Society Stocktaking 2008.* Geneva: ITU. Available at: www.itu.int/wsis/stocktaking/docs/2008/WSIS-Stocktaking2008-e.pdf

Markoff, J. (2008) Internet Traffic Begins to Bypass the US. *The New York Times*, 29 August. Available at: www.nytimes.com/2008/08/30/business/30pipes.html?_r=1

Mitas, S. (2008) Turkmenistan: Doors Opening, Doors Slamming. *Transitions Online*, 29 September. Available at: www.tol.cz/look/TOL/section.tpl?IdLanguage=1&IdPublication=4&tpid=11

OCCASION project: www.ist-occasion.org

Sato, K. and Harada, Y. (2007) New Proposal for a Silk Road Broadband Highway. Presentation at the Workshop on Broadband and ICT Development for Improved Communications in Central Asia, Tashkent, Uzbekistan, 21-22 June. Available at: www.unescap.org/icstd/events/RW_JUNE2007/SATO2.pdf

Sima, S. (ed.) (2007) *Special issues related to Southern Caucasus.* Porta Optica Study. Available at: www.porta-optica.org/files/publications/POS-D2.2v2_Special_issues_related_to_Southern_Caucasus.pdf

Simerska, L. and Fialova, K. (2004) *Bridging the Gender Digital Divide: A Report on Gender and ICT in Central and Eastern Europe and the Commonwealth of Independent States.* Bratislava: UNIFEM and UNDP. Available at: web.undp.sk/uploads/Gender%20and%20ICT%20reg_rep_eng.pdf

Trans-Asia-Europe (TAE) Optical Fibre Cable Network: taeint.net/en

Transparency International: www.transparency.org

Ure, J. (2005) ICT Sector Development in Five Central Asian Economies: A Policy Framework for Effective Investment Promotion and Facilitation. Paper presented at the UNESCAP International Conference on Strengthening Regional Cooperation for Managing Globalization, Moscow, Russian Federation, 28-30 September. Available at: lib_user5.unescap.org/tid/projects/globalize_ure.pdf

REGIONAL REPORT

South-East Asia

Madanmohan Rao
TechSparks
www.techsparks.com

Introduction

This report explores connectivity and access dimensions of the information society vision in South-East Asia, by presenting a scaleable framework for comparing the maturity of different information societies. South-East Asia is home to some of the fastest growing economies of the world, and some leading information and communications technology (ICT) companies; it adds its own tone and texture to the diffusion of ICTs worldwide. The region exhibits a wide diversity of telecom and broadcast environments, ranging from teledensity-poor Laos and Cambodia, to advanced info-societies like Singapore, where provision of basic universal telecom access is no longer an issue.

For the diverse countries of the region, focusing on the vision of the information society must occur in parallel with and buttress other socioeconomic goals – after all, the digital divide is in part a reflection of socio-political and economic divides generally. Overcoming the divide must therefore be concomitant to other targets, such as the Millennium Development Goals (MDGs) regarding hunger, poverty levels, education, gender inequality, infant mortality, health services and environmental resources.

Frameworks for analysing digital info-structure

The comparative framework used in this report is called the "8 Cs" of the digital economy, based on eight parameters beginning with the letter C: connectivity, content, community, commerce, culture, capacity, cooperation and capital. There are two ways of looking at ICTs: as an instrument, and as an industry. As an instrument, affordable and usable ICTs can indeed transform the way societies work, entertain, study, govern and live – at the individual, organisational, sectoral, vocational and national levels. As an industry, ICTs represent a major growing economic sector covering hardware, software, telecom/datacom and consulting services (see Table 1).

Table 1: The 8 Cs of the information society

	ICTs as an instrument	ICTs as an industry
Connectivity	How affordable and widespread are ICTs (e.g., PCs, internet access, software) for the common citizen?	Does the country have ICT manufacturing industries for hardware, software, datacom solutions and services?
Content	Is there useful content (foreign and local) for citizens to use in their daily lives?	Is content being generated in local languages and localised interfaces? Is this being accessed/used abroad?
Community	Are there online/offline forums where citizens can discuss ICT and other issues of concern?	Is the country a hub of discussion and forums for the worldwide ICT industry?
Commerce	Is there infrastructure (tech, legal) for e-commerce for citizens, businesses and government? How much commerce is transacted electronically?	Does the country have indigenous e-commerce technology and services? Are these being exported?
Capacity	Do citizens and organisations have the human resources capacity (tech, managerial, policy, legal) to effectively harness ICTs for daily use?	Does the country have the human resources capacity (tech, managerial, policy, legal) to create and export ICTs and set standards?
Culture	Is there a forward-looking, open, progressive culture at the level of policy-makers, businesses, educators, citizens and the media in opening up access to ICTs and harnessing them? Or is there nervousness and phobia about the cultural and political impacts of ICTs?	Are there techies, entrepreneurs and managers proactive and savvy enough to create local companies and take them global?
Cooperation	Is there adequate cooperation between citizens, businesses, academics, non-governmental organisations (NGOs) and policy-makers to create a favourable climate for using ICTs?	Is there a favourable regulatory environment in the country for creating ICT companies, allowing mergers and acquisitions, and links with the diaspora population?
Capital	Are there enough financial resources to invest in ICT infrastructure and education? What is the level of foreign direct investment (FDI)?	Is there a domestic venture capital industry? Are they investing abroad as well? How many international players are active in the local private equity market? Are there stock markets for public listing?

Table 2: Digital infrastructure in South-East Asia		
Country	Notable aspects of digital infrastructure and policies	Key challenges
Cambodia	1. National ICT policy formulation by national ICT development authority 2. International civil sector support for ICT projects and policies	1. Interdepartmental alignment on ICT initiatives 2. Local content in Khmer language
Indonesia	1. National education network 2. WiMAX trials for broadband internet access 3. Rapidly growing mobile penetration (11 operators, 100+ million subscribers)	1. Expanding digital access outside key islands like Java 2. Relatively low government spending on ICTs 3. Lack of interdepartmental coordination for ICT policy
Laos	1. Opening up of FDI to create telecom infrastructure 2. Growing mobile penetration (already exceeding landline)	1. Political/commercial isolation 2. Low telecom penetration in rural areas 3. Inadequate pace of regulatory reform 4. Low involvement of Laos diaspora in ICT initiatives
Malaysia	1. Strong government support for knowledge society vision, multimedia "super corridor" 2. Commercial WiMAX initiatives for broadband internet access 3. High mobile penetration	1. Political turbulence; impacts on free speech (e.g., arrest of bloggers)
Myanmar	1. Greater Mekong sub-region information superhighway project	1. Restrictive government policies towards free flow of information
Philippines	1. PLDT's Asian-American cable gateway 2. Cross-sector support for medium-term Philippine development plan (2005-2010) and Philippine cyber-services corridor programme 3. Support for voice over internet protocol (VoIP), ICT training, business process outsourcing (BPO) industries, telecentres 4. Widespread usage of mobile phones; short message service (SMS) capital of the world	1. Internet access in rural areas 2. Low broadband penetration
Singapore	1. "Intelligent Nation 2015" project, national broadband network 2. Active courting of global ICT industry 3. Strong government agencies, e.g., InfoComm Development Authority (IDA), Media Development Authority (MDA)	1. Overcoming broadband divide between upper and lower income groups 2. Dealing with issues of inappropriate content, digital piracy
Thailand	1. Active support from National Telecommunications Commission (NTC) 2. Healthy competition between infrastructure players 3. Licences issued for third generation (3G), WiMAX	1. Improving internet access outside major cities like Bangkok 2. Low broadband penetration 3. Political turbulence affecting investor climate
Vietnam	1. Regulations permitting more FDI in ICT sector 2. 60% mobile phone penetration, mobile virtual network operators (MVNOs); country has a very young population fuelling demand 3. Launch of first telecom satellite for Vietnam	1. High tariffs, low broadband usage

Digital info-structure access in South-East Asia

The 8 Cs framework can be used to tease apart some of the key challenges in implementing the vision of knowledge societies in South-East Asia. These include increasing ICT diffusion and adoption, scaling up ICT pilot projects, ensuring sustainability and viability of ICT initiatives, creating ICT industries, and systematically analysing research on the global information society. Table 2 shows some key aspects regarding ICT access and policy in South-East Asia.

The digital divide in the developing countries of South-East Asia (such as Laos and Cambodia) is most evident at the phase of connectivity. Steps to reduce this digital gap include lowering tariffs on the import of computers and modems, creating community internet access centres (with leased lines and shared devices) and other public access initiatives (such as public phone kiosks), and bringing access rates down by creating a favourable climate of competition between internet service providers (ISPs) and mobile operators.

A key challenge in the newly emerging economies of South-East Asia lies in creating a level playing field between government-owned or government-funded and private sector service providers. Costs of dial-up and leased lines are dropping, but could become more affordable. Organisational adoption of intranets and extranets is only slowly emerging in some countries in the region. Much potential lies in the

Table 3: Classification of Asia-Pacific information societies based on the 8 Cs framework

Type	Characteristics	Examples
Restrictive	1. ICT infrastructure is very limited 2. ICT usage is tightly controlled by government 3. Awareness of ICT among general population is very low	North Korea
Embryonic	1. ICT infrastructure is just being rolled out 2. Donor agencies are active in funding and providing human resources 3. Most ICT activity is driven by diaspora, NGOs	Afghanistan, East Timor
Emerging	1. Internet infrastructure exists in urban areas 2. Local capacities exist for ICTs 3. Policy bodies are being formed 4. Widespread digital divide exists 5. E-commerce is not yet widely prevalent	Nepal, Bangladesh
Negotiating	1. Widespread internet/wireless infrastructure exists 2. Local capacities and markets exist for ICTs, e-commerce 3. Government is "negotiating" benefits and challenges of new media (authorities exercise strong control over online content, search engines; political and cultural censorship of internet is practised)	China
Intermediate	1. Sizeable markets for internet, e-commerce, wireless exist 2. Digital divide is still an issue, donor agencies are active 3. Political climate is generally free of censorship for traditional and online media	India, Philippines
Mature	1. Large-scale penetration of internet, wireless 2. Mature business models for online content 3. Political climate is generally free of censorship for traditional and online media	Australia, New Zealand
Advanced	1. Large-scale penetration of broadband and wireless internet (including 2.5G, 3G) 2. Political climate is generally free of censorship for traditional and online media 3. Some ICT companies are major players in global market (e.g., wireless content models* are being exported)	Japan, South Korea

* The re-packaging of domestic content for wireless channels in other countries.

hands of public sector units, such as the power grid and railway authorities, who have existing secure cable connections across the region.

Special concerns arise in cross-country wiring for regions with mountainous terrain, large arid tracts, or with a high density of island space. Interesting developments to track on this front include the increasing feasibility of wireless access, ranging from cellular telephony and wireless local loop (WLL) to Wi-Fi/WiMAX networks and satellite links for voice and data traffic.

The digital divide also extends to content, in terms of number of websites, amount of local language content, and use of online content by key sectors such as government, education and healthcare. In today's world of social networking and broadband content, the boom in sites like YouTube, Facebook and MySpace seems to be inapplicable to some of the digitally challenged countries of South-East Asia. For instance, until very recently, a lack of standards for representing Khmer characters was a major obstacle for digital content growth in Cambodia. Other challenges arise in the case of languages for which internet domain names and email addresses must be typed in the Latin alphabet only and not in the local languages.

For the developing nations of South-East Asia, the extent of community stretches beyond local borders to the global diaspora population. Indeed, nations like India, South Korea and Taiwan are great examples where involvement from the diaspora community has helped bootstrap and globalise domestic ICT industries. This has yet to happen in a major way for countries like Laos and Cambodia.

As for capital investments in software, use of freeware and shareware packages and tools should be encouraged where possible, instead of relying on costly proprietary software solutions. These tools include the use of the Linux operating system and Apache Web servers for digital publishing. More open source forums are needed in the region; the United Nations Development Programme's (UNDP) Asia-Pacific Development Information Programme (APDIP) launched some notable projects in this area, and the e-ASEAN forum has helped move towards synchronisation and harmonisation of regional ICT initiatives.

The growth of internet users in the Asia-Pacific region is gaining momentum as emerging markets leverage mobile phones as a new and widely available form of access, according to the International Telecommunication Union (ITU) Asia Pacific Telecommunication/ICT Indicators 2008 report.[1]

In upper-middle- and high-income economies of South-East Asia, ubiquitous access is progressing through a competitive race to provide ever faster fixed broadband speeds, and the deployment of mobile broadband technologies at ever lower prices. In most of the region's low- and lower-middle-income economies, mobile phones have become a substitute for the shortage of fixed lines and fixed-broadband access. Thailand has five million users accessing the internet with their mobiles, which accounts for 40% of the nation's entire internet user base. Malaysia and the Philippines also registered double-digit figures for the percentage of internet users relying on mobile phone access.

The cost of handsets will continue to be a barrier in least-developed countries (LDCs), and is key to breaking the psychological "USD 10 barrier" for affordability. Mobile telephony operators are going deep into LDCs with bundled offers for connection and handsets. The only way to penetrate those regions is by ensuring affordability.

For rural access, needs assessment of information and knowledge requirements and aspirations in rural communities should be at the heart of any rural ICT for development (ICT4D) initiative. Issues related to design of the user interface, information architecture, language of presentation and communication of the information via alternative media (e.g., community radio) should occupy a key position. Knowledge management, generation and propagation models should be actively studied to help rural communities move from the information layer to knowledge via village telecentres.

Key to growing rural mobile access is not just creating networks and making handsets available, but also providing a wide range of applications such as news, commercial content and transactional services. Other strategies include providing local content in various languages and creating simpler tariff plans.

Regional comparison

Based on the 8 Cs framework, the countries of the Asia-Pacific can be divided into eight categories: restrictive, embryonic, emerging, negotiating, intermediate, mature, advanced, and agenda-setting. ICT diffusion amongst the population, strength of online content and cultural sectors, and the projection of domestic ICT industries globally progressively increase along the spectrum, as does openness of political expression (see Table 3).

References

Bhatnagar, S. and Schware, R. (2000) *Information and Communication Technology in Development: Cases from India.* New Delhi: Sage Publications.

Castells, M. (2001) *The Internet Galaxy: Reflections on the Internet, Business, and Society.* Oxford: Oxford University Press.

Gallagher, L. and Turnbull, G. (1999) *Telecommunications in Action.* London: The Regency Foundation.

Rao, M. (2002) *The Asia-Pacific Internet Handbook.* New Delhi: Tata-McGraw-Hill.

Quarterman, J. (1990) *The Matrix: Computer Networks and Conferencing Systems Worldwide.* Digital Press.

Ramanathan, S. and Becker, J. (2001) *Internet in Asia.* Singapore: Asian Media and Information Communication Centre.

Tan, F., Corbett, S. and Wong, Y. (1999) *Information Technology Diffusion in the Asia Pacific: Perspectives on Policy, Electronic Commerce and Education.* London and Hershey: Idea Group Publishing.

1 See: www.commsday.com/node/258

REGIONAL REPORT

The Pacific

Don Hollander
2020 Communications Trust
www.2020.org.nz

Introduction

This report looks at information and communications technology (ICT) empowerment in the Pacific. It concludes that the situation varies from country to country, and greatly within countries, but that no place is particularly well served or engaged to leverage ICTs to overcome the tyranny of distance that pervades the region.

Grouping the Pacific itself is a challenging task. Different international organisations include different countries and territories.

Broadly, the Pacific[1] can be divided into four basic groupings:

- The Polynesians in the Southeast Pacific (Cook Islands, American Samoa, Samoa, Tokelau, Niue, Tonga)
- The Melanesians in the Southwest Pacific (Fiji, Vanuatu, Tuvalu, Solomon Island, Kiribati, Nauru, Papua New Guinea)
- The Francophone countries and territories of the Pacific (New Caledonia, French Polynesia, Wallis and Futuna)
- The countries and territories of the North Pacific (Federated States of Micronesia, Palau, Northern Marianas, Guam, Marshall Islands).

Generally, the countries are small on virtually every measure: small populations (Niue and Tokelau with less than 1,500); small economies (Niue and Tokelau are barely viable economically, and certainly not without considerable amounts of external aid; Tuvalu and the Solomons are also very poor); and small land masses (Nauru, Tokelau and Tuvalu all with less than 100 square kilometres and meagre natural resources).

There are exceptions: Papua New Guinea has more than six million people and Fiji and the Solomons each have more than half a million. Papua New Guinea is also physically huge, certainly compared to the others, and has vast natural resources. Fiji's economy, despite four coups in twenty years, does very well. Guam, French Polynesia, New Caledonia and other territories strongly supported by a foreign state (e.g., France, the United States, New Zealand) also do fairly well.

Rather than look cursorily at each country, we will look at Samoa, often considered the star performer in terms of ICTs in the Pacific, and note aberrations from that model.

Samoa: A case study

Samoa has been the poster child for liberalisation and achievement in the area of ICTs and telecommunications in the region.

Political will

Around the turn of the century the prime minister of Samoa, Tuilaepa Aiono Sailele Malielegaoi, recognised the value that information technology and telecommunications could provide for his country as a key catalyst for prosperity, and took on the role of minister of ICTs. By doing this he set a foundation for going forward before delegating the role to others in his cabinet.

Few other national leaders in the Pacific have held ICTs with such high regard. The one exception is Jimmie Rodgers, who is the head of the Secretariat of the Pacific Community – the operational arm of the association of states and territories in the Pacific. Rodgers has seen firsthand the power that information can provide and is actively taking steps to empower people throughout the Pacific with access to the internet, particularly those in remote islands and communities.

Some movement has also been seen through the Pacific Islands Forum Secretariat's Regional Digital Strategy[2] and the Wellington Declaration,[3] produced by a forum of communications ministers meeting in Wellington in March 2006. There are other pockets of progress being made in the Pacific, but at a glacial pace.

Government monopolies

SamoaTel is the government-owned incumbent telecommunications provider in Samoa. It has a licensed monopoly on land lines and international circuits that is due to expire in July 2009.

Competition in Samoan telecommunications began last century when there was open competition from the private sector in the provision of internet services, with three internet service providers (ISPs) in 2000 offering consumers choice of provider and service plans. This number has since doubled. Samoa opened up cellular services to competition in 2006 when it issued three global system for mobile (GSM) licences – one to SamoaTel, one to the incumbent advanced mobile phone system (AMPS) provider Samoa Cellular, and one to Digicel.[4]

1 Pitcairn Island falls into the geography, but its population is so small that it is not included here. Easter Island is officially a part of Chile. The Chatham Islands are also in this space, at its southern extreme, but are really a part of New Zealand.

2 www.forumsec.org.fj/pages.cfm/economic-growth/ict

3 www.beehive.govt.nz/node/25341

4 Digicel promptly purchased Samoa Cellular Services, resulting in just two providers.

International services are still a licensed monopoly for SamoaTel, though Digicel does have the right to operate its own international gateway, but only for its own use.
The government has made clear its intention to privatise SamoaTel by the end of the decade, part of a long-term strategy to get the state out of areas where the private sector can operate.[5]

Other countries are also opening up their telecommunications markets, particularly for cellular and ISP services. Digicel is expanding its operations to Fiji, Papua New Guinea, Tonga and Vanuatu. Its entry into new markets has not been without controversy and significant engagement with the courts. But the people are voting with their phones and competition is warmly welcomed by all (except, perhaps, the incumbents).

Limited skills and knowledge

One other point associated with the government-owned telecommunications monopoly is the shortage of people who are independent and yet still capable of providing advice. The local carrier is often the only source of advice that small country governments have with respect to market organisations – and a dominant incumbent that promotes competition would be rare in any country.

When Samoa was recently presented the opportunity to connect to two undersea cables, the government-owned incumbent – the government's principal source of advice – recommended against it so that it could continue its stranglehold on satellite and microwave connections.

Fortunately for Samoa, other advice was taken, but restrictions in the contract and landing arrangements will mean that the future holds ongoing litigation. All this because of a lack of local independent expertise.

Connectivity

Samoa, like most countries of the Pacific, gets its connectivity through satellite. This service is relatively expensive and of relatively poor quality (high latency, echo and noise) and its capacity is constrained.

In 2008 there are several projects underway, or at least being considered, to bring undersea fibre to the islands. American Samoa is having an existing, unused cable rerouted to provide direct connection to New Zealand and Hawaii. And Samoa is planning on adding an associated undersea link for the 60 kilometres between American Samoa and Samoa – in this way piggy-backing on the new link.

Another initiative that will link many of the countries of the Pacific is sounding more positive, though nothing has yet been agreed. The French are planning on running links to their Pacific territories, and engagement is being sought from other territories along the path. This is being facilitated by Rodgers – showing how important individual leadership is in the Pacific.

Providing undersea fibre connections to each country will give a material boost to capacity. However, many of the countries consist of hundreds of small and scattered islands, some with very small populations indeed. Landing fibre into a capital will be enough of a challenge; getting more remote communities lit up is not realistic at all.

For many of these smaller islands and very remote communities, the Secretariat of the Pacific Community is running a project that will install small satellite earth stations, and provide services from there. Sustainability is a key focus, and in pilot projects in the Solomons the capital investment is being leveraged by a number of local users – schools, health clinics, banks, mining industries, and others – so that the monthly satellite costs will be recoverable. Maintenance and capital replacement will eventually be part of the programme.

Published strategy

Samoa started work on a national ICT strategy in 2002 and completed it the next year. This document was developed through extensive consultation throughout the country.

In the early part of 2000, the United Nations Development Programme (UNDP) was strongly advocating the development of ICT strategic plans, yet few were completed and even fewer to the level or extent of that in Samoa. Fiji, which already has a reasonably sized population and connection through the Southern Cross undersea fibre cable, is an exception. It is looking to grow a domestic ICT industry providing services to its neighbours.

Regulatory reform

Along with political will goes the need to create a fair and level playing field. While some countries may try to achieve this through pure market forces, it is not a successful model, particularly in small economies. Even New Zealand, after more than a decade of trying to use market forces and market competition law, has resorted to a regulator.

Samoa installed a telecommunications regulator in 2006. Since that time it has worked to reduce the powers of either a monopoly (SamoaTel) or a duopoly (SamoaTel and Digicel).

The regulatory environment does have short-term costs, as the incumbent dominant services provider is unnaturally

5 In 2008 the government sold its television operations.

precluded from dominating incumbents. It is a fine line that the regulator must walk, but it is particularly essential in small economies.

Tariffs

Many countries struggle financially to make ends meet. They often use their government-owned monopoly telecommunications providers to levy an indirect tax on communications. Many countries also see ICT equipment, including computers and software, as luxury goods and issue an import tariff – not to protect a domestic industry, but to generate revenue.

In 2002 the government of Samoa removed any tariff premium associated with ICT goods and treated them as general goods.

Other leadership

Besides political will, a successful deployment of ICTs within a country – infrastructure, supply and skills – must have leadership from within the community. In Samoa the embracing of ICTs is spread far and wide. Schools in remote villages, such as Leuluoega College (a high school), have seen their value and have diverted scarce resources to ensure that their students have at least rudimentary skills.

Samoa is blessed with a number of private sector entrepreneurs in ICT. Aitken Fruen is the CEO of iPasifika and Laeimau Oketevi Tanuvasa is the CEO of rival Computer Services. As long ago as 2002, Samoa's 180,000 people were served by more than 35 businesses actively competing in various parts of the ICT sector – and all but one were local initiatives.

Conclusion

ICTs can make a material difference in the prosperity of a country, even small island states in the Pacific. But this requires leadership, political will and patience. It requires a government that understands the value that ICTs and associated open and easy access to information provide. It takes individual leaders, inside and outside of government, who see the opportunities. And it requires a realisation that the local telephone company is not a different way to tax and inhibit growth, but a facilitator for growth – and trust that the total government tax take will increase as business and individuals prosper.

Samoa's leaders had that vision a decade ago, and have acted deliberately, diligently and patiently. The country's success serves to benchmark progress in the region. ■

ARGENTINA

Nodo TAU
Danilo Lujambio, Florencia Roveri, Carolina Fernández, Iván Kozenitzky, María Victoria Escobar, Flavia Fascendini, Eduardo Rodriguez and Melina Dachesky
www.tau.org.ar

Introduction

A global view on the policies related to the information society, from the standpoint of access, leads us to think about three fundamental aspects when we analyse the Argentine state of affairs. First, we need to analyse indicators and statistics reflecting physical access to technology; second, we need to evaluate the regulatory and legal frameworks (as well as those being debated); and last, we need to look at educational policies dealing with information and communications technologies (ICTs).

Physical access to technology

Infrastructure

In Argentina there are 16 million people online, which is almost 40% of the population. This percentage places our country far below more developed countries – such as the United States (US) at 72.5%, the United Kingdom (UK) at 68.6%, and France at 58.1% – but in a favourable position regionally. The only country in the region that surpasses us is Chile (44.9%).[1]

If we look at the information technology (IT) market, we see that in the last three years sales of computers have doubled (Clarín, 2007a). In part this is due to the fact that 30% of computers found in homes are old and cannot take advantage of new broadband connections.[2] It is also worth noting that many people first learn to use the internet at home, where they have access to computers (Clarín, 2007b). Two years ago, people used to have their first online experience in cybercafés and public telecentres.

These statistics account for an active market driven by commercial and business strategies. However, we ask: what is happening to the 60% of the population that has no access to the internet?

In our country, the internet is developing quickly: the number of users rose from 4.1 million in 2002 (Telefónica, 2003) to 16 million in 2007. However, this growth has not reduced the digital divide. In 2003, 73.5% of Argentine internet users lived in the urban region of Buenos Aires (INDEC, 2006), 63.6% were less than 30 years old, 57% of these were university students or graduates, almost all of them (94.3%) were professionals and 54.4% were male (Telefónica, 2003).

An official survey on cultural consumption stated that 47.2% of Argentines have never surfed the internet: these people are mostly women, under 50 years old, and from low socioeconomic sectors (Clarín, 2007c). Among those who do surf the internet, 86.6% do it in cybercafés. Another study asserts that low and middle socioeconomic groups, mainly adolescents and including street children, use cybercafés and telecentres (Contrera, 2007) – one reason why these centres are considered invaluable in reducing the digital divide (Finquielevich & Prince, 2007).

Universal service

The lack of access to a telephone line, especially in areas that the telephone companies consider non-profitable, is another factor that contributes to digital exclusion. In 2000 the Universal Service Trust Fund was created to guarantee the supply of telecommunications services to all inhabitants. In June 2007 Resolution 80/207 was passed, obliging telephone companies to contribute 1% of their income, backdated to when the fund was legally constituted. As a result, the government has presented the telephone companies with a USD 750 million bill, representing the contributions that have not been turned over since 2001.

In April 2008 the General Regulations for Universal Service were published in the Official Bulletin, requiring the main telephone operators – Telefónica and Telecom – to expand fixed-line telephony to the whole country in 60 months. Voices from different sectors suggest that what is really needed is for licences to be renegotiated, and for them to better reflect the potential for offering triple play services (i.e., broadband internet, TV and telephone access), amongst other major policy developments.

The merger of Cablevisión and Multicanal

In December 2007, the government approved a merger between Multicanal and Cablevisión, the main cable operators in the country, creating a new operator that has 47% of the cable television market and 620,000 broadband subscribers (La Nación, 2007). The listed shareholders of the new entity are the Clarín Group (60%) and Fintech Advisory, a US investment fund (40%).

Some of the conditions imposed by the National Commission for the Defence of Competition – the body that authorised the merger – relate to universal access:

- "Social tariffs" for paid digital television, but only valid for very poor zones in the Buenos Aires metropolitan area.
- Free cable television connections for public schools, hospitals, health centres and nursing homes, as well as police and fire stations (Clarín, 2007d).

1 Internet World Stats: www.internetworldstats.com
2 Prince & Cooke: www.princecooke.com/mercado.asp

- The laying of 3,000 kilometres of fibre-optic cable alongside national and provincial highways.

It is worth noting that the Clarín Group is the biggest and most influential multimedia broadcasting company in Argentina, and the merger has been seen as a concession by former president Nestor Kirchner to avoid media criticism. Some sources suggest that the merger had irregularities, which include the breach of cultural industries legislation (Lanata, 2008).

Community Technology Centres

The Community Technology Centres (CTCs) programme, implemented in 1999, was an initiative that aimed to increase public access to the internet.[3] The programme has remained unchanged for years, and has stagnated. However, the current government is attempting to revive it and has invited 50 CTC coordinators from different provinces to participate in a free "digital civics" course organised by the National Secretariat for Communications and academic institutions. Attempts have also been made to revive the programme's website,[4] but the site does not offer information on the policies to be implemented within the framework of the project or provide a schedule for future activities.

Legal and regulatory framework

The new broadcasting law

Broadcasting Law No. 22285 was part of the internal security legislation established during the last military dictatorship in Argentina. In 2005 there was a great step forward in the democratisation of communications when the national executive modified Article 45 of that law, which prohibited non-commercial entities from applying for licences.

In April 2008, President Cristina Fernández de Kirchner proposed a new broadcasting law, possibly as a consequence of official disappointment with the way big media houses had covered the economic conflict in the agricultural sectors (Katz, 2008). A change in the authority of the Broadcasting Committee, which regulates radio and TV frequencies, was followed by a round of consultations with different stakeholders, including the Coalition for Democratic Broadcasting, which had drafted a proposal called "21 Basic Points for the Right to Communication"[5] during the government of Néstor Kirchner, but had obtained no concrete results. The current president has shown an interest in using it as a basis for the new law.

Judging from discussions regarding the new law, the issue of digitalisation clearly offers fresh opportunities for new forms of citizen participation in media, but also poses the danger of media monopolies being formed.

Digital television

> "The radio spectrum is a good that belongs to the whole society (...) For a country as big as Argentina it undoubtedly has a strategic value" (Valle, 2008).

Argentina started discussing digital television in 1997. A commission created to investigate the matter determined that the US standard would be the best to adopt. The two main broadcasting channels tested this new format, but a schedule for the implementation of the new system was not set. In 2006 a new commission decided that the European standard would make more effective use of the radio spectrum. Many feel that the discussions have been influenced by different lobby groups, rather than focusing on the best strategic choice for the country. It was expected that there would be a cascade effect among the Southern Common Market (Mercosur) countries, and that all would try to adopt the same norm to share their cultural products via TV. The adoption of the European standard is seen as a way of encouraging the entrance of new television companies into Argentina.

Digital tax

At the end of 2007, the Association of Independent Musicians submitted a proposal for the creation of an Institute of Music which would "develop and expand musical activity in the country." This institute would be financed by a "digital tax" applicable to any format or medium that stores or reproduces music and images (such as CDs and DVDs, CD, DVD and MP3 players and recorders, and mobile phones).

The proposal provoked strong opposition in the blogger community, which organised a "No Tax in Argentina" campaign that led to the conclusion that the charge was not feasible.[6] Some argued that it would widen the digital divide, raising the price of technological goods; that it would legalise piracy; that the tax would be limitless and thus unfair; and that what would be collected would not go directly to the content creators (Berghella, 2008; La Barbarie, 2008).

Human capacity and training

Among government policy discussions, the issue of ICTs in education has been prevalent.

Digital literacy policies

The new Law of Education No. 26206, which regulates the national education system, was passed in December 2006. The law supports the idea that access to ICTs is important for equality and quality in education.

The government's programmes involve equipping and connecting schools, training teachers, and developing educational material, as well as promoting digital literacy in the classroom (Landau et al., 2007). The following public programmes stand out:

- The Programme for the Improvement of Secondary Schools aims to install computer infrastructure in the

3 For more information, see the Argentina country report in GISWatch 2007: www.globaliswatch.org/files/pdf/GISW_Argentina.pdf

4 www.ctc.gov.ar

5 www.coalicion.org.ar/index.htm

6 noalcanon.org/no-al-canon

classroom. Teacher training and the development of learning materials are also key issues.

- The Comprehensive Programme for Educational Equality (PIIE) develops strategies for the strengthening of urban fringe schools by providing equipment. Within the PIIE framework, the pedagogic strengthening programme trains teachers in schools where equipment has already been installed.
- The www.educ.ar portal initiative also installs equipment and connects schools to the internet, trains teachers and creates educational content. The portal is responsible for the Digital Literacy National Campaign and coordinates the Encuentro TV channel, which broadcasts high-quality educational content.

Apart from these programmes, the Ministry of Education signed an agreement with the One Laptop per Child (OLPC) initiative in 2006, although the implementation of this project has not run smoothly.

Despite all these initiatives, two aspects of digital literacy in the classroom still need to be strengthened: access and appropriation. Regarding access, there are noticeable differences between private and public school students. The difference between rural and urban students is still more noticeable. It is true that the policies to provide equipment have been strengthened, but resources remain scarce. Regarding appropriation, it is difficult to profit from the potential that ICTs have for improving education without adequate teacher training, and this needs to be improved.

It is worth mentioning that these government programmes operate independently from each other, which means the potential for synergies is lost.

Action steps

This report suggests that in Argentina there is no comprehensive public policy to deal with the digital divide. Policies that favour access to technologies by excluded population groups are very isolated, and have low impact. We believe that a great step forward would be approaching the problem from the point of view of universal access. Within the national government framework, the National Programme for the Information Society,[7] which has not been operational for a while, is now slowly moving forward. It is this programme that needs to look at the issue.

Regarding policies that define the regulatory and legal framework, there are issues that have been gradually taken up by different civil society organisations (see GISWatch 2007). In some cases, they have given rise to interesting processes that have influenced policy – particularly when specific proposals have been made. The collaboration of civil society in policy development processes should be encouraged.

Lastly, regarding educational policies, we feel that ICT initiatives have been uneven. This is partly due to the fact that real educational management in our country depends on the provinces and not on the national government (the level we have evaluated here). However, national plans should find ways of resulting in practical implementation on the ground. Reaching the underserved 60% of the country is difficult because the people who are excluded are the poorest, and live in the least populated areas. As a result, we believe that the public education system would be the best way to include them. ■

References

Berghella, V. (2008) ¿Canon digital en la Argentina? *Clarín*, 13 February. Available at: www.clarin.com/diario/2008/02/13/conexiones/t-01606184.htm

Clarín (2007a) Computadoras: se duplicaron las ventas en los últimos tres años. *Clarín*, 24 December. Available at: www.clarin.com/diario/2007/12/24/elpais/p-01801.htm

Clarín (2007b) Hay 2,8 millones más de usuarios de Internet. *Clarín*, 15 December. Available at: www.clarin.com/diario/2007/12/15/elpais/p-03602.htm

Clarín (2007c) Casi la mitad de los argentinos todavía no navegó por Internet. *Clarín*, 5 December. Available at: www.clarin.com/diario/2007/12/05/sociedad/s-03001.htm

Clarín (2007d). Confirman la adquisición de Multicanal por Cablevisión. *Clarín*, 8 December. Available at: www.clarin.com/diario/2007/12/08/elpais/p-03601.htm

Coalition for Democratic Broadcasting: www.coalicion.org.ar/index.htm

Contrera, E. (2007) La brecha digital se achica porque crecen los locutorios y los cíber. *Página 12*, 17 May. Available at: www.pagina12.com.ar/diario/sociedad/3-85094-2007-05-17.html

Finquielevich, S. and Prince, A. (2007) *El (involuntario) rol social de los cybercafés.* Available at: www.oei.es/tic/rolcibercafes.pdf

INDEC (2006) Accesos a Internet: Diciembre 2005. Available at: www.cnc.gov.ar/indicadores/archivos/INDEC_internet_03_06.pdf

Internet World Stats: www.internetworldstats.com

Katz, C. (2008) Argentina: The clash over rent. *Links – International Journal of Socialist Renewal.* Available at: links.org.au/node/453

La Barbarie: labarbarie.com.ar/2008/canon-digital-algunas-conclusiones

La Nación (2007) El Gobierno autorizó la fusión de Multicanal y CableVisión. *La Nación*, 8 December. Available at: www.lanacion.com.ar/nota.asp?nota_id=969301

Lanata, J. (2008) Enemigos íntimos. *Crítica de la Argentina*, 6 April. Available at: www.criticadigital.com.ar/impresa/index.php?secc=nota&nid=2290

Landau, M., Serra, J. C. and Gruschetsky, M. (2007) *Acceso universal a la alfabetización digital: Políticas, problemas y desafíos en el contexto argentino.* Available at: www.oei.es/pdfs/acceso_unuversal_alfabetizacion_digital_diniece.pdf

Prince & Cooke: www.princecooke.com/mercado.asp

Telefónica (2003) *La Sociedad de la Información en la Argentina.* Available at: www.telefonica.com.ar/corporativo/sociedaddelainformacion/pdf/014-127.htm

Valle, L. (2008) El estándar digital: un valor estratégico. *El Cronista*, 8 April. Available at: www.palermo.edu/ingenieria/eventos_noticias/nota_valle_tvdigital.html

7 www.psi.gov.ar

BANGLADESH

Bytes For All
Partha Sarker
www.bytesforall.net

Introduction

Bangladesh has a population of 138.23 million with a gross domestic product (GDP) per capita of USD 520 in 2007. Almost 76% of its population lives in rural areas where the literacy rate is about 56%[1] and where 41% of people live on less than one dollar a day. The country has continued to make considerable progress in ICT sector development. Some of this has been registered through the wider penetration of ICT usage, infrastructure enhancement and a favourable regulatory regime. According to the International Telecommunication Union (ITU), there are about 450,000 internet users in Bangladesh (as of August 2007), which is about 0.3% of the total population. But the growth in mobile telephony is phenomenal. Currently in Bangladesh, there are about 40 million mobile phone users, many of whom are accessing the internet using their cell phone connection.[2]

The situation in the fixed/public switched telephone network (PSTN) market is not that euphoric. About 80% of all land telephone lines are in Bangladesh's four major cities where only 20% of the population lives. By the end of 2007 PSTN subscribers grew to over 1.19 million compared to 1.01 million in June 2006. Bangladesh got connected to the SEA-ME-WE 4[3] broadband submarine cable in 2006. The data transfer capacity of the cable is 14.78 gigabytes per second (Gbps), of which 3.28 Gbps was being used until June 2007.[4] Despite its demographic profile, Bangladesh has done relatively well in some social indicators such as improving female literacy and school enrolment, reducing infant mortality, increasing access to safe water and sanitation, etc. But although telecoms is one of the largest contributors to the growth of GDP in Bangladesh, its relationship with social and human development indicators is often not studied, or is not taken into policy consideration.

Legal and regulatory framework

In their research paper, "Regulating for the Next Billion", Rajendra Singh and Siddhartha Raja (2008) argue that a regulator has to deal with both supply- and demand-side issues. On the supply side, telecom regulators are involved in three fundamental types of issues: interconnection, resource allocation, and revenue management. On the demand side, however, the task of the regulator is typically indirect, especially since there is no way to order users to do something. The regulator can, however, through control of the supply of ICTs, ensure that telecom services reach the underserved (universal service), that they are affordable (subsidies), or have some minimum standard (quality of service and interconnection) (Singh & Raja, 2008).

Before 1996, the telecom policy environment in Bangladesh was a bit dismal, with the absence of any regulatory body and the monopolisation of the telecom network either by the government or by one private network (i.e., Citycell). During the early 1990s, the Bangladesh government rejected an offer to be connected to an undersea internet cable on security grounds. In 1996 the government first started to offer wireless licensing and opened up the market for more than one player. One of the wireless providers to surface due to this process was GrameenPhone, a subsidiary of Grameen Bank, a major development organisation in the country. The Bangladesh Telecommunication Act (April, 2001) founded the Bangladesh Telecommunication Regulatory Commission (BTRC) and marked a new era in the telecom regulatory environment.

The major functions set for this regulatory body as identified by the act are:

- To regulate the establishment, operation and maintenance of telecom services in Bangladesh.
- To control and abolish discriminatory practices and ensure a level playing field for operators and healthy competition.
- To hear and resolve objections, disputes and complaints through public hearings and issue injunctions.

So far the regulatory body has licensed four international gateway service providers (IGSPs), six mobile phone operators, 185 internet service providers (ISPs) both in Dhaka and elsewhere, 21 very small aperture terminal (VSAT) operators, and six zonal PSTN operators. Recently it decided to process 116 community radio licences in the coastal and remote areas of Bangladesh. BTRC is also responsible for setting regulation to introduce next-generation telecom networks and services in Bangladesh. As part of this, BTRC recently started to provide licences for voice over internet protocol (VoIP) services (e.g., for call centre operation), third generation (3G) services, and WiMAX services.

Different legislations have resolved many telecom interconnection issues that are pertinent to wider telecom penetration in the country. For example, the Interconnection Regulations 2004 stipulated that an interconnection agreement should be executed within three months from the first

1 www.apdip.net
2 www.btrc.gov.bd
3 South East Asia-Middle East-West Europe 4
4 www.btrc.gov.bd

day on which the new operator starts providing telecommunication services. The Bangladesh Telecommunications Act 2001 also states that if interested parties, who are bound to execute interconnection agreements, cannot agree on the terms of such an agreement, any of them may approach the commission for judgment.

The deregulation of the telecoms sector has continued to fuel the competitive environment, especially in the mobile phone market. The six mobile phone operators are in fierce competition, a situation which has led to a call rate reduction to a level which is the lowest in South Asia. Some of the operators have started to offer a call for the equivalent of a mere USD 0.004 – the base rate offered by BTRC.

The private sector has 98% of the market share in the mobile telephony sector. But in the fixed-lined telecom market, the Bangladesh Telegraph and Telephone Board (BTTB), the incumbent operator, has 74% of the market share. In response, BTRC divided the country into five zones and has allowed for 35 licences to be granted to fifteen private sector PSTN operators under an open and transparent licensing system. In March 2006 BTRC invited bids from private operators so that it could award four licences to the private sector for operating in the central zone. The new operators started offering connections from September 2007. It is predicted that after the deregulation of the fixed-line telecom market in Dhaka City, the PSTN will grow more than 100% by the end of 2008.

The country's first call centre licensing process has been very open and transparent. Before issuing the licences, BTRC organised a public consultation to develop guidelines. To encourage youth employment and investment in call centre businesses, its guidelines proposed to issue the licences in three broad categories: call centres in Bangladesh, hosted call centres in Bangladesh (for companies without infrastructure) and hosted call centre service providers in Bangladesh. The licence fee was BDT 5,000 (approximately USD 70) for each category for an initial term of five years. BTRC issued licences to thirteen individuals and joint venture companies.

Auctions to issue licences for international gateways (IGWs), interconnection exchanges (IXPs) and international internet gateways (IIGs) were also held.[5]

Another institutional development with significant policy implications was the separation of Bangladesh Submarine Cable Company Limited (BSCCL) from BTTB. Prior to this, BTTB had long functioned as the regulatory body, service provider and infrastructure owner all at the same time. This division is likely to begin a new era in the telecommunications sector.

Physical access to technology

Bangladesh got connected to SEA-ME-WE 4 at a cost of USD 35.1 million. However, it started with an obsolete model of one operator being responsible for all international connectivity. Regulatory expert Rohan Samarajiva argued that in such a scenario, the regulatory agency should step in to ensure that a hybrid model is developed where BTTB builds capacity to reach major population or commercial centres and offers connectivity at non-discriminatory and cost-oriented terms to other operators (the "buy" option). He also argued that all operators be given the "build" option so that they can build a link to the cable station, co-locate equipment, etc. The offer of both build and buy options reduces the burden placed on regulation (Samarajiva, 2005).

Despite the availability of higher bandwidth, the growth of internet users was not significant in the last couple of years. Until last year, BTTB was the sole provider of bandwidth with a high operating cost. In February 2008, it reduced internet tariff charges by 20-40%, with an expectation that this would increase the internet usage level. According to the new tariff schedule, the monthly charge came down to about USD 10, from about USD 14. An annual lease for internet access up to two megabits per second (Mbps) came down to about USD 20,571 from its original ceiling of USD 27,428. But many experts believe that the price reduction is still not conducive to reaching a broader population with growing connectivity demand. The rate is still nine to ten times higher than the same bandwidth cost in India or Pakistan (Daily Star, 2008).

BTTB has already recovered the initial investment cost of setting up its submarine cable. Now there is a legitimate call from civil society for the government to drastically reduce internet charges to match other countries in South Asia. Some government bodies acknowledge the fact that the bandwidth prices fixed by BTTB are far too high and need to be adjusted. In a recent interview with *The Daily Star*, the chairman of BTRC, Manzurul Alam, called BTTB's bandwidth prices "abnormally high" and said they should come down to BDT 10,000 (USD 145) per megabit (Daily Star, 2008).

The government is also responding to growing bandwidth needs by allowing a second submarine cable to be developed. BTRC has already published guidelines, inviting proposals from private investors in this regard.

Locally relevant content

One interesting outcome of better connectivity is that it transforms the demand from connectivity to content. Bangladesh is at the transition of this development. As telecom institutions are being reorganised, and the market is expanding, an enabling environment is fuelling the appetite for content and services. This content need is being addressed by three separate trends:

- Availability of different content services via internet and cell phone connection
- Emergence of end-user innovation and user-generated content
- A push for localisation processes and standards.

5 www.btrc.gov.bd

Bangladesh's government is at the forefront of digital content publishing. The Digital Review of Asia Pacific 2007-2008 reports that the government, with support from the United Nations Development Programme (UNDP), has published many of its documents in digital format, both on the web (www.forms.gov.bd) and on CD-ROM. Most of these documents can now be downloaded free of charge. The downloadable documents include forms for passport applications, visa applications, citizenship, pensions, internet connections (through BTTB), birth registration, income tax returns and driving licences. However, out of 40 ministries listed on the government website (www.forms.gov.bd/eng/ByMinistry.aspx), only eight ministries have partially released their documents (Librero & Arinto, 2007).

Different non-governmental organisations (NGOs), depending on their areas of expertise, have produced digital content on development issues. The Development Research Network (D-Net),[6] for example, has produced a number of CDs on livelihoods following a consultation with rural communities. The International Rice Research Institute (IRRI) in Bangladesh has developed a "Rice Knowledge Bank" – a digital service for those who provide information and support for farmers (such as NGOs), which is also the first comprehensive, digital rice-production library containing an ever-increasing wealth of information on training and rice production.[7]

Different mobile phone carriers are also developing or providing value-added content services using the mobile network. GrameenPhone, one of the largest cell phone networks in Bangladesh, provides a range of news updates in collaboration with different news agencies. Its "cell bazaar" initiative provides a mobile phone-based marketplace, where users can buy and sell any item using the cell phone. Banglalink has launched a different type of service for SSC (similar to O level examination) candidates. They are managing a short message service (SMS) based registration process where candidates with a Banglalink number can register for an online examination. AKTEL, another carrier, maintains a multimedia messaging service (MMS) greetings portal through which AKTEL subscribers can send MMS greetings to other AKTEL subscribers, even if their handsets are not MMS-enabled.[8]

The decentralised structure of the internet has encouraged the growth of user-generated content and collaborative publishing based on collective knowledge. Writing and maintaining blogs and participating in different social networking sites (like Facebook or LinkedIn) has become quite a common practice among the younger generation in Bangladesh. The Bangladesh Open Source Network (BDOSN),[9] an informal network that seeks to popularise free and open source software (FOSS), has worked to facilitate Bengali (also known as Bangla) content on Wikipedia. As of January 2008, Bengali Wikipedia[10] had over 16,000 entries, one of the highest among the non-English versions of Wikipedia, and has been constantly referred to as a success story by the founder of Wikipedia.

Localisation has also gone a long way to make computing and the internet useful to the majority of the population. Bengali is spoken by 210 million people across the world, but no substantial local language application or standard was available before the late 1990s. Some Bengali fonts were developed for the Windows environment in a haphazard way, resulting in a lack of interoperability. As a result, keyboard mapping was different, which made localisation a cumbersome process. In 1998, Tanim Ahmed first solved the locale issue (bn.BD) and started a process of localising Linux.[11] Since then the major initiatives have been run by volunteers, although institutional initiatives have also entered the scene recently. The PAN Localization Project has helped establish the Center for Research on Bangla Language Processing at BRAC University in Bangladesh.[12] It has developed a 100,000-word list with tagging, verb and noun morphology, rich-text editor and spell-checker. A high-performance optical character recogniser (OCR) is also in the process of being developed.

Finally, the Right to Information Act creates legal entitlement for people to seek information and demand transparency in the activities of institutions, including government and non-governmental institutions. The government drafted the Act in 2002 but never placed it before parliament. The present government is trying to make some amendments and is planning to bring it out as an ordinance. Similar legislation has been enacted in 65 countries in Asia, including India and Pakistan.

Action steps

It is important that the government continues to play an effective regulatory role to balance the telecommunications sector both on the supply and demand side. It needs to encourage professionalism, competence and accountability, including in the incumbent operator.

It is essential for civil society organisations to understand and make themselves heard on issues of ICT and telecom regulation. Not too many organisations in Bangladesh have that capacity. Therefore capacity building on policy and regulatory issues may be an important step.

The priority in Bangladesh is moving from connectivity to content and services. As connectivity is improving, new content and services are likely to emerge. Civil society organisations need to be prepared to take part in this discussion and see what content and services can be developed to reflect the needs of the social development sector. ■

6 www.dnet-bangladesh.org/main.html

7 www.knowledgebank.irri.org/rkb/first.htm

8 mobiforge.com/blog/bangladesh-some-unique-services-telcos

9 www.bdosn.org

10 bn.wikipedia.org/wiki

11 bengalinux.org

12 www.bracuniversity.net/research/crblp

References

Asia-Pacific Development Information Programme: www.apdip.net

Bangladesh Open Source Network (BDOSN): www.bdosn.org

Bangladesh Telecommunication Regulatory Commission (BTRC): www.btrc.gov.bd

Bengali Wikipedia: bn.wikipedia.org/wiki

Center for Research on Bangla Language Processing: www.bracuniversity.net/research/crblp

Daily Star (2008) 20-40pc internet tariff cut. *The Daily Star*, 7 February. Available at: www.thedailystar.net/story.php?nid=22295

Development Research Network (D-Net): www.dnet-bangladesh.org/main.html

International Rice Research Institute – Rice Knowledge Bank: www.knowledgebank.irri.org/rkb/first.htm

Librero, F. and Arinto, P. (eds.) (2007) *Digital Review of Asia Pacific 2007-2008*. Sage/IDRC/Orbicom. Available at: www.idrc.ca/en/ev-116715-201-1-DO_TOPIC.html

mobiForge: mobiforge.com

Samarajiva, R. (2005) Making the most of submarine cable connectivity for Bangladesh. *The Daily Star*, 6 December. Available at: www.thedailystar.net/2005/12/06/d512061501104.htm

Singh, R. and Raja, S. (2008) Regulating for the Next Billion. In Samarajiva, R. and Zainudeen, A. (eds.) *ICT Infrastructure in Emerging Asia: Policy and Regulatory Roadblocks*. Sage India/IDRC. Available at: www.idrc.ca/en/ev-117916-201-1-DO_TOPIC.html

BOSNIA AND HERZEGOVINA

oneworld-platform for southeast europe (owpsee) foundation
Valentina Pellizzer
www.oneworldsee.org

Introduction

Bosnia and Herzegovina remains a small and complex environment where it is hard to implement reform any time it may affect the state. The simple fact that the state is based on collective or group rights more than on individual rights has its implications. It creates a sense of parallel and mutually obstructing realities. On one hand there are the declarations and agreements signed during national and regional conferences by government representatives, and on the other there is everyday life, which happens in a very disharmonious environment, where reforms are on standby or are applied partially, or have to pass through very invasive processes to comply with the political will and power of the three national communities (Bosniaks, Serbs and Croats) and their governing parties.

Because of this, the information and communications technology (ICT) policy environment is deadlocked by tensions around two bodies, the Agency for Development of the Information Society (AIS) and the Academic and Research Network (BIHARNET), both of which should be bodies operating at the state level.[1] However, the AIS has still not been officially established, after several proposals were rejected. A draft law is now waiting for parliamentary approval. The situation is more complex for the academic research network. BIHARNET, which was formally registered at the state level but is seen to be part of the Federation of Bosnia and Herzegovina (i.e., one of the two national entities), is almost frozen by opposing veto powers held by the two main nationalities sharing power: Bosniaks and Croats. At the same time, another academic and research network, SARNET in the Republika Srpska, acts on its own, and is in regional and international partnerships with other academic networks.

In this context, the growing use of the country's top-level domain (.ba) could be seen as a glimmer in the dark: a sign that Bosnia and Herzegovina could be seen, at least from a search engine point of view, as a united country. Currently the number of websites registered on the domain is 8,958. It is important to mention that while it was very common a few years ago to find public institutions with extensions like .net,[2] .org and .com., today we see an increase in the use of the .ba domain, especially at the municipalities level (e.g., www.opstinaderventa.ba, www.lukavac.ba). A change in approach is also visible in Republika Srpska, where the .ba domain appears together with the sub-domain .rs.[3]

Capacity: Do people understand how to use technology?

According to the eSEE [South-East Europe] Plus Matrix, as of June 2008 internet penetration in Bosnia and Herzegovina was 20%, with broadband services standing at 6%.

The relevance and importance of ICTs is something that citizens are learning. The integration of technology requires investment and strategic decision-making. In this regard, the commitment of Bosnia and Herzegovina is difficult to read. Even if it is true that almost 90% of schools have a computer lab, only 10% of them have broadband access. Pupils start learning about technology only in high school and there is no common curriculum for the whole country.

Looking at social networking, such as blogs or forum activities, we could say that people are getting more familiar with these. Last winter a civic movement successfully convened more than 10,000 people in Sarajevo using the power of the internet. For three months people protested by posting messages on blogs, forums and mailing lists, and using short messaging service (SMS), amongst similar tools.

Blogger.ba hosts more than 70,000 different blogs. Another portal, Bljesak,[4] has more than 3,162 users for a total of 8,835 themes. Also widely used is the portal Banjalukalive, with 2,016 members and more than 1,785 themes, even if the majority of them are still to do with entertainment or social networking. This year events made clear that blogs and forums are becoming the alternative and direct voice of the citizens. This voice is not always progressive, but it still reflects the need for communication and for having spaces for discussion.

1 Bosnia and Herzegovina encompasses two entities with their own governments and parliaments: the Federation of Bosnia and Herzegovina and the Republika Srpska. There is also one internationally supervised district, the Brcko District. This system of government was established by the Dayton Peace Agreement to guarantee the representation of the country's three major groups (Bosniaks, Serbs and Croats), with each having a veto on anything that goes against what is defined as "the vital interest of the constituent people".

2 The official website of the parliament of the Republika Srpska is www.narodnaskupstinars.net, which still uses the .net domain as a top-level domain. The same is true of the official website of the Republika Srpska (www.vladars.net).

3 As it is not a state, the Republika Srpska does not have its own internet domain name and its institutions prefer not to use the Bosnia Herzegovina top-level domain (.ba) – or indeed any other single top-level domain – and opt instead for a composite (e.g., www.rs.ba).

4 www.bljesak.info is one of the main portals run from Mostar.

Relevant content: Is there locally relevant content, especially in terms of language?

Content production can be roughly divided into three sectors: private sector content, civil society content, and public institution or official websites (Bosnia and Herzegovina has fourteen different levels of administration, so there is great potential for online content).

In all three sectors the issue of local content involves a cross-cutting issue: language. In Bosnia and Herzegovina there are three languages – Bosnian, Croatian and Serbian – and two alphabets (Latin and Cyrillic). At the same time, English is used at state level.

The question of language use, more than a language issue per se, reflects the nationalistic poison that is all around. Language is used to divide instead of bridging the divide. In fact, the languages are not so different that users cannot understand and actively participate regardless of the official language of the website. Very few sites are able to cover all the languages, because this requires time and resources and does not offer any real additional value. But the issue of online languages remains a potential trap that can be used at any time to split public opinion. Few are the groups who articulate their position around languages and content from an inclusive perspective, and elaborate and produce critical and alternative content.

Forums offer online spaces where people confront each other regardless of language. However, there remains a percentage of people who choose to register themselves as users with what they feel as "their" portals, reproducing in the virtual world the same nationalistic divisions of the real one.

Trust: Do people have confidence in the technology they use?

In the last year the use of technology has increased, while reflection on privacy, security and issues such as cyber crime remains very low. Bosnia and Herzegovina is still a country where the majority of computers have pirated software, and where it is possible to buy illegal copies of movies and cracked software on the main streets. The level of online public and commercial services is still low. The majority of public sites do not go further than offering downloadable forms, which need to be filled in and brought to the respective offices.

Bosnia and Herzegovina is currently defining laws and regulations regarding security, privacy and cyber crime, on its path towards European Union (EU) integration. In this regard it is following the world trend around security and public interest versus individual rights. What is missing is a public debate with spaces and opportunity for citizens to analyse the alternatives.

In the last two years the internet in Bosnia and Herzegovina has increasingly offered alternative information (via online media, forums, bloggers, internet radio, etc.). Anyone who can access an internet café, or has internet access at work or university, is potentially a content producer. All these spaces are providing alternative content which is very often opposite to the mainstream discourse. The fact that there is no debate around online laws and regulations could carry a cost in terms of freedom of expression. In a country organised around collective rights, content is under constant threat of censorship (e.g., there is a hate speech case related to the first Queer Festival in Sarajevo, which is happening during Ramadan).[5]

For a transitional state like Bosnia and Herzegovina, issues related to internet privacy, security and cyber crime are still far away from general concern and are often seen as something that experts need to discuss and find solutions to. This leads to strange events, such as a public official easily obtaining the real names of forum users who were publicly criticising her behaviour and revealing them during a TV show.

Action steps

If we look at the developmental trends in Bosnia and Herzegovina around the implementation of an ICT strategy, we have to say that public institutions have failed. While Bosnia and Herzegovina was the first country from the Western Balkans to approve an ICT strategy, it now lags behind countries such as Serbia and Macedonia.

The current focus at the state level is e-government, which means developing internal infrastructure for public institutions, and a more interactive and inclusive management of their services. When it comes to the education sector, the mosaic becomes more fragmented and splits into small pieces. In the overall process, citizens or civil society actors are not considered stakeholders, but more or less beneficiaries.

The nature of the internet is making citizens realise that there is a technology that can be used which is connected worldwide. But around the use and abuse of ICTs, and their dissemination, there is still no critical mass.

A critical focal point is developing around content production. State officials have mostly left the online space to be dominated by hate speech – such as the attack on the Sarajevo Queer Festival – without taking any steps to address and implement the country's anti-discrimination law. The regulatory agency has also not issued any fines. This shows clearly that the issue of content and privacy, when it comes to individual rights, will require citizens to either stand up and take responsibility, or silence their diversity. ◾

5 Many publications, including the popular *SAFF* and *Dnevni Avaz*, have used derogatory language in relation to lesbian and gay people. They have called for the organisers of the festival to be lynched, stoned, doused with petrol or expelled from the country. Death threats have been issued on the internet against individual gay rights activists. Appeals have also been made to the public to disrupt the festival (Amnesty International press release, 19 September 2008).

References

eSEE Plus Matrix: www.eseeinitiative.org

Omerovi, S. and Bambura, I. (2004) *Public Relations in Service of Local Governance: A Step Further. The analysis of capacities and needs of 11 BiH municipalities in the field of public relations.* Sarajevo: Mediacentar. Available at: www.soros.org.ba/docs_lokalna_uprava/public_relations_in_service_of_local_governance.doc

Regular monitoring of the following websites and portals:

www.sarajevo-x.com[6]

bljesak.info

mladi.info

www.bhtelecom.ba/portal.html

www.monitor.ba

www.ngo.ba

www.pincom.info

www.banjalukalive.com

www.cafe.ba

efm.ba/portal

radio202.ba/loc

www.oiabih.info/ba/informira/web_portal/index.shtml

www.radiosarajevo.ba

24sata.info

info.ba

bih-x.com

www.blogger.ba[7]

www.bljesak.info[8]

Forums from Bosnia and Herzegovina:

s14.invisionfree.com/SELONACELNIKOV_FORUM

www.kostajnica.com/discus/index.html

forum.prijedor.com/index.php

forumi.gradiska.com/index.php

forum.rskoming.net/index.php

forum.blic.net/index.php

www.banjalukalive.com/forum/index.php

forum.teol.net

www.banjaluka.rs.ba/forum

forum.mrkonjic-grad.com

www.celinac.org/forumi/index.php

www.kotorvaros.rs.ba/forum/index.php

www.teslic.info/index2.php?option=com_forum

srpskikupres.com/v-web/bulletin/bb/index.php

www.modrica.com/forum/forum_topi ... ID=36&PN=1

www.bijeljina.com/modules/newbb

www.lopare.net/forum/index.php

www.phpbber.com/phpbb/?mforum=ugljevikb

www.zvornik.info/diskusije

www.srpskosarajevo.com/forum

forum.sarajevo-rs.com

www.24casa.com/forum

www.elitesecurity.org

www.benchmark.co.yu/forum/index.php

www.mycity.co.yu/phpbb

forum.krstarica.com/index.php

manastir-lepavina.org/forum

www.pravoslavac.net/razgovori/index.php

www.sarajevo-x.com/forum

moforaja.com/board.php

www.mostarskaraja.com/board.php

www.forum.hr/index.php

www.index.hr/forum/default.aspx

www.iskon.hr/forum/index.jspa

6 One of the most visited online magazines in Bosnia and Herzegovina.

7 The main blogger community in Bosnia and Herzegovina, powered by sarajevo-x.com.

8 Internet magazine and forum.

BRAZIL

GPOPAI (Research Group on Public Policies for Access to Information), University of São Paulo
Pablo Ortellado
www.gpopai.usp.br

Introduction

Access to information and communications technologies (ICTs) in Brazil has grown steadily in the past years, with a few notable exceptions. Access to traditional media equipment, such as radio and TV sets, has almost become universal, although the presence of radios in Brazilian households seems to be declining. The new frontier in extending access to such media is now digital radio and TV, and the main regulatory issue has been the definition of standards. At the same time, access to computers and the internet continues to form the backbone of the country's public ICT policy.

The Brazilian Internet Steering Committee (CGI) has been surveying the use of ICTs for the past three years (2005-2007) and is now the main source of data relating to access to ICTs (CGI, 2008). Additional data is available from the National Household Sample Survey conducted by the Brazilian Institute of Geography and Statistics (IBGE), whose most recent available data is for 2006 (IBGE, 2007). These will be the main sources for reporting on the present state of access to ICTs in Brazil.

The country's key demographic, economic and social indicators are presented in Table 1.

Table 1: Main demographic, economic and social indicators

Population (2007)	183,987,291
Gross domestic product (GDP) per capita by purchasing power parity (2005)	USD 8,402
Gini index (2005)	0.57
Human development Index (2005)	0.800
Adult literacy rate (2005)	88.6%
Population aged 18-24 in higher education (2006)	12.1%

Key policy and regulatory challenges

After heated controversy, Brazil opted in 2007 for the Japanese standard ISDB for digital TV. The decision was received with strong criticism from civil society and academia for being a poor interactive standard, and not allowing greater plurality of broadcasters. In fact, the implementation of the standard was made in such a way that companies who were licensees of the analogue TV spectrum automatically retained the right to provide the new digital TV services. A similar dispute is now underway regarding the adoption of the digital radio standard, and civil society defenders of greater plurality are again objecting to the government's proposed standard, IBOC.

There is also ongoing dispute over the idea defended by TV companies of imposing technical protection measures (TPM) on digital TV broadcasting to limit the recording of aired content. The adoption of TPM to restrict copying of digital TV is being debated in Congress. The proposal is to limit copies of aired content to one high quality copy per TV set (Bill 6915/2006). Another bill being debated (Bill 89/2003) proposes to criminalise the circumvention of TPM.

A last point of controversy in digital TV is what to do with the spectrum now used for analogue broadcasting once the system is entirely converted to the digital standard. Civil society organisations are proposing that this portion of the spectrum should be considered a "commons" – an open spectrum to be used for citizens' networks (Silveira et al., 2007). TV companies, on the other hand, want to retain the right to use the spectrum for new services.

Certainly more impressive than the slight decline of analogue radios in households is the pronounced decline of fixed telephones (from 54% to 45% in the past three years). This might be explained by the accentuated rise in mobile telephones, whose presence in Brazilian households has risen from 61% to 74%. Mobile telephones are clearly the medium with the highest growth rate in households, especially among the poor. The CGI survey noted that 49% of the very poorest households (with monthly family incomes below USD 240) already have access to mobile phone devices, and 73% of those devices can be connected to the internet (although only 3% of them actually do). On the other hand, only 17% of the poorest households have fixed telephone lines. With the increased availability of internet services on mobile phone devices, this should clearly be a focus in policy for extending internet access.

A clearer point for policy regulation is the concentration of telecom operators. There has been heated debate since early 2008 on whether Brazilian authorities should allow the merger of telecom operators Oi and Brasil Telecom. On the one hand, the merger is criticised by some analysts for using public funds, and for concentrating the telecom market. Defenders of the merger, however, say that it will prevent the two smaller Brazilian companies from being acquired later by the largest operators in Latin America, the Spanish company Telefónica and the Mexican company TelMex. Additionally, it is argued that the new merged company will have a large share of public capital, and so the state will have greater power to intervene should the market become dysfunctional. It is now up to regulating agency Anatel to redefine the rules that will allow or block the merger.

Access initiatives

Not surprisingly, access to computers and the internet has been the main focus of recent public ICT policy. This includes offering subsidies for buying desktop and laptop computers, and providing public access to the internet.

There are two main policies for subsidising the acquisition of computers, both implemented at the federal level: the programme Computers for All and the complementary tax incentive law called *Lei do Bem*, and the programme One Computer per Student.

Since 2004, the Computers for All programme[1] has been giving tax exemptions to businesses and low-interest credit to consumers so that they can buy low-cost desktop and laptop computers with free and open source software (FOSS).[2] The programme aimed to sell one million computers annually, but data indicates it has failed to meet such high goals. In 2006, Computers for All was responsible for selling 530,000 computers. Surprisingly, an additional 1.5 million computers with FOSS software, but unrelated to the programme, were sold in 2006 too. In 2005, the programme was complemented by a tax exemption law (*Lei do Bem*) which, among other things, aimed at subsidising the acquisition of higher-end computers with or without free software. All together, these initiatives were largely responsible for the sale of over 10 million computers in Brazil in 2007. These figures make Brazil the fifth largest world market for personal computers.

The One Computer per Student programme is still in the planning stages. Originally inspired by Nicholas Negroponte's One Laptop per Child project, the programme aims at acquiring laptops for every student in the country. During an experimental phase in a few schools, the first attempts to implement the programme were thwarted in 2007 when bids for buying the laptops through a public tender did not match the government's budget.

Regarding access to the internet, public policies have been focusing on filling a gap clearly observed in surveys. Although 17% of Brazilians have an internet connection in their households, twice as many (or 34% of the population) had accessed the internet at least once in the three months prior to the CGI survey. This means that 17% of the population accessed the internet away from home: while at work, at school or in public or private internet access centres. Among the poor, the survey found that most access occurs in private venues, such as "LAN houses" and cybercafés.[3] When it comes to the very poorest Brazilians (with a monthly family income below USD 240), 78% of internet access is through these commercial venues.

Figures like these demonstrate the urgent need for policies to provide free and public access to the internet. There are several government programmes at municipal, state and federal level trying to provide free internet access to citizens. However, as the data demonstrate, such initiatives are deficient and uncoordinated. Among several ongoing programmes, four of them stand out: the GESAC programme, coordinated by the Ministry of Communications; the Culture Hotspots programme by the Ministry of Culture; the Telecentres programme in the municipality of São Paulo; and the newly announced Broadband in Schools programme.

The GESAC (Electronic Government – Citizens' Support Service) programme[4] aims to provide satellite internet access to communities with low human development index scores, through internet access centres. The latest available data indicate that currently there are 3,482 GESAC internet access centres offering over 22,000 terminals running free software in 2,145 different municipalities.

The Culture Hotspots programme[5] is somewhat different. It not only provides internet access, but offers multimedia equipment for cultural communities to produce and digitally record and share their content, mostly using free software. At this moment there are 781 hotspots across the country.

The Telecentres[6] are centres offering internet access to citizens in the city of São Paulo, also using free software. It is the largest municipal programme in Brazil, providing internet access in 273 centres with 5,400 terminals and 1,362,984 registered users. Although programmes such as GESAC, Culture Hotspots and Telecentres try to compensate for the lack of internet access in households, they seem to be out of sync with demand. While 78% of the poorest citizens who use the internet pay for access in places like cybercafés, only 8% of them access the internet in public centres.

To face this huge challenge, the federal government recently announced the new programme Broadband in Schools. This programme plans to install broadband internet infrastructure in all public schools by December 2010, thereby offering internet access to most school-going youth. The programme was the result of an agreement between the federal government and telephone companies, where the government replaced the contractual requirement that phone companies build telephone service points in every city, with the requirement that they build broadband infrastructure across the country and offer free access in every school until 2025. According to the federal government, 55,000 public schools will receive broadband internet connectivity, which will then be offered to the schools' 35 million students and staff members.

1 www.computadorparatodos.gov.br

2 Although the programme required that computers be sold only with free software, a survey of purchasers showed that 73% of them had switched to a Windows operating system after sale (ABES/Ipsos, 2006).

3 LAN (local area network) houses are essentially cybercafés devoted primarily to internet gaming.

4 www.idbrasil.gov.br

5 www.cultura.gov.br/programas_e_acoes/cultura_viva/programa_cultura_viva/pontos_de_cultura

6 www.telecentros.sp.gov.br

Critics of the programme say two things: that through this deal, the project of building a public broadband infrastructure was abandoned; and that by privately controlling the broadband infrastructure, telephone companies will be able to exploit commercial broadband services in remote locations with no market competition (Gindre, 2008). Finally, there is potential for policy extending internet access by making use of the FUST fund – a fund composed of 1% of the telcos' revenue, collected for the purpose of providing universal access to telecommunication services. Due to conflicting legislation and the use of the fund's resources to pay public debt, the fund has been barely touched since 2002.

Action steps

This short overview of the state of access to ICTs in Brazil, and policies for universalising access, could help define a few points for priority action:

- TPMs restricting the recording of digital TV content and the criminalisation of circumventing TPM restrictions are about to be voted on in Congress. At the same time, the standard for digital radio that might or might not increase the plurality of broadcasters is about to be defined by the Ministry of Communications. These require progressive intervention.
- The spectrum now used by analogue TV will be vacant and could be used for building open spectrum citizen networks.
- Policies on public internet access centres have failed. The very poorest Brazilian citizens are paying for internet access in cybercafés and have not been widely using the public centres. The FUST fund could be used to drastically improve the reach of public access policies.

References

ABES/Ipsos (2006) *Computador para Todos-2006.* Available at: www.abes.org.br/computadorparatodos.pdf

CGI (Brazilian Internet Steering Committee) (2008) *Survey on the Use of Information and Communication Technologies in Brazil.* São Paulo: Brazilian Network Information Centre. Available at: www.cetic.br/tic/2007/indicadores-cgibr-2007.pdf

Computers for All: www.computadorparatodos.gov.br

GESAC (Governo Eletrônico – Serviço de Atendimento ao Cidadão): www.idbrasil.gov.br

Gindre, G. (2008) Governo troca política de inclusão ampla por banda larga nas escolas. *Observatório do Direito à Comunicação.* Available at: www.direitoacomunicacao.org.br/novo/content.php?option=com_content&task=view&id=3090

IBGE (Instituto Brasileiro de Geografia e Estatística) (2007) *Pesquisa Nacional por Amostra de Domicílios: Síntese de indicadores 2006.* Rio de Janeiro: IBGE. Available at: www.ibge.gov.br/home/estatistica/populacao/trabalhoerendimento/pnad2006/sintesepnad2006.pdf

Culture Hotspots: www.cultura.gov.br/programas_e_acoes/cultura_viva/programa_cultura_viva/pontos_de_cultura

Silveira, S. A. et al.(2007) *Comunicação digital e a construção dos commons: Redes virais, espectro aberto e as novas possibilidades de regulação.* São Paulo: Fundação Perseu Abramo.

Telecentres: www.telecentros.sp.gov.br

BULGARIA

BlueLink Information Network
Doroteya Todorova and Milena Bokova
www.bluelink.net

Introduction

This report looks at the advances and changes being made in Bulgaria in its attempt to reach the level of information and communications technology (ICT) penetration seen in other European Union (EU) countries. Bulgaria became a full EU member on 1 January 2007. Though tremendous progress has been made in infrastructure development, the country still lags behind most other countries in the union.

This report has been compiled from information sources such as online newspapers, surveys and media publications, and interviews with a representative of the state institution responsible for ICT policy and a representative of the Internet Society (ISOC)-Bulgaria. After the accession of Bulgaria to the EU, Eurostat, together with the Bulgarian Statistical Institute (NSI), conducted a survey among internet users in the country. Some of the data of this survey was used to present in a qualitative way the progress the country has made in its attempts to increase ICT usage.

The government has set a number of priorities in the ICT sector, which include developing high-speed broadband internet infrastructure; modernising the public sector through e-governance; providing quality e-content for education; and improving Bulgaria's competitiveness in the field of science and technology. The State Agency for Information Technology and Communications (SAITC) is one of the bodies responsible for implementing the state policy at a national level. Another governmental structure in ICT policy implementation is the Communications Regulation Commission (CRC). The CRC is a specialised independent state authority, entrusted with the functions of regulation and control over electronic communications. In the context of equity and transparency, and in compliance with Bulgarian legislation, the CRC strives to promote competition in the country's telecommunications markets.

Physical access to technology

The SAITC is in the process of preparing a national programme for rolling out broadband internet access. After the programme is ready, it will be presented for approval to the Council of Ministers. The new idea is to include public-private partnerships in the process, so that broadband internet can become more accessible and not so dependent on state finances. The estimates made by the SAITC show that between USD 120 million and USD 170 million are needed to make broadband internet available throughout the country. Bulgaria is at the bottom of EU rankings regarding access to broadband internet – although a large part of the sector is not regulated and not included in official statistics.

There remain disparities in physical access to technologies between the big cities and the smaller remote areas of the country. A positive trend is the increasing amount of investment which is being made by private companies and by international donors. The Telecentres Project between the SAITC and the United Nations Development Programme (UNDP) has built a network of 103 public telecentres (or iCentres) in remote and economically underdeveloped areas. A mobile telecentre started operating in 2005, to reach difficult-to-access villages in the most isolated areas of Bulgaria. It has a satellite internet connection and provides essential services to businesses and individuals in these settlements.

Over two years the Bulgarian Telecommunications Company (BTC), the partly privatised state telecoms company, invested more than BGL 130 million (USD 100 million) in modernising its fixed network. By 1 January 2007, the telephone systems in 94 Bulgarian cities and towns, including all 27 regional capitals, had been converted to digital, and the BTC had changed about 400,000 subscribers' lines. The level of digitalisation in Bulgaria now exceeds 73% of all telephone lines. Where digitalisation has been carried out, the BTC clients can activate many add-on services such as call forwarding, call hold and conference calls. The network modernisation also created an opportunity for a significant expansion of the BTC asymmetric digital subscriber line (ADSL) internet network, and broadband communications services in general. BTC broadband internet service subscribers currently number more than 140,000 (1.75% of the Bulgarian population) in more than 300 towns and cities in Bulgaria. According to one of the biggest local area network (LAN) operators in the country, their subscribers number between 200,000 and 400,000, which is between 2.6% and 5.3% of the population. According to the i2010[1] mid-term review in Bulgaria, broadband penetration in January 2008 was 7.6%, the lowest in the EU and far below the EU-27 average of 20%.

In 2007 the number of businesses with access to the internet had increased by 14.5% compared to 2005. Due to infrastructure development and the need for high-speed internet, the use of dial-up internet has decreased by 21.5% and the use of ADSL has increased. In 2007, one fifth of all businesses had accessed the internet via mobile phones, whereas in 2005 none had.[2]

1 i2010 is the EU's umbrella strategy for developing ICTs.

2 National Statistical Institute: www.nsi.bg/Index_e.htm

A project for creating internet labs in all Bulgarian schools, known as i-Class, has been successful. The biggest impact of the project is felt in remote areas where the lack of highly qualified specialists has been overcome by setting up a control centre in the country's capital, Sofia. The centre provides services and solves technical problems remotely. A new pilot project for providing wireless internet in schools was launched on 22 April 2008. In its first phase it will include 31 schools.

The proportion of internet users among people fifteen years and older in Bulgaria reached 34.5% in 2007, but is still behind levels in other EU countries. Recent research by Nielsen Online showed that more than half of the users live in the three biggest cities of the country. The numbers of men and women users are equal, which suggests a gender balance in internet usage in Bulgaria (Koinova, 2008).

Though the above-mentioned improvements have increased the overall level of physical access to technologies in Bulgaria, a key challenge to the government still remains: the isolation of disadvantaged groups and ethnic minorities who still have limited access to technologies. Institutional websites have improved in the last couple of years, but they are still inaccessible to people with visual impairments, with the exception of the website for the Ministry of Transport. Users of the innovative software SpeechLab, which converts computer text to speech, have now increased to more than 1,500.

Affordability of technology and technology use

The availability and affordability of ICTs determines a country's ability to take full advantage of the knowledge and information revolution.

Though part of the EU since 2007, Bulgaria is considered one of its poorest members. According to the latest research from Eurostat, the level of wages in Bulgaria is the lowest among all EU countries. The low purchasing power of Bulgarian households, especially those from disadvantaged groups, hampers their ability to buy high-quality technology and software. As a result, despite greater competition among internet service providers (ISPs) and improved peering networks, the cost of access to the internet has dropped but still remains high for people from the disadvantaged groups. For example, the price for internet access through the major ISPs is around BGL 40 (USD 32) per month, which is very expensive for a country where the average monthly salary is USD 295.

A positive trend is the continuous rise in wages, especially in the ICT sector. ICT specialists have seen a 30% rise in their salaries in 2006-2007 (calculated in USD). Another trend is a reduction in prices in the capital, due to the number of ISPs and the competition they create. The limited use of wireless internet is explained by the high cost of equipment. Depending on its quality, set-up costs range from BGL 150 to BGL 250 (USD 118 to USD 197), with a monthly fee of BGL 24-180 (USD 18-142) (CRC, 2006).

According to the International Data Group (IDG),[3] ICT expenditure in 2007 in Bulgaria reached USD 113.42 per person, or 2.46% of gross domestic product (GDP). Compared with other Central Eastern European (CEE) countries, this is above average, but remains low due to the low purchasing power of Bulgarians as a whole. The Bulgarian ICT market in 2007 was worth USD 873.25 million. After Bulgaria became an EU member, the ICT market saw steady growth and IDG forecasts that the average growth for the period 2007-2011 will reach 13.4% a year.

According to ISPs, telecom charges still comprise a large percentage (approximately 70%) of internet access costs, presenting a serious disincentive to expanding their networks. The full liberalisation of the telecom market will bring significant changes in the provision of leased lines and access at the local level, resulting in a reduction in charges. The CRC continues to see growth in the number of ISPs. In 2006 the number of ISPs stood at 554, an increase of 42% compared to the previous year. In its yearly report for 2006, the CRC notes that small ISPs are being bought by bigger ones, and predicts that the internet market in Bulgaria will soon have fewer but stronger ISPs.

The computer hardware segment, which includes personal computers (PCs), notebooks, servers and peripherals, was estimated to be worth USD 224 million in 2005. With hardware still accounting for around 60% of national information technology (IT) spending, total sector value was estimated at USD 380 million in 2005. Overall, the total size of the IT market is expected by Business Monitor International (BMI) to increase to around USD 710 million in 2010, with services accounting for around 25% (BMI, 2008).

Human capacity and training

In general in Bulgaria there are relatively low levels of ICT skills in the population. A 2006 survey conducted by i2010 found that 66% of the population has no internet skills, compared to the EU average of 40%. However, this figure has improved considerably in Bulgaria.

According to the NSI, 70% of the people who use computers and the internet have never had formal computer skills education, though 37.7% of them claim that their ICT skills are satisfactory. These results are confirmed by the fact that most of the people interviewed are self-taught when it comes to ICTs, with the help of colleagues, relatives or friends.

Realising the need for higher IT skills, the government, together with other organisations, has started a series of skills-development projects. In 2006, the iCentres project developed and implemented the largest Bulgarian training programme. The target was the state administration, and 23,000 civil servants were trained on-site in core IT skills. The project expanded to 265 locations (every municipality), and 430 instructors conducted 2,500 classes in less than a year. In 2007, another 22,000 civil servants were trained

3 idg.bg

under the project. Materials and exams were also offered electronically, and e-learning is now a regular component of the project. It was expected that it would become the main way of training state employees in the future.

The iCentres Association signed a three-year contract with Microsoft for the training of trainers and of unemployed citizens in IT skills. At the same time, the project's partnership with Cisco resulted in the establishment of local Cisco Academies and the organisation of Cisco Certified Networking Associate (CCNA) courses for telecentre managers.

A joint project between the SAITC and the Podkrepa Confederation of Labour, which focuses on providing IT and business communication skills to disadvantaged groups, started in 2007. The aim of the project is to streamline the professional development of the target groups by providing them with new professional skills that can facilitate their access to the labour market.

The National Innovations Centre at SAITC has started a free ICT skills course for young people with disabilities. This course is part of the initiative to make ICTs available to as many Bulgarians from disadvantaged groups as possible. A project aiming to enhance employment opportunities of another disadvantaged social group in Bulgaria, the Roma minority, started on 2 February 2008. The project includes IT, language and business communication skills, amongst other components.

In the past few years, the non-governmental sector has been actively working to support human capacity development at the local level in Bulgaria. One of many examples is ISOC-Bulgaria, which took part in the SELF project,[4] working to create an interactive, easy-to-use and community-driven platform for educational and training material focused on free software.

Action steps

A Draft National Programme for Accelerated Information Society Development was drawn up in 2007. The programme emphasises the convergence of ICTs, electronic content, public services and an improved quality of life. It is in line with the European Information Society Policy Strategy, i2010. Six guidelines for development have been defined in the programme: ICT infrastructure and security; society and culture; economy and employment; research and development (R&D); education and training; and marketing the ICT sector. These guidelines will be connected to concrete projects, which are going to be described in the road map developed as a part of the programme.

According to Nelly Stoyanova from the SAITC, a "reasonable medium-term goal (e.g., until 2010) is bringing the state and private sector contribution to R&D expenditure to parity, while increasing the total amount to 1.0-1.2% of GDP. In the somewhat longer term, Bulgaria should aim at achieving a comparable position among the EU-8[5] countries as regards the EU's strategic goal of raising R&D expenditure to 3% of GDP."[6]

In order to allow Bulgaria to achieve its R&D potential, the creation and expansion of new firms in high-technology sectors is essential. It is therefore of utmost importance to ensure that the right conditions exist for new technology-based firms to flourish in the same way as they do in the EU and the United States.

In addition, the responsibilities of institutions in Bulgaria are changing. The emphasis is not so much on the restructuring of the economy, but on specific challenges that EU membership imposes. A key step in this direction is improving the awareness and confidence of businesses in the field of ICTs. Strong support is needed for the development of relevant skills and widespread network literacy.

The following are steps the government should take in order to narrow the gap between Bulgaria and other EU countries:

- Continue investing in infrastructure (broadband internet) development in order to increase the physical access and availability of ICTs to citizens.
- Continue current training programmes, and expand the ones focusing on disadvantaged groups.
- Develop an integrated policy on R&D and innovation, which links to other economic policies, such as those dealing with small business and investment. Since one of the least-developed ICT areas in Bulgaria is R&D, the government should develop public-private partnerships for increasing investment in R&D, including providing direct public support and guarantees for Bulgarian organisations which have successfully bid for projects under the EU framework programmes.
- The worrisome trend of Bulgarian students leaving the country continues (some 20,000-30,000 annually) and the government has to develop a strategy to stop or minimise this. The government should prepare a national programme aiming to attract young specialists to work in the ICT sector, which has a chronic shortage of qualified employees.
- There should be efforts to make the ICT industry more environmentally friendly by consuming less energy and resources and generating less waste. There is a need for policy development in this regard as well as R&D and implementation.

4 www.selfproject.eu

5 Poland, Czech Republic, Slovakia, Hungary, Estonia, Latvia, Lithuania and Slovenia.

6 Based on a 2008 interview with the BlueLink Information Network.

References

ARC Fund (Applied Research and Communications Fund) (2008) *Innovation.bg 2008 Report*. Available at: www.arc.online.bg/fileSrc.php?id=2445

BlueLink Information Network (2008) Interview with Nelly Stoyanova, representative of the SAITC.

BlueLink Information Network (2008) Interview with Julia Velkova, representative of ISOC-Bulgaria.

BMI (Business Monitor International) (2008) *The Bulgaria IT Report 2008*. Available at: www.businessmonitor.com/it/bulgaria.html

CRC (Communications Regulation Commission) (2006) *Annual Report*. Available only in Bulgarian at: crc.bg/index.php?lang=en

EIS (Europe Information Society) (2008) *i2010 Annual Information Society Report 2008*. Available at: ec.europa.eu/information_society/eeurope/i2010/mid_term_review_2008/index_en.htm

FlossWorld (2007) *Free/Libre and Open Source Software: Worldwide Impact Study*. Available at: www.flossworld.org/deliverables.php

International Data Group (IDG): idg.bg

JNN & Associates (2008) *White Paper of Bulgarian Telecommunications Services and Technologies*. Available at: www.jnn-marketing.com/WPTelecom.htm

Koinova, E. (2008) Nielsen Online issues first Bulgarian online report. *Sofia Echo*, 26 May. Available at: www.sofiaecho.com/article/nielsen-online-issues-first-bulgarian-online-report/id_29535/catid_67

National Statistical Institute: www.nsi.bg/Index_e.htm

SAITC (State Agency for Information Technologies and Communications) (2008) *I-integration of minorities*. Available only in Bulgarian at: www.daits.government.bg/?t=novina&id=119

SELF project: www.selfproject.eu

CAMEROON

PROTEGE QV
Sylvie Siyam Siwe, Serge Daho and Laurence Houssou
www.protegeqv.org

Introduction

With a gross domestic product (GDP) of USD 2,300 per capita (UNDP, 2008) and a population of about 16 million, the Central African country of Cameroon (otherwise known as "Africa in a shell") seems to have all the strengths necessary for a boom in the development and use of information and communications technologies (ICTs).

The country enjoys access to a fibre-optic backbone along the Chad-Cameroon pipeline, and a SAT-3 submarine cable landing point at the port city of Douala, with a capacity of 2.5 gigabits per second (Gbps) (MINPOSTEL, 2006). ICTs are seen by the government as a "miracle" tool able to stimulate growth, and the president defined the vision of a country "bracing up to adapt to the requirements of the information society" – which has included offering training for ICT specialists in higher education.

But the economic crisis faced by the country since the early 1990s has consequences for public investment, and influences people's physical access to ICTs, their ability to afford them, and their capacity to use them. As the national policy for the development of ICTs notes, "despite...the quality of its human resources, and the political stability it enjoys, the country remains one in which ICT penetration and usage are relatively low" (NAICT, 2007).

Physical access to technology

Audiovisual

The signals of 33 public radio broadcasting stations, managed by Cameroon Radio and Television (CRTV), reach 85% of the country (NAICT, 2007), while 39 private radio stations and 26 community stations help in improving country coverage and the diversification of programming (MINPOSTEL, 2006). Cameroon has one public television station, six private television stations and more than 200 private cable distributors (NAICT, 2007).

Teledensity

In the past five years, mobile networks operated by two private operators, Mobile Telephony Network (MTN) and Orange Cameroon, and since 2006, Cameroon Network (or CAMNET, a public operator), have expanded very fast, with the mobile penetration rate increasing from 7.1% in 2003 (MINPOSTEL, 2006) to 22% today (Bambou, 2008). The fixed telephone network covers 107 localities, and is operated exclusively by the semi-public corporation Cameroon Telecommunications (CAMTEL) (MINPOSTEL, 2006).

Internet services

Since 1998, users have been connected by very small aperture terminal (VSAT) satellite, public switched telephone network (PSTN), or by wireless. About 25 internet service providers (ISPs) offer services like website hosting, email, forums and internet protocol (IP) telephony. Access to broadband services has been easier since 2005, with fibre-optic cable laid along the Chad-Cameroon pipeline (MINPOSTEL, 2006) and the link to the SAT-3 cable. CAMTEL, the exclusive provider of SAT-3 bandwidth, operates eight internet nodes (Lange, 2008) and provides access of two megabits per second (Mbps) to ISPs. Cameroon has no internet exchange point (IXP) (NAITC, 2007). To improve access in rural areas, the government has set up a project to equip more than 180 telecentres by 2008 (MINPOSTEL, 2006).

Infrastructure

Generally, public and private administrations do not have a rational approach to their information management systems (NAITC, 2007). But the Ministry of Finance has improved the collection, processing and preservation of data by operating integrated systems for the management of public finances (called SIGEFI), the salaries of state personnel (SIGIPES) and customs (SYDONIA).

Production and services industry

All ICT access and maintenance equipment is imported. However, many small and medium enterprises (SMEs) offer design, production and marketing services. Content production in the audiovisual sector is rudimentary, and much of it is pirated. Videos and DVDs sold for 1,000 CFA francs (about USD 2) per unit come from neighbouring Nigeria.

Table 1: Cameroon telecom market statistics 2006

Number of national telecom operators	1
Number of mobile operators	2 (now 3)*
Number of ISPs	approx. 25 plus many informal ones
Fixed-line penetration	0.6%
Mobile penetration	14.5%
Internet user penetration	1.4%
Internet subscriber penetration	<0.1%

*Updated by the authors

Source: Lange (2008), BuddeComm

Affordability

Access to equipment

Around 53% of the population lives in urban areas (Tetang Tchinda, 2007) and radio penetration is relatively high, with 75% of urban homes and 55.1% of rural ones owning a radio (MINPOSTEL, 2006). The average radio set is affordable, costing about USD 6. It can be used in areas without electricity and does not require any expertise. Listening to radio programmes in English, French and local languages is a very popular pastime for families.

The price of TV sets starts at about USD 80, depending on the type and features offered. The use of a TV set is quite common – 26% of households have one, compared to 14% in the sub-Saharan African region as a whole (World Bank, 2006).

A computer costs about USD 560, inaccessible to the majority in a country where 48% of the population lives below the poverty line. In 2006, there were only 1.1 computers per 100 persons (World Bank, 2006), and 66.2% of institutions have no computer (MINPOSTEL, 2006).

The growth of mobile telephony has been rapid. Kits comprising a mobile handset, a SIM card and about USD 2 in airtime are sold by operators at less than US 45. In 2006, there were 12.7 mobile phone subscribers per 100 people, compared to 13.5 in sub-Saharan Africa in general (World Bank, 2006).

Services

Radio and TV signals are broadcast free of charge. Very diverse programmes and packages are offered by the private cable distributors at different prices, from a minimum of USD 11 per month.

Connectivity to the internet is offered by public and private operators at about USD 68 per month for households. Internet services are also offered by different operators through wireless technologies, but at very expensive rates: code division multiple access (CDMA) is sold by CAMTEL at USD 225, "Livebox" by Orange at USD 450, and WiMAX by MTN at USD 326. Navigation on the internet is now possible through mobile phones, but it is also expensive (e.g., USD 2.70 per hour with CAMTEL during daytime hours).

As a consequence, 86.1% of internet users say they use cybercafés, as against 28.2% accessing the internet in their workplace or at home. The cost of access in cybercafés is about USD 0.67 per hour (the cost of two loaves of bread), and affordable to the majority.

In urban areas, voice over internet protocol (VoIP) services are offered for between USD 0.06 and USD 0.12 per minute for a call to the United States and Canada, making it more affordable than local calls.

Regarding fixed-line phones, the cable network has a total capacity of only 164,000 lines (NAICT, 2007). Residential telephone installation charges have been reduced to USD 90 since 2005 and the rate for local calls during peak hours is USD 0.04 per minute (MINPOSTEL, 2006). So-called "call boxes", or points managed by one person owning two or three mobile phones and offering call services at USD 0.22 per minute for local calls, are very common in urban areas: there were about 20,000 in 2005 (Nana Nzepa & Tankeu, 2005).

Human capacity and training

Apart from radio and television sets, which do not need specific skills to operate, people are trained either in the formal training system or by informal means to use ICTs.

Formal education system

In 2003 the Ministry of National Education passed a decree making ICTs an obligatory part of the curriculum. Consequently, the National Pedagogy Support Unit created in the ministry was in charge of ensuring capacity building for teachers, including through distance learning (Tetang Tchinda, 2007). However, a great majority of teachers in the educational system are computer illiterate.

While the formal educational system does not provide adequate training in ICTs, major achievements are noticeable; for example, the establishment of sixteen Multimedia Resources Centres (MRC) in universities and some schools, and the interconnection of six state universities.

In higher education institutions (public or private), such as the African Informatics Institute, Nsiantou Institute, Ndi Samba Institute, and the Yaoundé I, Buea and Douala Universities, and many others offering training for ICT specialists, graduates are either specialised technicians (G.C.E. A Level + 2/3), engineers (G.C.E. A level + 4/5), or bachelors or masters in computer sciences.

Other solutions

Many employees of libraries, hospitals, civil society organisations, government and business do not have basic technical skills to use ICTs in their daily work. According to the National Agency for Information and Communication Technologies (NAICT), with current national training capacities, Cameroon can train about 35 engineers and 300 technicians annually, more or less. At this rate, and unless strong action is taken, Cameroon will not be able to have a critical minimum of specialists to sustain wide-scale ICT development and deployment (NAICT, 2007).

To overcome the inadequacies of the formal educational system, and to meet current demands, many "rapid training centres" of various calibres have been set up and offer different curricula. Among them:

- PROTEGE QV provides e-learning initiatives through radio-based training for women entrepreneurs.[1]
- ASAFE, a non-governmental organisation (NGO) located in Douala, seeks to advance and expand entrepreneurship among women by enabling them to access international markets.[2]

1 www.protegqv.org

2 www.asafe.org

- Agence Universitaire de la Francophonie (AUF) offers distance learning programmes to university students and lecturers.[3]
- SchoolNet Cameroon is an NGO that engages in collaborative educational projects using ICTs.[4]
- UNDP/TICAD (Tokyo International Conference on African Development) are undertaking a joint initiative to close the digital divide by equipping schools and NGOs with refurbished computers.

The African Informatics Institute is also involved in a programme aimed at training 100,000 women by 2012, in partnership with the UNDP and the Ministry of Women's Affairs.

What hinders ICT take-up?

Economic situation: Since the economic crisis in the early 1990s, public spending on ICTs has not been optimal. The total telecommunications investment in 2005 was 16.8% of revenue, compared to 36.0% for sub-Saharan Africa (World Bank, 2006).

Unsuitable regulation: Regulation should normally facilitate competition, promote private initiatives and reduce prices. However, there is a monopoly in fixed-line telephony, and there is little space for small private sector initiatives to take root. Added to this, the regulator is not entirely independent: it reports to the ministry and a management board appointed by the head of state (Lange, 2008).

Market density: Due to the low purchasing power and low population density in rural areas, it is difficult for private operators to invest there.

Incomplete decentralization process: A complete transfer of decision-making authority to local governments would have stimulated each local council to develop its ICT sector in line with the need for local development.

Lack of real ICT manufacturing industry: The existence of a local ICT manufacturing industry would impact on the affordability of equipment and the integration of technology into the everyday lives of citizens.

Electricity availability: The access rate to electricity is high in urban areas – 89.8% in 2006 – compared to only 27.3% in rural areas. The grid, which is operated by AES Sonel, the national company, has regular outages, which can damage equipment.

Lack of sensitisation and training: For 22% of institutions (and most administrations) this is a major obstacle to the promotion of ICTs in Cameroon. Most students say they can afford ICTs, but because they do not know how to use them, they cannot benefit from them properly.

Costs of access to technology and services: A full 52% of institutions and more than 50% of professionals in the educational, health and civil society sectors agree that their low purchasing power constitutes a real obstacle to the development of ICTs (MINPOSTEL, 2006). They also point out that there is an absence of political will to bring down prices, for instance, through lowering taxes. Most individuals (63.9%) think that poverty is a major factor blocking the development of ICTs in Cameroon (MINPOSTEL, 2006). According to a national survey on the level on penetration and usage of ICTs in Cameroon, an efficient strategy to reduce the costs of communication and equipment should include the reduction of taxes on goods and services in the sector.

The government says it is committed to reducing the cost of communication and ICT products (NAICT, 2007) by:

- Encouraging the setting up of multiple network operators with diversified products and services
- Reducing taxes and tariffs for the end-consumer
- Developing multiple access points and terminals.

Action steps

To expand the development and use of ICTs, the ministry in charge has set several objectives (MINPOSTEL, 2006). They include:

- Raising teledensity to 30% for fixed telephony and 50% for mobile telephony by 2015
- Achieving 100% radio and television coverage
- Reducing the cost of communications
- Implementing an effective infrastructure maintenance policy
- Raising the internet usage rate to 40% by 2015.

Our recommendations to improve access to ICTs coincide with some of these points. Our main points of action in order of priority are:

- Formulation and implementation of a suitable legal and regulatory framework to create a competitive environment
- Allocation of more funds to physical infrastructure in the public budget
- Reduction of customs and taxes on goods and services in this sector
- Training of personnel in use of ICTs
- Sensitisation of institutions to ICTs and popularisation of ICTs
- State subsidies to operators offering services in rural or remote areas
- The effective decentralisation of government to promote the provision of communication services at local levels. ■

3 www.foad.refer.org

4 www.iearn.org

References

Agence Universitaire de la Francophonie: www.foad.refer.org

ASAFE: www.asafe.org

Bambou, F. (2008) Cameroun: une minute de téléphone coûte plus cher qu'une baguette de pain. *Les Afriques*, 4 February. Available at: www.lesafriques.com

Budde.Comm: www.budde.com.au

Lange, P. (2008) *The Case for "Open Access" Communications Infrastructure in Africa: The SAT-3/WASC cable – Cameroon case study.* APC. Available at: www.apc.org/en/node/6142

MINPOSTEL (Ministry of Posts and Telecommunications) (2006) *Cameroon Scan-ICT Report: National survey on the level of penetration and usage of ICT in Cameroon.* Yaoundé: African Information Society Initiative. Available at: www.uneca.org/aisi/scanict.htm

MTN Cameroon: www.mtncameroon.net

NAICT (National Agency for Information and Communication Technologies) (2007) *National Policy for the Development of Information and Communication Technologies.* Yaoundé: NAICT. Available at: www.antic.cm/IMG/pdf/Cameroun_National_ICT_Policy_10-03-2008.pdf

Nana Nzepa, O. and Tankeu, R. (2005) Cameroon. In Gillwald, A. (ed.) *Towards an African e-Index: Household and individual ICT access and usage across 10 African countries.* Research ICT Africa. Available at: www.researchictafrica.net/images/upload/Chapter04Cameroon.pdf

Orange Cameroon: www.orange.com

PROTEGE QV: www.protegqv.org

SchoolNet-Cameroon: www.iearn.org

Tetang Tchinda, J. (2007) *ICT in Education in Cameroon. info*Dev/World Bank. Available at: www.infodev.org/en/Document.390.aspx

UNDP (2008) Human Development Report 2007/2008: Country Tables. Available at: hdrstats.undp.org/countries/data_sheets/cty_ds_CMR.html

World Bank (2006) ICT at Glance: Cameroon. Available at: devdata worldbank.org/ict/cmr_ict.pdf

CHILE

Women in Connection (Mujeres en Conexión), Diego Portales University
Patricia Peña Miranda
www.mujeresenconexion.org

Introduction

Like many other countries in Latin America, Chile today is bearing the fruits of more than ten years of public policies that promote universal access. These have included a national programme promoting the educational use of information and communications technologies (ICTs), digital literacy programmes for citizens, and a telecommunications legal framework that allows the entrance of new operators.

The continuity of many of these initiatives has given Chile a good reputation in the region, with impressive positions in indices like the World Economic Forum (WEF) Networked Readiness Index,[1] where it was ranked 34th among 127 countries in 2007-2008 – higher than any other Latin American country.

This was all the result of a vision that began during the administration of former president Eduardo Frei Ruiz-Tagle (1994-2000), and the formation of a special committee dealing with the information society in the early 2000s. This effort allowed the Ricardo Lagos administration (2000-2006) to develop a Digital Agenda (2004-2006), with the participation of the private sector, which included 34 programmes and initiatives.

Under the current administration of President Michelle Bachelet, the Chilean ICT development vision is facing some controversy, although there is a Digital Development Strategy 2007-2012 that sets 25 objectives and goals to promote the effective use of technology. The last United Nations Development Programme (UNDP) National Human Development Report on Chile, released in 2006, was dedicated to examining the impact of new technologies in Chilean society. The main finding of this study was that 50% of Chileans do not feel a part of the process, and the causes for this were cultural and subjective (UNDP, 2006).

Physical access to technology

Statistics indicate that almost 30% of Chileans have access to a computer with an internet connection on a daily basis in their homes, workplaces, schools or public centres (such as cybercafés). A recent telecommunications consumer survey (SUBTEL, 2008) showed that by June 2008, 1,405,510 Chilean households had access to fixed-line connections to the internet, and one in every three homes had access to broadband. Moreover, 79% of internet users access it in their homes, 53.1% at cybercafés, 50.5% at their workplaces and 28.1% at their schools.

In the 2008 Information Society Index developed by the International Data Corporation (IDC),[2] Chile retained its position as the country with the highest scores in Latin America. The index is based on variables like personal computer ownership, internet access and telecommunications services, as well as social variables such as education. Chile ranked 29th overall out of the 53 countries studied worldwide, and 26th with regard to internet access.

Table 1 shows the distribution of different ICT services in Chilean households. The percentages indicate the availability of the services according to socioeconomic level.

The Digital Strategy 2007-2012 shows the main goals achieved for the first Digital Agenda in Chile (2004-2006). These include:

- 1,095,000 internet connections
- 976,000 people trained between 2003 and 2006
- 68% of businesses connected
- 776 infocentre networks established.

The major programme for connecting public schools is Enlaces (Links), launched by the Ministry of Education. The programme has resulted in the provision of one computer for every 29 students, with 4,895 schools connected to broadband by 2006, 670 of them in rural areas. The programme decided not to participate in the One Laptop per Child (OLPC) initiative, nor is it considering free and open source software (FOSS) for education, although there are pilot projects exploring low-cost alternatives like Classmate, an Intel laptop.

The success of the Enlaces programme has been mixed. The last evaluation report (2004) revealed that it is an expensive programme with poor use made of the equipment installed. The average cost per student is USD 46 (47.8% higher than the international standard), and the average price for every computer installed between 2001 and 2003 was USD 1,450. The report also shows that only 13% of Chilean students use the computers three times a week, and that 9% use the internet three times a week.

When connectivity does not mean social inclusion

The UNDP report mentioned above found that 50% of Chileans do not feel included in the information society or consider themselves beneficiaries of new technologies. This shows us that it is not enough to guarantee access to technology in a developing country like Chile without

1 www.weforum.org/pdf/gitr/2008/Rankings.pdf

2 www.idc.com/groups/isi/main.html

Table 1: ICT services in Chilean households

Service	Socioeconomic level*					
	A/B/C1	C2	C3	D	E	Total
Telephone	88.2%	79%	59.7%	46.2%	19.6%	54.5%
Long-distance telephone service (carrier)	21.1%	16.7%	5.6%	4.7%	3.2%	7.8%
Mobile phone (prepaid or with contract)	96%	91.9%	88.7%	89%	86.8%	89.5%
Internet connection	75.9%	55.5%	28.8%	16.7%	4.6%	28.5%
TV (cable/satellite)	73.3%	54%	34%	25.9%	8.7%	33.5%
None of the services	0%	0.2%	0.8%	1.9%	5.4%	1.0%

*A, B, C1, C2, C3, D and E indicate socioeconomic levels with A being the highest income level, C2 and C3 medium income level, and D and E the lowest income levels.

Source: **SUBTEL (2008)**

promoting public policies for the social appropriation of ICTs.

The UNDP report is based on an analysis of trends in public policies in ICT development and a national survey conducted across the whole country. According to the report, 84% of adolescents between the ages of fourteen and seventeen feel that new technologies are accessible, while 50% of people eighteen and older do not.

The study also includes a subjective category that shows that 21% of people surveyed consider themselves absolutely excluded (for reasons including a lack of income, lack of interest and age); 18% have technological aspirations (they want to use technology, but cannot afford it); and 8% consider themselves "e-workers" (ICTs are used daily in their work environment) or "e-connected" (connected all day, a category made up mainly of young people with a high income). Slightly under 8% of respondents were classified as "e-gamers" (mainly students and young people) and as "technologically insecure" (those who do not use any kind of technology), while 5% said they use the internet modestly.

The main conclusion of the report was that despite the ICT access rate in Chile, there is limited appropriation. The main challenge for Chile is to promote not only a public policy centred on access to technologies, but to think about related cultural and subjective aspects and socio-cultural conditions.

To illustrate these findings, although the Enlaces programme promotes equality in the opportunity of access, an evaluation report from 2004 shows that there was little evidence to suggest these efforts had improved the quality of Chilean education.

On the other hand, since 2000 a digitised civil society has started to emerge, including bottom-up social spaces and networks in education, community telecentre and infocentre networks, FOSS organisations, organisations promoting digital rights, social and community media networks (radio, television and press), social wireless groups, web entrepreneurs, a bloggers movement, "hacktivists" and gender and ICT groups. These will all help to push the focus of public policies beyond a technocentric approach to access.

The political view: Digital Strategy for 2007-2012

After one and a half years without a digital agenda, in January 2008 the Bachelet government launched the new Digital Strategy 2007-2012.[3] The strategy was developed through a public participation process that included the input of citizens, professionals, consultants, activists and civil society organisations. The process included a blog to which people could post comments, proposals and contributions over a one-month period.

The main objective of the Digital Strategy is to "contribute to Chile's economic and social development by means of the potential offered by the use of [ICTs] to improve the quality of education, increase transparency, productivity and competitiveness, and provide better governance through greater citizen participation and commitment." President Bachelet has said about the government's vision: "Access to information in modern society is not the privilege of a few, but a basic resource for development, equality and democracy."

The strategy's Action Plan 2007-2012 has 25 objectives, including:

- Extending broadband connectivity to 2.3 million people
- Extending connectivity to 90% of rural areas
- Connecting 200 of the poorest neighbourhoods
- Developing entrepreneurial centres for the promotion of digital and ICT skills for entrepreneurs (micro, small and medium level)
- Extending local e-government services
- Reaching the goal of ten students per computer, improving digital educational resources, and promoting ICTs in the educational management of schools.

3 www.estrategiadigital.gob.cl

Action steps

In August 2007 civil society organisations opposed the government signing an agreement with Microsoft as part of its Digital Strategy, demonstrating that an active civil society focused on the information society is emerging in Chile. Civil society networks are working to promote issues such as digital rights, access to information and culture, and civil society input into public policies on ICTs.

Despite the Digital Strategy, we need to have a better understanding of how we want to continue growing in the different areas of ICT development over the next years, to be clear about our *sense* and *purpose*. Amongst other things, we need to promote the growth of a local software industry; public policies that allow the social and economic sustainability of community telecentres and Wi-Fi networks; new methodologies for digital literacy programmes for adults, elderly people, people with disabilities and indigenous communities; and the sustainability of the local ICT industry, especially at the small- and medium-enterprise level, and particularly regarding the production of content. ■

References

Government of Chile (2008) *Digital Strategy 2007-2012*. Available at: www.estrategiadigital.gob.cl

International Data Corporation (IDC) Information Society Index: www.idc.com/groups/isi/main.html

SUBTEL (Subsecretaría de Telecomunicaciones) (2008) *Encuesta Nacional de Consumidores de Servicios de Telecomunicaciones, Primer Semestre 2008*. Available at: www.subtel.cl/prontus_subtel/site/artic/20080902/pags/20080902114148.html

UNDP (United Nations Development Programme) (2006) *Desarrollo Humano en Chile 2006: Las nuevas tecnologías: ¿un salto al futuro?* Available at: hdr.undp.org/en/reports/nationalreports/latinamericathecaribbean/chile/name,3400,en.html

World Economic Forum (WEF) Networked Readiness Index: www.weforum.org/pdf/gitr/2008/Rankings.pdf

COLOMBIA

Colnodo
Olga Paz Martinez
www.colnodo.apc.org

Introduction

Colombia's information and communications technology (ICT) infrastructure is growing but is still not significant. During 2007 computer sales increased between 62% and 66%. In 2006 there were 4.6 computers per 100 inhabitants and by the end of 2007 this figure increased to 8.4 computers per 100 inhabitants.

In the coming years the Ministry of Communications is planning to increase significantly the purchase of computers by eliminating value added tax (VAT) on computers costing less than 1,740,000 Colombian pesos (USD 967) and by encouraging telecommunications companies to offer packages that include an internet connection and a computer.

As a way of offering equipment to the most deprived communities, the Computers for Education programme aims to increase access to ICTs in public educational institutions by promoting their usage and application in teaching. By 31 July 2008, this programme had given away 114,524 computers, benefiting 3,055,452 students in around 10,086 educational institutions. This represents 22.64% of the total number of public schools in the country.[1]

Between June 2006 and December 2007 there was a twofold increase in access to the internet. According to the Telecommunications Regulatory Commission (CRT), 13.2% of Colombians were internet users in June 2006. By December 2006, the figure was 22.8%, and in December 2007 it had risen to 26.9%. According to recent figures from Internet World Stats,[2] Colombia, with 45,013,674 inhabitants, has an access rate above the world average of 20%, and is even ahead of other Latin American countries such as Peru (26.2%), Brazil (26.1%), Venezuela (21.7%) and Mexico (21.6%). However, the access rate is still below countries such as Chile (44.9%), Argentina (39.3%), Uruguay (31.6%) and Costa Rica (35.7%).

While these statistics show that during 2006 and 2007 Colombia made a major leap in ICT coverage, internet usage is still limited to the main cities. At the same time there are no statistics available on the use of internet by age, occupation, gender, and rural or urban areas, nor research available on how and what people do with ICTs, in order to know which groups most benefited from the use of ICTs.

The Economist Intelligence Unit (EIU), in association with the IBM Institute for Business Value, recently published an e-readiness ranking which assesses a country's ability to promote and support digital business and ICT services. The rankings include criteria such as number of computer servers, websites and mobile phones, but also things like the citizens' ability to utilise technology skilfully. A total of 70 countries were included, and ranked on a scale from one to ten. The top countries were the United States (8.95), Hong Kong (8.91) and Sweden (8.85). Colombia slipped to 58th place in 2008, from 53rd in 2007, although its overall score was higher than in 2007 (4.71 versus 4.69) (EIU, 2008). This change of position can be explained by the fact that other countries made much more significant progress and their ranking is now higher.

Bridging the divide

Rural access

Although rural areas still have less access to the internet, due to a lack of service providers and of infrastructure that requires high financial investment, the Compartel programme – which aims to increase the coverage of ICTs in areas isolated from urban centres – has provided localities with less than 10,000 inhabitants with internet access through telecentres. Presently there are around 1,230 telecentres run by Compartel, and 265 telecentres already in operation have been upgraded.[3]

From 2007 onwards, Compartel has reformulated and included in its plans the design, execution and support of projects that aim to improve the social ownership of ICTs. This has to be highlighted as an important achievement because it will increase the impact of telecentres by improving the living conditions of users. The strategy involves promoting the use and appropriation of the existing ICT infrastructure in order to enable communities to use the available telecentres for fulfilling their business, economic and social needs. This strategy of ownership, promotion and training in the use of ICTs is implemented in alliance with other government initiatives and public and private institutions.

By 2008 Compartel is expected to have established 2,000 new internet access points in educational institutions and telecentres. Some of Compartel's achievements in the last year have been:

- 218 telecentres with 46 free virtual training courses provided by the National Learning Service (SENA), in which 9,370 people have registered.
- 64 telecentres taking part in a pilot virtual classroom initiative for coffee producers, in which 1,106 people have been trained.

1 www.computadoresparaeducar.gov.co

2 www.internetworldstats.com

3 www.compartel.gov.co

- In March 2008, in a public accountability event, Compartel highlighted the achievements of the project "Management of Knowledge and Exchange of Experiences between Community Telecentres and Compartel Telecentres in Colombia", coordinated by Colnodo, the Universidad Autónoma de Occidente and Compartel. This project was funded by Telecentre.org. It is important to mention that many of Compartel's achievements would not have been possible if it were not for its alliances with numerous organisations working on the development of telecentres and training.

To achieve some of the access goals, Compartel and the Ministry of Communications, through its Department of Access and Social Development, are implementing a project which aims to strengthen telecentres by promoting the exchange of experiences and training, and, amongst other things, sharing knowledge to strengthen the national telecentres network. For implementing this project the ministry has signed an agreement with Colnodo, which is coordinating the activities together with universities and private and public agencies.

In Colombia there are at least four types of telecentres that, despite their different ways of operating, share the same mission of providing ICT access to urban and rural communities and through this enabling the development process:

- Telecentres set up and supported by the national government (Compartel)
- Telecentres set up and supported by local governments
- Telecentres set up and supported by for-profit companies
- Telecentres set up and supported by civil society organisations and universities.

Another of Compartel's objectives is to provide connectivity services using a broadband connection for public agencies. In 2007, the coverage of public agencies was increased by 73%. In 2008 Compartel expected to set up 5,197 connectivity points using a broadband connection for public agencies. These points were to be set up in 3,467 schools and 1,730 public agencies such as hospitals, town councils and judicial offices.

Broadband services have been growing steadily in the main cities, and this market is saturated. However, there are just a few initiatives offering broadband services in small towns and in rural areas. Some towns located far away from the country's centre have no broadband service providers. As a result, the challenge for the Ministry of Communications is to promote access to these services in these areas.

E-government

The Connectivity Agenda,[4] a governmental policy aimed at the creation of a more competitive business sector, a modern government and a community with more development opportunities, is focused on the design and development of e-government. This strategy aims to create an efficient, transparent and inclusive government where citizens and enterprises have access to services through ICTs. The evolving e-government framework has the following stages, according to the Connectivity Agenda:

1. Information made available to the public through web pages
2. Basic interaction between the agencies and citizens
3. Advanced interaction between the agencies and citizens
4. Transforming the agencies so they can offer better and timely services
5. Citizen participation in public decisions.

Although stages one and two – information and basic interaction with the public – have been achieved in most of the government agencies, stages three, four and five have not been achieved yet. The goal is to reach them by 2010.

The Connectivity Agenda has made a great effort for all Colombian municipalities to have a website where citizens can get public information about administrative matters.

If there is an area in which Colombia has stood out it has been e-government. According to an e-government report compiled by Darrell West, professor of public policy and political science at Brown University, amongst 198 countries, Colombia leapt from 58th place in 2007 to 22nd in 2008. According to this report, Colombia is the third highest-ranked country in Latin America, behind only Brazil (10th) and Mexico (19th) – and even ahead of Chile (26th), which is widely recognised for its leadership in e-government (West, 2008).

Mobile phones

A good way to provide internet access is mobile phones. According to reports from the Ministry of Communications, the number of subscribers leapt from 2,256,801 in 2000 to 10,400,000 in 2004, 21,849,993 in 2005 and 33,941,118 in 2007. The number of mobile subscribers does not match the number of users, since one person can have more than one subscription. Still, what is happening at a national level and especially in rural areas shows that, thanks to mobile phones, the country has made steady progress in closing the gap between people with and without access to phones. Although in 2007 the sector did not grow at the same pace as previous years, it was quite dynamic and experienced the greatest profits given the broad range of services on offer, such as text messaging, audio, photos, images, etc. Technological advances also improved quality and allowed users to have more information saved on their mobile phones. However, connection to the internet via a mobile phone is still very expensive and not affordable for the great majority of users.

Another limitation is mobile content itself. This usually consists of publicity about products. Cultural or educational content or news is not yet available.

4 www.agenda.gov.co

Policy and legislation

National ICT Plan

The Colombian government has drawn up the National ICT Plan 2008-2019. Its goal is for all Colombians to be able to use ICTs in order to increase social integration and competitiveness by 2019.

The plan includes impact programmes for different social groups and sectors, focusing on issues like regulation, business competitiveness, and programmes for improving the appropriation and usage of ICT in key sectors.

Perhaps one of the most important aspects of the plan is the announcement made by the government of transforming the present Ministry of Communications into a Ministry of Information and Communication Technology, and a redistribution of responsibilities among different government agencies.

ICT Bill

In order to regulate technological and institutional convergence, the Ministry of Communications submitted an ICT Bill, which was already approved by the House of Representatives in June 2008, and will be discussed in the Senate in upcoming sessions. This bill defines the principles and concepts of the information society and the organisation of ICTs in Colombia.

With this bill the transformation of the present Ministry of Communications into a Ministry of Information and Communication Technology will be approved and a new agency will be created: the National Spectrum Agency, which will deal with all issues related to radio spectrum and its regulation.

eVision Colombia (2019)

This vision includes a strategy called "Moving forward towards a better informed society". The strategy holds the following promise: "In 2019, [access to] information will be a right...which in turn will promote economic development, social well-being, social equality and democracy. ICTs will be a means to access information freely, at a reasonable cost and from anywhere in the country."

The fundamental principles guiding this vision are content generation, dissemination of information, usage of information, and standards and best practices, within an institutional and regulatory framework that includes incentives. The 2019 framework also emphasises developing ICT infrastructure.

Action steps

In 2007 the national government issued a decree on technological convergence, which aims to attract new investors, scale up telecommunications infrastructure, and promote the development of new services. According to this decree, the biggest operators are required to offer connectivity access to third parties so they can also provide telecommunication services to the public. Because of the possibilities of convergence, operators have made significant financial investments in new networks and platforms. The country has also seen the merger of several companies and the takeover of small local companies by multinationals. One of the risks of these developments is that the telecommunication services of the whole country are being left in the hands of a few foreign companies. This situation needs to be monitored.

The ICT Bill aims to promote free competition among providers in the hope of reducing costs for the citizens and to catalyse widespread access to ICT services similar to that seen with mobile phones. However, there remain regions untouched by the market, where people's income is extremely low. In these regions it is important to have ICT access strategies led by the national or local government. This is the reason why telecentres continue to be a feasible and important alternative, and should be actively supported by civil society. ■

References

Agenda de Conectividad de Colombia: www.agenda.gov.co

Centro de Investigación de Telecomunicaciones (CINTEL): www.cintel.org.co

CRT (Comisión de Regulación de Telecomunicaciones) (2008) Informe Sectorial de Telecomunicaciones No. 10, May. Available at: www.crt.gov.co

CRT (2008) Informe Trimestral de Conectividad No. 12, May. Available at: www.crt.gov.co

Compartel: www.compartel.gov.co

Compartel (2008) Rendición de Cuentas, Ministerio de Comunicaciones, María Teresa Cuello, Gerente del Programa Compartel, 27 March. Available at: www.compartel.gov.co

Computadores para Educar: www.computadoresparaeducar.gov.co

Departamento Nacional de Planeación: www.dnp.gov.co

EIU (Economist Intelligence Unit) (2008) *E-readiness rankings 2008: Maintaining momentum*. Economist Intelligence Unit/IBM Institute for Business Value. Available at: a330.g.akamai.net/7/330/25828/20080331202303/graphics.eiu.com/upload/ibm_ereadiness_2008.pdf

Internet World Stats: www.internetworldstats.com

Ministry of Communications (2007) Decreto No. 2870 del 31 de julio de 2007 por medio del cual se adoptan medidas para facilitar la Convergencia de los Servicios y Redes en Materia de Telecomunicaciones. Available at: www.mincomunicaciones.gov.co/mincom/src/user_docs/Archivos/normatividad/2007/Decreto/D2870de2007.pdf

Sistema de Información Unificado del Sector de las Telecomunicaciones: www.siust.gov.co

West, D. (2008) *Improving Technology Utilization in Electronic Government around the World, 2008*. Washington: Brookings Institution Press. Available at: www.brookings.edu/reports/2008/0817_egovernment_west.aspx

CONGO, DEMOCRATIC REPUBLIC OF (DRC)

Alternatives
Caroline Tagny
www.alternatives.ca

Introduction

Africa remains a continent where access to the internet is uncommon and expensive. It is partly due to this that it faces real lags in its scientific, technological and social development. The Democratic Republic of Congo (DRC) is no exception. The deplorable state of communications infrastructure in the country is an undeniable deterrent to development and the fight against poverty. High-speed computer connections are via satellite, which is very costly. The rate is sometimes 1,000 times higher than in Europe!

The need to develop national backbone infrastructure in the DRC is not an isolated case. Many regional and international forums and institutions, including the New Partnership for Africa's Development (NEPAD), recognise that fibre-optic networks hold the solution to reducing the digital divide between the haves and have-nots. There have been a series of international, regional and local policy initiatives that all have the overarching goal of promoting the inclusion of citizens in the information society by assuring connectivity.

In the DRC, a national broadband backbone would enable an improvement in communications in a country four times the size of France, several regions of which continue to be very isolated. But national initiatives need to link to regional initiatives. For instance, the Pan African Research and Education Network (PAREN) was created to facilitate collaboration between universities and establish an Africa-wide broadband network. That said, PAREN's final design cannot be completed without a central interconnection point linking the different networks of West, East, South and North Africa. Being geographically central, the DRC can strategically position itself to become the core of these networks.

This report draws largely on a feasibility study produced in 2007 by Alternatives, in collaboration with the Association for Progressive Communications (APC), XitTelecom, and the non-profit multi-sectoral organisation DMTIC (Dynamique multisectorielle pour les TIC). Alternatives is an international non-governmental cooperation organisation that has been working in the DRC since 1998.

National context

After 30 years of dictatorship and two short presidencies, each interrupted by war, the DRC's first democratic elections were held in 2006, and Joseph Kabila was elected president. The DRC remains a country engaged in post-conflict reconstruction. While Kabila has identified five priority sectors – water and electricity, health, education, infrastructure, and employment – there has not been much change in any of these sectors over the past year. Proposed constitutional reforms have not progressed to any significant degree over the same period, and the government has been unable to implement its 2007-2011 agenda. National actors are reportedly preoccupied by the government's lack of transparency, specifically how it awards mining concessions and nominates the executive staff of public enterprises. Nevertheless, certain advances have been made to improve the state's efficiency and coordination capacities, notably through the reduction of government staff from 60 to 45 ministers and vice-ministers.

In 2006, the DRC's population was estimated at 62,660,551 inhabitants, giving it a density of on average 27 inhabitants per square kilometre. Households are concentrated in the mining region of Shaba and in lower Congo. Less than a third of the country's population inhabits urban areas.

Given the DRC's chronic deficit due to poor productivity and weak revenues, it is very vulnerable to external events. In recent years, macroeconomic indicators have stabilised given conditions imposed by international financial institutions regarding the liberalisation of commercial imports and exports. External aid accounts make up nearly half of the state's revenues.

Physical access to technology

In spite of the political crises that have plagued the DRC since its independence, as well as its failing economy, the information and communications technology (ICT) sector has grown, defying all predictions to the contrary. Between 1998 and 2006, the private sector invested more than USD 5 million in mobile technologies. Thousands of jobs have been created and the sector's fiscal revenues have contributed to putting the country on the path of economic growth.

Consisting of about 11,000 lines in Kinshasa, the fixed-line network is managed by the Congolese Office of Post and Telecommunications (OCPT). As it stands, though, the network is practically non-existent. A private operator, Congo Korea Telecom, has stepped in to sink fibre-optic cables linked to a satellite connection, but its network only serves an estimated 3,000 subscribers in the downtown area of Kinshasa.

The sector further developed thanks to the infrastructure of four mobile GSM telephone operators, which linked the country's main centres. The number of mobile subscribers has correspondingly surged from 20,000 in 1997 to approximately 4.5 million in 2007.

There are fifteen recognised internet service providers (ISPs) in the country, accounting for an estimated 140,625 users in 2005. The same year, wireless local area network (WLAN) subscribers were estimated at 24,000 and broadband internet subscribers numbered 15,000. According to World Bank statistics, in 2005 the average monthly cost for an internet connection stood at USD 93, or 40,641 Congolese francs (CDF). There are an estimated 200 cybercafés in the DRC, concentrated in Kinshasa and other large cities.

The absence of broadband is the main obstacle to the proliferation of ICTs. Public operators OCPT and the National Network of Satellite Telecommunications (RENATELSAT) have not had the capacity to develop a national backbone, even though it was part of their mandate. Alternatives' feasibility study, commissioned by OCPT, recommended the deployment of a 5,467-km network made up of 48 fibre-optic routes integrated with Congo's national electricity grid. It was also recommended that the fibre be laid alongside national roads and railroad tracks to help with its management and maintenance. Following up on the technical recommendations of the research, the government recently committed itself to a contract, in collaboration with the Chinese government, to build the line between the SAT-3 cable at Muanda and Kinshasa.

Legal and regulatory framework

On 18 February 2006 the president presented a new Constitution for the DRC, which stated:

> All people have a right to the respect of their private life and to the secrecy of their correspondence, telecommunication and all other forms of communication... This right is inalienable except in cases described by the Constitution.

In spite of its vagueness, we can deduce from this that the legislators intended to nurture a strong civil society and citizen protection. Communication is also presented as a fundamental human right.

Several laws and decrees regulate the ICT sector. Among other things, these laws establish a separation of responsibilities between the Ministry of Post and Telecommunications, the regulator, and public operators OCPT and RENATELSAT. The management of ICT development is conferred to the minister, while OCPT is designated as the manager of the .cd domain.

The construction of a national backbone does not need a different institutional configuration because the two existing state enterprises (OCPT and RENATELSAT) are sufficient to do the job.

Political will and public support

The creation of the Regulating Authority for Post and Telecommunications (ARPTC) was certainly one of the highlights of recent telecommunications reforms. Nevertheless, after four years of activity, the overall achievements of the ARPTC are not encouraging. The decisions taken by the new regulator are too few, have had little impact, and the paths that have been timidly opened have proven to have little relevance. Yet a number of factors weaken the regulator, including the minister's almost non-existent follow-up to technical recommendations put forward by it.

The backbone's use should be continuously overseen by the regulator, especially with regards to managing the conflicts that will certainly arise between operators over the transmission of their signals. But a general lack of cooperation between the minister and the ARPTC can have the effect of preventing the regulator from doing its job properly.

Policy, as it stands, consists of a draft telecom plan. However, work is being done by Alternatives and the multi-stakeholder non-profit organisation DMTIC, amongst others, to develop the country's first national ICT policy document.

Action steps

The DRC's strategic position at the heart of Africa holds implications for the development of Central Africa, and the continent more generally. The country's African responsibility requires linking up with different international transmission networks such as SAT-3, the West African Festoon System (WAFS), and the Eastern Africa Submarine Cable System (EASSy).

The construction of an internet backbone in the DRC will surely create economic synergies conducive to combating poverty, promoting national unity and relaunching the national economy. At the international level, the project is integral to the development of a global information society, the realisation of the Millennium Development Goals (MDGs), and the goals of NEPAD and the Common Market for Eastern and Southern Africa (COMESA).

It is important to guarantee the sustainability of the project through:

- Inclusiveness: The success of the project will depend on the participation of public and private sector partners.
- Efficiency: Measures should be taken to ensure that the project can attain its objectives, notably by rereading the present legal context and involving institutions in the day-to-day management of the project.
- Optimisation: In order to efficiently reply to potential demand for bandwidth and permit universal access to ICT services.
- Reliable framework: To guarantee sustainability, it helps to establish legal precedents, reliable institutions and a reliable economy.

The legal and regulatory framework is relatively capable of supporting the backbone. Mechanisms need to be put in place to ensure that the financing of the project is transparent, and the beneficiaries are clear. An open access approach is favoured. To do this, it is important that the backbone is not monopolised by any one institution, that it is managed contractually, and that there is transparency on all pricing. ■

Reference

Alternatives (2007) *Étude de faisabilité pour une dorsale Internet ouverte en République démocratique du Congo.* In collaboration with the International Development Research Centre (IDRC), Association for Progressive Communications (APC), Office Congolais des Postes et Télécommunications (OCPT), XitTelecom, and Dynamique multisectorielle sur les TIC (DMTIC). Available at: www.alternatives.ca/article2979 and www.rdc-tic.cd/?q=node/75

CONGO, REPUBLIC OF

AZUR Développement
Marc Foukou Mfoutou and Ngoko Yoka
www.azurdev.org

Introduction

As the whole world moves towards an information society, the Republic of Congo finds itself a slow starter. Having taken note of the important role that information and communications technologies (ICTs) play, the country is trying its best to organise itself in order to catch up, and, with difficulty, to reduce the digital divide that has grown over the years.

Estimated at more than three million inhabitants, the Congolese population is 51% female and 49% male. It is concentrated in the southern part of the country (more than 80%), where most people live in urban areas (66%). The average population density for the whole country is around 8.4 inhabitants per square kilometre.

The Republic of Congo is in large part covered by forests (60% of the country's territory) interspersed with savannas. It has a road network of 12,745 kilometres, and at least 10% of roads are paved. The Congo-Océan railroad (510 kilometres), completed in 1934, needs to be repaired. The principal airports are found in Brazzaville (Maya-Maya), the political capital, and Pointe-Noire (Antonio Agostino Neto), the economic capital, and the principal ports in Brazzaville (a river port) and Pointe-Noire on the Atlantic.

The Republic of Congo's economic activity is dominated by the petroleum sector. The share of the country's gross domestic product (GDP) contributed by crude oil production increased from 53.6% in 2002 to 70.4% in 2006. Transport and telecommunications contribute from 4% (in 2006) up to 5.1% of GDP.

The Ministry of Posts and Telecommunications, which is responsible for new technologies, worked on a national ICT strategy at the end of 2004, with the support of the United Nations Development Programme (UNDP). However, it was never adopted by the Council of Ministers, and as a result has become a dead document.

This national strategy has served as one of the information sources for this report, which is also informed by interviews with stakeholders in the ICT sector.

National ICT policy development

The national ICT policy formulated in 2004 aimed to reduce poverty and introduce the Congolese population to the information society era. To do this, several objectives were established:

- To accelerate the development of a viable and sustainable economic network which will contribute to job creation
- To support ICT access for populations living in cities and rural and disadvantaged areas
- To secure ICT infrastructure
- To define a legal and regulatory framework adapted to ICTs
- To develop ICT capacities and transform the educational system by means of ICTs
- To promote good governance by utilising ICTs.

However, implementation of the policy has not been easy. Over the last four years there have been three changes of ministers of postal services and telecommunications in charge of new technologies. At the same time, few institutions and non-governmental organisations (NGOs) in the Republic of Congo are involved in ICT policy and the ICT sector. Those that are involved work to popularise ICTs, to develop services by means of ICTs, and to educate the public about using ICTs for community development.

Civil society was involved in national discussions during the World Summit on the Information Society (WSIS) preparatory process in the Republic of Congo, but only one women's organisation contributed to the discussions. For some women's organisations, ICT policy is a technical area reserved to men, and they prefer to advocate for other causes.

Moreover, funding for work on ICTs is scarce for civil society organisations, as ICTs are not seen as a priority for development. Donors are keener to fund projects and programmes related to HIV/AIDS, peace-building and rural development.

Access to infrastructure

Landline telephones

The end of the National Office of Postal Services and Telecommunications (ONPT), the state-run monopoly operator, resulted in the creation of two public entities: SOPECO for postal services, and SOTELCO for telecommunications.

However, the telecommunications infrastructure inherited by SOTELCO was old, and consisted only of landline telephone services for the two main cities in the Republic of Congo, namely Brazzaville and Pointe-Noire. Practically all landlines are used by private companies, state administration, and in public call centres. The use of landline telephones disappeared from Congolese homes following the destruction of infrastructure during the socio-political troubles which plagued the country in the 1990s.

Mobile telephones

Celtel Congo was created in 1999. It was the first operator of the global system for mobile (GSM) network in the Republic of Congo. By 2008 it connected 760 cities and towns, and plans to connect 213 more locations by the end of 2008. Celtel has more than a million subscribers, out of the country's three million inhabitants.

MTN Congo, another mobile telephone company, was born after it bought and rebranded Libertis Telecom in 2005. Libertis Telecom had been operating in the country for six years. In seven years the company's capital stock increased from USD 20,000 to USD 10 million today. Investments by MTN in the Republic of Congo increased from USD 52 million in 2005 to close to USD 100 million in 2007. The investments are, in large part, concentrated on strengthening quality and the acquisition of new sites throughout the country. MTN presently covers more than 152 locations (towns and villages). It has already attracted some 500,000 subscribers.

Warid Congo is the third mobile telephone operator in the country. In 2006 it signed a partnership agreement with SOTELCO and began advertising its products and services in March 2008. Warid Congo plans to cover 44 cities and locations in the Republic of Congo within the next two years. For the moment, only Brazzaville, Pointe-Noire, Oyo, Ollombo and Dolisie are connected.

Internet access

Several internet service providers (ISPs) operate in the Republic of Congo: DRTVnet, A-Link, AMC Télécom, Dell Ofis, MTI and AlTech Congo. A growing number of cybercafés and telecentres operate in the main cities, namely Brazzaville, Pointe-Noire, Dolisie, Owando, Nkayi, Ouesso, Sibiti and Kinkala. However, the total number of cybercafés and telecentres is still low. While mobile telephone companies offer internet services for mobile phones and laptops, internet access in general is still limited to cities, and rural areas have almost no access.

Access should be boosted by the investment of USD 15 million in a pilot project using fibre-optic cables, which will be carried out in 2010.

Despite the noticeable presence of companies selling ICT products and consumer electronics, computers and other multimedia information technology (IT) equipment remain expensive. A recently formed community telecentres network has plans to advocate for affordable access to the internet and ICTs. The cost of internet subscriptions remains very high and out of reach for most Congolese citizens, ranging from USD 200 to USD 700 per month.

Use of ICTs

Access to ICTs has significantly changed Congolese society. The democratic era has changed the lifestyles of citizens and led to the liberalisation of the telecommunications sector. Currently, the country has more than one million mobile phone users. Cities that were once isolated and inaccessible are no longer so, thanks to mobile phones.

Companies that use ICTs are improving their performance. As a result of ICTs, many projects are being implemented. The banking sector is one of those which have experienced a significant change from the use of ICTs. Customers' payments are no longer performed manually. This not only reduces the waiting time for customers, but also improves working and living conditions of bank agents. Today, cards for automated teller machines (ATMs) allow users to carry out banking operations at any time.

The Congolese administration, including security services and public policing, have brought out computerised identity cards and biometric passports. The time for obtaining these identity cards has been significantly reduced from several months to a few weeks, or even days.

Several innovative services and jobs were also created through ICTs. These include the development of agencies for fund transfers through major localities of the country, and express parcel delivery services. In just five minutes, one can transfer funds to a family member or business partner located in most centres in the country. The transfer is automatic and is done using a phone and a computer.

ICT-related companies, mainly GSM mobile companies, are now amongst the biggest employers in the Republic of Congo. Formal and informal enterprises, including travel agencies, have sprung up as a direct and indirect result of mobile operators.

Access to the internet, although not at high speed and still quite expensive, facilitates the exchange of information and creates a climate of openness. It is now possible to have access to any kind of information on companies and services (e.g., products, special offers, flight schedules, night-time pharmacy hours, doctors, hotels, and restaurants).

ICTs have revolutionised the broadcast world of radio and television. For instance, computers enable TV and radio programmes to be prescheduled and broadcast. ICTs are also in the service of health, as in the case of a free line set up for information on HIV/AIDS by MTN and the National AIDS Committee.

Multimedia and digital technology has revolutionised the habits of the Congolese population. Mobile phones and digital cameras now film the events of society. Digital photos are developed quickly. Before, the process was quite long and involved expensive equipment and training.

ICTs have also made a considerable contribution to the revision of the electoral register and of state administration. In education, ICTs have proven themselves with the introduction of bar codes for examinations. Results for secondary schools and higher education institutions are now published on the internet. In the past, it could take several weeks, or even months, for students to access their results, especially for students living in rural areas.

Several other projects using ICTs are being implemented or planned. These include the incorporation of ICTs in immigration control and the computerisation of the port authority. However, the growing use of ICTs is not without its consequences, which include a resurgence of fraud at all levels, access to pornography on television and the internet, and cyber scams.

Capacity development

ICTs are not yet part of the national education curriculum. In some schools there are no computers for learners. Only the national university, Marien Ngouabi University in Brazzaville, has faculties or departments that have integrated computer training modules into their course work. The digital campus at the university, Agence Universitaire de la Francophonie (AUF), offers distance learning and provides both students and teachers with easy access to the internet – and this at reduced rates. There is also a distance-learning programme affiliated to Cisco in the faculty of sciences.

The Ministry of Technical and Vocational Education started a new course on computer science at a technical high school in Brazzaville two years ago. The aim was to increase the number of students with ICT skills. But, for the moment, students enrolled in this course do not have the opportunity to undertake undergraduate studies in computer science, as it is not offered at Marien Ngouabi University.

For a long time, students from the Republic of Congo have travelled abroad to study computer science at the postgraduate level. Most of them enrol in universities and colleges in the Democratic Republic of the Congo, France and in West African countries. This results in a brain drain, as most of them do not return, since employment is also a challenge.

Several NGOs, such as AZUR Développement, the IT Professionals Association (AIP), the Committee for the Promotion of Information Technologies in Congo (COPTIC), and the Congo Community Telecentres Network, provide access to computer equipment and training in basic computer skills. There are also several schools and private centres across the country training senior technicians in the field of IT, including the maintenance of networks and computer systems.

The mobile phone companies train their staff. Celtel Congo's training budget for 2007 stood at USD 1,578,000. In 2008, it spent USD 1,450,000 on training, apart from USD 60,000 spent by the group for the training of top management, making the total sum of one billion CFA francs devoted to the training.

State-owned enterprises such as the Congolese Informatics Office provide training and offer ICT-related services.

There are gender differences in ICT education. Men tend to study in technical fields, such as maintenance and networks, and are developers. Women engage more in training in basic computer skills. It is also a challenge for the very few women who study technical courses to find employment: most of them end up as secretaries.

Action steps

Being a developing country, the Republic of Congo is late in the appropriation of ICTs for development. Other African countries have successfully committed themselves to the promotion of ICTs, and the implementation of national strategies for the development of ICTs. Having recognised the role that they can play in economic and social development, the government should invest more and make access to affordable ICTs for the Congolese one of its priorities. In addition, there should be a gender-sensitive ICT policy. International organisations could support civil society organisations in order to achieve this.

The issue of electricity and roads is acute in the Republic of Congo. Because of this, ICT development must go along with the development of basic infrastructure such as roads and electricity, as well as training; otherwise all efforts will amount to little. The cost of access, including hardware and internet connectivity, must come down as well.

An appropriate legal framework is also essential to achieve these goals, as is the involvement of government at the highest level, and the involvement of civil society. ■

References

Ministry of Posts and Telecommunications (2004) *Stratégie nationale pour le développement des technologies de l'information et de la communication.*

Niombo, S. (2008) *Implication de la société civile des pays de l'Afrique centrale dans les politiques des TIC: le cas de la République de Congo.* Panos Institute West Africa.

OECD Development Centre/African Development Bank/United Nations Economic Commission for Africa (2008) *African Economic Outlook 2008.* OECD/ADB/UNECA.

Presentations by Celtel, MTN, Warid, MIGALE-SMS and COPTIC during Congo ICT Week, Brazzaville, June 2008.

COSTA RICA

Cooperativa Sulá Batsú
Kemly Camacho
www.sulabatsu.com

Introduction

According to the Constitution of Costa Rica, education, health, electricity, water and telecommunications are all universal public services. This policy, supported by a "solidarity state",[1] has resulted in power supply (91%) and land-line telephony coverage (65%) that ranks among the highest in the world.

Until now, telecommunication services have been a state monopoly handled by the Costa Rican Electricity Institute (ICE) and its subsidiary Radiográfica Costarricense (RACSA), the state-run internet service provider (ISP). Throughout the years, Costa Rica has carried out several pioneering efforts – some more successful than others – targeted at guaranteeing universal access to information and communications technologies (ICTs) for all citizens:

- Twenty years ago, the Educational Informatics Programme established computer labs in elementary and secondary schools to integrate computer use in the curriculum. However, a significant number of these laboratories are not connected to the internet, hindering the programme's pioneering potential. It has already been surpassed by other Latin American countries, where initiatives that started later have been able to provide connectivity.
- Since 2002, the costarricense.cr initiative has provided each Costa Rican citizen with a free email account and a personal website linked to their identification document number.
- The programme Communication Without Frontiers established public access points in post offices, banks and municipal government offices throughout the country.

These state-supported initiatives have had a positive impact on the country's position in Latin American ICT rankings. Several indicators from the Global Information Technology Report 2006-2007 produced by the World Economic Forum (WEF) illustrate this fact (see Table 1).

General position of the country

The investment in education as a universal right has had an impact on the population and shows in things like the level of the education system, the availability and quality of research centres, and the number of researchers and engineers. A country's educational quality has a bearing on its strategic uses of ICTs. As a result, it is included as a determining factor in the WEF report.

Costa Rica has a very good position regarding internet users and computers per 100 inhabitants, unlike broadband use. However, in the Cisco Broadband Barometer compiled by the Costa Rican High Technology Advisory Committee (CAATEC)[2] between December 2006 and December 2007, broadband penetration grew by 50%. This growth was experienced mainly in Costa Rican homes, followed by businesses. Little growth was experienced in educational centres and the public sector. Broadband also experienced greater growth in metropolitan areas compared to rural areas.

The indicators for telephony and internet servers place us at number one in the region. The figure for mobile subscribers is from 2004, and since then the percentage has more than doubled, with mobile networks reaching 57% of the population.

These data indicate that the universal access model was well on its way when the analyses were conducted. However, 2007 marked a radical change in access to ICTs for the Costa Rican population, owing to the adoption of the Central American Free Trade Agreement (CAFTA) between the United States (US) and a number of Central American countries, including Costa Rica. This substantially modifies Costa Rica's development model, especially regarding connectivity legislation included in CAFTA: the General Telecommunications Law and the Law to Strengthen and Modernise the Public Entities of the Telecommunication Sector.

Key transformations in the regulation of the telecommunications sector

It is too soon to precisely establish the effect that CAFTA will have, but ICT access will be unequivocally and strongly affected, as well as the information, communication and knowledge processes for different social groups.

CAFTA opens up the market in the three most profitable areas that the ICE controlled under the state monopoly model: mobile telephony, internet and networks. Telecommunication services change from being a public service sustained by the state, to being a service available to the public, sustained by the market. As a public service, they were cross-subsidised: the bigger consumers paid above-market prices to guarantee basic subsidised rates for people with fewer resources. With CAFTA, prices will answer only to the market, and only those with the resources to pay will be able to access the services.

1 The term "solidarity state" refers to the policy that those who have more pay more to subsidise those who have less. In this way universal access to basic services can be achieved.

2 www.caatec.org

Table 1: Costa Rica's ICT access status			
Indicator		Ranking within the LAC sample*	Ranking within the global sample (122 countries)
Infrastructure environment			
Telephone lines	32.09 per 100 inhabitants	1	38
Secure internet servers	61.7 per 1 million inhabitants	1	30
Availability of scientists and engineers	4.95 (from 1 to 7)	2	37
Quality of scientific research institutions	4.24 (from 1 to 7)	2	38
Individual readiness			
Quality of education system	4.12 (from 1 to 7)	1	40
Quality of public schools	3.73 (from 1 to 7)	1	50
Internet access in schools	3.08 (from 1 to 7)	9	81
Cost of mobile telephone call (USD)	0.05 per 3 minutes	2	27
Cost of broadband (USD)	2.06 per 100 kilobits per second (Kbps)	5	55
Individual usage (based on 2004 data)			
Internet users	25.42 per 100 inhabitants	1	45
Personal computers (PCs)	21.83 per 100 inhabitants	1	33
Broadband internet subscribers	0.66 per 100 inhabitants	10	60
Mobile telephone subscribers	25.45 per 100 inhabitants	17	87

* The Latin America and Caribbean (LAC) sample includes Chile, Uruguay, Mexico, Brazil, Argentina, Peru, Venezuela, Paraguay, Ecuador, Dominican Republic, Jamaica, Barbados, El Salvador, Panama, Colombia, Nicaragua, Bolivia, Guatemala, Honduras and Suriname.

Source: **World Economic Forum, *The Global Information Technology Report 2006-2007***

The functions of the Public Services Regulatory Authority (ARESEP), whose job it was to regulate public services and guarantee universal access, as well as those of ICE, which was responsible for implementing technical projects to fulfil ARESEP's mandate, have changed substantially. ARESEP will now regulate competition in the telecommunication market, and ICE will be just another service provider in the market. According to projections made by specialists, in five years' time ICE will lose 66% of its market share.

The principle of universal access to energy and telecommunication services is not compatible with market competition. Private providers will not operate at cost, much less subsidise populations that do not have the resources to access private services, because they are purely profit-oriented.

The purchasing power of the population is unequal, and the solutions proposed to solve this problem are remedial policies and programmes that give special conditions to the population sectors with the greatest need, particularly through a fund to attend to poor sectors called the National Telecommunications Fund (FONATEL). But this mechanism has already been tried unsuccessfully in other Latin American countries and has had little impact on providing access to ICTs for the most excluded population groups.

Moreover, following the rules on the dominant provider, it has been established that ICE's current infrastructure, built through years of public investment, will be used at cost by the enterprises that come to compete in the telecommunications market (Article 61, General Telecommunications Law). Costa Rica has excellent telecommunications and electricity infrastructure which has been developed by the state – that is, with the contributions of all Costa Ricans.

Although one might assume that the Costa Rican market is small – since it is a small country with a population of just over four million – it is a very dynamic market, precisely due to the high investment in infrastructure. Already other private enterprises working in Central America have expressed their interest in participating in the national market: Telefónica from Spain, América Móvil from México and Millicom from Sweden.

It is crucial for people and organisations interested in the social aspects of ICTs to monitor and follow up the deep changes that CAFTA and its telecommunications chapter will produce in the ICT access area, and amongst the Costa Rican population.

ICT access in the Costa Rican home

Table 2 illustrates coverage of different ICTs, both digital and non-digital, based on a 2006 household survey with a special ICT component (INEC, 2006).

Table 2: Home access to ICTs

Non-digital ICT	Coverage of total population	Urban	Rural	Digital ICT	Coverage of total population	Urban	Rural
Electricity	99.1%	99.9%	98%	Mobile	56.4%	65.1%	43.1%
Radio	84.9%	87.7%	80.8%	PC	28.2%	36.8%	15.2%
Television	93.7%	96.1%	90.1%	Internet access	9.8%	13.9%	5.2%
Land-line telephony	64.4%	74.4%	51.8%				

Source: INEC (2006)

Access to electricity, radio and television is widespread in Costa Rica. Even in an analysis by geographic region, access to the three services is similar in all regions, which is very uncommon in poor countries. This is related to the solidarity state model mentioned above.

However, there are important differences in rural and urban coverage for digital technologies, measured by the availability of computers and the internet. Nevertheless, the tendency is towards an increase in access to these tools. Since 2004, the consultancy firm CID Gallup[3] has been conducting studies for RACSA regarding access to technology in Costa Rican households. For 2008, the study indicates that 39% of households have a computer, which means that in two years there has been an increase of 11 percentage points in the availability of computers. Regarding connectivity, only 44% of the PCs are connected, which represents 20% of households, and a growth of 10 percentage points between 2006 and 2008.

According to a study by the University of Costa Rica's Programme on the Information and Knowledge Society (PROSIC), 90% of the country's young students use the internet, a percentage that grows to 99% for students between the ages of 21 and 24 (PROSIC, 2008). As in other countries, the digital-based technology that has had the greatest growth regarding coverage is mobile telephony, reaching 57% of the population.

According to 2007 data from ICE,[4] Costa Rica ranks third worldwide in individual mobile use (with an average monthly use of 181 minutes per client). Regarding the cost of a call, Costa Rica has the cheapest rate in Latin America and ranks 27th in the world (WEF, 2007). Two aspects have a bearing on this: the cost of the call (USD 0.04), and the fact that within the country mobiles can communicate without network restrictions and with a single rate regardless of where you are in the country.

Mobile messaging (texting) is even more common among Costa Ricans; the cost (USD 0.0027) together with the level of coverage has made this a popular form of communication. Between 2003 and 2006, texting increased 2.5 times, reaching an average of 252 messages per user per month.

Regarding ICTs and income analysis, households with larger incomes have a lot more access to ICTs. For example, in terms of mobile access, the highest income quintile shows a percentage of 86% and the lowest quintile 24%. The presence of computers in households follows a similar pattern: only 5% of the lowest-income households have a computer and none have connectivity, whereas 63% of the highest-income households have a computer and 30% have internet (PROSIC, 2007).

The CID Gallup report indicates that in households with internet connectivity, an average of three people use the internet. However, the same people often connect in public spaces such as study centres, office/working spaces and internet cafés.

It is worth mentioning the importance of the public use of ICTs. Internet cafés are particularly important, since there are over 800 of them in the country and they fulfil a major role in providing ICT access at low cost for communities.

Action steps

Due to the CAFTA-related changes in legislation, it will not be possible to know if the solidarity state model that supported access to ICTs as a universal right would have had the same impact as it did on other essential services in Costa Rica (such as electricity, education, land-line telephony and water, for example). It will be very important to monitor transformations in telecommunication services, and determine if the market will provide better services to the citizens than the universal access model that was being developed in the country. This is a good case study, since there is a baseline and historic documentation to which the future situation can be compared.

There are other countries with examples of good practices and lessons learned that Costa Rica should take into account before making drastic changes, especially regarding the use of telecommunication funds.

It will be difficult to sustain the idea of universal access to telecommunication services in the framework of market competition. However, it would be interesting to test some possibilities, and encourage citizen and civil society participation in this discussion. An orientation towards the social use and appropriation of ICTs is a good way to think about future actions. ■

3 www.cidgallup.com

4 www.grupoice.com/index.html

References

CAATEC (Comisión Asesora en Alta Tecnología de Costa Rica): www.caatec.org

RACSA (Radiográfica Costarricense S.A.): www.racsa.co.cr

CID Gallup: www.cidgallup.com

ICE (Instituto Costarricense de Electricidad): www.grupoice.com/index.html

INEC (Instituto Nacional de Estadística y Censos) (2006) *Encuesta de Hogares de Propósitos Múltiples*. Available at: www.inec.go.cr/IndexPantallaSet.htm

PROSIC (Programa Sociedad de la Información y el Conocimiento) (2007) *Hacia la Sociedad de la Información y el Conocimiento en Costa Rica: Informe 2007*. San José: PROSIC/Universidad de Costa Rica. Available at: www.prosic.ucr.ac.cr/informe_2007/index.htm

PROSIC (2008) *Los jóvenes costarricenses en la Sociedad de la Información: Avance de resultados*. San José: PROSIC/Universidad de Costa Rica. Available at: www.prosic.ucr.ac.cr/jovenes/jovenes.pdf

WEF (World Economic Forum) (2007) *The Global Information Technology Report 2006-2007*. Geneva: WEF.

CROATIA

ZaMirNET
Danijela Babic
www.zamirnet.hr

Introduction

The Croatian telecoms market has been shaped by the country's bid to join the European Union (EU), resulting in market liberalisation and the creation of a regulatory environment conducive to competition.

In most European countries, the public switched telephone network (PSTN), which has been developed over more than 100 years, is now declining in terms of the number of subscribers and revenue. However, according to a 2007 comparative report by Cullen International that looked at countries in South East Europe (SEE), Croatia still has growth in fixed telephony revenues, while the number of subscribers is more or less stable (Cullen International, 2007).

The digitalisation of fixed networks is crucial for the provision of value-added services and for increasing the quality of service for customers. Croatia has been 100% digital since January 2003. Competition is relatively strong, and alternative operators have taken more than 20% of the market share in the broadband access market (Cullen International, 2007).

The main strategic goal of the Croatian government in the area of broadband internet access is to achieve 500,000 broadband connections before the end of 2008 (a 12% penetration rate). Last year the number of broadband users rose to about 380,000 users, which means that the penetration achieved is 8% in relation to the number of residents, or more than 25% in relation to the number of households (e-Croatia, 2008).

The total number of internet users in the country in July 2007 (including broadband and other types of connections) amounted to 1,909,000, which means that internet penetration was at 43% (e-Croatia, 2008). According to the Cullen International report, in 2007 there were 1,684,600 internet users, or 37.94% of the population. There has been little change in the cost of access during this latest reporting period (2005-2007), so there is no visible correlation between lower costs and increased internet penetration rates. In fact, although Croatia has one of the highest access costs among SEE countries (second only to the former Yugoslav Republic of Macedonia) it has the highest internet penetration rate (Cullen International, 2007).

Results of a study published in 2006 showed that in terms of their availability on the internet, public services for business scored 60.41% and those for citizens scored 46.48% (e-Croatia, 2006).

The mobile market segment is growing significantly, with mobile penetration exceeding 100% of the population in 2007. Third generation (3G) and high-speed downlink packet access (HSDPA) services have been launched. Statistics suggest the mobile data market has reached critical mass and is entering a significant growth phase, an observation reinforced by news of the late 2007 launch of mobile voice over internet protocol (VoIP) services by one of the established mobile network operators.

Physical access to technology

The fact that Croatia has a very developed nationwide digital network, mainly owned or controlled by the incumbent operator T-Com, has not sped up the introduction of broadband in many rural and remote areas. In Croatia there are around 2,200 local exchange services, most of them with so few users or situated in areas so remote that installation of a digital subscriber line (DSL)/multiservice access node (MSAN) would not be profitable. They are therefore ignored by profit-driven private companies. Since even the incumbent operator is privatised, it is not realistic to expect that these remote areas and small exchange offices will become "broadband capable" anytime soon.

This creates unfavourable conditions for people and businesses in these areas where wireless solutions enabling mobile or satellite connections are the only option, because these are still very expensive in comparison to ADSL or cable broadband.

Being aware of the fact that broadband, without adequate content, is not enough to stop the depopulation of distant islands, the Ministry of Science, Education and Sports, the Central State Administrative Office for e-Croatia, the Croatian Telecommunications Agency, and the Croatian Academic and Research Network (CARNet) have developed a project which enables distance learning in regional schools on poorly inhabited islands by connecting them to schools on the mainland.[1]

In order to address the lack of physical access in rural areas, the Teleaccess Project is being implemented by the Central State Administrative Office for e-Croatia in cooperation with the business incubator Skrad-PINS d.o.o. and the local economic development agency LEDA Vinkovci. The Teleaccess Project[2] has established telecentres where citizens can use computers, access the internet and get acquainted with other modern technologies. The mission of the Telecentar, as these facilities are known, is to educate the population in local and rural regions through various interactive workshops and seminars, and to improve communication and

1 e-hrvatska.hr/sdu/en/ProgramEHrvatska/Provedba/Broadband.html

2 www.e-croatia.hr/sdu/en/e-hrv/vijest.html?h=/en/e-hrv/newLeftBanner/0

the practical use of new technologies, which will ultimately improve their competitiveness in the labour market. Similar projects were implemented in rural areas several years ago, but as initiatives by civil society organisations.

Despite good access statistics, the rural areas are not the only ones to face real access challenges. A significant number of people living in big cities are also deprived of a broadband connection to their home. This is because T-Com allegedly has an undeclared number of so-called pulse-code modulation (PCM) lines, where a single copper pair is divided between four or eight customers, offering telephone services that cannot even get a decent dial-up connection – not to mention broadband. At the same time, if the line is shared with several users, it becomes difficult for one user to switch to another operator. The incumbent is also refusing to give access to some local exchanges, and arbitrarily decides who will be allowed to switch to an alternative provider and who will not. According to a famous blogger specialising in telecommunications, T-Zombix, this situation results in a weakening of competition and effectively forces most of the competitors to shut down operations or at least slow down development.

Easy access to information and communications technologies (ICTs) is a prerequisite for participation in an information society. E-inclusion also refers to the extent to which ICTs help to equalise and promote participation in society at all levels (i.e., social relationships, work, culture, political participation, etc.) (Karzen & Karzen, 2007).

The implementation plan for the e-Croatia programme in 2008 is a key government document. The most significant part of this year's plan is the creation of a development strategy for e-management, with the aim of creating conditions for building a common platform for public administration. This will enable central authorisation and authentication services based on the electronic identity of citizens.

Generally, however, ICTs for inclusion in Croatia is still at its pre-infancy stages. One reason for this is the lack of capacity, particularly in the educational community. There is also a lack of awareness amongst policy-makers within the relevant ministries on e-inclusion issues and related best practices.

In June 2007, the Croatian Parliament passed a new strategy for people with disabilities for 2007-2015. Specifically, the document states: "For the full integration of disabled persons, it is necessary to ensure equal access to services, which indicates better accessibility to orthopaedic aid equipment, modern technologies and universal design."

However, most of the websites for public bodies are not completely accessible to persons with visual impairments. Also, e-learning systems that have been developed at universities in Croatia mostly neglect students with special needs.

An exception is the central governmental portal (www.mojauprava.hr) which is compliant with the standards set by the World Accessibility Initiative (WAI). It is also encouraging that key stakeholders, including non-governmental organisations (NGOs), private information technology (IT) companies and the state company for IT support (APIS-IT), as well as representatives of several university faculties, have expressed their interest in participating in activities related to e-inclusion, particularly e-accessibility, initiated by civil society. For example, the Croatian Association for the Blind has cooperated with the University of Zagreb's Faculty of Electrical Engineering and Computing to develop a "talking" software programme for the blind (currently being used by the University of Zagreb's School of Philosophy and the city of Velika Gorica's libraries) (Karzen & Karzen, 2007).

Legislation

SMP regulations

The concept of significant market power (SMP) is one of the central elements of the EU regulatory regime for electronic communications. Once an operator has been deemed as having SMP in a specific telecommunications market, it may subsequently be subject to asymmetric regulatory obligations.

In the 2003 acquis, an operator is presumed to be dominant in a relevant market only when its market share exceeds 40%. However, any final determination of SMP must take other factors into consideration, such as the control of "essential facilities" and the absence of potential competition. Furthermore, regulatory obligations on operators with SMP are not pre-defined in the legislation, but imposed by the national regulatory agency (NRA) after analysing the market (Cullen International, 2007).

In practice the regulator has no discretionary powers for imposing regulatory obligations on the relevant markets defined in accordance with the new EU regulatory framework. The primary law still defines a fixed set of regulatory obligations for SMP operators, in line with the rules of the open network provision (ONP) interconnection directive. Therefore, the new procedures will not be applied before the adoption of a new law based on the EU 2003 acquis, which was expected in early 2008 (Cullen International, 2007).

At a session held on 29 May 2008, the government accepted a draft proposal for the Electronic Communications Act. The new act provides further alignment with the EU legal acquirement.

According to T-Zombix, since nothing crucial has changed in the draft, the fact remains that the incumbent is still controlling all of the infrastructure.

On 14 September 2006 the NRA designated T-Com and its 100%-owned subsidiary, Iskon Internet, as jointly having SMP in the national market for fixed public telephony networks and services, and in the national market for transmission of voice, sound, data, documents, pictures and other media over fixed networks (Cullen International, 2007).

Access costs

Low-income tariff options for fixed-line telephony typically have monthly rental prices that are much cheaper than normal tariffs. The package also typically includes a limited number of free or cheap call units. Once this quota has been exhausted, the user has to pay tariffs that are significantly more expensive than the normal tariff. The low-income tariff package is therefore unattractive for normal consumers, but may meet the basic communications needs of a low-income family (Cullen International, 2007).

T-Com has a tariff scheme whereby all national calls are charged at the same rate as a local call. This means that while a three-minute local call in Croatia has a relatively high price, the price for a three-minute national long-distance call is relatively low – less than half of the European average (Cullen International, 2007).

A straight comparison shows that mobile tariffs for Croatia are below the EU median. However, a comparison that includes PPP (purchasing power parity) shows that the local tariffs are well above the EU average. International tariffs in Croatia are moderately higher than the EU average. Amongst SEE countries, the only country that has more expensive dial-up access than Croatia is Macedonia (Cullen International, 2007).

Action steps

At this stage, policy initiatives are required in order to ensure accessibility to all public e-services for persons with disabilities and the elderly. Relevant ministries should:

- Improve the capacity of public administrations for planning and implementing e-inclusion measures. In particular, this refers to the capacity to integrate accessibility requirements into the technical specifications of public procurement procedures.
- Ensure sufficient funding for civil society initiatives in the area of e-inclusion.
- In collaboration with all stakeholders, establish a continuous monitoring mechanism that focuses on the accessibility of public e-services.
- In addition, actions to raise awareness on data storage and privacy issues should be conducted by civil society organisations in collaboration with stakeholders from the business sector and relevant state agencies.

References

Cullen International (2007) *Report 4 – Country Comparative Report. Supply of services in monitoring of South East Europe: Telecommunications services sector and related aspects.* Available at: www.cullen-international.com/documents/cullen/cipublic/studies/balkan/report4comparative.pdf

e-Croatia (Central State Administrative Office for e-Croatia) (2006) *Benchmarking study: Online availability of public services.* Available at: e-hrvatska.hr/sdu/en/Dokumenti/StrategijeIProgrami/categoryParagraph/06/document/Bench_2006_english.pdf

e-Croatia (2008) *Broadband development 2008 action plan.* Available at: e-hrvatska.hr/sdu/en/e-hrv.html

Karzen & Karzen (2007) *ICT for Inclusion of the Disabled and Elderly as Marginalized Groups in Croatia.* ZaMirNET.

Teleaccess Project: www.e-croatia.hr/sdu/en/e-hrv/vijest.html?h=/en/e-hrv/newLeftBanner/00

ECUADOR

IMAGINAR, Infodesarrollo
Hugo Carrión
www.imaginar.org, www.infodesarrollo.ec

Introduction

Political instability in Ecuador has led to a lack of continuity in national development plans in the information and communications technology (ICT) sector. There have been several initiatives that have been cut off or that have not even been implemented.

The effects of this instability include the non-fulfillment of plans for the expansion of the fixed telephony network, the lack of supervision and control over the installation of public telephony in rural areas, the accumulated debt of telecommunications operators owed to the Telecommunications Development Fund (FODETEL), and the weak enforcement of programmes such as the roll-out of telecentres.

Nevertheless, there have also been some advances and positive initiatives in the country. The dramatic reduction of the cost of internet access and the incorporation into the new constitution of the right to access ICTs are signs of progress.

Physical access to technology

The rate of access to ICTs in Ecuador is one of the lowest in the region. According to data from the National Council of Telecommunications (CONATEL), as of August 2008, the country had a fixed-line telephone penetration of 13.39%. However, the percentage of mobile subscribers was 78.64%. This is a phenomenon that is repeated in many countries in the region, where cellular telephony has met the needs left unfulfilled by the scant coverage of fixed-line telephony.

On the other hand, according to the same source, internet access has a penetration of only 2.2%, while broadband penetration is only 0.7% – amongst the lowest in South America.

There are still a large number of subscribers who connect to the internet via dial-up access, although this is on a downward trend. Most people access the internet using asymmetric digital subscriber line (ADSL) technology. Other technologies that are beginning to emerge are coaxial cable television subscription networks and wireless access using cellular networks.

The rate of electrification in Ecuador is over 90%, so access to electricity infrastructure in itself is not a serious problem. However, there is evidence of a wide gap between urban and rural areas when it comes to ICTs. Access to fixed telephony and internet is concentrated mainly in large cities.

The Telecommunications Development Fund (FODETEL), which is responsible for promoting access to connectivity in rural areas, has not been able to fully implement its work because of a lack of available funds (money is still owed by telecommunications operators). Additionally, several projects involving the installation of telecentres have been delayed. The largest project, called PROMEC, was finally shut down this year because the operator responsible was unable to install the 1,120 telecentres it had committed to establishing.

Affordability of technology

Ecuador has amongst the most expensive internet access in the region, with prices last year which doubled and even tripled that of other countries. The response from operators was that the high cost was mainly due to the cost of international connectivity through the Pan-American cable, whose capacity was saturated. Other fibre-optic systems were available through Colombia and Peru, which further raised the cost of internet access in Ecuador.

Given this reality, the government created a special regulation to facilitate the installation of new submarine cable connections. As a result, in November 2007, Telefónica International Wholesale Services (TIWS) connected Ecuador via the SAM1 cable, with an investment of about USD 40 million. Rafael Arranz, the vice president of TIWS, said that the cost of internet access could be reduced by 30% to 40%, and appealed to value added service providers to "also do their part" in reducing costs.

While the results are beginning to be felt, the benefits have yet to reach users. Perhaps we have to wait longer, until internet service providers (ISPs) opt for alternatives for connectivity, and assume a portion of the responsibility of lowering costs.

The regional and global trend has been to reduce the unit cost of internet access. This means that the cost for each kilobit per second (Kbps) inevitably will decline. The cost of basic access in Ecuador is between USD 15 and USD 30, with speeds ranging from 256 to 600 Kbps. This does not differ very much from a regional average of USD 20 offering speeds of 300 to 600 Kbps. Andinanet, the largest ISP in Ecuador, publicly announced an offer of doubling the access speed annually while maintaining the same price for this access until the year 2010.

How much more can the cost of internet decline? That will be defined by market forces and state intervention to prevent distortions. The problem of international connectivity has apparently been solved, while suppliers on the domestic front should make efforts to keep the internet accessible and affordable. Companies, the government and universities are responsible for the development of applications and content that give meaning to the infrastructure, so that average citizens discover that the "network of networks" can improve their lives and that it is worth paying what it costs.

Legal and regulatory framework

Current legislation and regulations are outdated with regard to challenges such as the unbundling of the subscriber loop, allowing the installation and operation of convergent networks, and facilitating the development of community wireless networks, among other key issues. The existing regulatory framework is the result of six reforms to the Special Telecommunications Law issued in 1992. This law was created with the sole purpose of privatising the state telephone operator EMETEL. But after years of effort, little progress has been made. As a result there are two state operators with regional monopolies.

Nevertheless, 2008 has been a special year for Ecuador, because the National Constituent Assembly worked on the formulation of a proposal for a new constitution which was approved by popular referendum in September.

With regard to telecommunications, this included several aspects that deserve to be highlighted.

Article 16 surprised advocates by including within the rights of "good living" the right to universal access to ICTs, as well as equitable access to the use of spectrum frequencies.

Complementing this, Article 17 says the state "[s]hall ensure the allocation, through transparent methods and on equal terms, of radio spectrum frequencies..." This assurance of transparency is important. There are still valid complaints about the so-called "feast of frequencies" which involves more than 300 frequencies assigned without technical requirements being fulfilled. The assignment of the frequencies has been linked in the majority of cases with political and economic groups.

Article 261 declares that the state shall have exclusive responsibility over "radio spectrum and the general regime of communications and telecommunications, ports and airports." In this regard, while the opposition has denounced the proposed state control of telecommunications, the ruling party has claimed the right of the state to control these sectors, without excluding the possibility of concessions services. This disagreement will need to be urgently clarified by the new telecommunications law.

Article 313 says that the state "reserves the right to manage, regulate, and control the strategic sectors in accordance with the principles of environmental sustainability...and efficiency." It includes telecommunications and radio spectrum under the definition of strategic sectors. This has caused fear amongst private operators because in addition to the regulation and control of telecommunications, the state reserves the right to manage them.

Another surprise is Article 347, which includes the responsibility of the state to incorporate ICTs in education. It is noteworthy that the use of ICTs in education has been raised to the level of a constitutional principle. The implementation of this principle does not seem to be far off. The National Connectivity Plan 2008-2010, submitted in August, envisages an investment of USD 78 million for schools and other educational establishments in the next two years.

Finally, referring to natural resources (which includes radio spectrum), Article 408 mentions that the state is the owner. This article in particular has caused controversy with the statement that the state will "participate in at least 50% of the benefits of the use of these resources." While the media have reported that there is a proposal for the right to confiscate that violates the right to property, the defenders of the new constitution have argued that this is not the spirit of the proposal, although their explanations have not been entirely convincing.

It is also noteworthy that the new constitution facilitates the process of merging the telephone companies Andinatel and Pacifictel into a single public telecommunications company in the period of one year.

As we see it, the new constitution incorporates new and positive principles and rights. Moreover, several articles assign the state the role of regulator and administrator of telecommunications, granting it exclusive jurisdiction. A new regulatory framework for the sector should clarify issues of competition, the management of radio spectrum, and the form of participation of private operators, among other fundamental issues. Compared to the previous constitution, the new constitution definitely contains advances and important contributions to the telecommunications sector. However, there are a couple of points that must be clarified for some sectors.

In the political instability experienced in the country, the obsolete regulatory framework and weakness of the authorities, as well as the absence of a long-term vision, have all been determining factors that have shaped the current ICT landscape. Several plans, programmes and projects have been nothing more than declarations of good intentions. A dramatic example is the flat rate for dial-up internet access, which has remained unimplemented for five years and which now, in the year 2008, even seems unnecessary.

The National Plan for the Development of Telecommunications (2000-2005) was never implemented organically and never evaluated. As a result, we will never know if it served a useful function. The government recently adopted a plan for 2007-2012, containing 16 targets, 94 goals and 319 indicators. However, these have also not been measured.

The latest government initiative has been the National Connectivity Plan, which involves of an investment of almost USD 900 million over the next two years. We still need to know more details about the fate of these funds.

Action steps

To increase and improve physical access to technologies, the state must make the statement that access to ICTs is a right of all Ecuadorians a reality. The successful implementation of projects included in the National Connectivity Plan will be the best measure of this commitment.

As to the affordability of technology, efforts should be directed towards better understanding the cost structure of access and focusing on efforts to reduce service costs. It is also important to strengthen organisations so that they can advocate for better quality services and better prices on behalf of the consumer. Finally, the regulatory agency must have the necessary skills to incorporate, in a creative way, measures to regulate tariffs if so required.

Most actors recognise that one of the major challenges is the issuance of a new telecommunications law that responds to the reality of technological convergence and ensures universal service for citizens. It is therefore of vital importance to start a participatory process to discuss the principles of this new law.

"It is not the form of government which constitutes the happiness of a nation, but the virtues of the rulers and of the judges," said Aristotle. This could certainly apply to the case of Ecuador. Beyond the shortcomings of the legislation or its lack of being adapted and updated, the institutional weakness of the country's regulatory bodies and authorities has been a determining factor for the delay in the development of ICTs and telecommunications. "Regulatory capture", where bureaucrats favour particular interests, might explain many aspects of the situation in Ecuador. Large economic groups handle the mesh of interests in one of the most profitable segments of the country's economy. Corruption is no stranger to this sector, where the authorities are at least guilty of the sin of not acting.

References

National Connectivity Plan 2008-2010: www.conectividad.org/archivo/regulacion/Plan_Conectividad.pdf

National Council of Telecommunications (CONATEL): www.conatel.gov.ec

National Plan for the Development of Telecommunications 2007-2012: www.conectividad.org/archivo/regulacion/conatel/Plan_Desarrollo_Telecomunicaciones.pdf

New Constitution of Ecuador 2008: www.asambleaconstituyente.gov.ec/documentos/constitucion2008/constitucion_de_bolsillo.pdf

Solidarity Fund: www.fondodesolidaridad.gov.ec

Telecommunications Development Fund (FODETEL): www.conatel.gov.ec

EGYPT

ArabDev
Leila Hassanin
www.arabdev.org

Introduction

The telecom sector is a flagship of the Egyptian economy, and the government sees it as an important factor in enhancing the country's competitiveness regionally and globally. Therefore the telecom sector's infrastructure has been upgraded extensively over the last decade. To further its effectiveness, the government has been deregulating the sector in decisive steps: it is one of the most liberalised in Egypt.

Mobile communications, in particular, has been one of the sub-sectors in the telecom field to enjoy the greatest amount of liberalisation. Global system for mobile (GSM) services were first offered in late 1996 by the public company Arento (Arab Republic of Egypt Telecommunication). It was privatised and taken over by Mobinil[1] in May 1998. In November 1998, Click GSM, another private operator, was added to the sector, ending Mobinil's short monopoly. Click GSM then became Vodafone Egypt.[2] From 1998 until early 2007, when the third operator Etisalat[3] began operating, Mobinil and Vodafone had a duopoly of the mobile market in Egypt. The licensing of a third operator in 2006 was a move to increase competition and service coverage. The tendering process was a much-heralded event in Egypt and symbolised the government's earnest intent to pursue its liberalisation and privatisation plans for the telecom sector.

Mobile access has accelerated quickly in Egypt, with a population of close to 80 million (by end 2008), and one that has been underserved for decades when it comes to fixed lines. Mobile access now has the highest diffusion of all telecom services in Egypt. About one fourth of Egypt's population has mobile access, and about 40% of the adult population has a cell phone. Users surged from 200,000 in early 1999 to 3.4 million in 2001; and from 5.8 million at end 2003 to 7.7 million at end 2004, 12 million in 2005, and 17 million in 2007, according to the Egyptian Ministry of Communications and Information Technology (MCIT).[4] Other numbers quoted by the Egyptian government and the telecom industry put users at over 25 million for 2007.

The competition between mobile communication providers offered more services and incentives for users, which further spurred access. For example, Etisalat was the first operator to introduce third generation (3G) services in Egypt, followed closely by Vodafone. Etisalat claims that it had close to one million subscribers to its 3G network in less than two months (Yuan, 2008).

1 www.mobinil.com

2 www.vodafone.com.eg

3 www.etisalat.com.eg

4 www.mcit.gov.eg

Egypt has two main customer bases for mobile access: while the majority of users use prepaid and rely on text messaging, there is a limited, though important, high-end sector for local businesses and foreign investors. To serve the latter, mobile operators now offer the highest available 3G services – at present Etisalat offers up to 3.75G.

Part of the reason for the rapid increase in mobile diffusion has been the slow and limited capacity of Telecom Egypt,[5] the fixed-line incumbent, to expand its fixed services. Fixed telephone lines only increased from 7.5 million in 2000 to 10 million in 2007. Telecom Egypt is still the only fixed phone line provider, though a second provider is now in the pipeline as part of Telecom Egypt's privatisation process. The new fixed-line provider is not seen as a potential competitor to the mobile operators, as demand for mobile access has by now been deeply entrenched in Egypt.

Physical access to technology

The operating mobile networks in Egypt are:

- ECMS-Mobinil (GSM 900/1800, 2.5G)
- Vodafone Egypt Telecommunications S.A.E. (GSM 900/1800, 3G 2100)
- Etisalat Misr (GSM 900/1800, 3G 2100).

Currently, Egypt follows South Africa in having the highest number of mobile phones in Africa. Mobinil still leads the market, followed by Vodafone Egypt and Etisalat Misr. The entrance of Etisalat has markedly affected the provision of higher-end 3G services, which include high-speed mobile internet access, mobile television and video phone. Etisalat acquired its 3G licence in October 2007, after reaching an agreement with the national regulator, and was followed by Vodafone in early 2008. Their services cover Greater Cairo, Alexandria, Aswan, Sharm El Sheikh, Hurghada and Luxor. The user numbers for 3G services range between over 200,000 (GSMA, 2008) to the close to a million users reported by Etisalat (Yuan, 2008).

Despite widespread publicity for the new 3G services, the popularity of 3G in Egypt has market limitations. According to the MCIT, about 80% of the mobile customer base is interested in prepaid voice and texting services. For instance, in November 2007 Etisalat upgraded from 3.5G to 3.75G, which allows for high-speed uplink packet access (HSUPA), offering downlink speeds of up to 7.2 megabits per second

5 www.telecomegypt.com.eg

(Mbps), twice as fast as the earlier 3.5G downlink speeds. In early 2008, these high speeds were available in specific locations in and around Cairo only (even though coverage will be extended).

Mobile connection growth rates will most likely slow once the sector reaches saturation point, but an increase in services provided is foreseen, including high-end services.

National and international roaming

National roaming is an area where the competing companies collaborate. This collaboration allows a company to use the networks of its competitors until it builds an independent network of its own. In terms of network coverage, Mobinil and Vodafone have a fifty-fifty market share in Egypt. For the time being, Etisalat is using Mobinil's networks in the north, and Vodafone networks in the southern governorates.

For international roaming, the local mobile phone operators use GSM 900 networks and have roaming agreements with all major international operators. However, to date coverage is limited to Cairo, Alexandria and the Red Sea, from Suez to Sharm el-Sheikh, and the major towns along the Nile.

Mobile number portability (MNP)

Egypt introduced mobile number portability (MNP) in April 2008. MNP allows mobile phone users to retain their mobile telephone numbers when changing from one mobile network operator to another. MNP is provided by network software and service provider Telcordia's NPC and Giza Systems.

MNP will most probably elicit more competition in the high-end market, which has a lower threshold for customer retention.

Affordability and use

Although the entry of the third mobile operator Etisalat in 2007 was expected to introduce aggressive price wars between the providers, this has not materialized. Etisalat charges EGP 0.39/minute for prepaid and EGP 0.34/minute for postpaid. Mobinil offers prepaid services in the price range of EGP 0.35-0.45, while Vodafone offers the same services for EGP 0.39.

Instead of lower rates, operators are competing more towards offering wider coverage, improved service quality, voice clarity, and better customer service. The consumer is also being offered more perks due to competition. For example, Mobinil and Vodafone began offering lifetime subscriptions to their prepaid services that before were subject to termination if not promptly re-subscribed. Etisalat, being the newcomer, put forward lifetime free minutes to outbid its competitors' offers – in its plan, prepaid subscribers would get five minutes free per month for life (El Madany & El Sirgany, 2007).

Given general income levels in Egypt, it remains questionable whether 3G services will have a broad user base in the near future. And already the competition for prepaid subscribers (who are the majority) showed a decline of 12% in average revenue per user in 2007.[6] It is unlikely that incentives will attract more users to the prepaid market.

Trust in technology

From a purely technical standpoint, trust in technology is high in Egypt. Consumers offered a choice of providers are more assured that the competition will bring them higher quality of service and wider coverage, if not actually more competitive prices. Operators have been working on increasing their coverage, and on providing better services and better user tariffs (even if not as competitive as expected). Linked services like mobile banking are also being promoted. In general, for most middle-income Egyptians, and even those on the higher end of the lower-income bracket, having a cell phone is considered a necessity; and improvements in technology have made this possible.

Privacy concerns are another issue. The lack of privacy for information and communications technology (ICT) users, including mobile users, is a hot topic in Egypt, as in many countries these days. Cell phone users, until recently, were allowed to have anonymous user accounts. This changed in May 2008, when the National Telecom Regulatory Authority (NTRA),[7] citing public security reasons, requested mobile phone companies to block service to anonymous subscribers.

This move seemed to coincide with public strikes and upheavals that Egypt recently experienced due to rising living costs, especially as a result of higher food prices and low incomes. Many of these strikes have been organised using cell phones and the internet, which have been monitored by the government. Some activists tried to circumvent this by having anonymous connections – an option which has now been closed down.

In compliance with government measures, Vodafone has begun disabling text messaging capabilities for anonymous subscribers, and has asked them to come forward with their details. Mobinil linked the move to government plans for MNP. In general, subscribers are being told by the operators that their anonymous connections will be disconnected or suspended in the near future (Johnston, 2008).

Action steps

Egypt is pursuing its deregulation and liberalisation plan for the telecom sector in a timely and linear manner. Mobile communication, being one of the most progressive sub-sectors of the telecom field, has been enjoying a rapid increase in services and coverage, and at least some measure of competitive pricing since 1998. The mobile customer base has also grown rapidly over the years.

However, privacy issues are a concern. The Egyptian consumer is being actively encouraged by the government

6 Dun & Bradstreet's All Business: www.allbusiness.com

7 www.tra.gov.eg/english

to appropriate the latest technologies in order to grow the sector, but at the same time there is a lack of privacy in using the services, whether voice, text or content.

Given the present national, regional and international context, it is unlikely that there will be an easing up on privacy issues. In fact, more surveillance is expected. While there are limited public outbursts against the lack of mobile privacy in Egypt, these are neither strong nor numerous enough to force the government to reconsider.

References

Dun & Bradstreet's All Business: www.allbusiness.com

El Madany, S. and El Sirgany, S. (2007) Etisalat Launches Services May 1. *Daily Star Egypt*, 2 May. Available at: www.dailystaregypt.com/ ArticleID=6957

Etisalat Egypt: www.etisalat.com.eg

GSMA (GSM Association) (2008) GSMA Honours Egypt with Government Leadership Award. *GSM World*, 11 May. Available at: www.gsmworld.com/news/press_2008/press08_33.shtml

Johnston, C. (2008) Egypt asks mobile firms to bar anonymous users. *Reuters*, 5 May. Available at: www.reuters.com/article/latestCrisis/idUSL0562685

Ministry of Communication and Information Technology (MCIT): www.mcit.gov.eg

Mobinil Egypt: www.mobinil.com

National Telecom Regulatory Authority (NTRA): www.tra.gov.eg/english

Telecom Egypt (TE): www.telecomegypt.com

Vodafone Egypt: www.vodafone.com.eg

Yuan, Z. (2008) A Rising Sun Shines on the Nile River. *Huawei Service* (1). Available at: www.huawei.com/publications/view.do?id=3035&cid=5424&pid=2043

ETHIOPIA

Ethiopian Free and Open Source Software Network (EFOSSNET)
Abebe Chekol
www.efossnet.org

Introduction

Ethiopia is one of the poorest and least developed countries in the world, with an estimated per capita income of about USD 160 (World Bank, 2007a). With a population of 83 million, it is the second-most populous nation in Africa behind Nigeria. Amharic is the official language of the Ethiopian government, which follows a federal governing system with nine regional states.

Ethiopia's economy is largely based on agriculture, accounting for half of the country's gross domestic product (GDP), 60% of exports, and 80% of total employment. The share of agriculture, industry and services as a percentage of the GDP was 48%, 13% and 39% respectively in 2005 (World Bank, 2007a). The country's literacy rate is among the lowest on the continent, with only 42% of the adult population able to read and write.

Telecommunications was introduced in Ethiopia in 1894. Despite the very early introduction, Ethiopia has one of the most underdeveloped information and communications technology (ICT) infrastructures on the continent.

Table 1: Physical access to technology

Fixed telephone lines per 100 inhabitants (May 2008)	1.15
Mobile cellular telephone subscribers per 100 inhabitants (May 2008)	2.46
Computers per 100 inhabitants (2006)	0.31
Internet subscribers per 100 inhabitants (May 2008)	0.04
Broadband internet subscribers per 100 inhabitants (May 2008)	0.002
International internet bandwidth (Mbps) (2006)	2.79
Percentage of population covered by mobile cellular telephony (2006)	10
Internet access tariffs (20 hours per month), in USD, and as a percentage of per capita income	USD 12 and 92
Mobile cellular tariffs (100 minutes of use per month), in USD, and as a percentage of per capita income	USD 7 and 53
Radio sets per 100 inhabitants (2001)	18.35
Television sets per 100 inhabitants (2003)	0.79

Source: ITU Telecommunications Indicators Database (2007), ETC Company Profile 2007

This report reviews the current ICT infrastructure and access in Ethiopia and assesses the appropriateness of technology to communities and organisations. It also reviews locally relevant content, applications and services available for use by citizens and organisations. It then concludes with a review of important issues discussed in the report and provides recommendations as a way forward.

With an average of 1.15 main telephone lines per 100 inhabitants (the African average being 3.77 and sub-Saharan African average being 1.65), Ethiopia is ranked 32nd out of 53 countries. The number of computers per inhabitant is 0.31, a dramatically low figure even compared to regional figures for Africa averaging 2.24.

While the capacity of the landline telephone network is 1,123,281, the number of subscribers is 913,821. With a waiting list of over 100,000 in 2006, it shows that the current capacity might not be enough. Mobile network capacity has grown to 2,311,803, while mobile subscribers reached 1,935,000 in May 2008, which shows an 83% usage of the capacity.

Internet users in Ethiopia as of December 2007 totalled 164,000, with a 0.2% penetration, representing 0.4% of the users in Africa.[1] Under the rural connectivity project, between 2005 and May 2008, the Ethiopian Telecommunications Corporation (ETC) connected 10,353 villages. With regard to broadband, since its introduction in 2001, capacity has grown to 2.5 Gigabytes (Gbps), although the maximum speed that is available for subscription is 512 Kilobytes per second (Kbps). The number of subscribers reached 1,341 by May 2008.

The national state-run radio broadcaster, Radio Ethiopia, claims 80% coverage. It broadcasts in Amharic, Oromiffa, Tigrigna, Afar, Somali, Arabic, English and French. Another national station is Radio Fana, which also claims 80% coverage. The ruling government party, the Ethiopian People's Revolutionary Democratic Front (EPRDF), owns it. This technically makes it a private station. There are also three more recently licensed commercial radio services: Zami Public Connections (FM 90.7), Adei Promotions and Tinsaye Kinetbebat (FM 102.1) and Fana FM 98.1. There have been two new community radios set up, one in Dire Dawa and one in Yirgalem. At a regional level, there are now twenty state-owned services together with the eleven educational radio-broadcasting transmitters run by the Education Mass Media Agency (EMMA).

1 Internet World Stats Usage and Population Statistics: www.internetworldstats.com

Ethiopian Television (ETV) is the only TV broadcasting service in Ethiopia, with two channels. The first serves the whole country and the second broadcasts to Addis Ababa and its surrounds only.

A relatively small advertising market has made it difficult for investors to come forward to start up stations. In addition, the number of people with radio receivers is still relatively small. A recent survey found that around half (48.3%) of the population owns a radio set.

The main modern source of energy in Ethiopia is hydropower, and the Ethiopian Electric Power Corporation is the sole energy service provider in the country. Only 17% of the population uses electricity, 50% of which is consumed in Addis Ababa, and much of the rest in other urban areas (Admassie & Taye, 2007).

Key access programmes

The ICT infrastructure – both internet protocol (IP) and non-IP based – described in this section comprises the core programmes through which ICT-based activities and initiatives are being delivered.

WoredaNet is a terrestrial and satellite-based network whose prime objective is to provide ICT services to government at the federal, regional and *woreda* (district) levels. Currently over 565 *woredas* are connected to the network, and through the network are linked to regional and federal government offices. Moves are taking place to link *kebeles* (the lowest level of government administration) and it is reported that 6,000 are currently connected and 18,000 will be connected by the end of 2008.

One application of WoredaNet is videoconferencing facilities during court hearings held at the Federal Supreme Court,[2] as well as district-level courts. The Federal Supreme Court was one of the winners of the 2007 Technology in Government in Africa (TIGA) Awards, organised by the United Nations Economic Commission for Africa (UNECA) and the Canadian government in recognition of achievements that have led to changes at national, regional or provincial level (UNECA, 2007).

SchoolNet is a satellite-based network that covers secondary schools across Ethiopia.[3] Currently 668 secondary schools are connected to a gateway that provides video and audio streamed educational programming. Access to the internet is available through a downlink-only very small aperture terminal (VSAT) satellite connection. The fact that SchoolNet has one-way downlink capability only limits the ability of students to download useful material of their own choice.

The Engineering Capacity Building Programme (ECBP) in the Ministry of Capacity Building is undertaking a trial in which they are implementing 5,000 low-cost laptops in selected schools. This project uses the XO machines produced by the One Laptop per Child (OLPC) Foundation, designed for use by children in developing countries to provide them with access to knowledge (Chekol, 2007).

Another project is HealthNet, which enables health practitioners throughout Ethiopia to access a wide range of information services that are crucial to health care. Established by SATELLIFE in 1994 in collaboration with Addis Ababa University Medical School, there are 62 points that are connected and making use of HealthNet's services.

AgriNet is a broadband network linking 50 agricultural research centres, of which 34 fall under regional governments and are provided with communications linkages through eight VSATs.

Community radios have significant potential to reach communities. The government recently invited people seeking community radio licences to apply. There have been two new community radios set up, one in Dire Dawa and one in Yirgalem.

Various forms of telecentres have been widely deployed, often as pilot projects. The Ethiopian Information and Communication Technology Development Agency (EICTDA) estimates that there are 0.03 telecentres per 100 people. However, like many other countries in Africa, telecentres in rural areas have proved difficult to sustain once start-up funds have run dry.

The use of open standards is crucial for a country like Ethiopia. In this regard the Ethiopia Free and Open Source Software Network (EFOSSNET), established as an informal network of ICT professionals in February 2005 with support from UNESCO and the Catalysing Access to ICTs in Africa (CATIA) programme in association with APC, has been promoting FOSS in Ethiopia through training, research and consultation. The current level of awareness of FOSS in Ethiopia, including policy sensitivity to the issue of free software, can be attributed to the activities of EFOSSNET.[4]

Locally relevant content, applications and services

Based on a UN e-government survey, Ethiopia's e-government readiness index is 0.1857, which reflects improvement compared to the 2005 index, which was 0.1360. However, Ethiopia showed a decrease in its rank worldwide, from 170th in 2005 to 172nd in 2008 (United Nations, 2008). The e-government index is a composite measure of three areas: the web measure index, telecommunication infrastructure index and human capital index.

The key challenges for e-government in Ethiopia, as is the case for many other African countries, include the overall literacy rate, the development of telecommunication infrastructure, and the government's commitment to a more transparent and citizen-centred form of governance (Kitaw, 2006).

Through the public sector reform programme, government institutions began to provide information and services online. Some of the major content, applications and services provided by the government are delivered through the WoredaNet, SchoolNet, AgriNet and HealthNet programmes.

2 www.federalsupremecourt.gov.et

3 www.schoolnet.et

4 www.efossnet.org

Conclusion

Ethiopia faces a challenge in adopting and fully benefiting from the current ICT revolution and knowledge economy. Studies have indicated that a successful transition to a knowledge economy can be attained through four pillars: the prerequisite economic and institutional regime; education; information and communication technology; and innovation (World Bank, 2007b). In this regard, Ethiopia places significant emphasis on the first three areas, but there is little or no progress in the area of innovation other than a national science and technology innovation policy, drafted by the Ethiopian Science and Technology Agency in October 2006, which has yet to be approved (ESTA, 2006).

ICT infrastructure development has also been the biggest constraint in the use of ICTs in education (Hare, 2007) and business (Admassie & Taye, 2007), amongst other sectors of the economy.

Furthermore, a lack of resources, language barriers and a low level of skills and capacities, including awareness of the benefits of ICTs, are major hurdles to ICT development in the country. Most rural communities in Ethiopia, which form more than 80% of the population, have not woken up to the issues of the information society. The government and other stakeholders need to act together to enable Ethiopia to join the knowledge economy. The government, for its part, needs to open up the ICT market and create an enabling environment for the private sector to flourish.

References

Admassie, A. and Taye, W. (2007) *The Role of ICTs in Enhancing Trade and Economic Growth in Ethiopia*. Addis Ababa: UNECA.

Chekol, A. (2007) *Ethiopia Implementation Report: September 2007 to February 2008*. Addis Ababa: Engineering Capacity Building Programme (ECBP).

EFOSSNET: www.efossnet.org

ESTA (Ethiopian Science and Technology Agency) (2006) *National Science & Technology Innovation (STI) Policy*. Addis Ababa: ESTA.

ETC (Ethiopian Telecommunications Corporation) (2007) *Company Profile*. Addis Ababa: ETC.

Federal Supreme Court of Ethiopia: www.federalsupremecourt.gov.et

Hare, H. (2007) *ICT in Education in Ethiopia*. World Bank/infoDev. Available at: www.infodev.org/en/Publication.402.html

Internet World Stats Usage and Population Statistics: www.internetworldstats.com

ITU (International Telecommunication Union) (2007) *World Telecommunication/ICT Indicators Database*. Geneva: ITU.

Kitaw, Y. (2006) *E-government in Africa: Prospects, challenges and practices*. ITU/EPFL. Available at: people.itu.int/~kitaw/egov

SchoolNet: www.schoolnet.et

United Nations (2008) *The United Nations e-Government Survey 2008: From e-Government to Connected Governance*. New York: United Nations. Available at: unpan1.un.org/intradoc/groups/public/documents/UN/UNPAN028607.pdf

UNECA (United Nations Economic Commission for Africa) (2007) African government innovation in information technology rewarded. Press release, 2 May. Addis Ababa: UNECA. Available at: www.uneca.org/eca_resources/news/2007/070502tiga.htm

World Bank (2007a) *World Development Report 2007: Development and the Next Generation*. Washington: World Bank.

World Bank (2007b) *Building Knowledge Economies: Advanced Strategies for Development*. Washington: World Bank.

INDIA

IT for Change
Vivek Vaidyanathan and Gurumurthy Kasinathan
www.itforchange.net

Introduction

In the India country report for GISWatch 2007, we provided an overview of the Indian information and communications technology (ICT) sector, covering areas such as telecommunications, telecentres, community radio and the Indian information technology (IT) industry. This year's report looks at the theme of access, focusing on physical access to technology and the legal and regulatory framework, with special reference to community radio and ICTs in education policies.

In terms of physical access, this report will look at the increase in mobile telephony that has propelled India to second place globally in terms of mobile connectivity. Rural teledensity has registered an impressive growth rate. These developments have mostly been due to low talk-time tariffs, the availability of low-cost handsets and proactive measures by the government to boost rural connectivity.

The roll-out of the government-promoted Common Service Centre (CSC) telecentres has crossed the 50% mark. While it is too early to comment on how these centres will eventually turn out, we present the case study of another state-run e-government telecentre model (E-Gram), which appears to be a good instance of balancing social and economic goals.

In the section which addresses the legal and regulatory framework, we consider community radio. A year and a half after the enactment of the Community Radio Act, licences are just about to be issued. We examine the reasons for this delay, and offer points that need to be considered by the government and community radio sector to properly promote community radio.

A National Policy on ICT in School Education (NPISE) is being formulated, a process which highlights certain complexities relating to policy-making in the fields of ICTs and development. Development actors are often unwilling to engage with ICTs, believing that they undermine developmental principles and processes, while governments are under pressure to frame policy to regulate the use of ICTs. There is also a new set of actors – ICT for development or ICT4D organisations – who are eager to push for the use of ICTs in different sectors such as health and education. Policy-making tends to be distorted due to the different levels of participation by these actors. In the case of NPISE, technology companies who would gain from specific policy choices are part of the policy-making structures, themselves coordinated by ICT4D practitioners, while a large group of well-known education activists in India are conspicuous by their absence.

Physical access to technology

Mobile telephony

India has the world's second-largest wireless network with 261.09 million connections. This figure dwarfs fixed-line connections, which stand at 39.42 million (Prabhudesai, 2008).

Proactive government measures to boost rural connectivity

Over the past year, national teledensity has registered an impressive growth rate and stood at 26.22% at the end of March 2008 (TRAI, 2008). The boom in mobile telephony, aided by government intervention to improve rural connectivity, low talk-time tariffs, and the availability of low-cost handsets, has helped to boost rural teledensity from 2% in 2007 to 8% in 2008 – an increase of 300% within the span of one year (iGovernment Bureau, 2008). The government has set a target of around 25%, which seems possible to achieve given recent governmental measures to boost rural connectivity. Amongst other things:

- The rules surrounding the use of universal service obligation (USO) funds for promoting rural teledensity have been liberalised. The government has promised to use USO money to fund innovations which will boost rural connectivity, and has called on technology innovators to demonstrate their technologies in pilot projects. The government will fund the commercial roll-out of successful projects (Philip, 2007).
- The government is actively thinking of bringing in "niche operators" to cater for rural connectivity.[1] It has proposed that these operators should be allowed to set up services in rural areas that have less than 1% teledensity, and that they be spared paying spectrum fees (Thomas, 2008).
- The approval by the government to allow private telecom operators to share infrastructure with a view to bring down costs and boost telecom investment in rural areas is bearing fruit. This can be gauged from the recent tie-up between Bharati, Idea and Vodafone, to create a company which aims to set up 70,000 towers in two years, accessible to all operators (Borpujari, 2007).

Cheap talk-time tariffs and low-cost handsets

In 2006, companies like Bharat Sanchar Nigam Limited (BSNL) and Bharati-Airtel launched schemes such as the

1 Niche operators essentially operate in small areas such as a district, and offer mobile and broadband services.

One India plan, which allowed customers to make calls anywhere in India for just one rupee (INR 1)[2] per minute. Over the past few months there have been a series of price cuts in talk-time tariffs (popularly referred to as airtime in countries like the United States) by all major telecom players, which puts affordable mobile telephony in the hands of consumers. And it is the state-run telecom player BSNL which has not only matched the competition but bettered it. In addition to cutting subscriber trunk dialling (STD)[3] charges on mobile and fixed-line phones by up to 50%, BSNL has reduced STD rates for rural customers to 80 paisa[4] per minute, and has brought down the entry-level cost of its flagship Super One India Plan from INR 799 (USD 20) to INR 499 (USD 13), which should bring in further customers (Business Standard, 2008). It has also announced that it is doing away with monthly rental charges in rural areas to boost rural connectivity.[5]

Cellular service providers have also been bundling low-cost handsets along with their mobile connections. Reliance Communications was the first to offer handsets in the range of INR 777 to INR 888 (USD 19 to USD 23) (Prabhudesai, 2007) while Spice Telecom is offering handsets for INR 599 (USD 15). The trend of bundling low-cost tariffs with low-cost handsets is a low-margin/high-volume business. It is expected that by 2010 the number of mobile users in rural India will be as high as 167 million users, and this business model will go some way in helping reach this figure. Figure 1 shows the projected growth rate of low-cost handsets in India (Gupta, 2007).

Figure 1: **Growth in low-cost handsets**

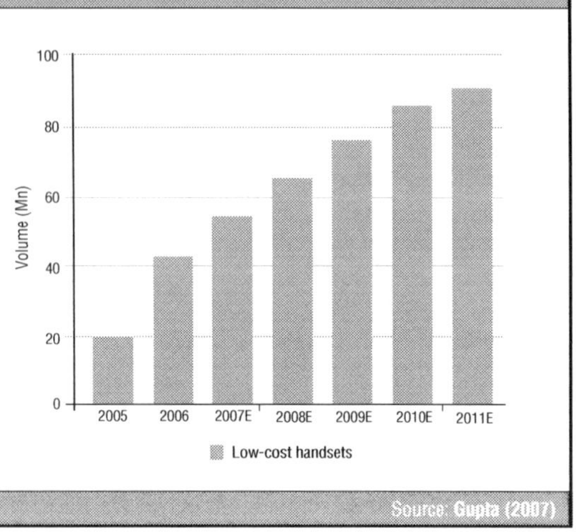

Source: Gupta (2007)

The net effect of all these measures is that it is has brought down the prices of mobile connectivity and allows even poor people to get connected.

Common Service Centres

The CSCs form an integral part of India's National e-Governance Plan, and are the delivery points to access government services. This programme aims to provide internet connectivity through 100,000 centres to the 600,000 villages of India and is quite ambitious in its goals. As per the latest statistics given by the Ministry of Communications and Information Technology (MCIT), over 61,000 centres have been rolled out, and the rest (40,000) will be rolled out by the end of the year (MCIT, 2008). In quite a few cases, contracts for these centres have been bagged by private enterprises, such as Reliance Communications in West Bengal (EFY News, 2007), and UTL and Orion e-Gov Services Consortium in Jharkhand.[6]

While it is too early to comment on how these centres will turn out, one challenge would be balancing the delivery of government services and social services with limited revenue possibilities through commercial services. IT for Change (ITfC) had an opportunity to study a relatively new e-government telecentre project initiated by the state government of Gujarat.[7] The project, called E-Gram (or E-Village), aims to digitise the state's Gram Panchayats – local government bodies at the village level – and provide services to rural citizens.

The E-Gram initiative in Gujarat

The E-Gram telecentre initiative is a relatively new one, first piloted in 2001 in one district, but now extended to all districts of Gujarat. The project aims to digitise all the Gram Panchayats in the state. An E-Gram centre is located in a public space, usually a Panchayat office. Each centre has a computer with an internet connection.

While the aim of E-Gram was to digitise Panchayats, the centres that we visited had achieved that and much more, which makes it worthy of mention.

How E-Gram is making a difference:[8]

- E-Gram is one of those few e-government initiatives which links key development sectors to digital technologies, while other similar projects tend to be driven by IT departments independent of a developmental frame of reference. This project works in close proximity to line departments in order to collate and digitise information in the health, education, and social services sectors, amongst others.

2 1 USD = approximately INR 40, so one rupee is USD 0.025 or 2.5 cents.

3 Subscriber trunk dialling refers to a system allowing subscribers to dial trunk (long distance) calls without operator assistance. For more information, see en.wikipedia.org/wiki/Subscriber_trunk_dialling

4 1 rupee = 100 paisa.

5 BSNL: www.bsnl.in/newsdetailed.php?news_id=419

6 Government of Jharkhand, Ministry of Information Technology, Common Services Centre Scheme: www.jharkhand.gov.in/depts/infor/infor_csc.asp

7 The case study on E-Gram draws from an ongoing study by ITfC, funded by the Social Science Research Council, New York.

8 For a more detailed account of the E-Gram operations and the results of our visits, see www.indiatogether.org/2008/may/gov-telectr.htm

- The second promising feature of this project is that while its operations are outsourced, the government retains control over operations. As a result, the profit goals of the private operators are reasonably balanced with social objectives.

Measures for success of the project, as defined by the project itself, include close linkages between development priorities and technology, a good public-private partnership mix, and decentralised governance. These appear to have been achieved to a reasonably satisfactory level by the project, which sets a good example for others to follow.

Legal and regulatory framework

Community radio

Experiences in India and in other parts of the world suggest that community radio stations give communities an opportunity to voice issues that are of importance to them. They can also be used to mobilise communities on various social issues. Some of the community radio stations in operation in India are Namma Dhwani run by Myrada and Voices[9] (in the state of Karnataka), Ujhas Radio run by Kutch Mahila Vikas Sangathan (Gujarat), and Sangam Radio run by Deccan Development Society (Andhra Pradesh). Many community radio stations have been operated by state-run institutions, such as universities or broadcasting agencies.

The government of India enacted its Community Radio Policy in 2006 to enable community-based institutions to apply for radio licences. Since the enactment of the policy, over 150 institutions have applied for community radio licences, of which 76 have been granted letters of intent, which is a preliminary step towards securing broadcast rights (Ministry of Information and Broadcasting, 2008). However, to date just a single community radio licence has been issued (Iyer, 2008).

Community radio activist Sajan Veniyoor points out some of the reasons for the delay.[10] He says that while campus radio station[11] applications are processed through a single clearance system, approval of community radio station applications have to go through four ministries, each of which have their own requirements. Even after these clearances come through, there are separate applications for obtaining spectrum and wireless frequency (Ministry of Information and Broadcasting, 2006).

Veniyoor points out that these complexities have led to a situation where a licence which should have been procured within a year is not anywhere close to being approved.

9 Namma Dhwani Community Media Centre: portal.unesco.org/ci/en/ev.php-URL_ID=14615&URL_DO=DO_TOPIC&URL_SECTION=201.html

10 Interview by email with Sajan Veniyoor conducted on 11 June 2008.

11 Campus radio stations can be set up by recognised universities and pre-date the current community radio policy.

National policy on ICTs in education

Early this year, the Ministry of Human Resource Development (MHRD) initiated a process of formulating a National Policy on ICT in School Education (NPISE). Given the huge potential and (pedagogical) complexities in using ICTs in education, such policy guidelines are quite necessary. However, for meaningful policy formulation, it is essential that the process be driven by education experts who are familiar with the education contexts, challenges and priorities in the country, and who can visualise how ICTs can assist in meaningful academic transactions.

In the case of the NPISE, the policy-facilitating process has been outsourced to private ICT4D[12] organisations which do not appear to have the requisite experience in Indian education. Moreover, the policy-drafting group is dominated by technology vendors, and has very few educationists, even though India has a strong and active education community. Perhaps as a consequence of these structural lapses, the policy draft conspicuously lacks linkages to accepted education philosophies and perspectives,[13] as well as critical challenges being faced today in Indian education.[14] Also missing in the draft policy are possibilities such as the One Laptop per Child (OLPC) scheme (an alternative to the Intel PC, produced specially for use by schools, with features such as robustness, a user interface configured for children, and wire mesh internet access possibilities which makes connectivity easier), open source applications (though at least two states in India have already announced their preference for open source), and open access/open content.

ICT in school education is really a curricular decision, and ICT in education policy is education policy rather than IT policy.[15] What is needed is for education experts to engage with technological possibilities, rather than have technologists with little understanding of education driving this policy.

The issue points to a central principle of policy-making – that public policy needs to be driven by accepted public principles, rather than private or commercial interests, and that the role of public institutions in this process is important. Especially in the context of policies relating to use of ICTs,[16] this has often been ignored and needs correction.

12 Those with a technology or generic "technology in development" background, rather than any expertise in development or education.

13 The National Curriculum Framework, 2005, is one such landmark document in the Indian education scene. It includes a position paper on education technology which has been ignored in the policy draft. Available at: www.ncert.nic.in/sites/publication/schoolcurriculum/NCFR%202005/contents2.htm

14 Such as the dismal state of teacher education or the highly centralised nature of the public school system, which curtails autonomy and local curriculum development. The use of ICTs in education needs to address these challenges.

15 The complete details of the policy-making process and a full set of events can be obtained on the ITfC website: www.itforchange.net/index.php?option=com_content&task=view&id=204&Itemid=1

16 For instance, in many states, e-government road maps are being made by IT consultants who may not have much familiarity with governance and political processes and structures. These roadmaps often diverge from stated constitutional and governance goals, especially those relating to equity and social justice.

Action steps

The one point which stands out in this year's report is the phenomenal increase in rural teledensity, which has gone up from 2% to 8% over the period of a year. Considering the fact that for the last few years the figure of rural teledensity was stagnant at a little over 1%, the present growth rate is nothing less than remarkable. Clearly, proactive measures taken by the government and the availability of low-cost handsets, coupled with cheap talk-time tariffs, are working in connecting rural India. It is too early to comment on the roll-out of CSCs, though undoubtedly it is a programme unique in its scale and ambition.

On the regulatory front, the policy planning and implementation process could be strengthened for the NPISE and community radio policy, respectively, by involving sectoral partners and experts and making the process more consultative.

Specifically, for community radio:

- At this stage, what is probably required is expediting the process of issuing licences as a priority. The single clearance process currently available to campus radio applications could be extended to all community radio applicants.
- Funding seems to be another challenge. The costs associated with setting up a radio station are high, and there are calls for the government to set up community radio support funds which would provide assistance to those licence holders who need it the most. The Namma Banuli scheme enacted by the Karnataka government, which subsidises the cost of starting community radio stations and provides training, is a step in this direction (Radio Duniya, 2008).
- For its part, civil society is doing whatever it can to bring together the community radio sector and address the issue. The formation of the Community Radio Forum, an organisation that promotes community radio by addressing policy issues, and provides training to community radio station operators on practical aspects of programming, editing and broadcasting, is one initiative. But there is room for other interventions.
- Other challenges – such as lifting a ban on broadcast news and current affairs, as well as restrictions on foreign funding – need to be faced down the road. But for the present it would suffice to say that the real challenge lies in ensuring that licences are issued, and the entire process of policy-making becomes more clear and transparent. ■

References

Borpujari, U. (2007) A towering biz for telecom. *Deccan Herald*, 24 December. Available at: www.deccanherald.com/Content/Dec242007/eb2007122342788.asp

Business Standard (2008) BSNL reduces STD rates. *Business Standard*, 9 June. Available at: www.business-standard.com/common/storypage_c_online.php?leftnm=10&bKeyFlag=IN&autono=39554

EFY News (2007) Reliance bags West Bengal's E-governance project. *EFY News Network*, 9 May. Available at: www.efytimes.com/efytimes/fullnews.asp?edid=18811

Gupta, R. (2007) Low cost handset: Connecting Bharat with India. *iGovernment*, 6 November. Available at: www.igovernment.in/site/low-cost-handset-connecting-bharat-with-india

iGovernment Bureau (2008) Rural tele-density logs 8% growth in India. *iGovernment*, 14 March. Available at: www.igovernment.in/site/rural-tele-density-logs-8-growth-in-india

Iyer, A. (2008) Satara based MVSS is first NGO to get CR licence. *Radioandmusic.com*, 25 July. Available at: www.radioandmusic.com/content/editorial/news/satara-based-mvss-first-ngo-get-cr-licence#story

MCIT (Ministry of Communications and Information Technology) (2008) Common Services Centre Status at a Glance (May 1, 2008). Available at: www.mit.gov.in/default.aspx?id=825

Ministry of Information and Broadcasting (2006) Policy Guidelines for Setting Up Community Radio Stations in India. Available at: mib.nic.in/CRS/CRBGUIDELINES041206.pdf

Ministry of Information and Broadcasting (2008) Letters of Intent issued against New Guidelines (announced in December 2006) as on 30.4.2008. Available at: mib.nic.in/CRS/crsloi090508.htm

Namma Dhwani Community Media Centre: portal.unesco.org/ci/en/ev.php-URL_ID=14615&URL_DO=DO_TOPIC&URL_SECTION=201.html

Philip, J. (2007) DoT to fund innovations in telecom technology. *Times of India*, 26 December. Available at: infotech.indiatimes.com/Tech_News/News/DoT_to_fund_innovations_in_telecom_/articleshow/2651573.cms

Prabhudesai, A. (2007) Indian telecom industry surprised by Reliance offers! *Trak.in Indian Business Blog*, 3 May. Available at: trak.in/tags/business/2007/05/03/indian-telecom-industry-surprised-by-reliance-offers

Prabhudesai, A. (2008) India overtakes U.S. to become 2nd largest wireless network in the world. *Trak.in Indian Business Blog*, 26 April. Available at: trak.in/tags/business/2008/04/26/india-overtakes-us-to-become-2nd-largest-wireless-network-in-the-world

Radio Duniya (2008) Namma Banuli (India) community radio scheme. *Radio Duniya*, 13 February. Available at: radioduniya.in/news/news-details.asp?News=Namma-Banuli-(India)-community-radio-scheme&NewsID=13472&NewsCategeory=community%20radio

Thomas, T. (2008) DoT to allow niche operators in rural areas. *The Hindu Business Line*, 27 March. Available at: www.thehindubusinessline.com/2008/03/27/stories/2008032752270400.htm

TRAI (Telecom Regulatory Authority of India) (2008) India becomes second largest wireless network in the world. Press release, 25 April. Available at: www.trai.gov.in/trai/upload/PressReleases/566/pr25apr08no43.pdf

JAMAICA

Caribbean Programme in Telecommunications Policy and Management, University of the West Indies
Hopeton Dunn
hopetondunn@gmail.com

Introduction

Jamaica is known around the world as a picturesque Caribbean country with unique creative talents, athletic prowess and a distinctive and vibrant cultural environment. But beyond the postcard images and engrossing music, it is a country making important strides in information and communications technologies (ICTs), while still wrestling with other important social and economic challenges.

As the largest English-speaking country in the region, Jamaica is a leading member of the Caribbean Community and Common Market (CARICOM). The recorded population at the start of 2008 was 2.68 million, with about 1.3 million of that number representing the labour force (Statistical Institute of Jamaica, 2008). The officially estimated unemployment rate is 10.2%. Approximately 20% of the population is deemed functionally illiterate (Statistical Institute of Jamaica, 2008; UNDP, 2008).

Classified as a country with "medium" levels of human development, Jamaica was ranked 101st of 177 countries in the 2007/2008 Human Development Index (UNDP, 2008). In terms of business development, the country is 63rd out of 173 in the World Bank's "ease of doing business" index, and 11th in terms of "ease of starting a business" (World Bank, 2008).

The country has made important strides in terms of access to ICTs over the past decade. It boasts one of the highest teledensity levels in the world among both developing and developed countries. Survey data from 2007 confirmed that 94% of low-income Jamaicans were users of the mobile phone (Dunn, 2007), with an even higher level among other social classes. According to the industry regulator, the Office of Utilities Regulation (OUR), Jamaica's overall phone penetration level was 106 phones to every 100 inhabitants in 2006 (PIOJ, 2007). This is a substantial improvement on fixed-line teledensity ratios of fewer than 20 lines per 100 people less than a decade ago.

This is accounted for in part by a decade-old liberalisation policy, and the resulting price reductions generated through competition in the delivery of mobile telecommunications services. The Telecommunications Act (2000) enabled new competitive entrants to challenge the once monopoly provider Cable & Wireless in a rapidly expanding, but still small, telecoms market. Companies such as the Irish-owned Digicel Jamaica, and the US-controlled consortium Centennial (now MiPhone, owned by America Movil), generated rapid rate reductions for mobile calls, and helped foster the growth of prepaid credit services using heavy media marketing and reductions in the price of handsets.

In line with global patterns, many owners of fixed-line phones switched entirely to cellular phones, leading to an estimated 15% reduction in fixed-line ownership in Jamaica between 2005 and 2007. The entry in 2006 of triple-play provider Columbus Communications, trading as Flow, has brought additional competition to the fixed-line services market, but in a manner that seeks to combine this service with the provision of digital subscriber television and high-speed internet to homes.

Improving ICT access

The country's global competitiveness in the growth of broadband and other ICT services appears to be faltering, despite promising early trends and the phenomenal expansion in mobile voice telephony. In 2005 Jamaica's ranking fell from 59th to 85th in the UN E-Government Survey. Similarly, its e-readiness ranking has fallen from 46th in 2007 to 49th in 2008, despite a marginal improvement in the actual e-readiness score. Other recent ICT indices have shown Jamaica to be 45th in the 2006/2007 Network Readiness Index and 54th in the International Telecommunication Union (ITU) 2007 Digital Access Index.

Whereas the World Bank recorded overall internet usage among Jamaicans at 46.4% in 2006, usage among low-income groups is only 21% (World Bank, 2006; Dunn, 2007). In the case of household broadband penetration across all socio-economic groupings, levels are dismally low at approximately 13% (Budde, 2007). As fixed lines are the primary means for household internet connectivity, a fixed-line teledensity of 14.3% (Budde, 2007) foreshadows the relatively low internet uptake. While there is potential for expanding access via mobile broadband, and through new fixed-line provider Flow, effective access will remain elusive without adequate policy provisions and resourcing.

Slow uptake of the internet could also be attributed to the fact that most Jamaicans are lacking affordable hardware for internet connectivity, with a national stock of only 6.7 computer units per 100 persons in 2006 (World Bank, 2006). This contrasts with almost universal mobile penetration, and a high number of television sets, which stood at 70% of Jamaican households in 2006 (World Bank, 2006).

In terms of network connectivity, Jamaica's telecommunications system boasts advanced international submarine cable and satellite links into local digital networks, including a national fibre optic ring and increasing but still limited WiMAX coverage. The actual usage of this high-end infrastructure, however, is confined mostly to middle- and upper-income persons and businesses. It is expected that more WiMAX spectrum will become available in 2009 for residential areas, when the results of a spectrum auction in the 2.5 gigahertz (GHz) band begin to take effect. However, this proposal, led by the Spectrum Management Authority (SMA), may require an expansion in the range of spectrum capacity being auctioned if the initiative is to make a real impact on public WiMAX access.

Approaches to universal access

Universal access, in its original manifestation, referred to a "situation where every person has a reasonable means of access to a publicly available telephone" (Intven, 2000). As the concept has evolved, universal access is now also used in reference to internet connectivity. Targeted access initiatives should consider not only physical access to ICTs, but also the cost and training required to increase levels of information literacy and core competencies in the utilisation of digital media. The challenge is to secure not just formal access, but also effective access, as discussed by Wilson (2006) and by Barclay and Duggan (2008). This approach would mitigate the scenario in which, as "developing countries and organizations struggle to keep pace with the competitive pressures of globalization, it is becoming apparent that mere physical access to ICT solves only a small part of the puzzle" (Barclay & Duggan, 2008). Digital effectiveness would be enhanced through fostering an environment of effective access, creative innovation and knowledge-sharing.

Legal and policy reforms

Jamaica's legal and regulatory framework for telecommunications and ICTs includes the centrepiece Telecommunications Act (2000), which is currently in need of reform. There is also the Fair Competition Act, the existence of the Office of Utilities Regulation (OUR), the SMA, a National ICT Strategic Plan, Universal Access Fund (UAF) provisions and a new e-transactions law. This Electronic Transactions Act, which was approved by Parliament in April 2007, is aimed at promoting confidence and security in electronic transactions. The Act gives legal validity to electronic documents and digital signatures. However, its counterpart pieces of legislation, the Cyber Crimes Bill and the Data Protection Bill, have remained under deliberation for years without approval. This piecemeal and stop-start approach is symptomatic of the tendency, not unique to Jamaica, for ICT legislation to lag well behind industry innovations and create a drag on global competitiveness and on public and investor confidence. The failure to reactivate the Jamaica Telecommunications Advisory Council, provided for in the Telecommunications Act, as well as ministerial changes, may be contributing factors to an apparent lack of sustained public policy coordination in the sector.

The country has however benefited by being the first in the Anglophone Caribbean to begin the process of liberalisation, which started in 1998. Following a period of contentious and protracted negotiations and litigations, the government of Jamaica and Cable & Wireless struck an agreement in September 1999 for the opening up of the sector to competition on a phased basis. This set the pattern for similar arrangements in other countries in the Caribbean region, and opened the way for the entry of additional regional service providers, initially in the mobile sector.

This process of phased competition took place between 2000 and 2003 (Dunn, 2000). The number of telecommunications licences issued by the government increased from two in 1999 to 426 by 2007. Similarly, the number of internet service providers (ISPs) grew from 45 in 2001 to 80 in 2006 (PIOJ, 2007). Despite liberalisation, and the number of early ISP start-ups, the cost of high-speed internet connections (and attendant hardware systems) has not been reduced significantly enough to inspire an explosion in popular internet usage.

Universal access provisions

An important provision in the Telecommunications Act was the inclusion of universal service obligations (USOs) on provider companies, and the establishment of a Universal Service Fund (in practice referred to as a Universal Access Fund or UAF). However, no clear mechanism existed for the financing of the USOs and the floating of the fund. In 2005, the government mandated a universal access levy to be imposed on incoming international calls. This order, which came into effect in June 2005, required mainly external carriers to pay USD 0.02 per minute for calls terminating on mobile phones, and USD 0.03 per minute to fixed-line phones. The aim of the levy was to provide universal broadband internet services to Jamaicans. By 2007 the UAF had collected JMD 2.556 billion, the equivalent of USD 36.5 million (UAF, 2006; Government of Jamaica, 2008).

Funds collected through the USO levy are used to finance a national e-learning project called e-Learning Jamaica, with the objective of utilising state-of-the-art ICTs in Jamaican schools in order to improve the quality of education. While the e-Learning Jamaica project evidently faces no shortage of money, its pilot phase has made a slow and halting start, with limited reported impact to date on the learning environment and the ICT sector.

Among the challenges faced by the project was limited prior exposure to technology amongst the majority of the island's teachers in the secondary school system. This meant that the capacity to use the technology effectively did not exist. At least one lesson to be learnt from this experience, even if as yet inconclusive, is that financial resources are a necessary but not a sufficient condition for the growth and expansion of ICT learning in the global South. Careful strategic planning, deliberate and early exposure to information literacy among trainers, and the need for more detailed pre-planning, are among the requirements for successfully launching national-level e-learning initiatives. As it turns out, Jamaica's central government has started to call on the accumulated levy resources of the UAF for use within the consolidated fund from which general government expenditure is drawn. The e-Learning Jamaica project may in the future have to compete for resources that were originally designated for its sole use.

E-Powering Jamaica: ICT roadmap

In terms of broader ICT strategy, the overarching approach is articulated in a five-year national ICT plan entitled E-Powering Jamaica 2008-2012 (Dunn & Duggan, 2007). The plan aims at integrating ICTs at all levels to form a knowledge-based and educated society. It identifies eight specific but interconnected areas for strategic emphasis, as set out in Figure 1.

Making the transition

In order to redress the rich-poor imbalance in internet access in Jamaica, gaps in accessibility, availability and affordability of broadband connectivity need to be addressed. There is also a need to better utilise avenues of connectivity that are already available. The mobile phone has a small screen, but can serve as an important gateway to economic and social opportunities for the poor, who have adopted it as their technology platform. Although commonly seen as a channel for "useless chatter", empirical data are emerging to suggest that the mobile handset is more often a link to economic survival, and is used for things like job hunting, telework, or as a micro-business tool for low-income Jamaicans (Dunn, 2008).

As in many countries in Asia and Latin America, Jamaican entrepreneurs have been experimenting with mobile phone business possibilities, including the resale of credit, phone repairs and "unlocking", and the marketing of mobile attachments, as well as with m-banking services. These initiatives, like micro, small and medium enterprises (MSMEs) the world over, may hold the keys to increased youth and inner-city employment.

But such initiatives also require capital and management expertise. Agencies willing and available to extend low-interest loans and conduct suitable training appear far too limited in number, and too traditional in their social reach and policies. Yet, as we have argued elsewhere, the mobile phone may offer an opportunity to help transition the mass of low-income users into more widespread mobile broadband usage (Dunn, 2008).

It now appears clear that the Jamaican universal service levy needs to be re-purposed from solely providing e-learning support to schools, to incorporate other goals such as helping finance young and emerging creative industry entrepreneurs in the nascent ICT sector. Low-cost loans for computers, and more widely available management and information literacy training, could help establish more small cybercafés and telecentres in rural and low-income urban areas that are currently underserved. The increase in MSMEs in the ICT sector would not only increase broadband connectivity, but also assist low-income persons with business start-ups that could lead to greater economic independence and global marketing.

There is also the need for greater understanding among citizens of the ways in which the internet and other ICT tools can be empowering as well as socially challenging. An emphasis on youth ICT training, low-cost business start-up credit, encouragement of innovation, and appropriate forms of information literacy in schools are among sustainable ways of seeking to make the transition from the existing high mobile voice penetration in Jamaica to an environment of greater access to other productive broadband applications for citizens and small business operators.

Figure 1: **Strategic roadmap of ICT development for Jamaica**

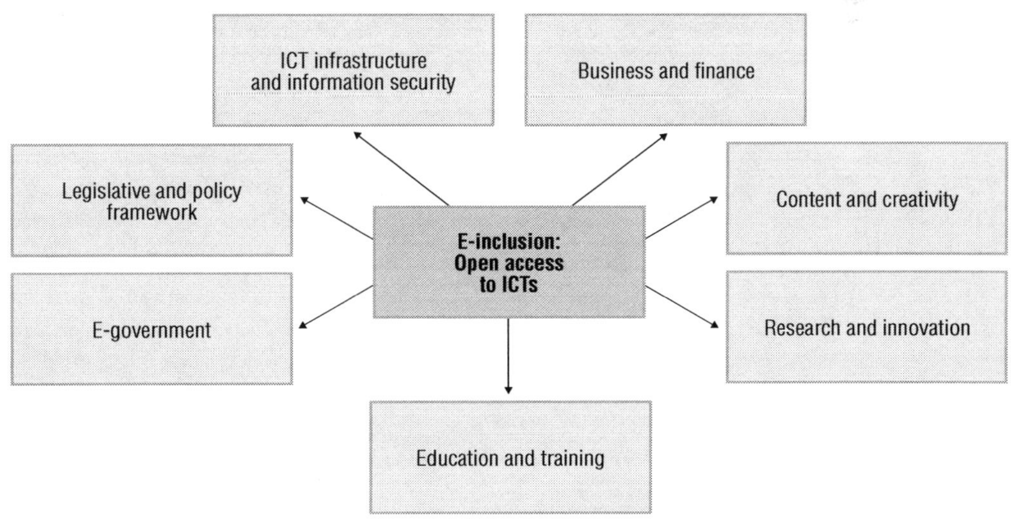

Source: **Dunn and Duggan (2007)**

Action steps

Jamaica has successfully transitioned from limited voice telephony access ten years ago to virtual ubiquity of voice telephony within the population. Universal access policies must now be redirected to attaining effective popular broadband access, legislative reforms, and inter-linkage of ICTs with entrepreneurship, cultural products and improved services delivery. Some of the steps that need to be taken include:

- The re-purposing of a portion of the UAF towards youth entrepreneurship in ICTs, through micro, small and medium-size cyber enterprises, and through research and innovation.
- The establishment of incubators for the best young Jamaican ICT minds, in order to arrive at unconventional, yet appropriate, uses of Web 2.0 and other emerging ICT technologies.
- Fast-tracking "digital switchover" in the free-to-air broadcast and subscriber television sectors.
- More and better digital broadband usage among the creators of cultural content, and the fostering of a culture of active internet usage, including the systematic uploading of local content and more widespread engagement in global online marketing.
- The provision by private sector service providers of more broadband-enabled mobile devices at low cost (with low connectivity costs as well) in order to stimulate higher levels of broadband penetration and effective access in the shortest possible time.

References

Barclay, C. and Duggan, E. (2008) Rethinking the Digital Divide: Towards a Path of Digital Effectiveness. Proceedings of the 41st Annual Hawaii International Conference on System Sciences.

BuddeComm: www.budde.com.au

Dunn H.S. (2000) *Telecommunications and Information Technology: Their Impact on Employment and Trade Unions in the Caribbean*. Kingston: FES.

Dunn, H.S. and Duggan, E. (2007) *E-Powering Jamaica: National ICT Strategic Plan 2007-2012*. Kingston.

Dunn, H.S. and Johnson Brown, S. (2007) Information Literacies and Digital Empowerment in the Global South. Report prepared for UNESCO on the occasion of the International Association of Media and Communication Research (IAMCR) 50th Anniversary Conference 2007.

Dunn, H.S. (2007) *Mobile Opportunities: Poverty and Telephony Access in Latin America and the Caribbean. Jamaica Country Study*. TPM-MSB, UWI.

Dunn, H.S. (2008) "Wha' a Gwaan?": Research Report on a Qualitative Study of Mobile Telephony and Poverty in Jamaica. TPM-MSB, UWI, Mona.

Government of Jamaica (2007) The Jamaica Telecommunications Policy 2007 (Draft). Kingston: Ministry of Industry, Technology, Energy and Commerce.

Government of Jamaica (2008) Ministry Paper: Performance of the Universal Access Fund Company Limited (UAFCL) for Financial Year 2006/2007 and Focus for Financial Year 2007/2008. Available at: www.memt.gov.jm/PDF%20Files/Ministry%20Papers%202007/UAF.pdf

Intven, H. (ed.) (2000) *Telecommunications Regulation Handbook: Module 6*. Washington: *info*Dev and the World Bank.

PIOJ (Planning Institute of Jamaica) (2007) Vision 2030 Jamaica: National Development Plan, Information and Communications Technology Sector Plan. Kingston: PIOJ.

Statistical Institute of Jamaica (2008) Jamaican Statistics. Available at: www.statinja.com/stats.html

Sullivan, N. (2007) *You Can Hear Me Now: How Microloans and Cell Phones are Connecting the World's Poor to the Global Economy*. San Francisco: Jossey-Bass.

UNDP (United Nations Development Programme) (2008) Jamaica: The Human Development Index - going beyond income. Available at: hdrstats.undp.org/countries/country_fact_sheets/cty_fs_JAM.html

UAF (Universal Access Fund Company Limited) (2006) Sensitizing the Jamaican Diaspora on the Universal Service Levy.

Wilson, E. (2006) *The Information Revolution and Developing Countries*. Cambridge, MA: MIT Press.

World Bank (2006) ICT at a Glance: Jamaica. Available at: devdata.worldbank.org/ict/jam_ict.pdf

World Bank (2008) *Doing Business 2008: Comparing Regulation in 178 Countries*. Washington: World Bank and the International Finance Corporation.

KAZAKHSTAN

Andrew Beklemishev

Introduction

Kazakhstan is the ninth largest country in the world in terms of size but is one of the countries with the lowest population density, with a little over fifteen million people living in its vast territory. Rich in natural resources – mainly oil, gas, and metal ores, including large deposits of uranium – Kazakhstan has an economy that is largely dependent on the extraction of these resources. Surging oil, gas and metals prices on world markets in recent years allowed the country to enjoy nearly 10% growth in gross domestic product (GDP) in 2002-2006. However, it was affected by the world's financial liquidity crisis in 2007, due to a dependency on credit from abroad by the banking sector.

The country's booming financial and construction sectors were affected the most. GDP increased by only 8.5% that year and economic growth is expected to slump further in 2008. Growth of money supply and increasing food prices have caused a spike in the inflation rate, which was 18.8% at year-end 2007.[1] Experts expect the economy to improve only by the end of 2008, given the government continues its reforms and is able to manage the inflation rate and provide assistance to the troubled sectors of the economy.

Rapid economic growth in recent years, high literacy levels, the president's long-term vision and new government programmes were among the key driving factors for increased computer and internet penetration in Kazakhstan, allowing the country's information society to develop. Rising disposable incomes allow Kazakhstanis to buy computers. Decreasing internet tariffs – although still relatively expensive compared to European Union (EU) member states (Political Intelligence/Internews, 2006) – and an increase in the availability of broadband internet in large cities allowed for easy access to global information and promoted information sharing and interaction between citizens. The implementation of two state programmes – the Programme on Reduction of Information Inequity and the Programme on Implementation of Electronic Government in the Republic of Kazakhstan – is expected to provide access to key government services in the near future for all, but especially to underserved and vulnerable groups (Beklemishev & Tsekhovoi, 2006).

Physical access to technology

In order for the information society to develop successfully, the freedom of access to information has to be ensured. In the digital age, the most efficient means of access to information are digital: telephones, mobile phones, computers, information kiosks, etc. It is therefore important to look at the availability of technology in a country as a prerequisite for the development of the information society – both the hardware available and the services that go with it, such as internet access. It is also always necessary to keep in mind that the technology in itself is not enough for the information society to thrive.

Fixed-line and wireless communication technologies include various options for connectivity, but all are dependent, in one way or another, on the country's communications "backbone" – a system of networks of various operators that connect cities and connect to the networks of other countries. In Kazakhstan, this backbone is formed by the networks of seven major operators and consists mostly of fibre-optic lines, although satellite and wireless radio relay connections are widely used as well.

Kazakhtelecom, the largest telecom operator in the country and a de facto monopoly, has the largest network by far, which includes fibre-optic lines connecting all major cities of the country and connections to all bordering countries. The total length of this fibre-optic network is close to 12,000 kilometres, with maximum data transmission rate capabilities of ten gigabits per second (Gbps) between three of the largest cities, and one Gbps between other cities (Kazakhtelecom, 2007). Some of the other major operators have built their own fibre-optic networks and are continuing investment in this activity, while others are relying on Kazakhtelecom's infrastructure.

Satellite communications are used widely in Kazakhstan, providing a cost-effective way to cover large distances. Some telecom operators, such as Nursat (owned by Kazakhtelecom), rely almost exclusively on digital satellite connectivity as the backbone for their networks. Very small aperture terminals (VSATs) are very popular and provide both internet and voice services; their number exceeds thousands of installations. Kazakhstan launched its own satellite in 2007, called KazSat-1, and plans to launch at least another three in the next few years. These will, supposedly, eliminate the country's need to use other satellites and will provide a wide range of satellite-based services for its citizens, including digital television, internet and voice connectivity. Experts have argued against the need for such investment, despite the government's firm position.

Fixed-line telecommunication is the most basic way to access information. However, in addition to regular voice communications services, additional services can be provided using the basic telephone line, such as voice over internet protocol (VoIP) telephony, dial-up networking and broadband

1 Economist Intelligence Unit: www.eiu.com

internet access using integrated services digital network (ISDN) and digital subscriber line (DSL) technologies.

Fixed-line penetration in Kazakhstan reached twenty lines per 100 inhabitants early in 2008, and is expected to reach 23% by year-end, according to the Agency for Informatization and Communications of Kazakhstan (AIC).[2] At the same time, mobile penetration has reached 78 users per 100 inhabitants, making mobile communications a preferred choice.[3] This does not necessarily mean that nearly 80% of Kazakhstanis use mobile services, as mobile operators report only the numbers of active subscriber identity module (SIM) cards, and some people are known to have over five such cards registered in their name. It is, however, safe to assume that over half of the country's population uses mobile phones and, according to the mobile operators, nearly 100% of the country's population is living under the coverage of mobile communications networks.

The AIC recently announced that internet penetration in Kazakhstan reached 11% early in 2008[4] and is expected to reach 15% by year-end. These figures are believed to be exaggerated, although a level of 8% is thought to be quite reasonable by the experts. The primary reason for low internet penetration in Kazakhstan, and its small growth rate, is the slow pace of liberalisation of the telecom sector. Kazakhtelecom, a de facto state-owned monopoly, controls most of the country's telecommunications infrastructure, owns most of the key players in the market, and enjoys favourable relationships with the government and legislature. Internet access tariffs offered by Kazakhtelecom are quite high compared to those of EU member states, especially for businesses, and are considered generally expensive for the population at large. Recent government-mandated decreases in the price for DSL-based broadband access have improved the situation slightly, although more drastic measures are necessary.[5]

The computer literacy level in Kazakhstan was estimated at a little less than 10% in 2007, while computer penetration was no more than 5% that year, according to the AIC. These two numbers are key to understanding the reality of internet penetration in the country: a computer illiterate person with no computer will have a much tougher chance of using the internet. The state Programme on the Reduction of Information Inequity was adopted in 2007 and aims to increase both computer literacy and computer penetration in the country. Two government-subsidised projects were launched at the end of 2007 that promise to supply citizens with affordable computers. One is implemented by the private sector, and another, called "Ashyk Alem" ("Open World" in Kazakh), is implemented by the AIC itself. The latter provides a bundle that includes a locally assembled personal computer (PC), Microsoft's Vista Starter Edition software, and ten hours of dial-up internet access for around USD 350. It can be argued that a lowering of customs tariffs for computers, as well as other incentives, are more efficient ways to increase computer penetration levels than direct subsidies. However, efforts like Ashyk Alem still deserve praise for decreasing the country's digital divide.

Access to the internet using wireless technologies such as Wi-Fi and WiMAX is starting to pick up in Kazakhstan – but mostly in the three largest cities, including the capital, Astana, and Almaty, the country's largest city. A small number of Wi-Fi hotspots were introduced in these cities, mainly at hotels, restaurants and cafés. New hotspots will be appearing soon. Kazakhtelecom has introduced the Megaline Wi-Fi service to Astana and Almaty. The service offers prepaid access to Wi-Fi hotspots, installed and owned by Kazakhtelecom in numerous locations, and is starting to gain popularity among businesspeople on the move. Independent telecom operators are starting to introduce WiMAX-based access to the urban population.

Another option for internet access in Kazakhstan is internet cafés that are present in most cities and some rural communities. Prices are generally affordable and attract a lot of students and young adults. Public access centres are starting to appear in libraries and government service centres. Government-sponsored information kiosks are being installed at every major KazPost office (the national postal service provider), Akimats (an equivalent to a mayor's office), as well as other public venues, and promise much in terms of access to information, especially in rural areas. A lack of access to the world wide web will be among the hindering factors for the wide use of these kiosks by citizens.

The last but most undervalued option for access to the internet in the country is mobile telephony. There are three major mobile telecom operators in Kazakhstan that cover nearly 100% of the population: two offer services based on the global system for mobile communications (GSM) standard and one uses code division multiple access (CDMA). A fourth mobile operator is growing fast and also offers GSM-based services. The GSM operators offer internet connectivity using general packet radio service (GPRS) across most of the country, and EDGE (enhanced data rates for GSM evolution) in large cities. There is talk of rolling out third generation (3G) services in the near future. However, these services are not promoted enough, and users are usually unaware of their benefits.

Political will and public support

Governments can play a key role as drivers and facilitators for the development of the information society. Many leaders have made the development of the information society, through increased use of information and communications technologies (ICTs), a priority. However, it is often difficult to translate a grand vision into specific programmes, and even more difficult to implement them without losing the initial target. Governments often end up conducting reforms for

2 www.aic.gov.kz

3 Kazinform Agency: www.inform.kz

4 Kazinform Agency: www.inform.kz

5 Kazakhtelecom's "best offer package" is ADSL connectivity of 256 kilobits per second (kbps) for a USD 40 monthly fee which includes 10 Gb of traffic (as of June 2008).

the sake of reforms, without getting the private sector and civil society involved to the extent necessary.

Kazakhstan recognised the need to develop modern information technologies very early in its development, and has continued to advance this approach through the creation and implementation of various programmes and strategies. Initiated by the president of Kazakhstan in 2001, the first state programme concerned with development of the information society was called the Programme on Formation and Development of National Information Infrastructure for 2001-2003. This led to an e-government strategy in 2004, two e-government programmes for 2005-2007 and 2008-2010, two telecom sector development programmes for 2003-2005 and 2006-2008, and the Programme on the Reduction of Information Inequity for 2007-2009.

The two state programmes on telecommunications sector development helped to establish modern infrastructure in the country. Telecom sector deregulation, liberalisation, the increase of competition, and infrastructure development were and are among the top priorities of both programmes, and although some of the targets were not achieved (or were achieved only nominally), the programmes have significantly facilitated the development of ICT infrastructure in the country.

Kazakhstan's e-government development strategy consists of the two e-government programmes mentioned above, and includes four stages: "informational" (2005-2006), "interactive" (2006-2008), "transactional" (2008-2009) and "the information society" (2009) (Beklemishev & Tsekhovoi, 2006). Some government agencies already provide interactive services, with a certain degree of success. For example, it is already possible to submit tax forms electronically and to check whether tax payments have cleared the system or whether there are any tax liabilities outstanding. All of this is done in real time using digital signatures, which sets Kazakhstan apart from many other countries. It is estimated that over 80% of businesses in Kazakhstan submit their tax reports electronically. The implementation of the e-tax system has certainly motivated many businesses to harness ICTs and became a driving force for the computer training of many accountants and businesspeople. However, the e-tax system is still far from achieving its goals of efficiency, ease of use and transparency.

There are many other e-government services already available in Kazakhstan, most of them informational. The vast majority of these services, unfortunately, remain of little value to citizens and businesses. There are two main reasons for this. One involves the supply side, the government itself, which offers services that are either incomprehensive or of little value to the consumer of these services. There seems to be a disconnect between the real needs of citizens and businesses and the government's perception of what is of the most importance to these citizens and businesses. The second reason has to do with the demand side: the number of Kazakhstanis who understand what e-government is and, moreover, are aware of its advantages, is very small. Low computer literacy and internet penetration rates only add to the problem.

In an effort to promote e-government services and to increase access to communication infrastructure and information resources, the Programme on the Reduction of Information Inequity has three main goals: a 20% computer literacy rate; a 20% internet penetration rate; and an increase in the role ICTs play in the life of the average citizen. These goals are being realised through the creation of training centres, public internet access points, information kiosks, and a reduction in internet access tariffs and the cost of computers. As a part of the programme, the government plans to implement mandatory information technology (IT) testing in schools, colleges and universities, covering a total of a million students – 6.6% of the entire population. The government claims to have educated over 800,000 people by mid-2008 under this programme.[6] Overall it plans to educate and train over two million people in three years, thereby increasing the computer literacy rate from the current 5% to 20%.

Action steps

There are various options available for access to information in Kazakhstan, but many still need to be developed. The fact that nearly 90% of the population does not use the internet and is computer illiterate means that the situation is far from satisfactory for the information society to develop. Infrastructure needs to be continuously improved. The ICT sector needs to be developed using free-market approaches, and the government needs to ensure competition, deregulation and fair use of the resources available (such as radio frequency spectrum).

Largely disadvantaged inhabitants of smaller cities and rural areas spread across the vast territory of the country make up more than half of Kazakhstan's population, and are yet to experience the wonders of today's technology. It is these people that should be targeted by state programmes, as it is they who are most affected by the digital divide.

It is, however, most important that consumers have the freedom of choice of information channels based on their abilities, needs and preferences.

The possibility of reaching the majority of the population using mobile telephony with little investment is not recognised in the country. Kazakhstan can take advantage of its mobile infrastructure and leapfrog to mobile internet without the heavy investments in fixed-line infrastructure.

The leadership of President Nursultan Nazarbayev was crucial in getting ICT development on the government's agenda. The new government programmes discussed above prove that the government is keen to bring about the necessary changes to implement e-government services and improve the ICT infrastructure.

However, it is also clear that the government's priorities are not aligned with those of businesses and citizens. It often

6 Kazinform Agency: www.inform.kz

seems that the implementation of e-government initiatives is done for the sake of e-government itself and not to address the population's specific problems.

The government has yet to analyse the real demand for its services by citizens. It is necessary to align priorities and to get the respective stakeholders involved in both the design and implementation of the various state ICT initiatives, including the introduction of e-government services. Stakeholders should be well informed of the government's plans, and understand both the positive influence ICTs can have on society and the technology choices that can be made. Only then will they be keen to get involved and offer all the support they can in making these ICT initiatives possible. ■

References

Agency for Informatization and Communication of the Republic of Kazakhstan: www.aic.gov.kz

Beklemishev, A. and Tsekhovoi, A. (2006) *Status of Information Communication Technologies in Kazakhstan, Volume 2, 2004-2006*. Almaty: UNDP Kazakhstan.

Economist Intelligence Unit: www.eiu.com

Kazakhtelecom (2007) *Annual Report 2007*. Available at: www.telecom.kz

Kazinform Agency: www.inform.kz

Political Intelligence and Internews (2006) *Final Report: Monitoring of Russia and Ukraine (priority 1) and Armenia, Azerbaijan, Belarus, Georgia, Kazakhstan and Moldova (priority 2): Telecommunications and the Information Society*. Brussels: European Commission.

KENYA

Kenya ICT Action Network (KICTANet)
Alice Wanjira
www.kictanet.or.ke

Introduction

The 1990s are considered the era of the greatest policy reform in communications technology that the world has ever witnessed. National carriers were privatised, and new competitors and services were authorised (Ayogu, 2003). Kenya has been part of this dramatic change. The information and communications technology (ICT) sector in the country is now fully liberalised, offering opportunities for the country's economy and opening up access to the rural areas. The ICT sector in the country is optimistic, civil society and business are proactive in the field, and the government's commitment to ICTs has achieved regional and international recognition.

Yet like most developing countries, the good mixes with the bad. The fixed telephone service provider, Telkom Kenya, has 330,000 lines, with a teledensity of 0.16% in rural areas and 4% in urbanised areas. This number of subscribers is gradually dropping due to the poor quality of the service and lack of compliance with universal service obligations. On the other hand, the mobile sector is expanding rapidly. The number of subscribers has grown from 5.3 million in 2005 to 7.3 million by December 2006, an expansion of 36.5%. By March 2008, the number of subscribers had risen to 11,989,007 with a penetration rate of 32.25%. Then again, the development of the internet in Kenya has not been as robust as the telephony sector. A Communications Commission of Kenya (CCK) internet study (2007) found that there are only 1,650,000 internet users, even though the internet was introduced in 1993. This is out of a population of some 37 million.

Since 2003, ICTs have remained amongst the Kenyan government's top development agendas. This is evident in various national plans and initiatives, such as The East African Marine System (TEAMS, 2007-2009), the Digital Villages project, and the e-Government Strategy (2004-2009). The Kenya e-Government Strategy provides a road map for the implementation of ICT initiatives and outlines a process for the modernisation of government. This is likely to impact on relationships between citizens, businesses and government. The potential of ICTs to store, process, retrieve and disseminate vast amounts of data and information will continue to provide opportunities for increased transparency, accountability and efficiency in government operations.

According to the 2005 World Public Sector Report published by the United Nations Department of Economic and Social Affairs (UNDESA), over 90% of the 191 UN member countries operated government websites. It is notable that e-government is closely linked to and shares similar characteristics with e-commerce and e-business in terms of the use and implementation of internet technology. It re-engineers inter- and intra-organisational processes and structures, generating new services, products and channels for the end-users. E-government holds promise for improved delivery of many types of public services, as well as disseminating information about government operations. It promises to improve communication between citizens and government, enabling more direct participation in decision-making. It is important that ICTs, and the internet in particular, function in a secure manner so users have confidence that they will work in a reliable and safe way. Security and trust in the online environment has therefore become an important goal for policy-makers.

A study conducted by Pyramid Research in 2000 noted that for most people in Africa, electronic interaction with government is usually through ICT intermediary institutions or other public access venues, typically the local district office, post office, community centre, cybercafé, library or school. This is unlike industrialised countries where citizens interact electronically with government at home or the workplace. For many Kenyans, this study still resonates, and many citizens continue to rely on intermediary institutions. The degree of trust that exists between citizens and these institutions tends to have considerable impact on how ICTs are used to achieve development objectives.

A UN Global E-Government Readiness Report (2005), based on a study conducted by UNDESA, notes that African countries face numerous challenges to fully adopting and adapting to e-government services, and seizing the opportunities presented by ICTs in general. Key challenges cited in the report are: the overall literacy rate; the commitment of government to genuine transformation; the development of communication infrastructure; and cyber security. Through e-government, citizens are required to reveal personal information and communicate with officials in a very impersonal way compared to telephone calls or face-to-face encounters, which are more interactive. The study suggests further that issues of security, trust and public confidence determine whether citizens feel comfortable enough to make use of and work with e-government services. On the other hand, under the appropriate conditions, ICTs can contribute to enhancing trust and trustworthiness by expanding access to public information and, thereby, promoting openness, transparency and accountability in public administration.

Similarly, in order for consumers and small and medium enterprises (SMEs) to benefit from e-commerce and e-business, they need confidence in the security of online transactions. As access to the internet diversifies, from personal computers (PCs) to mobile phones and other wireless devices, there will be an increasing concern about the protection of assets and privacy in this networked world. These aspects will become important in a digital age based on convergence of technologies and systems.

In Kenya, ICTs – particularly computers – are still poorly understood by many people, even though they have become a ubiquitous part of daily life. There is a good deal of technophobia, a lack of skills, as well as general unease in the face of computers, especially with the older generation, and also in the case of many policy-makers. Amongst other things, this is due to bad personal experiences, socialisation, culture, news of large-scale computer failures, and a mindset gap (Mundy et al., 2001).

How government actions/inaction can contribute to a lack of trust in ICTs

The extent to which what a government does and does not do can lead to distrust in technology can be illustrated by two examples:

Kenya National Examination Council

In 2007, the Ministry of Education blamed computers for a mix-up of the national examination results for over 40,000 national secondary schools. A committee constituted to look into the matter attributed the problem to the Kenya National Examination Council's (KNEC) outdated computer software. The ministry did not admit to professional negligence and sheer incompetence. It explained the national shame by blaming computers. By doing this it implied that the barriers to ICT adoption are a result of poor information technology (IT) equipment, lack of financial resources to purchase up-to-date computers and software, and poor infrastructure, rather than constraints such as a lack of skilled personnel.

This demonstrates the tension that can exist between technology and government, and how technology can be used as a scapegoat. Processing power and good software can make government more user-friendly and sometimes also more efficient, but technology on its own cannot compensate for the incompetence and mistakes of politicians and bureaucrats.

The Kenya Terrorism Bill

The terrorist attacks in Kenya in 1998 and 2002, compounded by the global anti-terrorism campaign, resulted in the initiation of an anti-terrorism bill published in the Kenya Gazette on 3 July 2003. If this bill is enacted, it will be a criminal offence to "collect", "make" (produce and make available on a website), or "transmit" (by email, voicemail or any other telecommunication method) any record of information of a kind likely to be useful to a person committing or preparing to commit an act of terrorism. This clause is followed by the statement that "it is a defence for a person charged with an offence under this section to satisfy the court that he had a reasonable excuse for his action or possession."[1] This is likely to affect the use of the ICTs, particularly the internet. The challenge will be for users to discern what constitutes information likely to be "useful" to terrorists. Civil society critics argue that this, together with other provisions of the bill relating to increased powers of search and seizure by the police, will lead to a growing sense of distrust and uncertainty in using the internet in Kenya.

Managing risk: Privacy and security

In providing services to the public and carrying out various other functions online, governments collect and use a wide range of personal information about their citizens. These include data regarding income, education, health, property ownership and employment. Governments are therefore obligated to protect the privacy and security of the identity and personal information that they acquire, not only because of the right to privacy recognised by international laws, but also because trust is a critical factor of any successful online programme, whether in the field of e-commerce or in the field of e-government.

An Organisation for Economic Co-operation and Development (OECD) study into e-governance found that privacy and security are often cited as major concerns of internet users and major reasons why many non-users still avoid the internet (OECD, 2008). Individuals and businesses will not use e-government services unless they are assured that the information the government collects will be used responsibly and protected from abuse. To promote trust in online applications most effectively, policy-makers must address privacy and security issues in the planning and design of online services and application phases. Privacy and security measures included from the design phase are generally easier to implement. If the legal and technical challenges associated with identity are not successfully addressed, the quality of social interactions both online and in the physical world will deteriorate, further affecting trust in government and technology.

The way risks are managed is therefore one important aspect of whether people trust electronic governance, at least in terms of the protection of personal data. Victims of cyber crimes, for example, would be less supportive of national computerised files. Therefore, business and government will have to adopt highly concrete and effective rules of fair information practice in order for programmes using personal information to be seen by the public as acceptable.

The OECD study notes that despite a growing awareness of security problems and a corresponding growth in security measures taken, security incidents are still widespread and are not abating. Fraud with credit or debit cards is a serious barrier to engaging in e-commerce, which raises challenges for businesses to convince consumers that e-commerce can be conducted in a safe online environment.

Although the Kenyan government has begun to deal with issues of cyber security through various bills, including the Kenya ICT Bill 2007, there is still a lack of comprehension about the extent of the destruction that can be brought on by cyber crime.

1 Suppression of Terrorism Bill, 2003, Part II, 5.

The pending legislation that deals with issues of internet privacy and security are the following:

- The Kenya ICT Bill 2007: This bill aims to facilitate the development of national infrastructure to enable universal access; establish a regulatory framework for the carriage and content of communications under convergence; promote a plurality of news, views and information; and create a framework for increased investment in and application of ICTs. The bill contains a clause that holds cyber criminals liable for crimes and proposes an enforcement framework that would involve cyber inspectors. It does not adequately cover the issues of privacy or data protection. The government has proposed the development of a separate data protection bill.
- Consumer Protection Bill 2007: This bill aims to "establish a regime of consumer protection law, in order to provide comprehensive consumer protection and appropriate legal recourse to aggrieved consumers." It proposes to "codify and consolidate consumer laws in Kenya; to prevent unfair trade practices in consumer transactions..." The bill attempts to protect consumers from unfair practices and provides legislative provisions that would apply to all consumer transactions. It has specific safeguards for protection of consumers who use the internet for goods or services and defines an "internet agreement" as a "consumer agreement formed by text-based internet communications." This is to encourage public confidence and trust regarding internet-related transactions.
- Electronic Transaction Bill: The overall objective of the bill is to create an enabling legal environment for consumers, businesses, investors and government that will facilitate and promote the use of electronic transactions which are conducted using various types of ICTs. The bill aims to encourage the use of ICTs, including e-government and e-commerce services. It also aims to protect the privacy of the public and the interests of consumers and investors from abuse.

Action steps

The above-mentioned OECD study notes that citizens have more confidence in a system of government where there are widespread opportunities for civic participation and the protection of human rights. However, government websites rarely facilitate unmoderated public feedback, and there are very few published public reactions to policy proposals. There is also little use of discussion forums, electronic mailing lists and bulletin boards. As a result, the overall impact of the internet seems to have failed to improve transparency of government decision-making, increase access to policymakers, or facilitate public participation in policy-making. Most Kenyans still depend on radio as their source of information. Traditional methods like letters, written submissions, and informal face-to-face meetings continue to dominate communication.

Citizen trust is an important catalyst of e-government adoption, which depends heavily on the internet. Lack of confidence and trust in government cannot be compensated for by ICTs. For Kenyans to use the internet and other ICTs to communicate and conduct business electronically, it will depend on the level of confidence and trust in people, in organisations and indeed in the technology they use. Technology on its own will not bring reform, but it can make changes easier, cheaper and more effective.

Trust is about risk management, which often means that the government needs to be proactive, even in seemingly innocuous regulatory changes. For example, in 2015, Kenya will introduce digital broadcasting. Digital broadcasting has emerged as a globally accepted standard for next-generation mass media. While digital migration is a very significant technological turning point, it will force the take-up of new technology, which cannot be accomplished without having an effect on issues of trust and public confidence in legal and regulatory relationships.

Embracing new technologies will involve much more than organisational and technical issues or regulatory frameworks. It will include ethical dimensions of state-citizen interaction, in which trust, consent and democracy are crucial. And the absence of clear attention to these in the current policy-making processes is a cause for action.

References

Ayogu, M. (2003) *Strengthening National Information and Communication Technology Policy in Africa: Governance, Equity and Institutional Issues.* ATPS Special Paper Series No. 13. Available at: www.eldis.org/go/topics/resource-guides/governance/key-issues/e-government/e-government-and-public-sector-reforms

CCK (Communications Commission of Kenya) (2007) *Annual Report 2006/2007.* Available at: www.cck.go.ke/annual_reports/CCK%20Annual%20Report06-07.pdf

Government of Kenya (2006) Kenya Terrorism Bill 2006. Nairobi: Government Printers.

Government of Kenya (2007) Kenya ICT Bill 2007. Nairobi: Government Printers.

Government of Kenya (2007) Kenya Consumer Protection Bill 2007. Nairobi: Government Printers.

Kitaw, Y. (2006) *E-government in Africa: Prospects, challenges and practices.* ITU/EPFL. Available at: people.itu.int/~kitaw/egov

Mundy, D., Kanjo, C. and Mtema, P. (2001) Meeting training needs for information age reform. In Heeks, R. (ed.) *Reinventing Government in the Information Age.* London: Routledge.

OECD (Organisation for Economic Co-operation and Development) (2008) *Measuring Security and Trust in the Online Environment: A view using official data.* Available at: www.oecd.org/dataoecd/47/18/40009578.pdf

United Nations (2005) *Global E-Government Readiness Report 2005: From E-Government to E-Inclusion.* New York: United Nations. Available at: unpan1.un.org/intradoc/groups/public/documents/un/unpan021888.pdf

UNDESA (United Nations Department of Economic and Social Affairs) (2005) *Unlocking the Human Potential for Public Sector Performance: World Public Sector Report 2005.* Available at: unpan1.un.org/intradoc/groups/public/documents/UN/UNPAN021616.pdf

KOREA, REPUBLIC OF

Korean Progressive Network Jinbonet
Jisung Kim
www.jinbo.net

Introduction

The Republic of Korea – more commonly known as South Korea – is one of the top ranking countries in terms of access to broadband internet and mobile telephones. According to the International Telecommunication Union's (ITU) 2007 statistics, the number of internet users per 100 inhabitants is 72.2, the number of broadband subscribers per 100 inhabitants is 30.62, and the number of mobile cellular subscribers per 100 inhabitants is 90.2. Reading from the same statistics, in 2006, the percentage of the population covered by a mobile signal was 99%. According to the Organisation for Economic Co-operation and Development (OECD), in 2006 the percentage of households that had broadband access was 94%.

Geographically, there are about 30,000 people who live in areas where wired broadband access is not available. Other than them, almost all citizens in Korea can subscribe to internet access services. Such high geographical coverage is mainly due to a population concentrated in relatively small urban areas and aggressive investments in telecommunication infrastructure by the government and private companies.

Since the early 1990s, the government has put various policies in place to ease the digital divide. Early government efforts included regional ICT roll-out initiatives and computer education for farmers and fisherpeople. However, a comprehensive digital divide policy was only implemented with the formulation of the first five-year digital divide plan in 2001. The second five-year plan (2006-2010) is currently in progress. The second plan's major goal is raising the score of each vulnerable population group measured by a digital divide index that the Korean government has developed to 80% of that of the general population.

The most vulnerable populations are people with disabilities, farmers and fisherpeople, the elderly, and low-income population groups. Among these, farmers and fisherpeople and the elderly are lagging further behind than people with disabilities and low-income groups. Within each group, people who are older and less educated experience a greater sense of the digital divide.

The most significant socioeconomic factors affecting access for people with disabilities, low-income groups and farmers and fisherpeople is age, while for the elderly it is education.

In general, in these groups, people who score lowest on the digital divide index do not use the internet.

Digital divide index

In 2004, the government developed a digital divide index to quantitatively measure the digital divide. Since 2004, it has annually conducted status surveys and published its results in a survey report and in a white paper (KADO, 2008).

The survey involves face-to-face interviews with 15,000 individuals: 3,000 respondents each from the general population, people with disabilities, farmers and fisherpeople, the elderly, and low-income earners.

The questions used in the interview cover the issues shown in Table 2.

Table 1: Growth of broadband access, 2001-2007

	2001	2002	2003	2004	2005	2006	2007
Subscribers per 100 inhabitants	18.47	21.83	24.22	24.82	25.32	29.08	30.46
Households with broadband access (%)	56.9	68.2	66.7	85.7	92.7	94.0	n/a

Source: **OECD Broadband Statistics**

Table 2: Categories for measuring the digital divide

Access		Accessibility of personal computers (PCs) and internet; type of PC; type of internet connection; ownership of other information and communications technology (ICT) devices
Capacity		Competence in the use of PCs and the internet
Usage*	Quantitative	Usage of PCs and internet; hours of PC use
	Qualitative	Helpfulness of PCs and the internet in daily life; usage of PCs and the internet in the recommended areas of use

* Usage score = (0.6 × Quantitative usage score) + (0.4 × Qualitative usage score)

Table 3: 2006-2007 digital divide indexes

	People with disabilities		Low-income*		Farmers and fisherpeople		Elderly**		Average***	
	2006	2007	2006	2007	2006	2007	2006	2007	2006	2007
Aggregate	26.1	24.0	27	24.5	50.2	45.4	41.6	37.4	38	34.1
Access	14.6	11.2	20.4	15.8	30.5	23.3	17.1	9.9	19.8	13.5
Capacity	39	36.6	32.9	32.4	70.9	69.5	67.6	66.3	57.1	55.5
Quantitative usage	32.2	31.9	30.7	30.0	61.9	57.6	58.3	55.6	49.7	47.2
Qualitative usage	38	36.7	35.1	32.8	68.9	68.0	60.5	59.4	53.6	52.0

* Beneficiaries of the NMLSS (National Minimum Living Standard of Security System). For example, in 2007, a household that has four family members and an income less than KRW 1,205,535 was eligible for the NMLSS.
** Age over 50.
*** Weighted by the size of each group.

The digital divide index[1] is the difference between the score[2] of vulnerable groups and that of the general population. Before the calculation is done, the score is normalised based on the assumption that the score of the general population is 100. Therefore, the larger the digital divide index value, the larger the digital divide. The survey also includes a digital divide index in each category, using each category's scores.

The 2006 and 2007 survey results show that the gap in physical access is getting smaller in all of the population groups. However, in the capacity and usage categories, vulnerable population groups score only about half of that of the general population. The gap is especially large for farmers and fisherpeople and the elderly.

While the survey reports that age and education have the most significant influence among socio-demographic factors on an individual's achievement in access to and use of ICTs, income, occupation and gender influence the level of ICT take-up too.

When vulnerable populations are segmented further by age and education, there is a clear difference between the sub-groups. Except for people with disabilities, people who are 30 or older, with no high school education, scored less than 80% compared to the general population. Excluding the elderly and farmers and fisherpeople who have a college degree education or more, people who are 60 and over also scored less than 80%. In the low-income population group, excluding college graduates, people who are 40 or above scored less than 80%. Low-income individuals consistently scored less even compared to individuals of the same age and education level from the other population groups.

The most striking characteristics of people who score less than 80% compared to the general population is that they do not use the internet. Amongst these, only 1.2% of people with disabilities, 1.4% of low-income groups, 0.6% of farmers and fisherpeople, and 0.3% of the elderly use the internet. In contrast, almost 100% of people who scored more than 80% compared to the general population in the four population groups use the internet. Therefore, digital divide policy in Korea should be focused on providing incentives for people who do not use the internet to use it, and removing barriers that prevent them from using it. The survey identified the top five reasons for people not using the internet. These were: "Not knowing how to use it and difficulty of usage"; "Difficulty of use by physically handicapped people"; "No need to use it"; "Not knowing what to do with the internet"; and "No time for use".

Capacity and training

The fact that many internet "non-users" state that they do not need to use the internet or know what to do with the internet implies that they might not recognise the benefits of using the internet. According to the survey, of the people who think they do not need to use the internet, only 12.5% of them recognise the benefits of the internet, but still do not feel they need to use it. The remaining 87.5% are not aware of the benefits of using the internet, and because of this they do not think they need to use it.

Among the reasons for not using the internet, "not knowing how to use it and difficulty of use" was the most frequent. It suggests that many also feel uncomfortable about computers and the internet.

The government has launched a number of training programmes in the past, including PC training programmes in rural areas in the early 1990s, and a broad-based programme that aimed to train 27 million citizens from 2001 to 2004. At present, various ministries carry out their own training programmes targeting vulnerable population groups. Even with these training programmes in place, people still do not know how to use the internet, or why they need to use it. This indicates that training-related policies should be re-examined and redesigned.

Most of the training programmes have been done in classrooms that are set up in facilities such as social work institutions, educational facilities, or agricultural technology transfer agency offices. There are some training programmes

1 Digital divide index = {1 – (Vulnerable population score/General population score)} × 100

2 Aggregate score = (0.3 × Access score) + (0.2 × Capacity score) + (0.5 × Usage score)

Table 4: Scores (as a %) by age and education compared to the general population		People with disabilities	Low-income	Elderly	Farmers and fisherpeople
Age 10-19	Middle school graduate and below	113.4	120.4	-	-
	High school graduate	133.8	128.1	-	-
	College graduate and above	-	-	-	-
Age 20-29	Middle school graduate and below	92.5	91.8	-	113.7
	High school graduate	120.0	119.6	-	111.7
	College graduate and above	132.6	124.3	-	127.4
Age 30-39	Middle school graduate and below	89.2	56.1	-	59.4
	High school graduate	107.5	90.4	-	105.4
	College graduate and above	124.6	118.4	-	120.1
Age 40-49	Middle school graduate and below	63.5	50.6	-	58.6
	High school graduate	89.1	76.3	-	90.7
	College graduate and above	124.6	97.7	-	123.3
Age 50-59	Middle school graduate and below	46.5	36.1	55.3	46.3
	High school graduate	74.6	64.3	86.3	75.2
	College graduate and above	105.2	67.9	119.9	106.7
Age 60+	Middle school graduate and below	27.9	22.2	40.8	29.7
	High school graduate	47.1	31.8	68.2	53.5
	College graduate and above	70.8	36.7	93.0	81.2
Average		76.0	75.5	62.6	54.6

carried out at homes by instructors or online. Online training programmes serve more and more trainees every year. An online training course usually lasts ten to fifteen hours, and face-to-face training twenty to sixty hours. Courses can be roughly categorised into three types: the first includes courses oriented toward daily life skills, such as online banking, online shopping, word processing, and internet searching; the second type includes courses that are targeted at specific population groups such as people with disabilities or the elderly; and the last type includes courses that develop capacity necessary for jobs or starting businesses. The government support for the training facilities covers the costs of instructors, equipment maintenance, broadband subscription and miscellaneous operational costs. While the number of training facilities is increasing, support for instructors is limited, and this in turn limits access to the training programmes offered. The government recognises the shortage of instructors and is trying to train voluntary instructors.

Since online courses are meaningless to people who do not use the internet, more home-visit training opportunities over and above face-to-face classroom training must be provided. It is highly unlikely that farmers and fisherpeople would be able to attend classes, even if the number of training facilities and classrooms is significantly increased, because some of them still live far from these locations. People with disabilities or the elderly could also experience difficulties in getting from their homes to training venues.

Appropriate technology

The survey found that a lack of attention to the access needs of people with physical disabilities and the elderly is also preventing take-up. The Korean population is aging very quickly compared to other countries. The ratio of the elderly in the low-income and the farmers and fisherpeople population groups is also higher than the general population.

Compliance with web content accessibility standards and guidelines is still very low. According to an evaluation of e-government sites of 198 countries conducted by Brown University (West, 2007), Korea received the most points overall. However, when one looks at the rating for each category – Online Services, Publications, Databases, Privacy Policy, Security Policy and W3C Disability Accessibility[3] – Korea scored 100% in all categories except W3C Disability Accessibility, where it scored 0% (the average was 23% for all 198 countries).

Article 20 of the Anti-Discrimination against and Remedies for Persons with Disabilities Act, which was enacted in April 2007, prohibits discrimination against persons with

3 Based on the standards recommended by the World Wide Web Consortium (W3C).

disabilities by individuals, legal persons or government agencies in accessing electronic or non-electronic information. The article provides a base for obliging institutions to use accessibility standards and guidelines that have already been prepared by the national standardisation authority. However, the article is no more than a declaration because it lacks specific requirements and enforcement power.

According to a government estimate, about 360,000 individuals among people with disabilities need some sort of aiding device to use ICTs. In the last four years, however, national and local government agencies provided devices in only about 23,000 cases.

A promising way to encourage internet non-users is to develop new information access environments using home appliances such as digital TVs. The home appliance approach can also help the elderly who feel uncomfortable with the keyboard interface and operating systems.

Action steps

- Provide more home-visit training programmes for people who have physical or geographical difficulties in attending training venues.
- Provide more tech support services for citizens that can help solve everyday technology needs and problems.
- Increase the financial support for instructors and support staff involved in training programmes.
- Compliance with web content accessibility guidelines should be made mandatory, at least in the government procurement of information systems and devices.
- Increase the financial support for devices that aid people with disabilities in accessing ICTs.
- Support the development of home appliance-based information access technologies, and provide financial assistance for buying and using these appliances, in addition to the current support for PCs and internet subscription. ■

References

Choi et al. (2004) *2004 Research of Digital Divide Index and Status.* Seoul: Korea Agency for Digital Opportunity & Promotion.

Choi et al. (2008) *2007 Research of Digital Divide Index and Status.* Seoul: Korea Agency for Digital Opportunity & Promotion.

ITU ICT EYE: www.itu.int/ITU-D/ICTEYE

KADO (Korea Agency for Digital Opportunity & Promotion) (2008) *2008 Digital Opportunity White Paper.* Seoul: Korea Agency for Digital Opportunity & Promotion.

Korean Statistical Information Service: www.kosis.kr/eng

National Assembly of the Republic of Korea (2007) *Anti-Discrimination against and Remedies for Persons with Disabilities Act.* Available at: www.humanrights.go.kr/english/information/legal_materials_03.jsp

OECD Broadband Statistics: oecd.org/sti/ict/broadband

Shim et al. (2008) *Survey on Computer and Internet Usage.* Seoul: National Internet Development Agency of Korea.

West, D. (2007) *Global E-Government, 2007.* Providence: Taubman Center for Public Policy, Brown University. Available at: www.insidepolitics.org/egovt07int.pdf

KYRGYZSTAN

Civil Initiative on Internet Policy
Tattu Mambetalieva and Zlata Shramko
www.gipi.kg

Country situation

Kyrgyzstan (or the Kyrgyz Republic) is 199,900 square kilometres in size with a population of a little over five million. Located in the northeast of Central Asia, it borders China, Kazakhstan, Uzbekistan and Tajikistan, rendering it completely landlocked. Most of the country is mountainous (93%), and the average altitude is 2,750 metres above sea level. The highest altitude is 7,439 metres (Peak Pobedy), the lowest 394 metres.

After having gained independence in 1991, Kyrgyzstan implemented a number of large-scale projects focused on establishing a digital communications network and providing access to the global communications network for Kyrgyz users. Despite these efforts, around 30% of rural settlements still lack telephone services. The number of mobile network subscribers is constantly growing, although this has not become a very widespread service. In order to overcome this problem, a universal access programme was launched, which included e-centres and a rural access project, both aimed at reducing the digital divide between rural and urban areas.

Internet penetration in Kyrgyzstan is improving each year, a process facilitated by surmounting many regulatory barriers and the establishment of public access centres and internet cafés. The number of popular and affordable internet telephony services is constantly growing as well.

The market for computer and telecommunications equipment is well developed, but the software market is much less advanced. The large volume of counterfeit software and gaps in governing software development processes present grave problems for this sector.

The mass media is reasonably developed in Kyrgyzstan. Hundreds of distant towns and villages in the country have gained access to a television signal as a result of a satellite television project. However, difficulties in securing a frequency range for broadcasting, as well as financial constraints and pressures, affect the variety of public information, its independence, and national audience coverage.

Citizen access to government information is also problematic: the information is still very scarce, and its provision often involves complex bureaucratic difficulties.

Kyrgyzstan has a unique experience in that it formulated its development policy on information and communications technologies (ICTs) collaboratively. The country has adopted a national strategy called Information and Communication Technologies for Development in the Kyrgyz Republic. Despite some criticism, this document has played a crucial historic role in providing an understanding of ICTs as a working tool for development and in unifying disparate stakeholders in the field. A strong, collaborative and truly multilateral ICT community in Kyrgyzstan, represented by the private sector, civil society actors and government institutions, is capable of successfully defining the development direction in the near future, and creating a new, effective strategy, as well as developing the corresponding practical action plans.

The country's telecommunications legislation was adopted in 1998. However, the legislation is now outdated. Amongst other things, it does not allow for independent regulation, curtails real competitiveness in the market, and has not kept pace with changes in technology. As a result, preparatory work is being done in order to draft a new telecommunications law. This process is unique: for the first time the business sector is asserting its rights through legislative reforms. However, there is still a need to attract international consultants in order to help develop appropriate telecommunications policies.

Access, affordability and political will

The importance of ICTs for living and development can be seen in the efforts by many countries to assure equal access for users to telecommunication infrastructure, ICT services and products. Universal access approaches vary from country to country depending on state policy and economic status, as well as on the infrastructure resources of a territory.

Determining a set of universal services appropriate to the present day capacity of the country is an issue of the day in Kyrgyzstan. In this regard, it is important to keep the strategic priorities of economic development and the development of a social state in balance.

Telephony

The Kyrgyz population has around 428,000 primary telephone lines: 349,000 home phones and 79,000 business phones. The number of pay phones has grown to 1,545, having increased 3.5 times compared to 2002, when the total number of pay phones across the country was 432.

The local telephone network in Kyrgyzstan is mainly provided by the national operator JSC Kyrgyztelecom. Kyrgyztelecom has implemented a number of projects over the years focused on establishing modern digital telecommunications infrastructure. In spite of this, a year ago the fixed-line teledensity in Kyrgyzstan was only around 84 lines per 1,000 people. The relatively low ratio is explained by the fact that almost two-thirds of the population resides in mountainous rural areas. Currently almost 30% of the 6,000 settlements located in the rural areas of Kyrgyzstan do not have telephones.

Providing local fixed-line phone service is an unprofitable venture for Kyrgyztelecom. This is due to the low prices set both for the capital Bishkek and for the outlying regions – the prices are lower than the cost levels. Losses are significantly higher in the rural areas because of the higher cost of operations and even lower prices to end-users. The price of an annual phone bill for the urban population ranges between USD 12.60 and USD 15.50 (without taxes), and in rural areas between USD 4.70 and USD 7.00. The need to subsidise local telephone service forces Kyrgyztelecom to utilise cross-subsidies, which leads to higher prices for long-distance phone calls than alternative operators can offer.

These alternative operators – such as Saima-Telecom and Winline – have an opportunity to effectively compete with Kyrgyztelecom in terms of pricing for intercity and international communications. Intercity and international long-distance services are currently provided by fifteen operators. The market share of Kyrgyztelecom in this market segment is constantly decreasing, while other network operators use the Kyrgyztelecom infrastructure to various extents for providing their own services. Alternative operators for fixed-line telephonic communications mostly provide their services in Bishkek and its vicinity, focusing on the richest clients.

For example, Saima-Telecom's network covers around 40% of the city. The company provides its services via fibre-optic cable. Since 2005, it has offered asymmetric digital subscriber line (ADSL) internet connectivity. In 2006 the company began implementing a project that created a new-generation network in Bishkek, unifying such services as traditional telephony, internet protocol (IP) telephony and broadband internet access.

Another alternative fixed-line telephone operator, Winline, is the owner of a major communications network and is able to provide local and long-distance telephone services through wireless telephone terminals with an independent feed. The company offers services to the residents of Bishkek and the Chui region – mostly surrounding Bishkek city. Experts estimate that alternative operators have the aggregate of at least 5,000 telephone lines.

Mobile communications

Kyrgyzstan has experienced rapid growth in mobile communications over the past several years. According to official International Telecommunication Union (ITU) data, in 1999 the number of users of mobile networks was no greater than 2,600, but the number of mobile users had risen to 263,400 in 2004, 541,700 in 2005, and exceeded 560,000 in 2006.

Despite this dynamic development, it should be noted that the adoption of mobile communications in the country still remains relatively low. The 2006 figure still represents only 10% of the total population. When mobile communications services first appeared in Kyrgyzstan in the 1990s, only the people with the highest levels of income could afford them. Gradually, as the competition strengthened, cell phones became more affordable to the wider population.

Presently in Kyrgyzstan there are nine registered mobile service providers. Six of these are operating. Every year there is tougher competition for the less solvent groups of the population, and the revenues of the mobile network operators per user are constantly declining. The average cost of a one-minute phone call on a mobile phone within the same network ranges from six to twenty cents (depending on the tariff, zone, and call category), which makes mobile communications affordable for the general population.

The market of additional mobile services is developing very rapidly in Kyrgyzstan. These services include multimedia messaging service (MMS) and wireless application protocol (WAP) access that makes it possible to download music and videos and receive postcards and various information items through short message service (SMS) subscription, as well as to take part in SMS games. It should be noted that at this point there are relatively few WAP websites in the .kg domain, and subscribers mostly use Russian information and entertainment WAP sites.

Internet

The total number of internet users in Kyrgyzstan over the last few years has increased annually by 100,000 people on average. Today it totals over 550,000 – which means each tenth resident of Kyrgyzstan has become an internet user. Notably, the number of regular users is only 150,000. Growth in the dial-up segment has practically stopped, while there has been an increase in the number of ADSL broadband subscriptions. The total number of subscribers to all internet providers combined is currently estimated at 16,000. Approximately 10,000 of these are corporate users. The cost of hourly dial-up internet access ranges on average between USD 0.40 and USD 0.80 (without taxes) during the day and between USD 0.10 and USD 0.30 (without taxes) at night. At the same time, the average monthly income in Kyrgyzstan remains very low (around USD 60), which is the major socioeconomic factor hindering growth. Another barrier to development is a low level of home computer ownership: the Expert Consulting Agency estimates that the total number of home computers in the country amounts to about 80,000.

There are over 150 centres offering public access to the internet in Kyrgyzstan, including internet cafés and free public access centres. The latter, together with a number of higher education institutions offering public access, are financed by international donor organisations and positively contribute to the number of internet users in the country.

Hardware and software

There is a major disparity in the hardware and software markets in Kyrgyzstan: the software market is much less developed. While Kyrgyz users have an opportunity to use most of the newest software products and programmes, sometimes even before their colleagues from other countries, according to experts, 99% of these are pirated. The major factor explaining the current situation, apparently, is not a resistance on the part of users to purchase licensed products, but the mere fact that they cannot afford to buy them due to limited financial resources.

Another reason for the lack of development in the software market is the lack of any system of software governance – software installation in the corporate and even in the state sector occurs on an ad-hoc basis. At the same time, free and open source software (FOSS) is only used by some companies.

Targeted work on promoting and disseminating FOSS in the country has begun. For example, an initiative for developing FOSS, called Free and Open Source Software Support in the Kyrgyz Republic,[1] has developed FOSS training courses to train non-governmental organisations and educational institutions, amongst others. FOSS localisation is also being done to encourage wide public use, including in schools.

Factors affecting physical access to technology

- Geography: Kyrgyzstan is primarily a mountainous country. This makes many parts of the country hard to reach, with high costs involved in rolling out telecommunications.
- High concentration of telecommunication services in the capital: 80% of the volume of ICT services are provided in Bishkek city, where 20% of the country's population resides. The remaining 20% are offered in the regions where 80% of the population lives (half in cities or towns).
- Low density of telephone lines in rural areas: Teledensity in rural areas is 1.5% to 2%, which is roughly four to five times less than the country average (8%), and twelve to sixteen times less than the capital (25%).
- Disproportionate development of the internet network: Since the level of poverty is considerably higher in the outlying regions, the more remote a village is from the capital, the fewer the customers. This makes some areas relatively unprofitable for operators.
- Poor quality of services: The quality of available services in the regions (e.g., the stability of cellular communication, quality of TV and radio signals, transfer, etc.) is much lower than in the capital, because of the less-developed infrastructure.
- High cost of telecommunication services: The purchasing capacity of the population greatly influences the situation. High tariffs for international and intercity services (despite the ongoing restructuring of tariffs for international, intercity and local communication services) restrict access for many Kyrgyz citizens.
- Insufficient widespread access to wireless communication facilities: Apart from fixed telecommunication lines, other communication facilities are seldom used and not always used effectively.

Action steps

Several attempts have been made to broaden universal access. One of these attempts was when providers initiated a fund to finance setting up communication centres (e-centres) in remote areas and rural settlements. However, this initiative was not successful, despite the fact that around 30 centres were set up. One of the problems is that the centres were not business-oriented and self-sustainable. The operators were carrying most of the costs, and there was mass closure of the centres when the funding finished.

Another model was attempted with the support of the United States Agency for International Development (USAID). It proposed setting up e-centres which were to provide paid communication services to people, including paid computer literacy courses. This project was more successful, as its e-centres became self-sustainable. However, expansion of the centres has been very slow, as the providers do not extend their coverage networks to remote areas and villages.

It is critical for the development of universal access in Kyrgyzstan for one of the key ICT players – either government or business – to exert political will. One of them must assume responsibility for the development of access to ICTs in the country, and consequently undertake appropriate commitments.

Current legislation does not make any provisions relating to universal access, except for political declarations by government leaders who declare the priority of universal access development. Concrete proposals are necessary.

1 www.unix.kg

References:

Association of Communication Operators, Association of Internet Clubs, Civil Initiative on Internet Policy (2004) *Public Expertise and Systematization of the Current Legislation of the Kyrgyz Republic in the Information and Communication Technology Sector.*

Civil Initiative on Internet Policy (2006) *Kyrgyzstan ICT Overview.* Bishkek: CIIP. Available at: www.internetpolicy.kg

Civil Initiative on Internet Policy (2007) Kyrgyzstan Overview: Country report for the OpenNet Initiative project. Bishkek: CIIP. Available at: www.internetpolicy.kg

Ershova, T. and Hohlov, Y (2006) *Global Internet Policy Initiative Contribution to Information and Communication Technology Application for Development in Kyrgyz Republic: Case Study.*

Expert Consulting Agency (2004) *Analysis of the Information and Communication Technology (ICT) Sector of Kyrgyzstan.* Bishkek: Expert Consulting Agency.

Government of Kyrgyzstan (2002) Национальная стратегия "Информационно-коммуникационные технологии для развития Кыргызской Республики" (Presidential Decree "On the National Strategy for Information and Communication Technologies for Development in the Kyrgyz Republic"). Available at: www.gov.kg/index.php?name=EZCMS&menu=2906&page_id=105

ICT Council under the President of the Kyrgyz Republic and United Nations Development Programme (UNDP) (2003) *Information and Communication Technologies (ICT) Industry Survey in Kyrgyzstan.* Bishkek: UNDP.

ITU (International Telecommunication Union) (2006) *World Information Society Report 2006.* Geneva: ITU.

National Statistical Committee (2005) *Current State of ICT Development and Use in the Kyrgyz Republic: 2001-2004.* Bishkek: NSI.

Public Information Center under the Administration of the President of the Kyrgyz Republic (Общественный Информационный Центр при Управлении делами Президента Кыргызской Республики) (2006) Обзор состояния сектора ИКТ в Кыргызстане.

Soros Foundation Kyrgyzstan (2003) *Approaches to Telecommunications Services Affordability Policy Development in Kyrgyzstan: Materials and Recommendations.* Bishkek: Soros Foundation Kyrgyzstan.

United Nations (2005) *Global E-Government Readiness Report 2005: From E-Government to E-Inclusion.* New York: United Nations. Available at: unpan1.un.org/intradoc/groups/public/documents/un/unpan021888.pdf

MEXICO

LaNeta
Olinca Marino
www.laneta.apc.org

Introduction

Mexico is currently living through a very difficult social and economic process, putting both urban and rural areas under pressure. Violence is part of daily reality, including a high rate of femicide (more than 6,000 women have been killed since 1999 in mostly unsolved gender-specific murders) (Univision, 2007). There are hundreds of deaths related to drug trafficking, and kidnapping gangs have grown across the country. The only constant is the lack of a guarantee of fundamental rights.

Family income has declined, limiting people's access to diverse goods and services, including information and communications technologies (ICTs). According to information published by the Federal Consumer Protection Agency (PROFECO), the cost of a "basic food basket" has jumped from the equivalent of 16.8 minimum wage days of work in December 2006 to 23 days as of May 2008 (Di Constanzo, 2008). This situation has worsened the plight of Mexican families.

The country's federal administration frequently privileges the interests of big capital and the market over the interests of the majority of citizens. The government has tried to sell off national resources such as coastlines, oil, gas and telecommunications frequencies, to mention but a few, to the highest bidder – be it Mexican or foreign capital.

Access to ICTs

Due to the economic and social conditions of the country, ICTs continue to be tools used by the privileged sectors in Mexico. The country's uneven state of digital access is due to differences in income, age, gender, urbanisation, and socioeconomic disparities between regions.

Country statistics are overwhelming. Mexico is home to the second richest businessman in the world: his name is Carlos Slim and he earns USD 30.13 million a day (Bill Gates earns USD 5.4 million daily) (Galán, 2008), whereas the daily minimum wage of a Mexican worker is just under USD 5.

It is no coincidence that telecommunications is one of Slim's most successful business areas. He is owner of Telmex and America Móvil, suppliers of telephony and internet not only in Mexico, but also in several Latin American countries. Slim made his fortune in the 1990s, when the then state-owned telephone company Telmex was sold to him at a very low price, paving the way for huge profits later on. Besides Slim, a number of other Mexican families are also well recognised for their monopolistic business practices (e.g., the Salinas Pliego, Arango and Azcárraga families).

In 2007, two respected sources regarding internet access and ICT use offered us differing data. The Survey on Availability and Use of Information Technologies in Households carried out by the National Institute of Statistics, Geography and Informatics estimated that there are 20.8 million internet users in Mexico, while the Internet User Habits Survey conducted by the Mexican Internet Association (AMIPCI) placed the number of users at 22.7 million (AMIPCI, 2007). The difference of almost two million users is far from negligible.

In spite of this imprecision, it is clear that the majority of internet users in Mexico are young, with 63% aged between 12 and 34. Meanwhile, 47.6% of internet users are women, whereas men constitute 52.4%. While the gender divide does not appear significant, a combination of socioeconomic factors does limit women's access to internet. For example, besides the usual technical, educational and family patterns that benefit men more than women, many men have access to the internet and ICTs in their workplace, while many Mexican women work in the manufacturing and services sectors in positions that do not involve computers, the internet, or ICTs generally. The low access to internet amongst the general population as a whole is also explained by a combination of other factors, such as a lack of skills in the use of technologies, the cultural rejection of ICTs, and a lack of awareness of their specific benefits (Tello, 2008).

On the other hand, 92.4% of internet users are located in urban areas, whereas only 7.6% are in rural areas. There are also differences between regions. Northern and central Mexico have lower poverty indexes compared to southern Mexico, because of the high concentration of economic activity in these regions. As a result, northern and central Mexico's investment in computers relative to gross domestic product (GDP) is greater than the national average. Southern Mexico and some areas of central Mexico, which have higher rates of poverty and lower investment, are also regions with a high density of indigenous populations. All this means that a woman over 40 years of age living in a rural area will have very precarious access to technology.

In an attempt to promote ICTs as a driving element of the economy, the government has taken care to position technologies in the field of market competitiveness, placing little emphasis on the potential social benefits of ICTs for the general population. But despite privileging ICTs and the market sector, surprisingly, Mexico has not been able to consolidate ICTs in the world of Mexican business. According to the 2007-2008 Global Information Technology Report, produced by the World Economic Forum in cooperation with the international business school INSEAD, Mexico dropped nine places in the Networked Readiness Index, from 49th in 2006 to 58th worldwide. Two fundamental reasons for this decline were given: the federal government's limited use of ICTs and inadequate administration in the education sector (Cervantes, 2008).

In Mexico the low penetration of ICTs in business is notable. This varies according to company size, geographic region and economic sector. Reasons cited by various sources include telecommunications regulation, broadband rates, the unequal sizes of companies, and the lack of financing to acquire computer equipment. For this reason, there is a deep digital divide amongst Mexican companies compared to other countries (Tello, 2008).

On the other hand, the same report indicates that Mexico's broadband penetration has expanded. In 2008, broadband users increased by almost 5%. However, the costs are still high for the majority of the population. This is corroborated by the Organisation for Economic Co-operation and Development (OECD) Communications Outlook 2007 report, which states that Mexico is the country with the most expensive broadband prices of all 30 OECD member states. The cost ranges from USD 52.36 to USD 802.65 a month. By comparison, at the international level, Sweden's broadband costs range from USD 10.79 to USD 46.74 a month (OECD, 2007).

Since mobile telephony is experiencing the greatest growth in the telecommunications sector in Mexico, it could be deduced that it is the service offering the greatest access in the country. There are 589 handsets per 1,000 inhabitants, amounting to 64.6 million lines for the third quarter of 2007. This means that mobile telephony experienced a growth of 19.4% over the previous twelve months (Competitive Intelligence Unit, 2008). This growth is interesting, since it has occurred despite high service costs. Operators who offer cost-effective time rates (per second) are very few. The majority of them charge per minute, which increases costs for users. This is a critical issue for consumers. It seems that a lot of people have phones, but do not use them very frequently.

Setting the digital agenda

Without doubt, Mexico needs a digital agenda in order to ensure equitable access. At present a comprehensive digital agenda in the country does not exist. Instead, at the federal government level, there are a series of uncoordinated programmes and initiatives in different ministries. These programmes are spread across the National Development Plan, its corresponding sectoral plans, and individual state development plans. However, a proper inventory of these programmes does not exist, preventing an analysis of the course that the state has undertaken to lead the country towards a digitally developed society (Política Digital, 2008).

The official initiative involving universal access and governmental information over the last seven years has been e-Mexico, which attempted to create a system of satellite connectivity that offered services to the education and health sectors in particular, amongst other government sectors. However, since it was implemented by the Ministry of Communications and Transport, it did not receive support from either the Ministry of Education or the Ministry of Health (Hofmann & García-Cantú, 2008). E-Mexico has not been successful, in spite of several governmental efforts. At present, government agencies are discussing a new strategy for universal access that takes advantage of WiMAX and Wi-Fi connectivity for schools, health centres and government offices across the country. The State Networks for Education, Health and Government, a new version of e-Mexico (without the satellite), and the University Corporation for the Development of the Internet (CUDI) will be the principal implementers of the project.

In terms of content, e-government services try to facilitate access to state information for the general population. However, these sites are infrequently updated, and are not coordinated; they are a reflection of the deeper limitations of the Mexican e-government initiative, until now plagued by a lack of coordination in buying equipment, a lack of a regulatory framework, and, evidently, a lack of joint strategies within the government.

In any digital agenda, a fundamental element is access to public information. Mexico initiated that process some years ago. But transparency in Mexico is "practiced with difficulty, and in most of the territory does not reach a satisfactory level," a recent investigation by the Economic Research and Development Centre (CIDE) concluded (Zócalo, 2007).

Another point that any digital agenda must include is the right to communicate. Access to ICTs without the right to communicate is a contradiction. The rights of indigenous people, women and citizens in general to communicate; the right to be informed; the rights of journalists to practice their profession without risking their lives; the right to access ICTs in accordance with the vision and needs of different groups: all must be guaranteed. In short, a digital agenda should be focused on people, and not only defined by the market.

Governmental support for ICT research is also a key aspect. The Mexican government does not offer the necessary support, leaving the responsibility to academics and the research sector. However, as Guillermo Rodríguez Abitia, the director of the Centre for Information Technologies Development at ITESM-CEM says: "At present most of the companies dedicated to information technologies are service providers to big companies, and consequently conduct little research" (Investigación y Desarrollo, 2008).

Some academic research initiatives have been launched. The National Autonomous University of Mexico (UNAM), for example, is trying to connect diverse Mexican institutions nationwide and define a 20-year road map for the ICT sector. The UNAM network has also established agreements with the Ministry of Economy to implement knowledge management offices in educational institutions, which would address the country's telecommunications needs.

The federal government's firm steps in favour of proprietary software companies – the government has, for instance, renewed its partnership with Microsoft Mexico – does not favour a policy of broad access. At the same time, the federal government has announced specific guidelines for state spending. Two points stand out:

- Federal institutions must stop buying ICTs. Within a period of 36 months, all ICTs should be obtained via rental service contracts with commercial companies (Diario Oficial de la Federación, 2006).
- While the guidelines allow for state agencies to choose between free and open source software and commercially restricted licence solutions, because these agencies are forced to enter into service agreements with commercial companies, software is controlled by the provider. Already there are numerous reports of companies prohibiting the use of free software in federal contracts.

The country's digital agenda should also pay attention to specific groups of the population. There are currently no specific guidelines for women, young people, native language speakers or differently-abled people, to mention a few.

On this point, a decree was published in May 2008 establishing Mexico's compliance with the UN Convention on the Rights of Persons with Disabilities. Among other points, the convention obliges Mexico to adopt measures that ensure ICT access, including access to the internet, for people with disabilities. This is very important for the country, since approximately 10.3 million people have some type of disability (Álvarez, 2008), but currently have no facilities for using basic services, like making emergency calls or consulting official information. Under the convention, Mexico is committed to making public information available in accessible formats, including, for example, producing TV programmes with subtitles. Even though the impact of the convention is not yet visible, its fulfilment means a hope of guaranteeing the freedom of expression for people living with disabilities.

Action steps

In Mexico, public policies favouring the citizenry are fundamental to ensuring effective ICT access for the general population. We should consider what Tello says: "[A] society with cables is not the same as one that is prepared to access, evaluate and apply information. The aspiration to become a knowledge society necessarily implies that, in addition to network access, people have real access to information, that they know what to do with it, and that they have the capacity to transform it into knowledge, and this into tangible benefits" (Tello, 2008).

At present, several laws are pending, perhaps the most urgent being the law on radio, television and telecommunications. While the Supreme Court of Justice resolved an issue of conflicting articles in June 2007, the delays in its approval have been due to political reasons – despite recommendations from international human rights organisations.

Mexico requires a public policy that responds to social needs and generates value for people. For example, it is essential to increase national spending on ICTs. It is also essential to reduce mobile telephony and broadband costs. At the same time, it is crucial to break the monopolies of telecommunications companies. Social ICT projects, like digital villages, are also important.

Finally, citizens need to regain trust in public information. A controlled mass media, the publication of contradictory information, and the assassination of journalists have eroded public confidence.

The promotion of social networks to encourage participation, strengthen identity and build transparency is also fundamental. Mexican women and men face the challenge of creating a regulatory framework that ensures access to ICTs, and makes society's participation viable in the rebuilding of the country. ■

References

Álvarez, C. (2008) Telecom y discapacidad: ¿a quién le importa? *Razón y Palabra*, 20 May. Available at: www.cem.itesm.mx/dacs/publicaciones/logos/telecom/2008/may20.html

AMIPCI (Asociación Mexicana de Internet) (2007) *Hábitos de los usuarios de Internet en México*. Available at: www.amipci.org.mx/estudios.php

Cervantes, S. (2008) México reprueba en tecnologías. *El Universal*, 9 April. Available at: www.el-universal.com.mx/finanzas/vi_63650.html

Competitive Intelligence Unit (2008) *Telefonía Móvil*. Available at: www.the-ciu.net

Diario Oficial de la Federación (2006) Decreto que establece las medidas de austeridad y disciplina del gasto de la Administración Pública Federal. 4 December.

Di Constanzo, M. (2007) Con Calderón, la pérdida en el poder adquisitivo del salario mínimo es del 27%. *Secretaría de la Hacienda Pública*. Available at: secretariadelahaciendapublica.blogspot.com/l

Galán, V. (2008) Carlos Slim gana 1.25 mdd por hora. *CNNexpansión.com*, 7 March. Available at: www.cnnexpansion.com/actualidad/2008/03/07/slim-gana-251-000-dolares-por-hora

Hofman, A. and García-Cantú, M. (2008) Una estrategia nueva para el acceso universal en México. *Política Digital*, No. 45, August-September.

Investigación y Desarrollo (2008) Informática, se busca una agenda nacional. *Investigación y Desarrollo*, September. Available at: www.invdes.com.mx/activacion-inf.asp?CategoriaID=1&MesID=5&YearID=11&SubCategoriaID=1530

Organisation for Economic Co-operation and Development (2007) *OECD Communications Outlook 2007*. Paris: OECD.

Política Digital (2008) Las estrategias digitales – la nacional y las estatales – que no existen. *Política Digital*, 28 February. Available at: www.politicadigital.com.mx/?P=leernoticia&Article=437

Tello, E. (2008) Las tecnologías de la información y comunicaciones (TIC) y la brecha digital: su impacto en la sociedad de México. *Revista de Universidad y Sociedad del Conocimiento*, 4(2). Available at: www.uoc.edu/rusc/4/2/dt/esp/tello.html

Univisión (2007) Alerta por feminicidios en A. Latina. *Univisión.com*, 11 October. Available at: www.univision.com/content/content.jhtml?cid=1314856

Zócalo (2007) El acceso a la información en México a media tabla: CIDE. *Revista Zócalo*, No. 94, December. Available at: www.laneta.apc.org/zocalo/index.shtml?cmd[30]=c-2-94&cmd[31]=c-2-94

NIGERIA

John Dada and Bala Dada
Fantsuam Foundation
www.fantsuam.org

Introduction

This report provides an update of ongoing and planned information and communications technology (ICT) initiatives in Nigeria, and suggests areas that deserve attention. Going by the series of activities since the last report on Nigeria (GISWatch 2007), it appears that the level of awareness within policy circles and the country at large has been raised. This report looks at two areas of ICT development in Nigeria: physical access to technology and human capacity training.

The new government of President Musa Yar'Adua came into power on 29 May 2007 and has initiated the review and/or reversal of some ICT policies and actions of the previous administration:

- Reversal of the initial agreement on issuing a licence to Nigerian Communication Satellite (NIGCOMSAT) Ltd. (Aluko, 2008).
- Review of the National Rural Telephony Project (NRTP) (Binniyat, 2007).
- Revocation of the sale of Nigeria Telecommunications Ltd. (NITEL) and its mobile subsidiary, Mobile Telecommunications Limited, to the Transnational Corporation of Nigeria (TransCorp) (Onyedika et al., 2008).
- Creation of two new ministries – the Ministry of Communications and Information Technology (MCIT) and the Ministry of Information – out of the Ministry of Information and Communications.
- Scrapping the Nigerian Broadcasting Commission (NBC), whose functions were to be transferred to the regulator, the Nigerian Communications Commission (NCC) (Nwankwo, 2008).

Physical access to technology

Nigeria boasts a broad base of ICT infrastructure, but access to the technology remains a critical factor in its effective contribution to the nation's development.

Among the available technologies are wireless broadcasting technologies (radio and television), fibre-optic cables, metallic cables, mobile networks and satellite. The Nigerian National Petroleum Company (NNPC), Power Holding Company of Nigeria (PHCN), NITEL and Globacom have provided the backbone networks.

However, Nigeria is still essentially a rural country: 70% of its 140 million people live in rural areas. It is therefore important to assess ICT infrastructural availability in this context.

In terms of access, the global system for mobile (GSM) has become ubiquitous in most Nigerian cities. This is one of the reasons why Nigeria now has the fastest growing telecoms market in Africa. By April 2008, Nigeria's GSM subscriber base had increased to 47,205,063. In 2001 the teledensity ratio was 0.73%, but this has steadily increased over the years to 33.72% in April 2008.

The remarkable growth in the industry has seen an inflow of USD 12 billion in foreign direct investment from 2001 to April 2008.[1] But the increase in GSM subscriptions has not been matched with improvements in service quality: entry costs and tariffs are still high, as are complaints about poor service delivery. This explains why the Nigerian regulator has given subscribers a voice through the Telecom Consumer Parliament. The "parliament" has complained of an inability to recharge airtime, a high rate of dropped calls, poor audio quality, call interference, non-delivery of short message service (SMS), multiple billing systems for SMS, and poor customer care services. The regulator had to impose bans and fines on some Nigerian telcos because they were taking on many more customers than their infrastructure could cope with, leading to the poor service quality (Wireless Federation, 2007). The regulator acknowledges these deficiencies, but says they are due to the inability of the service providers to expand and meet demand.

According to the NCC, mobile coverage also only extends to 20% of the country, covering largely urban and peri-urban areas. Out of Nigeria's 76.53 million phones, about 13 million are in rural areas, serving 80% of the population. To bridge this gap, the NCC plans to offer fixed wireless access (FWA) telephony licences, allocated on a geographical basis, to ensure coverage of underserved populations. Fixed wireless access is the use of wireless technology to replace copper to connect subscribers to the telephone network (Trinkwon, 1996).

The Nigerian regulator's decision in 2003 to unify fixed and mobile licences became a disincentive for fixed-line operators, because new unified access operators were not under any obligation to provide rural connectivity. This concern partly informed the awarding of a contract of USD 93 million in 2006 to the National Information, Communication and Education Programme (NICEP), in the high hopes that it would significantly reduce the rural-urban information gap in Nigeria. Galaxy Backbone, a private sector initiative, was mandated to use a combination of satellite and very small aperture terminal (VSAT) to facilitate infrastructural access

1 Nigerian Communications Commission: www.ncc.gov.ng

for people in rural Nigeria (This Day, 2008). As at June 2008, the company has started the installation of 5,000 nodes for the VSAT network in the 36 state capitals and 774 local government areas.

It was also partly in recognition of the need to reach the underserved rural population that the government set up the National Poverty Eradication Programme (NAPEP)[2] through its Rural Communication Programme (RCP). The aim of NAPEP was to ensure that Nigerians in rural areas would be within one-day walking distance from a telephone. The regulator has also proposed a new licence category for fixed-line services in so-called short distance charging areas (SDCAs), or those with less than 1% teledensity, which may also be attractive to some private investors.

Besides these, the NCC now has two major strategies for the roll-out of broadband access throughout the country: the Wire Nigeria (WiN) project, through which it will subsidise the building of a core, high-capacity fibre-optic layer, and the State Accelerated Broadband Initiative (SABI). The Accelerated Broadband Initiative was designed to make broadband infrastructure available in all the 36 state capitals of the country as well as urban and semi-urban centres. The regulator's intention is to use SABI to provide wireless broadband services in Nigerian cities as widely as possible in order to stimulate demand and increase usage, at affordable prices. The WiN project will provide fibre-optic cable backbone infrastructure across the country to complement SABI.

Human capacity training

The level of awareness within the Nigerian government of the role ICTs can play in national development has gone past the stage of debating ICTs versus other development challenges, such as combating disease and poverty or ensuring food security and potable water. There is now an appreciation that connectivity is essential for development and that high-level human capacity training, such as is available through university education, is essential to meet these development challenges. Sustainable, long-term development is only possible where there are adequately trained scientists, engineers, doctors, and businesspeople, all products of Africa's universities (Juma & Moyer, 2008). The underutilisation of the existing capacity of the wired and wireless networks in Nigeria is partly due to low skills, or lack of adequately qualified personnel, and the poor state of the nation's universities.

However, a major achievement has been the completion of Nigeria's ICT-for-development (ICT4D) draft policy document. This comprehensive document will go a long way to address the gaps in the levels of physical access to technology and human capacity training in Nigeria.

2 www.napep.gov.ng

Action steps

Civil participation

The participation of civil society in ICT development is crucial. Yet the country's recent track record of civil participation is not looking good. Since its inception in 2004, the Freedom of Information Coalition has provided a voice for civil society in Nigeria. The GISWatch 2007 report for Nigeria mentioned that this coalition was at the forefront of lobbying for the passage of the Freedom of Information (FOI) Bill. The bill was unanimously passed by the Nigerian Senate on 15 November 2006, but suffered an unforeseen setback when the former president declined to support its enactment into law. The FOI – a cornerstone of democratic government in any country – had been pending before the National Assembly since 1999, and was re-presented to the new National Assembly in 2007. On 29 April 2008, the House of Representatives, for the fourth time in two months, refused to debate the bill.

In 1996, the previous administration saw the possibility of using community radio to address the high illiteracy rate in Nigeria. With 51% of the population illiterate, the 2008 Education for All (EFA) Global Monitoring Report suggests that Nigeria may not achieve the EFA goals – which include increasing adult literacy by 50% – by the 2015 deadline (UNESCO, 2008).

In our GISWatch 2007 report, we said that the government's decision was still pending following a report by the Community Radio Policy Drafting Committee, which was submitted to the federal government on 12 December 2006. But nothing further has been heard about it.

These omissions need to be addressed by civil society.

A different kind of power

One of the reasons two GSM operators, Celtel and MTN, argued in their legal action that the NCC should not impose fines on them for persistent poor quality of service was that poor power and security infrastructure has led them to incur huge installation and running costs (AAGM, 2007).

Whatever the ICT infrastructure is, it needs to have enough power to make it accessible for use at any time of day or night. The power situation in Nigeria has not improved under the new administration, despite huge financial investments. The new minister of energy recently intervened and released 600 electricity transformers of various capacities, electrical breakers, switches, and cables locked up in storage at the Power Holding Company of Nigeria (PHCN) in Abuja for ten years (Binniyat, 2008). The power sector has also been tabled before the National Assembly for investigation.

GSM for development

As a largely private sector-driven enterprise, the Nigerian mobile sector remains the major driver of the Nigerian ICT industry. However, it does not have the development orientation that is needed for rural connectivity. As a result, the exponential growth of GSM in Nigeria may have been at the expense of underserved rural communities, because most GSM operators have not gone beyond urban areas where it has been possible for them to recover most of their investments. The licensing strategies that have promoted the mobile phone revolution may have actually exacerbated the urban-rural digital divide, and inadvertently worked against the government's vision of providing affordable access to unconnected rural dwellers.

GSM is also an expensive technology, whose limitations for carrying data do not make it competitive with other technologies, such as fixed lines, fibre optic and other high-speed data services. This means that the recent GSM growth may not translate into sustained ICT growth, nor facilitate Nigeria's effective participation in the global economy.

The regulator has to find ways to bring competition to rural telephony in order to engage the private sector. The regulator is responsible for the administration of the Universal Service Provision Fund (USPF), which provides incentives to operators to extend services to less lucrative, unserved and underserved rural areas. The USPF was established in 2002, and is funded by contributions of 5% of the gross revenues of all major telcos; but it has up to USD 800 million unspent.

National ICT4D policy

The challenges and opportunities for Nigeria's ICT development are enormous, and these are best anchored within a national policy. The renewed efforts by the Nigerian IT Development Agency (NITDA) to provide a roadmap for ICT4D initiatives is a step towards getting ICT-enabled development down to the grassroots. This policy needs a comprehensive public awareness programme to encourage buy-in, and the government's commitment to more coherent infrastructural development and deployment.

Nigerian universities are often located in peri-urban or rural communities. Getting adequate connectivity to the universities can therefore be one way of providing affordable access to the rural population. One of the goals of the USPF has been to underwrite the costs of infrastructural deployment by private operators. This policy needs to be applied more vigorously with verifiable targets given to the selected operators.

At the same time, access for different disadvantaged groups needs attention. For instance, physical access is of fundamental importance for people with disabilities – a key point of focus for the current administration. However, one year on, there is not much evidence of a policy dealing with the issue, although the new ICT4D policy holds out some hope.

With Nigeria's population of 140 million still largely rural dwellers, the 50 million phone subscribers and 10 million internet subscribers do not amount to adequate coverage. A technology that can provide affordable broadband at the last mile of connectivity must be promoted (Oruame, 2008). The move by the regulator to issue spectrum licences in the 2.5-gigahertz (GHz) band (which so far has been used for broadcasting) will open up the market, and will hopefully encourage more private operators to explore last-mile access. The NCC, in addition to its efforts with WiN and SABI, has also endorsed WiMAX broadband access.

Physical access to technology is not an end in itself. The main purpose for access must be kept in clear focus: it is the access to content that is important. The exchange of information and knowledge through these technologies is what will bring about development for Nigeria. All of these require the implementation of an integrated and sustained human resource development programme, as recommended in the draft ICT4D policy. ■

References

AAGM (2007) Nigerian Communications Commission/Operators – Who Blinks First? *This Day*. The Financial Times Limited Asia Africa Intelligence Wire/Factiva.

Aluko, B. (2008) Nigcomsat, NCC Disagree Over Licence Issuance. *Nigerian Muse*, 19 January. Available at: www.nigerianmuse.com/projects/TelecomProject/Nigcomsat_NCC_Disagree_Over_Licence_Issuance

Binniyat, L. (2007) Bureaucracy threatens $400m national rural telephony project. *Vanguard*, 13 August. Available at: www.vanguardngr.com/articles

Binniyat, L. (2008) Minister Orders Distribution of 600 Transformers. *Vanguard*, 1 April. Available at: 72.3.244.61/stories/200804010359.html

Nigerian Communications Commission: www.ncc.gov.ng

Nkanga, E. (2008). Nigeria: Seeking Lower Cost of Broadband Access. *This Day*, 11 June. Available at: allafrica.com/stories/200806120177.html

Nwankwo, B. (2008) Task Force Recommends Separate Ministry for ICT. *Leadership*, 17 April. Available at: allafrica.com/stories/200804170369.html

Onyedika, N., Eke, E. and Mbamalu, M. (2008) FG Revokes Sale Of NITEL. *The Guardian*, 17 February. Available at: www.guardiannewsngr.com/news/article01//indexn2_html?pdate=170208&ptitle=FG

Oruame, S. (2008) Nigeria gears up to auction 2.5GHz spectrum. *InfoWorld*, 16 June. Available at: www.infoworld.com/news/feeds/08/06/16/Nigeria-gears-up-to-auction-25GHz-spectrum.html?source=gs

This Day (2008) FG Paid N5bn Rural Telephony Project Without Agreement. *This Day*, 25 April. Available at: allafrica.com/stories/200804250207.html

This Day (2008) GSM – FG Says Quality of Service Has Improved. *This Day*, 11 June. Available at: allafrica.com/stories/200806120091.html

Trinkwon, D. (1996) *The Technology of Fixed Wireless Access*. Available at: www.citi.columbia.edu/wireless/!citi_fw.htm

UNESCO (2008) *Education for All by 2015: Will we make it? EFA Global Monitoring Report 2008*. Available at: portal.unesco.org/education/en/ev.php-URL_ID=49642&URL_DO=DO_TOPIC&URL_SECTION=201.html

Wireless Federation (2007) Globacom pays fine. *Wireless Federation News*, 26 September. Available at: wirelessfederation.com/news/globacom-pays-fine-nigeria

PAKISTAN

Bytes For All
Shahzad Ahmad, Shahida Saleem, Rabia Garib and Fouad Bajwa
pakistanictpolicy.bytesforall.net

Introduction

A developing nation of over 164 million people,[1] Pakistan faces some of the most unique development challenges in the world. Alternatively listed as an A+ investment country, and then as the "most dangerous place on earth", the country has see-sawed between optimistic economic reports, violence, political instability and uncertainty. While claims of outstanding macroeconomic performance during the last few years abound, the incidence of poverty has, in fact, substantially increased. According to an estimate, close to 57 million people live below the poverty line – and this estimate includes 11 million people pushed below the poverty line over the last three years. The situation is likely to worsen in the years to come, especially in the wake of rising food and oil prices.

Despite all the odds, overall, 2007 saw a strong foreign investment influx, with over nine billion dollars invested in the telecom sector alone (Pakistan Times, 2007). As such, the influence and potential of information and communications technologies (ICTs) has never been more apparent, especially through their effect on the economic and social polity of the country. While Pakistan ranked 63rd with a score of 3.7 out of 10 on a recent e-readiness rating (EIU, 2007), the information technology (IT) and IT-enabled services sectors boast an impressive 61.18% growth in exports, making Pakistan a country to watch very closely. Efforts to bridge the digital divide continue, and the official information until the third quarter 2007 shows considerable progress has been made in the area of physical access. This includes mobile phone growth – over 89 million people now have mobile access (PTA, 2008) – and broadband expansion (150,000 connections). The growth of broadband is being triggered by market demand and aggressive plans of the various commercial players. Some operators are also rolling out nationwide WiMAX infrastructure. Pakistan's teledensity increased from 4% in 2003 to 51% in 2007 (both mobile and fixed lines). Mobile phones have become an important technology in ICT for development (ICT4D) initiatives.

Yet despite the claims by the government that it provides access from the mountains to the coast, there is an evident gap in the provision of access, and a dearth of an ICT culture. Whatever infrastructure is available is driven by market dynamics and commercial interests, and its quality is seriously questionable. As a result, remote areas are still far from enjoying a thriving backbone and the fruits of technology magic. While capacity has increased, the beneficial use of ICTs by the majority is still a grave concern.

Being the frontline state in the "war on terror" and a playground for international powers, Pakistan is suffering acutely as the war takes its toll on all aspects of development. Due to the worsening law and order situation, and in the name of national security, a huge population is deprived of quality access and of ICT-based development opportunities. Censorship and surveillance in the name of national security are on the rise, even in the new democratic regime. This also limits the effective use of ICTs and has negative implications on business and general ICT use.

Convergence of various ICT-related policies is a great challenge. Some very weak, undemocratic and draconian policies, and, above all, a lack of a coordination mechanism among various custodians of different policy sets are other issues. A people-centred approach to policy development initiatives, as well as implementation and monitoring, is totally missing. With the new democratic government in place, it is hoped that steps will be taken in the right direction to bring about change and positive impacts, taking into consideration inclusive approaches to policy development and governance.

Contextualising access

Pakistan seriously lags behind in harnessing the potential of ICTs, mainly due to an outmoded regulatory regime and a lack of focus and coordination in addressing ICT challenges and opportunities. While the new government seems committed to removing barriers to development, and attempting to improve access, the fact remains that a comprehensive, coordinated ICT policy, driven by the input and commitment of all stakeholders and sectors, remains lacking. Unfortunately, the existing policy has not helped any implementation efforts and has failed to show tangible results in any area. Besides neglecting the inclusion of all public and private sector stakeholders, it was not directly linked to other national development plans, and as such lacked the integrated vision and consensus required for real impact.

The fact that the Pakistani population is 67% agrarian and rural means that most of the ICT capacity and culture is only available to 33% of the country's citizens. An even smaller percentage actually benefits from technology because there is a significant lack of local language content, literacy and skills amongst the general public. If the urban regions are analysed, it can be seen that a majority of people are living in poverty. It is only the middle and upper classes that are participating in the ICT industry and related developments.

1 Population Census Organization: www.statpak.gov.pk/depts/pco/index.html

Therefore, Pakistan has to ask: how much ICT capacity and culture has really been developed? How can the government devise a strategy to help in further increasing ICT adoption and usage by the rest of the population?

After the fall of the military dictatorship, Pakistan is now entering a new era of social and economic development. This era should essentially be driven by innovation and access to ICTs. In the globalised market, where China and India are its major competitors, Pakistan has to shine by overcoming different challenges, such as fighting corruption and inducing good governance practices.

Physical access to technology

The goal to empower citizens with ubiquitous and universal access to ICTs is still a distant dream. This is not to say that there are no current policy initiatives. The Universal Service Policy (USP) developed by the government, with the main objective of providing basic access to telecommunications to poor and underprivileged communities across Pakistan, is a key component of the current ICT4D efforts in Pakistan.

The USP advocates the following goals:

- To make voice telephony affordable and internet access available to progressively greater proportions of the Pakistani population
- To foster conducive conditions and an enabling environment in which teledensity can grow
- To jumpstart the broadband and ICT markets to facilitate e-services.

In terms of penetration of ICT services, targets for 2010 were set as follows:

- 85% of the population should have telecommunications coverage and access to e-services, if desired
- 5% teledensity in rural areas
- 1% broadband penetration
- Preferably one telecentre for every 5,000 people, or at least one telecentre for every 10,000 people in Universal Service Fund (USF) contract areas.

Moreover, by the end of 2015, 95% of the population should have telecommunications coverage.

Unsustainable business models and a lack of local content and real connectivity, however, continue to pose major barriers to the implementation of USP targets. Efforts to utilise ICTs to achieve larger development goals remain mainly on paper. Substantial efforts by both the private sector and key government entities such as the Planning Commission and Ministry of IT will be decisive in determining whether ICTs will play a role in Pakistan's human and social development in the future.

Human capacity and training

Prerequisites to successful ICT programmes are the awareness, capacity and ICT literacy of users. ICT literacy has been introduced into the public school curriculum, but a lack of infrastructure in the schools prevents the new curriculum from being implemented. Many private sector and non-profit organisations, including Oracle (ThinkQuest), Ko-Ordination Group (with 3,000-plus ICT literacy centres), and Pehla Qadam (which offers an ICT-based literacy toolkit), have taken matters into their own hands and are striving towards imparting ICT literacy.

The government, through the Ministry of IT's Electronic Government Directorate, as well as other ministries, has started several very important projects with potentially wide-scale impact, specifically in the areas of transparency, accountability, and facilitation of access to ICTs. However, implementation hurdles and a lack of integration of appropriate agencies have prevented achieving the potential levels of impact to date.

A very vital part of the overall national development vision is the creation of qualified manpower in higher education. Stunning advances made in the last few decades in the fields of IT, biotechnology, material sciences, health sciences, renewable energy and other disciplines are rapidly changing the face of the globe, leading several countries on the path of social and economic development.

The Higher Education Commission (HEC) has undertaken a systematic agenda for reform, which includes categories such as faculty development, excellence in learning and research, relevance to national priorities and improving access.

So far the HEC has been able to set up the Virtual University[2] and Allama Iqbal Open University.[3] The Virtual University is Pakistan's first university relying completely on modern ICTs. It was established by the government as a public, not-for-profit institution. The aim was to provide affordable world-class education to aspiring students all over the country. Using free-to-air satellite television broadcasts and the internet, the Virtual University allows students to follow its rigorous programmes regardless of where they live. Over 750,000 students (growing at 14% a year) currently benefit from the distance-based learning programmes. This is over three times more than all the students of all the other universities put together.

Locally relevant content, applications and services

In ICT-enabled societies, there are two major challenges that every culture and society struggles to deal with: the unimpressive amount of credible, verifiable and accurate information that is available for free download, and the dearth of information that is available in a language that a local population can understand. With the potential for information overload that Web 2.0 offers, if a community is not pushing the right information out, hundreds of thousands of content aggregators are inadvertently recycling bad information which is already out there on an ongoing basis.

2 www.vu.edu.pk

3 www.aiou.edu.pk

The most challenging task is local language content availability. This space is being filled by individual initiatives, and more materials are being made available for specific applications. These include education, health, training, social websites and other information sites. Innovations like machine translation sites[4] are creating new opportunities for start-ups, as is the release of Urdu Language Tools by the Centre for Research in Urdu Language Processing.[5] It is envisioned that this will be instrumental in outreach of e-services to the majority. The centre, having already successfully developed the Urdu lexicon, speech recognition system and fonts, is now also coordinating the PAN Localisation project for seven Asian languages.

Action steps

- While the government is committed and work has begun on integrated policy formulation, the road ahead is long and arduous. A serious united effort by all stakeholders will have to take place in order for any real progress in the ICT policy area to be made. Isolated pockets of effort must be mainstreamed for scaling up and mass impact. A core group including the USF, Ministry of IT, Higher Education Commission, Pakistan Software Houses Association, civil society and private sector representatives must lay out a long-term roadmap and then serve as monitoring agents to ensure its implementation. Without a cohesive and integrated effort, the small pockets of activity, and the lessons learnt, will never be able to benefit the majority.
- The government has to generate the capacity of its citizens to embrace and engage technology and employ its uses in various avenues of life. Once this has been achieved, a culture of technology becomes the driving force for future ICT industry development and growth. The impact of such an industry has both social and economic effects, as technology becomes a daily life tool rather than simply a gadget-based fascination for its users. Pakistan has never had a strategy nor an ICT policy that focused on creating an ICT culture and increasing capacity on an ongoing basis in line with the changing social and economic environment. This needs to be taken up by all the stakeholders as critical.
- Access to online content is increasing, and with various stakeholders getting a stronger grasp of media convergence, perhaps more incentives could be given for a stronger focus on citizen journalism to generate larger amounts of local content. If there are not enough proactive initiatives taking place to produce fresh content, there are more chances for outdated content to return and haunt us. The web never forgets and stories on it stick. At the same time, Pakistanis who understand technology are adept at creating innovative platforms which can be shared by larger groups to inspire discourse and instigate discussion for change. The change is already happening, and it is only a matter of time before the creation of local content will be more streamlined.
- The importance of the local language must be stressed at all levels, regardless of whether it is a barrier to entry for a large part of the Pakistani population or not. The preservation of the local language is critical for maintaining a community's cultural identity and history.
- Pakistan's strategic direction should be building a society based on the foundations of creativity, innovation and emerging disciplines. This can only be achieved through increasing the capacity, usage and appropriation of ICTs. It also has to be realised that an innovative knowledge-based economy can only be achieved by cultivating, nurturing and retaining the top talent in the important and emerging creative classes. These include the youth, scientists, engineers, designers, writers and businessmen and women that serve as the source of growth in the country's knowledge economy. Unless Pakistan is positioned both locally and globally as an innovative and technologically advanced nation, it will never be in a position to become a talent magnet and retain its own creative human resource base. Opportunity should be demand-driven. In order to create that demand, the government must dedicate and mobilise its resources and fuel critical change throughout the country with increased transparency and accountability. ■

References

Allama Iqbal Open University: www.aiou.edu.pk

Centre for Research in Urdu Language Processing: www.crulp.org

EIU (Economist Intelligence Unit) (2007) The 2007 e-readiness rankings. Available at: www.eiu.com/site_info.asp?info_name=eiu_2007_e_readiness_rankings

Government of Pakistan Population Census Organization: www.statpak.gov.pk/depts/pco/index.html

PTA (Pakistan Telecommunication Authority) (2008) Telecom Indicators: Mobile Cellular Services. Available at: www.pta.gov.pk/index.php?option=com_content&task=view&id=650&Itemid=603

Pakistan Times (2007) Pakistan telecom sector attracts $ 9 Bln investment. *Pakistan Times*, 19 February. Available at: www.pakistantimes.net/2007/02/19/business1.htm

Virtual University: www.vu.edu.pk

4 www.paktranslation.com

5 www.crulp.org

PARAGUAY

Radio Viva FM 90.1
Arturo Enzo Bregaglio
www.radioviva.com.py

Introduction

Sixty-one years of delays and one flower

Paraguay, located in the Southern Cone region of South America, is a country where the socioeconomic development model is so unequal and unfair that almost 80% of its land is in the hands of less than 10% of the population. Out of a population of almost six million people, over 2.1 million live in poverty and nearly 1.2 million in extreme poverty.

For every 100 Paraguayans, 33 live in poverty and 20 survive on a monthly income of PYG 200,000 (about USD 40). According to the Ministry of Education and Culture, 97% of children between the ages of six and eleven are enrolled in primary school, although the school enrolment rate drops to 54% in the case of children twelve to fifteen years old. In the meantime, 8% of children aged five to fifteen work on the streets (MEC, 2005, p. 17).

Carrón (2007) estimates that about 116,000 people left Paraguay for other countries during 2006 alone. Of these, 2% were fifteen years old or younger, 10% were between fifteen and nineteen, and 73% were between twenty and 39 years old.

Even though Paraguay is a member of South America's Mercosur trade bloc, and a partner in the binational hydroelectric entities Itaipu (Brasil-Paraguay) and Yacyreta (Argentina-Paraguay), which provide much of the energy for the Southern Cone, it suffers a higher development asymmetry compared to its regional partners, and the different development indicators show very clearly that there are many things still to do.

The election of former Catholic bishop and pro-poor advocate Fernando Lugo on 20 April 2008 is seen as a hopeful sign for more egalitarian development. However, he has a tough task ahead, with challenges that include corruption and historical inequalities, both of which are responsible for the "misfortune of Paraguay", as the famous Paraguayan writer Augusto Roa Bastos put it.

The design of new social policies, especially in health, housing and education, face structural problems such as budget restrictions and a lack of investment.

The proposal of agrarian reform to benefit poor farmers is faced with a production structure based on only a small number of landowners who produce and export soybeans on a large scale, and cattle farming that results in the export of meat to large markets, especially Chile and Russia. Paraguay is the fourth largest exporter of soybeans worldwide, and meat is the third highest source of national income. Another major economic support is remittances from Paraguayans scattered throughout the world, on which many depend.

There is no doubt that the new political scenario in Paraguay has as its principal challenge the consolidation of democracy. It is crucial that it does not result in an authoritarianism that secures its early death.

Physical access to technology

Paraguay is a country with a subtropical climate and rainfall that exceeds 1,000 mm annually. A lack of roads makes travelling between villages, departmental capitals and Asunción, the capital of the country, difficult.

A lack of investment and the high levels of corruption for over six decades are evident to anyone who travels through the country in three aspects:

- Poor road infrastructure, with only three main routes for the whole country.
- Fixed-line telephone infrastructure that is no longer sufficient for all the cities of the country. For some in rural areas the nearest telephone is 70 kilometres away.
- Abundant electricity, produced by the Itaipu dam, which is unfairly distributed between the two states that own it: Paraguay and Brazil. The base of this inequity is the Treaty of Itaipu itself, signed in 1973, by the dictators of Brazil and Paraguay. The treaty establishes an equal distribution of electricity, but since Paraguay does not have the proper infrastructure to use the full provision of electricity, the country is forced (according to the treaty) to sell the rest only to Brazil at prices much lower than market prices.

To illustrate the challenges faced with physical access to technology, consider what happens on the border between Paraguay and Brazil. Since the days of the bandits in the 17th century, Paraguay's borders, particularly with Brazil, have been thin and permeable lines. Beginning in 1950, during the Stroessner regime, what began as a programme of settlement of the rich eastern territory of the country became a sale of land to landowners and foreign companies. Motivated by the offering of cheap and fertile soils, large and medium-sized Brazilian producers acquired extensive portions of land in Alto Paraná, Canindeyú and Caaguazú. Under these circumstances a particular group called *Brasiguayos* developed, whose identity evolved with specific ethnic, linguistic, political and economic features. The *Brasiguayos* became consolidated as a powerful group in the area, controlling great parts of the production and affecting public policies. Because of them, many cities along the border use Portuguese as their primary language in business and everyday life.

In terms of the integration of Paraguayan peasants and the *Brasiguayos*, the data reveal a situation that is not very encouraging. There are currently two different productive models, two cultures, and two modes of accessing new technologies.

On the one hand, the *Brasiguayos*, with greater financial resources and a better understanding of technology, create opportunities for large-scale production and high profitability. They use new technologies provided by the Brazilian private sector, and get internet access through Brazilian internet service providers (ISPs). They use the internet regularly to manage the prices of their products, to analyse markets and economies, and to compare market demand in both Paraguay and Brazil.

On the other hand, the poor Paraguayan peasants, without techniques to improve their crops, and with less land every day, are dissatisfied with this situation. Access to new technologies is almost non-existent, and the connectivity offered in some cities by Paraguay's state telecommunication company, COPACO, is slow, costly and outdated, and generally inaccessible to the Paraguayan peasantry.

Another case worth noting: Paraguay is currently inhabited by more than 85,000 indigenous people (DGEEC, 2002). Not long ago, in March 2004, there was a meeting between members of an indigenous organisation and a family from the indigenous Totobiegosode forest tribe, who had come out of the wilderness to establish contact with the modern world for the first time (ABC Color, 2004). The living conditions of most indigenous groups are marked by a lack of access to land, lack of access to basic social services, hunger and dependency on various forms of government hand-outs.

These few examples illustrate the dramatic nature of the encounter between two worlds. They are also symbolic of a greater divide. The difficulties that Paraguay is facing in an integration process that is both *internal* and *external* are more than obvious in the cases reported. This reality demonstrates that integration cannot be conceived as the simple task of incorporating access to new technologies.

What is needed is for the new Paraguayan government to measure tensions that originate in political, social and environmental policies. They require state and binational agreements that guarantee a pluralistic and democratic coexistence.

The impact of the legal and regulatory framework

Paraguay is one of the few countries in Latin America where the control of telecommunications – and therefore internet services – remains under the control of the state, and there have been no reforms or proposals aimed at changing this scenario.

During the last days of 1994, with the enactment of the new Telecommunications Law 642/95, the National Commission of Telecommunications (CONATEL) was established. But far from being a body representing various sectors of society, as the International Telecommunication Union's (ITU) "Blue Book" recommends, it is a body that reports directly to the president, and has directors appointed by the will or recommendation of the president without consulting parliament, or any other sector of Paraguayan society.

COPACO retains a monopoly over fibre-optic internet services, while CONATEL grants licences to a dozen companies for the provision of new services. The criteria for awarding the licences are not very different from those that governed during COPACO's total monopoly, and the result is a process with dubious transparency, which has ensured "free competition without a free market."

As a consequence, the telecommunications services that are provided in Paraguay today have the following features:

The fixed telephone network is growing very slowly, and the cost of the service is expensive. Installation in some cases takes several years, and in some areas of Asunción or its suburbs, it never gets done.

Of the country's seventeen departments, only about four to five important cities have fixed-line services. These services can be described as "moderately acceptable" in quality, and have similar problems to those that occur in the capital, such as lags in installation time.

There is virtually no fixed-line rural telephony. COPACO services only reach urban areas located in the regions outside the capital.

In the meantime, multinational mobile companies are multiplying rapidly. By 2006, the number of mobile subscribers far exceeded fixed telephony users.

Precarious state control and a lack of price regulation has meant that consumer rights have been neglected, and citizens have had to accept bad contracts and poor quality services.

Internet access became available through private companies that are expanding in Asunción with long-term investment plans, and without state control. The network has primarily been set up in Asunción and neighbouring areas, but also extends to some large cities in other departments. The network reaches about 2.6% of the total population of six million.

The sectors with the greatest connectivity overall are the private sector, some divisions of the state and municipalities in Asunción, a limited number of universities, non-governmental organisations (NGOs), cooperatives and private users.

The service offered by any of the private operators depends on the bandwidth offered by COPACO, which is typically unstable, slow and expensive.

Over the past two years COPACO has decided to get into the market to compete with the private sector companies in order to lower the costs of service. However, this is considered unfair competition by other market players, because COPACO still controls the main telecommunications infrastructure in the country.

Finally, we should point out that one of the main factors influencing the telecommunications environment is that the government has not carried out the reforms and restructuring that other countries underwent in the 1980s and 1990s. The decentralisation of the management of telecommunications is one of the pressing issues on the agenda of the new government.

Action steps

The information society is no longer a topic of academic discussion and has become an important part of the agenda of development policies in almost all countries in the world. The adoption of this new paradigm based on information and communications technologies (ICTs) is closely related to the degree of a society's development. However, technology is not just a product of development, but also, to a large extent, one of its engines: it is a development tool.

There are a number of development possibilities in terms of ICTs that that show potential in the most backward country in the region. These include the potential of using and optimising new technologies in some 100 telecentres throughout the country and deepening the experiences of technological convergence between ICTs and radio through greater coordination between various stations for coverage of events of national significance (this takes advantage of the fact that radio remains the most widely used medium in Paraguay).

While the decentralisation of internet services currently handled by the government monopoly is a must, there is also a need for increased coverage of ICTs in the media, including coverage of the relationship between youth and ICTs (68.3% of the population is under 30 years old).

We can suggest the following action points:

- Promote and encourage national dialogue on the role of technological change and innovation in economic and social development.
- Generate proposals that promote the decentralisation of internet use and the democratisation of access to radio spectrum in order to end the state monopoly.
- The popularisation and democratisation of access to science and knowledge and the application of this to the social needs of Paraguay.
- Promote policies of science, technology and innovation in accordance with policies of macroeconomic stability. These should be in line with social policies that address poverty and inequality.

References

ABC Color: www.abc.com.py

Carrón, J. M. (2007) La emigración paraguaya en el contexto de la globalización. Paper presented at the Third Paraguayan Population Congress, Asunción, 22 November.

DGEEC (Dirección General de Estadísticas, Encuestas y Censos) (2006) *National Household Survey*. Asunción: DGEEC. Available at: www.dgeec.gov.py

MEC (Ministerio de Educación y Cultura) (2005) *Education Statistics*. Asunción: MEC. Available at: www.mec.gov.py

PERU

CONDESAN (Consortium for the Sustainable Development of the Andean Ecoregion)
Jorge Bossio
www.condesan.org

Introduction

The Peruvian telecommunications sector is regulated by two institutions: the Ministry of Transportation and Communications (MTC), which is mainly responsible for the development of policies and granting licences to operating companies; and the Supervising Agency for Private Investment in Telecommunications (OSIPTEL), which is mainly responsible for regulating and supervising competition within the sector.

The telecommunications public services market has been characterised by a growing number of operators. The most dynamic and competitive segments have been those that require the least amount of investment, such as services that do not need to deploy "last-mile" networks. Other segments that require the most investment in infrastructure (landline, public, and mobile telephone services) are provided by only a small number of operators.

Despite the important growth observed over the last few years, recent data published by the National Institute of Statistics and Information (INEI, 2008) show that more than 40% of Peruvians only have access to radio and television at home.

Policies of expansion and competition

Changes introduced in the area of regulation foster the development of convergent services, reduce entry barriers, and as a result, facilitate the entry of new operators into the market (Razo & Rojas Mejía, 2007). In 1998, through Supreme Decree 020-1998-MTC, the telecommunications market was opened to competition. Recently, in 2007, the Supreme Decree was modified, with a new set of guidelines aimed at: (i) consolidating competition; (ii) reducing the gap in infrastructure; and (iii) expanding services to rural areas. The new guidelines established the following goals for the year 2011:

- To reach a teledensity of twelve landlines and 60 mobile lines for every 100 inhabitants
- To expand telephone services (landlines and/or mobile lines) in all districts at a nationwide level
- To achieve a million broadband internet connections
- To promote convergence.

The tools for achieving these goals include policies on tariffs, transparency, retail sales (and resale), promoting the legal registration of businesses, interconnection, spectrum management, number portability, and universal service.

Mobile services

The most obvious result of the new competition policies can be seen in the mobile sector (Gallardo et al., 2007). The total number of mobile phones increased during the year 2007 from 8.7 million to 15.4 million, representing the highest rate of growth in the last ten years (76%). As a result, the goal of 60 lines for every 100 inhabitants was reached in the first quarter of 2008. Due to this fact, in February 2008, the MTC modified the telephone penetration goals to 80 mobile phone lines and fifteen landlines for every 100 inhabitants.

The results from the National Household Survey during the first quarter of 2008 (INEI, 2008) confirm that 51.5% of Peruvian homes own at least one mobile phone, which means a 15.6% growth compared to the results obtained the previous year. The growth in urban areas outside of Lima has come close to 22 percentage points, reaching 66% of homes in these areas.

Regarding rural areas, mobile phones are used by 17% of households. However, this does not necessarily imply that the phones have service coverage in these areas; rural dwellers primarily use mobile phones when they travel to or are in the proximity of urban areas.

Landline telephone services

As a result of the allocation of the 450 megahertz (MHz) band to Telefónica Móviles, the company assumed responsibility for the installation of 350,000 wireless land lines during the year 2008. This would go some way to reaching the goal of 15% penetration, but would not be enough to achieve it entirely, which is why an additional effort by the private sector is deemed necessary.

Overall growth in the public telephone system seems to have come to a standstill. After showing growth rates between 14% and 19% in 2001-2003, the installation of public telephones has slowed to 8% or lower. This could be due to the alternatives that have appeared in the country's main cities over the last few years, such as public call centres and informal mobile phone rental services. In 2008 OSIPTEL ordered a reduction in prices for calls made from public telephones, which has been followed by initiatives by telephone companies aiming to reverse the downward trend in usage.

Nevertheless, even when it constitutes the best communication alternative for those who do not subscribe to personal landline or mobile telephone services (Barrantes, 2007), the public telephone system does not form part of the goals established by the policy guidelines.

Universal access policy

In Peru universal access is guaranteed by means of the Telecommunications Investment Fund (FITEL). Between 1998 and 2001, FITEL held successful tenders for four projects. The reverse bidding process was aimed at providing targeted subsidies for operators. The subsidies provided a portion of the capital investment costs and the costs of specific stages of implementation and operation.

After 2001, FITEL found itself at several crossroads. Firstly, rural operators faced competition due to the expansion of city operator services (in the areas of both public and mobile telephony), which seriously affected their economic sustainability. Torn between the projects' sustainability and the expansion of its network, the question FITEL faced was: should the investment made in these projects be protected or should the market be left to do its job?

Secondly, FITEL found itself debating incentives for investment and the allocation of funds. Should it be careful when it selected areas for intervention so as not to interfere with the expansion plans of commercial operators? If it did this, unspent money in the fund would increase, while many rural areas would remain unserved. How would it justify the apparent inefficiency in expenditure and the growth of the fund?

Thirdly, the question of the kinds of services that should be considered universal services was raised. Should access to the internet be included in its plans? Should mobile telephone services be included?

The final hurdle involved the choice between a small local operator and a large national operator. Which should be the model for business? Should small independent operators be promoted, or was it preferable to give incentives for large operators to expand their networks from the cities to the rural areas?

Unfortunately, the administration was unable to solve these issues effectively. In its attempt to do so, it created mechanisms that aimed to define the path to be taken, such as policy guidelines to promote greater access to telecommunications services in rural areas (Supreme Decree 049-2003-MTC). This clearly indicated a commitment to a model of small companies dedicated to rural telecommunications, and to taking into consideration access to the internet and other elements of human development as part of FITEL's objectives.

However, soon after, while faced with the pressures to speed up implementation and to mobilise funds (by means of 040-2004-MTC), it was established that telecommunications operators could present projects that aimed to use their own contributions to the fund and that those projects would not require approval by the ministry. This was considered a blow to the universal access policy (Saravia, 2005).

In five years (2001-2006), FITEL was only able to evaluate and award funds to one pilot project – a telecommunications operator in the Andes. Finally, the management of the fund was transferred to the MTC by means of Law 28900 in November 2006.

The new administration of FITEL funded three large projects that focused on the provision of internet access and multi-services via broadband networks. These projects were inherited from the previous administrators of the fund and reevaluated and promoted by the current one.

In June of 2008, the MTC proposed a new regulatory framework for telecommunications in rural areas (Ministerial Resolution 242-2008-MTC/03). With this regulatory framework, MTC aims to consolidate the inclusion of broadband and the development of capabilities within the defined objectives of universal access. In it, some definitions are established regarding areas of intervention, rural operators, and MTC authority to promote investment. As this report was being written the proposal for the regulatory framework had not yet been approved.

Use of ICTs

Mobile access

Only 60% of mobile users are subscribers to a mobile service (Barrantes, 2007). The other 40% of users – mainly women and young people with low incomes – tend to borrow phones or rent phones from *chalequeros* (informal dealers). Mobile phones are associated with the possibility of keeping in contact with family and friends, with job opportunities, and with saving time.

Statistics show that users are cost-conscious. Mobile phones tend to be used during reduced-rate hours, and "flashing" – where you alert someone to the fact that you want to be called using caller ID, without actually connecting – is common amongst the lowest income earners.

Incoming call traffic represents more than 70% of total traffic on prepaid phones. However, the origin of that traffic is changing: in 2004, the calls terminated in mobile networks were mainly from landline phones (41%) and public phones (30%), but by the end of 2007, mobile networks originated 44% of the incoming traffic.

Regarding outgoing calls, on-network traffic represents 81%, followed by 12% to landline telephones, and only 7% to other mobile phone networks. This preference has been steadily increasing at a rate of approximately 6 percentage points per year since 2004, when the proportion of on-network outgoing call traffic was 63%. This can probably be attributed to price reductions and promotions.

Finally, it should be emphasised that the outgoing call traffic from postpaid phones has traditionally been higher than from prepaid phones, despite the fact that postpaid phones constitute only 10% of the total number of phones in service. This situation has changed since 2007 as a result of aggressive campaigns and promotions that focus on prepaid phone clients. Outgoing prepaid call traffic during 2007 reached 48% of the total, an upward trend which continued in the first quarter of 2008.

Internet access

A significant number of Peruvians access the internet using telecentres or cybercafés. The latest report released by the

INEI (2008) regarding the penetration of ICTs found that only 6.9% of Peruvian households have access to the internet. Despite this, 30% of the population over six years old claim to use the internet, and 75% of them access the net mainly at cybercafés.

The use of cybercafés in Lima is in decline and is being substituted by other access options such as home access and institutional access (Apoyo, 2007). In contrast, in rural areas the use of cybercafés is on the rise (INEI, 2008). The internet user profile in Peru reflects the current conditions of social exclusion: only 23% of women are internet users compared to 31% of men.

According to a recent independent report (Apoyo, 2007), 58% of residents of Lima consider themselves to be regular internet users; 92% of the population from the highest socioeconomic level claims to use the internet compared to 38% from the lowest socioeconomic level. Gender imbalances are found within the city, where only 52% of women claim to be users versus 64% of men. The average profile of the internet user in Lima is most definitely that of a man between twelve and 35 years old, with a mid-level socioeconomic status. The primary uses of the internet are for communication purposes (78.5%) and for finding information (74.7%) (INEI, 2008).

There is little information available regarding the use of the internet in rural areas. The primary activity related to the internet is communication with friends and family members, mainly by means of chatting. Email is used sparsely; in fact, only 2.7% of those surveyed considered it to be a substitute for telephone service, preferring other services such as traditional mail. Other uses of the internet, such as getting work-related information or information related to productive activities or services in general, altogether constitute only 10% of the reasons for using the net (Bossio, 2005).

Action steps

Even while the Peruvian economy is growing, the uneven distribution of wealth and the conditions of inequality and exclusion still remain quite striking.

Regarding access to telecommunications services, FITEL's intervention, and the expansion of mobile networks, have allowed for telecommunications services to be available to the majority of the population. However, it is important to take into consideration that access to these services and technologies is not the only factor that is important. The existing inequalities and exclusions based on culture, language, education, age and gender, as well as physical and mental disabilities, require greater attention. Given that the digital divide is a part or an expression of a larger social divide, it cannot be approached only from the perspective of technology. Peru seems to be moving forward in this regard, even though mostly in theory rather than in practice.

On the other hand, the globalisation of telecommunications companies' operations, and the search for economies of scale, both by operators and manufacturers, pushes developing countries towards the adoption of new technologies in urban areas even when there is no service readily available for "older technologies" in underserved areas. This presents a risk as well as an opportunity: the risk of widening the gap between those who do and those who do not have access to these services, and the opportunity for the excluded populations to "leapfrog" stages of development. For this to occur, there would need to be a stronger coordination of public policy to promote competition, the expansion of services, and a consolidated fight against poverty.

In the same way, the policy of universal access must take into account not only the coordination of sectors in the deployment of infrastructure (roads, energy, water and sanitation), but also sectors that are engaged with the development of human capabilities and the development of appropriate content (education, health, manufacturing, trade, etc.). ■

References

Apoyo (2007) *Usos y Actitudes hacia Internet.* Lima: Apoyo Opinión y Mercado.

Barrantes, R. (2007) *Oportunidades móviles: pobreza y acceso a la telefonía en América Latina y el Caribe. El caso de Perú.* Lima: DIRSI. Available at: www.dirsi.net/files/peru_final.pdf

Barrantes, R. (2008) *Convergencia y universalización de los servicios de telecomunicaciones: agenda pendiente.* CEPAL.

Barrantes, R., Agüero, A., Galperín, H. and Molinari, A. (2007) *Asequibilidad de los servicios de telefonía móvil en América Latina.* Lima: DIRSI. Available at: www.dirsi.net/files/finals/asequibilidad_de_los_servicios_de_telefona_mvil_en__amrica_latina.pdf

Bonifaz, L. and Bossio, J. (2006) Perú. In Stern, P. and Townsend, D. (eds.), *Nuevos modelos para el Acceso Universal de los servicios de Telecomunicaciones en América Latina: informe de países.* Washington: World Bank.

Bossio, J. (2005) Uso de internet... aún lejos de metas de desarrollo. *TIC para el desarrollo.* Available at: tic_rural.blogspot.com/2005/08/uso-de-internet-lejos-de-metas-de.html

Gallardo, J., López, K. and González, C. (2007) *Perú: Evolución del Acceso, la Cobertura y la Penetración en los Servicios de Telefonía.* Lima: OSIPTEL. (Reporte N° 1 SGI-GPR 2007).

INEI (2008) Las Tecnologías de Información y Comunicación en los Hogares: Enero-marzo 2008.

Razo, C. and Rojas Mejía, F. (2007) *Del monopolio de Estado a la convergencia tecnológica: evolución y retos de la regulación de telecomunicaciones en América Latina.* Santiago de Chile: CEPAL/División de Desarrollo Productivo y Empresarial.

REGULATEL (2005) Panorama General de la Situación de la Banda Ancha en América Latina y su Evolución Temporal.

Saravia, M. (2005) *Acceso universal en el Perú: Futuro de FITEL en riesgo.* Lima: ITDG. Available at: www.itdg.org.pe/publicaciones-ver.php?codigo=198&idcate=13

Stephens, R., Bossio, J. and Ngo, J. (2006) Expanding the frontiers of telecom markets through PPP in Peru: Lessons for pro-poor initiatives. *Gridlines,* 5.

Webb, R. and Fernández-Baca, G. (2007) *Perú en Números.* Lima: Instituto Cuanto.

ROMANIA

StrawberryNet Foundation
Rozália Klára Bakó
www.sbnet.ro

Introduction

This report focuses on two issues: access to information and communications technologies (ICTs) in Romania, and the legal and policy context shaping ICT access. Building on the GISWatch 2007 country report conclusions,[1] we found these issues the most pressing, and therefore the most useful to assess. A key assumption was that the ICT sector in Romania had improved in terms of dynamic development, increased visibility, and funding opportunities due to European Union (EU) accession. The report was compiled through desk research and empirical analysis (participant observation at major ICT events and interviews with key actors, during May-June 2008).

The Romanian ICT sector registered a market value above EUR 7 billion in 2008, making a 10% contribution to the country's gross domestic product (GDP).[2] The sector has attracted substantial investments, high quality human resources and public prestige (Baltac, 2008).

Romania's EU membership since January 2007 has facilitated access to structural funds for ICT development. Public and private partnerships have strengthened in ICT policy-making processes and infrastructural investments: a well-organised and vocal business advocacy drive acted as a catalyst for ICT development initiatives. At the same time, civil society actors' involvement became more visible: the 2008 eLiberatica Conference[3] on free and open source software (FOSS) attracted more public attention than in 2007, and a well-publicised internet education project was implemented during 2007 and 2008 by the Center for Independent Journalism (CJI)[4] and the Association for Technology and Internet (APTI).[5]

The main factors affecting ICT use negatively, according to interviewed media, law and ICT actors, were the lack of practical education, an unsettled regulatory framework and poor self-regulation when it comes to content, both at the individual and institutional level.[6] Infrastructural access, and geographic-, gender- and age-divide issues were not part of mainstream ICT discourse in Romania.

ICT access in Romania

The dynamic ICT development from 2002 to 2007, driven by EU accession requirements and pushed by the business community,[7] had broader benefits for individuals, organisations and society at large. A visible process of digital inclusion took off, funded by public and private actors. Major funders of ICT development projects and programmes in Romania were the EU, the World Bank, the United States Agency for International Development (USAID), the Center for International Private Enterprise (a non-profit affiliate of the US Chamber of Commerce) and the Ministries of ICT and Education. Western organisations acted as role models in Romania, with a louder voice in the business sector (Bakó, 2007).

Infrastructural access to ICT improved substantially: telephony and internet services penetrated even remote communities – this due to the implementation of a universal service directive in 2004 (Manolea, 2008). Under EU accession pressures, the telecommunications market was liberalised from 1 January 2003. In four years, competing fixed-telephony service providers secured a 28.7% market share, as shown in Table 1.

The fixed-telephony penetration rate was 19.8% on 31 December 2007, according to regulatory authorities (ANRCTI, 2008), compared to a 90.5% penetration rate for mobile telephony (Secmerean, 2008).

Access to internet services experienced constant growth from 2005 to 2007, in terms of an increase in internet service providers (ISPs) and better quality services. In two and a half years, the number of ISPs almost doubled, as shown in Table 2.

The internet penetration rate has increased steadily, from 5.5% in 2005 to 26.9% in 2007. It is still low compared to other EU member states, but the growth rate is substantial, as shown in Table 3.

1 www.globaliswatch.org/node/3445

2 Ministry of Communications and Information Technology (MCTI): www.mcti.ro

3 www.eliberatica.ro

4 www.cji.ro

5 www.apti.ro

6 User-generated content needs self-regulation rather than institutional intervention, which would limit free speech.

7 See GISWatch 2007.

Table 1: Fixed-telephony market structure (2004-2007)

Indicator	31 Dec. 2004	31 Dec. 2005	31 Dec. 2006	31 Dec. 2007
Market share of incumbent operator (%)	98.9	90.3	80.6	71.3
Market share of competing providers (%)	1.1	9.7	19.4	28.7

Source: **www.anrcti.ro**

Table 2: **ISPs in Romania (2005-2007)**						
Indicator	30 Jun. 2005	31 Dec. 2005	30 Jun. 2006	31 Dec. 2006	30 Jun. 2007	31 Dec. 2007
No. of ISPs	692	981	1,154	1,412	1,389	1,338

Source: **www.anrcti.ro**

Table 3: **Growth in internet penetration rate in Romania (2005-2007)**						
Indicator	30 Jun. 2005	31 Dec. 2005	30 Jun. 2006	31 Dec. 2006	30 Jun. 2007	31 Dec. 2007
Total access (%)	5.5	8.5	11.7	15.3	21.0	26.9
Broadband (%)	2.4	3.5	5.5	8.2	10.8	14.8

Source: **www.anrcti.ro**

Table 4: **Dedicated internet broadband penetration rates in the EU, at 31 December 2007**				
Indicator	Denmark (high)	Bulgaria (low)	EU-27	Romania
Penetration (%)	36.6	7.6	20.0	9.9

Source: **www.anrcti.ro**

As for the dedicated broadband internet penetration rate, compared to other EU member states, Romania ranked amongst the lowest third, as shown in Table 4.

The most far-reaching digital inclusion programme in Romania is the Knowledge Economy Project. It was started by the Ministry of Communications and Information Technology (MCTI) in partnership with the Ministries of the Interior and Education, and is funded by the World Bank (2006-2010). The total amount of funds allocated to this initiative is USD 70 billion.[8] An important component of the programme is the creation of 200 so-called Knowledge Centres in small, disconnected communities across Romania. The next step in the programme involves targeting small business communities and local authorities and encouraging them to set up business-to-business (B2B) and business-to-consumer (B2C) relationships.

Another important governmental initiative was presented at the FOSS conference eLiberatica: the development of open ID in Romania (Teodorescu, 2008). The MCTI is negotiating with major telephony operators and commercial banks to get involved in providing digital identity for Romanian citizens. This would offer easy, safe and affordable access to electronic services provided by governmental agencies and businesses.

ICT businesses in Romania make a well-organised, articulate, and vocal community. The sector attracts expertise, attention, resources and prestige, interviewed experts said. Key ICT business players are organised informally in a lobby group (Tech 21 Coalition), which monitors laws and regulations in the ICT sector and raises its voice for members.

Open source communities have also strengthened their voices. The Romanian Open Source Initiative,[9] a non-governmental organisation (NGO) created in 2007, organised two conferences aimed at mainstreaming FOSS for businesses, government, users and developers. The first eLiberatica Conference (2007) focused on general issues relating to FOSS, with participants from the open source business community (e.g., IBM, Sun Microsystems, eZ, Mozilla Foundation, Gartner) and high-profile developers from the international FOSS scene. The second conference reached a broader audience, including businesses, government officials, media, and international and local developers.

Romania's EU membership (from 1 January 2007) opened up access to structural funds for ICT development. The total amount of money dedicated to strengthening the sector is EUR 559 billion, with an EU contribution of 68.5%, and co-funding from the public and the private sector, as shown in Table 5.

The EU funding is targeted at three main areas: developing ICT use, strengthening electronic services, and sustaining the e-economy, with a more substantial resource allocation to ICT use, as illustrated in Table 6.

The developmental objectives of the structural funds were clearly set for each field, according to specific country needs:

- Projects aimed at better ICT use should facilitate broadband access for small, disconnected communities and for schools.
- Projects aimed at developing electronic services should focus on e-government, improve the interoperability of electronic systems and look at e-learning and e-health applications.
- Projects promoting the e-economy are expected to produce electronic systems for efficient business management and for B2B operations management (e.g. e-payment, e-commerce, e-tenders).

8 Finantare.ro: www.finantare.ro

9 www.rosi.ro

Table 5: **EU structural funds for Romanian ICT development (2007-2013)**

Total amount (EUR)	EU contribution	Public co-funding	Private co-funding
559 billion	383 billion	86 billion	90 billion

Source: **www.mcti.ro**

Table 6: **EU structural funds allocation priorities for Romanian ICT development**

Total amount (EUR)	ICT use	Electronic services	E-economy
383 billion	149 billion	119 billion	115 billion

Source: **www.mcti.ro**

There is increasing public attention on ICTs in education. Education and media experts found ICT-related education too theoretical and knowledge-based, rather than skills-oriented (Baltac, 2008; Av'dani, 2008). High schools and universities are focused on developing sophisticated programming skills, whereas the proficient, ethical and data-sensitive use of the internet is not on the "digital immigrant" educators' agenda (Prensky, 2006).

There is a lack of gender and FOSS mainstreaming in official ICT discourse. Government representatives challenged at eLiberatica 2008 on poor FOSS visibility in public discussions declared defensively that the neutrality principle does not allow them to promote either proprietary or free software solutions.

Legal and regulatory framework

The strengths and weaknesses of ICT policy in Romania are connected to EU accession pressures, market development trends and regulatory institutions' lack of capacity (Manolea, 2008). The sector's main strengths, according to Manolea, are substantial efforts made to catch up with EU legislation dealing with liberalisation and a simplification of the authorisation processes for ICT businesses. The main weaknesses concern legislative and functional instability. Legislative instability is a result of too quick and unprepared an alignment with EU legislation, which did not consider the specific country regulatory framework. As a result, an avalanche of ICT-related laws were issued by the government, skipping any consultation process (Manolea, 2008). Functional instability refers to an unclear and unsettled regulatory framework which makes it difficult for government stakeholders to do their work.

Personal data protection and right to privacy issues are expected to raise debates and concerns due to the boom in e-commerce (Jugastru, 2008). Although they copy the EU directives on the matter, the laws and regulations adopted in Romania are problematic: those dealing with personal data storage are too weakly justified, others dealing with control mechanisms for safe data storage are not clearly set, and guarantees for protecting personal information are not sufficient.

A World Bank-supported project for South East Europe funded the creation of a CD-ROM on ICT-related public policies in Romania, targeted at the ICT business sector. The state secretary at the MCTI declared at the launch that Romania could become a leader in the ICT field in the region, and a role model to other countries (MCTI, 2008).

Developing responsible communication practices on the internet was an important issue mainstreamed by civil society actors, particularly the Center for Independent Journalism and the Association for Technology and Internet. Education and self-regulation are seen as the best ways to reach this goal, according to one media expert (Av'dani, 2008). Governmental authorities should not intervene to limit internet content; instead, individual and institutional actors should be educated towards self-regulatory practices (CJI, 2008).

To conclude, there is an increase in awareness and more frequent discussions on ICT policy issues amongst professional and institutional actors in Romania. The fact that eight Romanian law and ICT experts recently contributed to a book on the information society in Europe, focusing on ICT policy (Péron, 2008), is significant proof of this.

Action steps

Two keywords highlight priorities in terms of ICT access and policy: *education* and *participation*. They are interconnected and refer to both issues analysed in this report.

Education is an important catalyst for strategic ICT use: universities have to develop their ICT curricula with a more practical approach that focuses on skills rather than theoretical knowledge (Baltac, 2008). It is also necessary to educate wider audiences (citizens and organisations) so that they can properly benefit from the information society (Brad, 2008).

Civil society actors should get involved in educating young people about the internet in terms of using it more professionally, and issues such as personal data protection (Av'dani, 2008).

Strengthening partnerships and adopting a multi-stakeholder approach to ICT development is a must in order to enable inclusive and transparent regulatory processes, ICT policy experts believe (Manolea, 2008; Jugastru, 2008).

More effort should be made to encourage FOSS and gender mainstreaming in Romania, and civil society organisations and governmental actors should be systematically involved in this process.

Finally, ICT policy in Romania needs a more settled regulatory framework, more transparency and more public participation. ■

References

ANRCTI (Autoritatea Nationala pentru Reglementare in Comunicatii si Tehnologia Informatiei) (2007) *Piata de comunicatii electronice din Romania.* Available at: www.anrcti.ro

Association for Technology and Internet (APTI): www.apti.ro

Av'dani, I. (2008) De la non-reglementare c tre auto-reglementare pe Internet. Presentation at the CJI workshop *Bune practici in comunicarea pe Internetul romanesc,* Bucharest, 19 June.

Bakó, R. (2007) Information Society Discourse in Romania: Role Modeling Western Factors. *Electronic Journal of Radical Organization Theory.* Available at: www.mngt.waikato.ac.nz/ejrot/cmsconference/2007/proceedings/criticalviewsacrosscultures/proceedings_criticalviewsacrosscultures.asp

Baltac, V. (2008) Universities and the Information Society. In Péron, F. (ed.), *L'Europe dans la societé de l'information.* Brussels: Larcier, pp. 205-214.

Brad, R. (2008) Un seul réseau de communication – un seul monde – un internet. In Péron, F. (ed.), *L'Europe dans la societé de l'information.* Brussels: Larcier, pp. 29-36.

CJI (Centrul pentru Jurnalism Independent) (2008) *Bune practici in comunicarea pe Internetul romanesc.* www.cji.ro/articol.php?article=440

eLiberatica: www.eliberatica.ro

Finantare.ro: www.finantare.ro

Jugastru, C. (2008) La protection des données personnelles et le commerce électronique – la situation en droit roumain. In Péron, F. (ed.), *L'Europe dans la societé de l'information.* Brussels: Larcier, pp. 185-204.

Manolea, B. (2008) Réglementation des communications en Roumanie – peut-on parler d'un succes? In Péron, F. (ed.), *L'Europe dans la societé de l'information.* Brussels: Larcier, pp. 37-56.

MCTI (Ministry of Communications and Information Technology) (2008) *Sectorul IT&C romanesc promovat ca exemplu de buna practica in regiunea Europei de Sud-Est.* Available at: www.mcti.ro

Péron, F. (ed.) (2008) *L'Europe dans la societé de l'information.* Brussels: Larcier.

Prensky, M. (2006) Listen to the Natives. *Educational Leadership,* 63(4), pp. 8-13.

Secmerean, E. (2008) Rata de penetrare a telefoniei mobile, 108%. *Business Standard,* 11 March. Available at: www.standard.ro/articol_34059/rata_de_penetrare_a_telefoniei_mobile__108.html

Teodorescu, C. (2008) For the First Time in Europe: Digital ID Providers and OpenID Services for Romania. Presentation at the eLiberatica Conference, Bucharest, 29-31 May.

RWANDA

Rwanda Development Gateway Centre, National University of Rwanda
Emmanuel Habumuremyi
www.rwandagateway.org

Introduction

Rwanda, a densely populated, landlocked country in East Africa, lies south of the equator and covers 26,338 square kilometres. In 2008, the population was pegged at 9,139,919 (CNE, 2008). Dominated by very young people, with about 63% of the population living below the poverty line of USD 1 per day, there is a rapid population growth of 2.9% per annum. The country's commitment to gender equality has resulted in a high representation of women in decision-making positions. Along with recent legal reforms, these changes hold the potential of alleviating the unequal share of challenges facing the population.

Despite the 1994 genocide and challenges of poverty, Rwanda is hailed in the region as having the highest level of commitment and a unified approach to ensuring information and communications technology (ICT) diffusion and exploitation for development. The country is trying to find the path that will set it on course for achieving the objectives laid out in its Vision 2020.

Today, Rwanda boasts an internet exchange point (IXP), an ICT park, a national computing centre, and a telemedicine network that connects hospitals and universities in an attempt to transform and expand health services to underserved areas. However, despite a high level of political commitment to taking ICT development forward as a priority area, the current trend reveals several gaps. These relate to access to adequate infrastructure, affordability of ICT services, and weak coordination of ICT initiatives.

This report considers how far Rwanda has come in its plan to move from an agricultural-based economy to a knowledge-based economy through developing competitive, service-based industries.

Policy context

Rwanda started developing an integrated ICT policy in the late 1990s, with the vision of making ICTs a key part of its global socioeconomic development planning and policy. Known as the National Information and Communication Infrastructure (NICI) plan and policy, the plan is to be implemented in five-year phases with a different focus for each phase. The current NICI II plan (2006-2010) serves as a point of policy reference. It also serves as a framework for the government's long-term goal to transform the country into an information-rich, knowledge-based economy by pursuing an ICT-led socioeconomic development policy (Government of Rwanda, 2006, p.13).

The country has gone through major economic and telecommunications reforms that were aimed at increasing the competitiveness of the telecommunications industry and attracting foreign investment. Amongst them, the Rwanda Utility Regulatory Agency (RURA) was established with a mission to promote fair competition, to improve quality of services, and to create an enabling environment that attracts investors with the intention of improving the provision of services to citizens. This step was taken in accordance with the universal access obligations set by the International Telecommunication Union (ITU).

Rwanda has based its ICT policy on the Common Market for Eastern and Southern Africa (COMESA) model ICT policy, which was developed to serve as a guide for the harmonious development and application of ICTs within member states. To this end, a Rwanda-Tanzania "digital bridge" policy framework was developed to provide affordable, ubiquitous and high-quality services, and to build a competitive regional ICT sector, while creating an enabling environment for sustainable ICT diffusion and development.

Physical access to technology

Rwandatel, the main fixed operator and internet service provider, has a fairly extensive national microwave backbone that covers the capital Kigali and the main urban and semi-urban areas. It has built a fibre ring around Kigali city, as well as a link from Kigali to Butare in the southern part of Rwanda. It also has a code division multiple access (CDMA) network on top of its microwave backbone. MTN Rwanda-Cell and Rwandatel have both started to lay fibre to the east, close to the Tanzanian border. The current MTN network is estimated to cover 75% of the country, including Kigali and smaller, rural towns.

The government is currently rolling out fibre optics along all the main roads, a process which will be completed by 2010. From the main fibre-optic trunk, internet will be carried to the countryside via wireless technologies. It is expected that the combination of fibre-optic backbone and 3.5 gigabytes per second (Gbps) WiMAX wireless will cover the country and make Rwanda the most communication-wired country in East Africa (RIEPA, 2007). The first phase, covering 134 kilometres, is already underway (New Times, 2008). The power utility company Electrogaz has also decided to establish a private fibre-optic network alongside its grid.

Besides these, the Karisimbi project plays a significant role in enhancing electronic communications and broadcasting capabilities, not only in Rwanda, but also in nearby areas in neighbouring countries. This project seeks to provide low-cost, high-capacity communications capability to both rural and urban populations, and will expand coverage for mobile phones, internet, TV and FM radio, and reach many beneficiaries. It also seeks to offer air safety and surveillance capabilities through a Communication Navigation Surveillance/Air Traffic Management (CNS/ATM) system, which has already been endorsed by COMESA. Once fully operational, the project is expected to reduce the cost of communications in Rwanda on average by about 50%.

Various initiatives in Rwanda are underway to increase the population's access to ICTs. For example, the government is deploying multi-purpose community telecentres throughout the country to facilitate the spread of ICTs in the community (RITA, 2007).

Another government initiative is the ICT Bus Project being developed by the Rwanda Information and Technology Authority (RITA) and scheduled to commence late this year. The programme will use two buses, each with a fully equipped computer laboratory, that will act as mobile computer labs that will benefit farmers, traders, students, women, youth groups, entrepreneurs and other rural-based Rwandans (RITA, 2008).

As for the Rwandan private sector, the Scan ICT survey (Gatera, 2007) shows that ICTs in business is in its infancy stage. A number of businesses are aware of ICTs but are not using them, and only a few of them have a website presence.

Before June 2004, internet service providers (ISPs) were using international operators to carry their local as well as international traffic. The high cost of the satellite links and delays in connection made the situation unbearable, and limited the growth of the internet in Rwanda.

In October 2003, the Swedish International Development Cooperation Agency (SIDA) assisted Rwanda in the establishment of an internet exchange point (IXP). The Rwanda Internet Exchange (RINEX) project entered into operation in February 2004. RINEX keeps local traffic local and saves international bandwidth (Gatera, 2007).

Some ISPs were reluctant to connect to RINEX because they thought that the IXP would be managed by Rwandatel, since it is hosted there. This threat has been relieved a bit following a statement by RINEX management ensuring its neutrality. There is also a need for developing an IXP policy at the national level that guarantees its sustainability.

Licence application processes have been a problem for new telecommunication companies wanting to operate in Rwanda. Delays in processing applications are common, a situation which also contributes to delays in driving ICTs forward in the country.

Recent research by Research ICT Africa (RIA) has shown Rwanda has very poor scores across a range of technical areas, from tariff regulation, to interconnection, to spectrum management. This reflects, according to the authors, the "general lack of capacity in the regulator, as well as lack of a visible regulatory environment that involves not only the regulator, the Ministry of Communications and private operators, but also civil society and academics" (Esselaar et al., 2007, p. 45).

Appropriateness of technology

As communications facilities are mostly found in the cities where telecom operators are based, radio is the dominant source of information in Rwanda, because of its ease of use and access for more than 94% of the population living in rural areas (RITA, 2007). The lack of adequate power supply in remote areas also hinders the development of communications facilities.

Nevertheless, the health sector in Rwanda has started to use ICTs to deliver information focused on safe and efficient care. Another project is TRACKNet, a database used to collect AIDS data from the field, using cell phones with interactive voice response (IVR), general packet radio service (GPRS) and short message service (SMS) technology (Index, 2008).

The One Laptop per Child (OLPC) project is also worth mentioning. Currently 5,000 laptops are being distributed to all primary school children within five years. The project's implementation faces some challenges, such as reaching rural areas. For Carine Umutesi, who is in charge of the project at RITA, sensitisation campaigns targeting the schoolchildren and teachers will be key to the success of the project. The other major challenge is the lack of pedagogical materials on the laptop. The English versions are not understood by every child. Another issue is that technology is changing so fast that the OLPC programme might become redundant very quickly.[1]

Action steps

A number of initiatives, projects and activities are being carried out by the public and private sector. However, the organisations carrying out these initiatives are not collaborating or communicating, leading to a duplication of some of the activities (DICTM, 2008). It is recommended that the government put in more effort to encourage synergies. In particular, RITA's authority to manage and oversee all ICT initiatives should be strengthened.

The level of ICT awareness is quite low amongst the general population, and even within some organisations. Although the use of mobile phones is quite widespread in Kigali, there is a general lack of knowledge about the benefits of using other ICT technologies (DICTM, 2008). It is recommended that the government of Rwanda support and encourage civil society organisations to take on the roles of awareness raising, sensitisation and encouraging the uptake of ICTs in society.

At the moment, Rwanda's ICT sector is growing fast and the situation is likely to continue into the next few decades. The government of Rwanda's commitment to ICTs is seen by Rwandans as noble. The introduction of ICTs with a view to contributing to Rwanda's socioeconomic development is a long-term strategy and at present the country is still building the foundations of an information-based economy. Efforts

1 From an interview with the author, 30 April 2008.

made now will realistically only have a serious impact on overall standards of living several years down the line.

The development of human capacity in the ICT sector is, however, a critical issue that must be given immediate attention. Along with human resource development programmes, the curricula developed in higher education institutions should be designed to meet Rwandan labour market requirements and the demands of changing technologies, particularly in the ICT sector (World Bank, 2007).

References

CNE (National Electoral Commission) (2008) Final Voter List Statistics. Available at: www.comelena.gov.rw/index.php?&Effectif

DICTM (Danish ICT Management) (2008) Support to RITA and RURA for Monitoring Competition and Developing Regulatory Framework within ICT services (funded by the UNDP). Kigali: DICTM.

Esselaar, S., Gillwald, A. and Stork, C. (2007) *Towards an African e-Index 2007: Telecommunications Sector Performance in 16 African Countries.* Johannesburg: Research ICT Africa (RIA). Available at: www.researchictafrica.net/images/upload/Africa_comparativeCORRECTED.pdf

Government of Rwanda (2006) *An Integrated ICT-led Socio-economic Development Plan for Rwanda 2006-2010: The NICI-2010 Plan.* Kigali: MININFRA.

Gatera, E. (2007) *Scan ICT Baseline Survey Report. ICT Indicators: Measuring Usage and Penetration (Draft).* National Institute of Statistics of Rwanda (NISR).

Index (2008) Pioneering ICT in Rwanda's Health Care System. *The Index Magazine*, January, pp. 18-23.

New Times (2008) Business Sector to Foot Bill for Fibre Infrastructure in Rwanda. *The New Times*, 15 August. Available at: www.balancingact-africa.com/news/back/balancing-act_419.html

Nsengiyumva, A., Habumuremyi, E. and Haba, S. (2007) *Pro-Poor ICT Project Report – Rwanda: A Community-driven Network.* Kigali: UNDP.

RIEPA (Rwanda Investment and Export Promotion Agency) (2007) ICT Sector Profile. Available at: www.rwandainvest.com/spip.php?article88

RITA (Rwanda Information Technology Authority) (2007) *Business Plan Model for the Multipurpose Community Telecentres.* Kigali: RITA.

RITA (2008) *ICT Buses to bridge the digital divide in Rwanda.* Available at: www.rita.rw/spip.php?article132

World Bank (2007) ICT at Glance: Rwanda. Available at: devdata.worldbank.org/ict/rwa_ict.pdf

SENEGAL

APC West and Central Africa ICT4D Network
Coura Fall
www.apc.org

Introduction

In July 2008, legislation governing the development of an information society in Senegal was signed by parliamentarians in the National Assembly. This legislation includes:

- A law which lays down the main trends of the information society in Senegal by supplementing current legislation regarding information and communications technologies (ICTs)
- A law on cyber crime
- A law dealing with the protection of private data
- A related law dealing with electronic transactions (e-commerce).

This new legislation is proof of the political will in Senegal to develop an inclusive information society to the benefit of all the country's citizens.

Country situation

In Senegal, telecommunications contributes significantly to the improvement of macroeconomic indicators and the development of social and economic activity, with a contribution of 8% to the country's gross domestic product (GDP). The sector recorded a growth in value of 22.5% in 2006. While the fixed-line telephone market performed well, the internet sub-sector grew by 60.4% in the same year.

Senegal's advanced telecommunications network makes the country an attractive location for businesses establishing a presence in Africa. The domestic market is small but offers cheap labour, low operational costs, and a modern and affordable telecommunications infrastructure.

Mobile services were introduced in 1996 and competition in that sub-sector began two years later. Since the introduction of competition, the number of mobile subscribers has grown dramatically, with cellular lines now representing more than 85% of all telephone lines. Internet usage has doubled every year since 2003 when asymmetric digital subscriber line (ADSL) services were introduced. There is already extensive investment in fibre-optic infrastructure. Overall market penetration of broadband is still low, making it an attractive opportunity as ICT companies look to compete for new licences to operate.[1]

At the end of 2006, there was one national telecommunications company, SONATEL; two mobile phone companies, TIGO and Orange Senegal (SONATEL's cellular branch); and 412 internet hosts. A new licence has been granted to the Sudan Telecommunications Company (SUDATEL), which will shortly start offering fixed-line, mobile and internet services.

Policy and regulation

In 1985, telecommunications in Senegal was completely reformed. The post and telecommunications activities of the Senegalese Post and Telecommunications Office were separated, and SONATEL was established.[2] In 1996, new legislation outlined the basic policy governing the telecommunications sector. In 1997, SONATEL's capital was partially privatised, with 42.33% held by France Telecom, 27.67% still owned by the government, 20% public-owned, and 10% employee-owned.[3]

This privatisation did not drastically change the ICT sector, since SONATEL maintained its control over all telecommunications services. In 2004, the incumbent's monopoly ended but by 2006, the second national operator (SNO) was still unannounced. Senegal made commitments under the World Trade Organisation's basic telecommunications agreement to introduce a regulatory structure promoting fair and healthy competition between operators.

Universal access

Universal access and services in Senegal are one of the few areas privatised. SONATEL provides a type of franchise opportunity for small operators to set up a pay phone, fax, internet or other communications access services in rural areas. The opportunity seems to work well for rural communities by creating local access to ICTs, and encourages entrepreneurship among small businesses and individuals who run the telecentres. Table 1 offers a snapshot of ICT usage data for 2006.

Participation

Telecommunications are reaching even the most rural parts of the country. With a secure infrastructure and modern network, even small and medium businesses can survive in the Senegalese market. The following are just a sample of some of the ICT programmes and organisations operating in the country.

A leading-edge Senegalese business that provides local farmers with up-to-the-minute market prices for their crops through their mobile phones has won two major African ICT awards. Manobi-Senegal was named most innovative

1 Budde Comm: www.budde.com.au

2 National Information and Communication Infrastructure (NICI) in Africa Country Profile: Senegal

3 Novatech 2006 Investor Profile: Senegal

Table 1: ICT usage 2006		
Service	Number of users	Teledensity (Pop. 11.9 million)
Fixed-line	266,600 (2005)	2.24 %
Mobile	2,218,906	18.6%
Internet	540,000	5%

company, and was also selected the overall organisational winner at the African ICT Achievers Awards. Manobi's founder and CEO, Daniel Annerose, started the internet and mobile service company with support from the Acacia initiative of the International Development Research Centre (IDRC), the communications company Alcatel, and SONATEL.

Farmers in remote areas of Senegal were provided with wireless application protocol (WAP)-enabled cell phones that allowed them to connect to the internet to check strategic market information and compare competing local buyers' offers for produce. Subscribers have received, on average, about 15% higher profits for their produce after having covered costs, including the price of Manobi's service. Acacia's contribution has been to put in place a method for collecting the necessary market information and to test how the system was accepted by the farmers. The World Bank has subsequently also supported Manobi in extending the cellular network to include market information related to the fisheries sector.

Telecentres are another initiative with a major impact. SONATEL launched the first four pilot telecentres in Dakar in 1992. Ten years later there were over 15,000 privately owned telecentres in Senegal, more than in any other country in Africa. Since 1997, SONATEL no longer provides public telephone services, but instead has been licensing telecentres, which are operated by small businesses. Most of these centres only provide access to public telephones, but an increasing number of them have faxes, computers and internet access. Telecentres now constitute up to 30% of SONATEL's annual revenues. To foster further growth, SONATEL provides a 40% discount on services to telecentres. There are already around 6,000 telecentres in Dakar alone and over 30% of all telecentres are located in rural areas. Together, these make up over 7.5% of SONATEL's total fixed lines.

Senegal was a beneficiary country for the Digital Freedom Initiative (DFI). DFI volunteers are working with United States (US) businesses and the Senegalese government to implement several internet-based initiatives, such as an electronic payment system and basic information technology (IT) training for Senegalese merchants.

The DFI has also identified and developed a variety of ICT-enabled training materials, which have been used to help improve cybercafé operations, business management, and market access for dozens of small and medium-sized enterprises in Senegal. DFI is now working to leverage its investment in these materials to have them used countrywide. The programme is run by the government.

The Senegalese Information Technology Association (SITSA) is the first national association to represent the information industry and professionals in Senegal. SITSA was created in 2003 by representatives of most of the information technology and services companies in Senegal. They decided to work cooperatively to create a new association to promote the ICT industry nationally and internationally.

E-commerce is at its early stages of development in Senegal. The country's first experience with e-commerce was launched by Trade Point, an initiative of the United Nations Conference on Trade and Development (UNCTAD) to facilitate international trade. Trade Point uses the internet to promote matchmaking between Senegalese businesses and international partners.

In September 2008, kheweul.com, an ICT company, launched a project that created 200 websites for musicians, drawing on local expertise.

SONATEL and the Gambia Telecommunications Company (Gamtel) launched a new prepaid card, called *Carte Sama Yai*, aimed at Senegalese living in Gambia. The card allows them to communicate with their families back in Senegal more easily, and at an affordable price.

The Group for Population Studies and Education (GEEP), a non-profit organisation, has established a project known as Youth Cyberspaces. The objective of this project is to support an existing network of family life education clubs active in secondary schools. The project offers network access in order to improve communication among the club's members. It also serves as a vehicle for the distribution of different educational tools that are related to reproductive health, environmental management, population, etc. There are twenty active clubs in different parts of Senegal. IDRC/Acacia funds this project and linkages have been established with the World Links programme.

The Ministry of Education and SONATEL signed an agreement that establishes preferential terms for access to the internet to make it more affordable for learning institutions. Discounts vary depending on the type of connection, but can go as high as 75%. Installation costs are also discounted. SONATEL is directly responsible for invoicing the schools.

Political will and the role of the president

Senegalese President Abdoulaye Wade is effectively the cantor of ICTs in the country. It is Wade who is promoting the idea of a universal access fund in Senegal, and who supervises the e-government initiative.

Senegal has started a three-phase roll-out of its e-government initiative, which entails networking 63 administrative buildings, connecting 35 department capitals, expanding the network nationwide, and incorporating value-added e-government applications.

Senegal is divided into eleven regions and 35 departments, and there are 11,000 villages spread throughout the country. These are not yet connected to one another via a government intranet, which results in a higher cost of communication between government entities. The roll-out of e-government services will first reduce intergovernmental operating costs, and, with the application of value-added services and e-government applications, will create an efficient, low-cost government that is more accessible to constituents.

The governmental intranet has been envisaged as carrying voice, video and data. This network is based on a fibre-optic loop which joins together eight principal nodes. It will offer:

- High-speed access to the internet
- Internet protocol (IP) telephony
- Advanced services: conference calls, video conferencing, and an online directory
- A server and portal based on free software, as well as a tool for productivity and effectiveness for all the public authorities.

Conclusion

Even if Senegal has one of the best telecommunications infrastructures in Africa, and despite all the political will in the world, this infrastructure is largely underutilised for various reasons. The prices of services are relatively high because of the absence of competition in international fixed telephony and the internet, as well as limited competition in the mobile telephony sector. Moreover, innovation is restricted by regulation which consolidates the dominant position of SONATEL. The question of rural telephony is largely ignored, and the digital divide between cities and rural areas is still significant.

Various reforms were never led within a participative framework. Civil society's engagement with policy processes has not been active or influential. Even when all stakeholders were invited to a two-day national consultation process, recommendations from civil society were not included in the decisions.

The relationship between government and civil society or the private sector is, however, being consolidated. The regulator has included them in a task force set up to manage the universal access fund. The most important objective for Senegalese civil society is to be a part of this group and advocate for changes in policy direction that will benefit citizens' practices of freedom, and the effective use of ICTs in development processes.

References

ADIE (Agence de l'Informatique de l'Etat): www.adie.sn

APIX (Agence Nationale chargée de la Promotion et de l'Investissement des Grands Travaux): www.investinsenegal.com

ARTP (Agence de Régulation des Télécommunications et des Postes): www.artp-senegal.org

Budde Comm: www.budde.com.au

Computer Frontiers (2007) Sub-Saharan Africa Information and Communications Technology Conference, San Francisco, USA.

National Information and Communication Infrastructure (NICI) in Africa Country Profile: Senegal.

Novatech 2006 Investor Profile: Senegal.

OSIRIS (Observatoire sur les Systèmes d'Information, les Réseaux et les Inforoutes): www.osiris.sn/rubrique212.html

SOUTH AFRICA

SANGONeT
David Barnard and Jan Moolman
www.sangonet.org.za

Introduction

As in the rest of Africa, a primary aim of the telecom reform process in the early 1990s in South Africa was to open the telecom market to new entrants, especially mobile service providers, network operators, internet service providers (ISPs) and data network providers. Increasing affordable access to telecommunications in the interest of social and economic development was a key goal. In 2006, the Department of Communications, which is responsible for policies for telecommunications and communications in South Africa, announced its three-year strategic plan, which included the goal of "enabling the reduction of the cost to communicate" (Esselaar et al., 2006, p. 12). Despite this, access to and the high costs of communications in South Africa remain critical challenges.

It is in this context that this report outlines the growth and use of the mobile phone as an appropriate technology in South Africa. Given the complexity of this area, it offers only a snapshot of some of the innovative uses of mobile technology in the country.

Growth of mobile

In 2001, the number of mobile phone subscribers in Africa passed the number of fixed-line subscribers. According to *African Telecommunication/ICT Indicators 2008*, the number of mobile subscribers in Africa has increased dramatically in recent years. In 2007, the African continent added over 60 million new mobile subscribers, and mobile phones represented 90% of all telephone subscriptions (ITU, 2008).

Africa remains the region with the highest annual growth rate in mobile subscribers. At the beginning of 2008, there were over 250 million subscribers on the continent. Mobile penetration has risen from just one in 50 people at the beginning of this century, to almost one third of the population today. Mobile subscribers are also now more evenly distributed across the continent. In 2000, South Africa accounted for over half of all Africa's mobile subscribers, but by 2007, almost 85% were in other countries (Goldstuck, 2006).

In South Africa, mobile phones have become the preferred medium of telephony since their introduction in 1994. At the same time, fixed-line subscribers have fallen by more than 10% from their peak in 2000. Arthur Goldstuck (2006) of World Wide Worx argues that this has been a direct result of three key factors:

- The disastrous roll-out of fixed lines by Telkom
- Limited options available from Telkom for fixed lines
- The high cost of fixed-line rentals.

While Telkom met the letter of the law in terms of its universal services obligations set in 1997 to deliver 2.8 million lines in five years, the spirit of the law was a different matter. By 2002, Telkom had to disconnect 40% of the 2.1 million lines it delivered over the previous four years due mainly to non-payment (or non-affordability).

Key players in the mobile market

The South African mobile phone market is dominated by two operators, namely Vodacom and MTN. Both operators were licensed in 1993. A third provider, Cell C, was licensed in 2001.

By the end of 2007, Vodacom recorded 24.3 million subscribers in South Africa, and a total subscriber base of 33 million across its networks operating in South Africa, Tanzania, the Democratic Republic of Congo (DRC), Lesotho and Mozambique. It has an estimated market share of 56% in South Africa, and its customer base is made up of 3.4 million contract customers, 20.8 million prepaid customers and just over 100,000 community service phones (Vodacom, 2008).

At the same time, MTN recorded 14.8 million subscribers in South Africa, but had a total subscriber base of 61.4 million across its 21 operations in Africa and the Middle East. MTN had an estimated market share of 36% in South Africa and its customer base is made up of 2.5 million contract customers and 12.3 million prepaid customers.[1]

Cell C operates in South Africa only and recorded 4.8 million subscribers by the end of 2007 (Guest, 2008).

Mobile and innovation for development

However, even with the ubiquity of access, the challenge to South Africa and other African countries is how best to adapt and translate growth and innovation in mobile technology in support of specific development challenges.

With two out of every three South Africans owning a mobile phone, these devices are the easiest and least expensive way to communicate, and far more pervasive than the internet – clearly an appropriate technology for the context. As a result, mobile phones are being harnessed by individuals and organisations to monitor elections, raise money, support advocacy campaigns and encourage citizen journalism.

Mobile phones are also bridging the digital divide in developing countries at a rate much faster than most other interventions to date. They span socioeconomic and cultural boundaries and are revolutionising the way people organise

1 MTN: www.mtn.co.za

themselves and do business. Mobiles are changing the ways people communicate, and they are changing the way civil society works.

Mobile success, driven largely by competition, is also spawning new services such as micro-payment prepaid recharging, single rate interregional roaming and the uptake of m-commerce applications.

Mobile banking

Mobile banking and payments worldwide are receiving significant attention from the banking industry and mobile operators. It is a convergence of two very powerful industries that provides a much more pervasive and accessible channel for the delivery of banking, payment and other financial services. Mobile transacting has a number of advantages over more traditional banking methods as it breaks down geographical constraints and offers advantages such as immediacy, security and efficiency. In South Africa, 31% of unbanked people have a mobile phone, and a further 17% have access to a mobile phone.

In June 2008, the Competition Commission released a report by the Banking Enquiry Panel, which was chaired by Judge Thabani Jali. The panel made 28 recommendations to increase competition in the banking sector to bring down costs, of which nine relate specifically to the National Payment System (NPS) and five relate directly to the automatic teller machine (ATM) network. The Commission's recommendation to open up access to the NPS is seen as the catalyst the mobile payment industry needs to bring online transactions to the majority of the population (Vecchiato, 2008).

According to Leon Perlman, chairman of the Wireless Application Service Providers Association, the findings to open up the NPS are consonant with similar initiatives in many developing countries to provide ubiquitous and affordable banking and payment services using mobile phones (Vecchiato, 2008).

Given the vast potential of mobile technology to transform the banking landscape in South Africa, a number of service providers are already active in this field.

Wizzit offers a secure and efficient mobile payment banking solution to unbanked and under-banked people in the country. The product offered is a low-cost transactional bank account that uses mobile phones for making person-to-person payments, transfers and prepaid purchases. In November 2007, the International Finance Corporation (IFC), a member of the World Bank, announced that it will acquire 10% of Wizzit as part of its efforts to extend banking services to the poor (ITWeb, 2007).

Another South African company, Fundamo[2], develops and deploys m-banking applications which enable secure financial transactions to take place through mobile phones. With m-banking gaining momentum throughout the African continent, Fundamo has already provided solutions and supporting services to providers in South Africa, Kenya, Botswana, Zimbabwe, Zambia and the DRC. It is also expanding to other markets, such as Brazil, through a reseller licensing agreement with Brazilian banking solutions company BSI Tecnologia. This will allow BSI to sell Fundamo's mobile technology into the Brazilian market. Fundamo has also signed a global partnership agreement with management consulting and technology services company Accenture, to accelerate the worldwide adoption of mobile wallets.

All the main commercial banks in South Africa have introduced mobile banking solutions in recent years in an attempt to roll out services to the unbanked market based on the pervasiveness of mobile phones.

Other applications of mobile technology

There are a number of other examples of appropriate mobile technology applications in South Africa.

M4Girls is a pilot project launched by Nokia together with the Department of Education and Mindset Network. It uses Nokia 6300 mobile phones loaded with educational material to help improve the mathematics performance of Grade 10 girl learners. In addition to the initial pilot using mathematics, Nokia and Mindset are developing digital content in other key subjects such as English and information technology (IT) (ITWeb, 2008).

SMSweb offers an unlimited short message service (SMS) to schools so they can send important messages directly to parents via SMS. About 250 schools across the country already use the service. In 2007 more than four million messages were sent to parents.

FishMS is an SMS-based service from the Southern African Sustainable Seafood Initiative that provides information about the status of global fish stocks to consumers. Users text the name of a fish they are considering buying and are immediately advised as to whether the fish was sustainably harvested, or whether they should think twice before buying it.[3]

MobiDic, short for Mobile Dictionary, is a service that enables users to access dictionary content via their cellular phones. It was launched by SABC Education, a branch of the state broadcaster, in partnership with the Gauteng Economic Development Agency (GEDA) and Biza Telecoms, a black empowerment information and communications technology (ICT) company. The objective of MobiDic is to assist users in improving language skills and enhancing reading and writing abilities. By simply sending a word for which the user needs an explanation to a premium-rated short code number, they instantly receive a definition in return via SMS.[4]

SIMpill is a solution for the wireless monitoring and support of patients on chronic medication. It incorporates wireless technology to monitor and remind patients with chronic conditions to take their medication as prescribed, as well as helping health organisations to be more efficient and cost-effective in their patient care.[5]

2 www.fundamo.co.za

3 wwf.org.za/sassi

4 www.sabcmobile.co.za/mobidic

5 www.simpill.com

MXit is an instant messaging service which cuts the cost of an SMS, priced at up to 80 cents to send a one-word message such as "hello", by 100,000 times to just 0.0008 cents. More than six million South Africans – mostly under the age of 25 – are using MXit. New users are signing up at the rate of more than 10,000 a day. There are no set-up or sign-on fees, but users need mobile phones capable of running on general packet radio service (GPRS) or third generation (3G) technology. Once logged on it is possible for people to interact with other MXit users as well as with online chat communities such as MSN Messenger, ICQ, AOL Messenger and Jabber. Both parties must be logged on to the MXit network to send a message. Because one only pays for the data or information that one sends and receives and not for the access to the internet, using a service like MXit becomes very cheap.[6]

Call Me allows Vodacom subscribers to send up to five messages per day, free of charge, requesting a call back from the receiver. Services such as these have emerged in response to consumer behaviour where users would have previously "flashed" the person they wished to speak to by ringing their phone once and hanging up. Call Me formalises the process and helps minimise network traffic through fewer prematurely disconnected calls.[7]

Smile Communications is testing a service aimed at giving customers their own telephone number even if they do not own a handset. Individuals are offered free telephone numbers and voice message boxes. The trial run is being held in the Gamalakhe community, near Port Shepstone in KwaZulu-Natal. Customers will be given a secure PIN code so they can use any Smile phone. Once they log in, they can make low-cost calls and operate a voice mailbox with free message retrieval. Having a personal number means the customer can be contacted directly, though the incoming caller will need to leave a voice message, unless the user logs on to a Smile phone at a prearranged time to answer the call (Stones, 2008).

This service is a variation on another initiative to make telecoms affordable for people that required the cellular operators to hand out four million free subscriber identity module (SIM) cards to the poorest people in South Africa. Vodacom, MTN and Cell C agreed to give away the cards in exchange for spectrum access, but got bogged down by administrative and technical hitches. The cards were useless without a handset, so the owner had to borrow a phone. Though the cards gave the recipient a cellular number, they were not loaded with airtime so users still had to pay the high retail rates for prepaid airtime.

Action steps

Clearly, the mobile market and the potential of mobile technology to increase access and communication holds much promise for South Africa and other developing countries. However, despite the tremendous growth of mobile, there remain significant obstacles to its uptake. High prices and the fact that most older and cheaper phones are not enabled with key technologies are just two of these obstacles.

In June 2008 the Independent Communications Authority of South Africa (ICASA) gazetted regulations aimed at preventing consumers from being locked into long-term contracts with mobile operators – a longstanding criticism of networks. According to the new regulations, consumers will be given the option to choose the period of their mobile phone contracts, from six, twelve, eighteen, to 24 months. The new regulations became effective on 17 August 2008.

This move, as well as efforts in the policy and regulatory environment to promote increased competition, and more affordable pricing and licensing, point to a recognition of the need to support the growth of the mobile sector in the country. ■

References

Cape Argus (2008) SMS system helps schools, parents. *Cape Argus*, 30 June. Available at: www.capeargus.co.za/?fSectionId=3571&fArticleId=vn20080630055754502C368889

Esselaar, S., Gillwald, A. and Stork, C. (2006) *South African Telecommunications Sector Performance Review 2006*. LINK Centre Public Policy Research Paper No. 8.

Fundamo: www.fundamo.co.za

Goldstuck, A. (2006) *The Hitchhiker's Guide to Going Mobile: The South African Handbook of Cellular and Wireless Communication*. Cape Town: Double Storey Books.

Guest, K. (2008) Cell C's turnaround proves profitable. *ITWeb*, 16 April. Available at: www.itweb.co.za/sections/financial/2008/0804161031.asp?O=FPTOP&S=Telecoms&A=TEL

ITU (International Telecommunication Union) (2008) *African Telecommunication/ICT Indicators 2008: At a Crossroads*. Geneva: International Telecommunication Union.

ITWeb (2007) World Bank arm buys into Wizzit. *ITWeb*, 21 November. Available at: www.itweb.co.za/sections/business/2007/0711211042.asp?S=IT%20in%20Banking&A=ITB&O=FRGN

ITWeb (2008) Mobile phones to teach Maths. *ITWeb*, 8 April. Available at: www.itweb.co.za/sections/telecoms/2008/0804081343.asp?A=CEL&S=Cellular&O=FPPN

MTN: www.mtn.co.za

Stones, L. (2008) Free cellphone numbers. *Business Day*, 22 April. Available at: mybroadband.co.za/news/Cellular/3566.html

Vecchiatto, P. (2008) Commission opens mobile payment industry door. *ITWeb*, 26 June. Available at: www.itweb.co.za/sections/financial/2008/0806261040.asp

Vodacom (2008) Vodacom results for the period ended December 31, 2007. Press release. Available at: www.vodacom.co.za/mccrdetail.do?id=1084&action=detail

6 www.mxit.co.za

7 www.vodacom.co.za/services/callme_about.jsp

SPAIN

Pangea
Leandro Navarro
www.pangea.org

Introduction

Information and communications technologies (ICTs) constitute a market where diverse industries, producers and consumers converge, but also a public space where citizens and organisations live and interact. Although the ICT market is huge and involves a large part of the population, the ICT public space as a social structure where citizens and organisations exercise the right to communicate is fragile and underdeveloped. In this context, this report focuses on appropriateness of technology and locally relevant content, applications and services.

Access to technology

Access to ICTs is widespread in Spain (Atkinson et al., 2008; OECD, 2008), but the quality varies significantly between urban and rural areas. In urban areas, particularly in large cities, several operators offer voice and high-speed, good-quality internet access, while rural areas have fewer options, lower quality and even no coverage at all. The market for ICT services is dominated by the former monopoly operator Telefónica – 81.8% of fixed phone lines were operated by Telefónica in 2006, according to the Telecommunications Market Commission (CMT) – and competition is the most fragile in less populated areas. Although the government has institutions that monitor and regulate the market, and several organisations defend the rights of citizens or specific groups (such as musicians and other professional content creators), Telefónica's de facto monopoly is entrenched, with limited and artificial competition among service providers. At the same time, the quality of ICT services is controversial, specifically those from telephony and internet operators, who register a high number of complaints.

Low-cost telephony and internet access at low speed, equivalent to a connection over a phone line, is practically universal except in particularly remote areas. The most widespread technology for accessing the internet at high speed, accounting for roughly 79% of all high-speed internet connections, is asymmetric digital subscriber line (ADSL). ADSL registered 6.6 million lines in 2008 (CMT, 2008; OECD, 2008) in a population of 45 million. Mobile access is the fastest growing technology. This includes the offerings of data services from commercial mobile telephony operators (general packet radio service [GPRS] and third generation [3G]), commercial operators offering Wi-Fi services, and a few community-based organisations offering open networks based on Wi-Fi technology, particularly in areas where commercial operators provide little or no service at all.

Wireless community networks are a remarkable development, illustrated by Guifi.net,[1] with near 5,000 nodes in 2008. Guifi.net is a network owned by its users, and operates beyond commercial operators. It is mainly established in a rural area where ICT services by commercial operators are not sufficiently offered. It is clear proof of how an open network can be established and maintained by a community, and how it contributes to the social and economic development of the area.[2] Local governments and local businesses are also involved, showing how a public-private-commercial partnership can be established and sustained. These networks have become an incentive for commercial operators to provide ICT services in underserved areas, as open networks enlarge considerably the population of educated users demanding advanced ICT services.

There is also a growing number of content applications and services, as more and more people have access to and use the internet regularly. There is an ongoing effort by the public administration to allow citizens to interact with it via the internet – for instance, at the European Union (EU) and national level with a plan for the development of the information society and convergence with Europe (2006-2010), known as "Plan Avanza". In practice, however, many services have yet to get off the ground, particularly for tax-related issues. The electronic identification card for citizens, containing a chip with an X.509 certificate that can be used for electronic authentication, has been introduced. The recently introduced laws regarding electronic services (LSSI, 2002 and LISI, 2007, based on EU directives) have established a stable legal framework for businesses and citizens dealing with content, applications and services. But this has come at the price of introducing obligations and bureaucracy for internet providers and restrictions to freedom of expression and privacy that are considered excessive by some people and organisations.

There is growing awareness of free and open source software (FOSS). This is suggested by the adoption of FOSS applications such as Firefox, the number of local Linux distributions, particularly for schools and universities, the number of FOSS-related events, and active discussions on FOSS adoption by public administrations.

Content created in Spain is mainly written in the "Spanish" language (Castilian), but a notable exception is the introduction in 2006 of the .cat domain name system (DNS) top-level domain. This was established to serve the needs

1 www.guifi.net

2 For more information see: www.comesfa.org/WCL_EN

of the Catalan linguistic and cultural community. Some 30,000 domains have been registered in only two years of operation.

Local content

There are other languages spoken in Spain besides Castilian. These include Aranese (*Aranés*), a variant of Occitan, in Catalonia; Basque (*Euskera*) in the Basque Country and Navarre; Catalan (*Català*) in Catalonia, the Balearic Islands and in the Valencian Community; and Galician (*Galego*) in Galicia. There are also other languages that do not have any official status, with fewer speakers and lower popular demand for their recognition in their regions, or insufficient legal and institutional support. As a reference, the number of articles on Wikipedia in various languages of Spain is as follows: Castilian 386,000, Catalan 124,000, Galician 38,000, Basque 28,000, Occitan 14,000, Asturian 11,000 and Aragonese nearly 10,000. All these "minor" languages have an asymmetric relationship to Castilian, as they do with the rest of the European languages spoken in the EU.

Several linguistic communities in Spain have made their presence felt in EU institutions since the start, but the visible lack of institutional support from the Spanish government has meant that there has been no effective use of these languages in EU institutions or on websites. This was exemplified by the European Year of Intercultural Dialogue 2008.[3] While this initiative aimed to "explore the benefits of our rich cultural heritage and opportunities to learn from different cultural traditions," 27 countries but only 23 languages were represented – and only Castilian was represented among the languages in Spain.

This contradicts the objectives of Spain's National Strategy for the European Year of Intercultural Dialogue: "To help this intercultural dialogue to become established as a permanent and dynamic process within Spanish society and to make this process a fundamental mechanism ensuring and facilitating the application of the goals stipulated in the UNESCO Convention on the Protection and Promotion of the Diversity of Cultural Expressions."[4] This failure to represent the plurality of languages in Spain was particularly striking in an intercultural campaign. The cost of translation is one of the arguments used, but there are counter examples, such as www.europarl.cat, where the whole website for the European Parliament has been translated into Catalan and put online by a single person to show how feasible it is. The result is that languages such as Latvian or Estonian (with less than two million speakers) are official, whereas Catalan, with more than nine million speakers, is not recognised at the European level.

Private copying levy

The private copying levy, a fee for private copying, is charged on the purchase of various recording media and hardware, such as CDs, digital cameras and scanners.[5] This is done to compensate content producers for the private copying of acquired content, which is legal in Spain. It was established a decade ago, and ratified after an intense controversy during the reform of the copyright law passed in December 2007. New tariffs have been in effect since 20 June 2008. This levy is collected without considering the use of the media and distributed in a rather arbitrary way. It is supported by the traditional media industry that relies on the distribution of physical products (CDs and DVDs), but has been rejected by a large part of the population, industry and professional organisations.[6] However, an innovative community of artists has emerged adopting alternative models for the distribution of their artistic productions.

Action steps

There are a number of barriers hindering the participation and involvement of citizens in the information society, as well as solutions to overcome them.

Traditional channels are still used by the public administration, which does not take advantage of the opportunities for transparency and openness afforded by ICTs.

Citizens need to be empowered and public administrations forced to be transparent. Every state action or budget must be announced, documented and debated in public using blogs, open forums, and other internet-based platforms.

The access infrastructure and the networks are owned and exploited by private companies, with some support from governments in less profitable areas. Citizens have little information about and no control over the functioning of the networks that support the internet as a public space.

More dialogue and more support (legal and economic) is needed to facilitate, develop and promote the involvement of citizens and citizen organisations in the governance of the networks. This requires establishing plans, forums, follow-up mechanisms, reports, etc.

Citizen networks – networks created by citizens for self-service such as wireless community networks – must be explicitly supported and protected, not just left in a legal limbo or seen as unfair competition to commercial operators. They are a viable alternative way for building networks that are open and owned by the community, particularly by places and people who are not the focus of commercial offerings. Laws should support and protect these citizen initiatives, with measures such as the allocation of additional spectrum, facilitating the legal establishment of the networks, and introducing legal and fiscal incentives for their development. This should especially be the case in rural areas and in areas where they serve people otherwise excluded from commercial offerings.

3 www.interculturaldialogue2008.eu

4 www.interculturaldialogue2008.eu/fileadmin/downloads/documents/133-nationalcampaigns/national_strategy/strategy_spain_en.doc

5 For more information see: en.wikipedia.org/wiki/Private_copying_levy

6 Todos contra el canon: www.todoscontraelcanon.org

The network, software and content industries fight for monopolies by courting political power.

Regarding networks, more effective policies need to be developed that reduce the advantage of dominant operators and create true and more open markets. The need for this is particularly clear with Telefónica, which is the de facto monopoly operator in Spain. Alternative operators need to be better supported.

Regarding software, the adoption of free software by the public administration should be encouraged. Monopolistic pressures from companies with anti-competitive practices such as Microsoft should be discouraged.

Regarding content, alternative, innovative and small content creators should be protected from the large national and international media groups. It is also necessary to open a dialogue between government, content creators, content consumers and citizens to find an acceptable agreement among them to regulate the content market. Research needs to be conducted on new business models for the media industry that are ethically and commercially more acceptable and fair, as an alternative to the unfair and regressive current levy model.

There is an urgent need to establish policies to promote the diversity of languages online. As technology is not neutral, a decision should be made at all the political levels to use the internet to save, digitise, enhance and promote the cultural heritage of the country's many languages, major and minor, officially recognised or not. Otherwise the internet can become a tool that erodes the rich cultural heritage of linguistic diversity. ■

References

Atkinson, R., Correa, D. and Hedlund, J. (2008) *Explaining International Broadband Leadership*. Washington: ITIF. Available at: www.itif.org/index.php?id=142

CMT (Comisión del Mercado de las Telecomunicaciones): www.cmt.es

European Parliament alternative website in the Catalan language: www.europarl.cat

European Year of Intercultural Dialogue: www.interculturaldialogue2008.eu

European Year for Intercultural Dialogue – Spanish National Strategy: www.interculturaldialogue2008.eu/fileadmin/downloads/documents/133-nationalcampaigns/national_strategy/strategy_spain_en.doc

Guifi.net: www.guifi.net

OECD (Organisation for Economic Co-operation and Development) (2008) Broadband Statistics. Available at: www.oecd.org/sti/ict/broadband

Todos contra el canon: www.todoscontraelcanon.org

Wireless Commons Licence: www.comesfa.org/WCL_EN

SWITZERLAND

comunica-ch
Wolf Ludwig
www.comunica-ch.net

Introduction

With a total of 7.5 million inhabitants, Switzerland ranks among the smaller countries in Europe. It is comparable to the municipality of London (7.5 million). It is a federalist country composed of 26 cantons (FSO, 2008) with a high degree of autonomy. It is also subdivided in four linguistic and cultural areas: a Swiss-German part (5.1 million inhabitants), a Swiss-French part (1.8 million), a Swiss-Italian part (325,000) and a Reto-Romanic part (35,000). Political consensus between these cultural areas is difficult and mostly time consuming.

For this survey basic data was collected from the Federal Office of Communication (OFCOM), the Swiss Federal Statistical Office (FSO) and the Federal Delegate for Informatics. There is a great variety of material on issues regarding the development and state of the national information society from different sources (governmental as well as non-governmental). The federal government announced its first strategy on the information society in 1998 – a strategy which has been perceived by some stakeholders as "ambitious". It was revised in January 2006 (OFCOM, 2006), but was still criticised by civil society members as "too pragmatic, without any visionary approach" (Ludwig, 2006). The government played a proactive role in the World Summit on the Information Society (WSIS) process between 2002 and 2005, with Switzerland hosting the first summit in December 2003 in Geneva. Switzerland was among the few countries at the time to include civil society in its governmental delegation (at least during the Geneva phase).

The challenge and economic potential of information and communications technologies (ICTs) were realised in the late 1990s, and the enormous expectations that surrounded them were dumped with the dot.com crash that followed the first hype of the "New Economy". To better assess the economic and social importance and implications of ICTs, the FSO started to systematically collect, verify and publish data over the years. The FSO conducted a survey called Use of Internet in Households in Switzerland in 2004. For the first time it used the model questionnaire (Community Survey on ICT Usage) that is recommended by the European Union's (EU) statistic authorities (Eurostat) to improve the comparability of indicators and results in a broader European context. Special emphasis was laid on access to technologies and levels of usage in Swiss households (for family members from the age of fifteen upwards). The results were published in 2006 (FSO, 2006). According to Yves Froidevaux, scientific collaborator at the FSO, additional and complementary data is regularly collected by private internet research institutions like WEMF/REMP,[1] NET-Metrix[2] and IGEM/Publica Data AG.[3] The next FSO survey is expected to take place in 2010.

The data and indicators collected for this report have been verified by other sources, including stakeholders from government, business and civil society in Switzerland. Several interviews were conducted with government officials, civil society actors and experts from the Swiss Academy of Engineering Science (SATW).[4] The main goal of the report was to establish if there were differences and potential contradictions between national strategies, action plans, indicators, and the various intentions of stakeholders, and the realities on the ground regarding the implementation of the information society in Switzerland. Our questionnaire emphasised access to infrastructure, the digital divide, and the exclusion of marginalised groups.

Country situation

Switzerland is known to be a wealthy country with a comparatively good technical infrastructure that covers most of the country. Its ranking in the United Nations Conference on Trade and Development's (UNCTAD) Digital Divide Report: ICT Diffusion Index 2005 (UNCTAD, 2006) ranged from position 14 in 1997, to 5 in 2001, to 7 in 2004.

In the second half of the 1990s, mobile telephony in Switzerland saw considerable growth. A boom in mobile applications, combined with advancements in internet technologies, had an impact on the national infrastructure. While the number of lines connected to the public switched telephone network (PSTN) increased continuously until 1995, mobile technology has taken over. Analogue technologies were slowly but steadily replaced by integrated services digital network (ISDN) technologies (FSO, 2007).

Physical access to technology

In 2005, more than 62% of internet users had access to the internet via broadband technologies: 1.7 million Swiss were subscribed to a broadband connection, which signifies a penetration rate of 23 subscribers per 100 inhabitants. According to these figures, Switzerland ranges above Organisation for Economic Co-operation and Development (OECD) countries (an average of 13.6 per 100 inhabitants) but behind countries like Korea, the Netherlands and Denmark,

1 www.remp.ch/de/internet/index.php

2 www.net-metrix.ch

3 www.publicadata.ch

4 www.satw.ch

where more than 25% of the population have access via broadband (FSO, 2007).

In 2006, about 71.8% of the population over fourteen years of age claimed to have used the internet at least once over the last six months. These people constitute a so-called "largest user circle". In the same time frame, about 48.3% of the people interviewed stated that they used the internet daily or almost daily ("heavy users"). About 12.3% said they used the internet several times per week ("medium users"). These last two groups make up an "inner circle".

In 1997 only 7% of the population used the internet on a regular basis. This increased to 57.3% in 2005 and 60.6% in 2006 (FSO, 2007).

Other indicators show an increase in household expenditure on ICT hardware and services: on average CHF 294 per month – roughly the same amount in USD – or 3.8% of total household expenditure in 2004 (FSO, 2007).

According to the latest findings of NET-Metrix-Base (2008), about 77% of the population over fourteen used the internet in the last six months. In comparison with neighbouring German-speaking countries Austria (69%) and Germany (63%), Switzerland is leading in terms of online penetration (NET-Metrix-Base, 2008). But this tells only part of the story. Distinctions regarding access and usage are still evident at a second glance. The FSO's 2004 household survey reaches three significant conclusions:

- There is a large discrepancy in internet access between households due to disparities of income and education. As both variables are closely linked to each other, a lack of skills is a fundamental reason for differences in internet usage.
- Age, gender and education are key variables in the digital divide. The typical internet user is young and male, with a higher level of education. The use of the internet is increasing amongst previously excluded groups generally. However, the digital divide still persists, and is even intensifying for people with low incomes and lower levels of education. This broadening divide is observed on the European level as well (Demunter, 2005).
- A considerable number of households with a computer are still not connected to the internet and do not want to be connected. This is related to high internet access costs and a lack of skills.

Human capacity and training

In the course of the 1990s, more and more young people entered ICT professions and studied ICTs at high school and university. But since 2004 there has been a remarkable backlash in the field (FSO, 2007). There are now fewer ICT professionals recruited per year (2,500 graduates) compared to the number retiring (more than double). Experts blame a "lack of consistent effort in the teaching curriculum" or observe a "lousy reputation of ICT professionals." Measures to change this are being taken, but may take years to show results. Outsourcing ICT needs is now common for Swiss businesses (NZZ Online, 2007a).

E-accessibility and e-usability

Disparities in access are not based on culture or language, but follow well-known socioeconomic distinctions like age, gender, income and education. For instance, the fact that access in the Swiss-Italian part (Ticino) differs from other linguistic regions is seen to be because of regional age structures rather than due to factors of language (or even income). Other vulnerable groups who lack digital integration are people with disabilities, single-parent families or those with immigrant backgrounds.

The Access For All Foundation argues that technologies help to reduce barriers but create new ones at the same time.[5] The foundation is dedicated to overcoming these barriers, and considers itself a link between the government, ICT industry and disadvantaged people, including those with disabilities. It is also the independent certification office for accessible websites in Switzerland. Accessibility standards in compliance with those of the World Wide Web Consortium have been developed and are available. However, according to a recent survey submitted by the foundation, many official websites for cantons and municipalities still do not cater for people with disabilities. Among the better ones are those of the federal government and its offices (NZZ Online, 2007b).

The share of older adults aged 50 and over who use the internet on a regular basis – so-called "silver surfers" – is still remarkably low: only 37% belong to the "inner circle", according to the WEMF/REMP figures for 2006.[6] The Swiss Council of Seniors (SSR)[7] describes this situation as a "ticking time bomb" (NZZ Online, 2007b).

Legal and regulatory framework

The Swiss telecom market has been increasingly liberalised over the last few years. Besides the incumbent Swisscom, which traditionally had a dominant market position, there are several other private enterprises in the fixed-line and mobile sectors with growing market shares. Some observers argue that the recent liberalisation of the so-called "last mile" – previously controlled by Swisscom – may stimulate further competition in the ICT market and improve access options. But this argument is not shared by all actors among civil society. Some of them fear a decrease in public services in peripheral and mountainous areas of the country.

Action steps

Good infrastructure (high-speed broadband) and increased access for the majority of the Swiss population in the various parts of the country are evident. However, access to and use of the internet and online services differ depending on age, gender, income and education, as well as among people with disabilities.

5 www.access-for-all.ch

6 www.remp.ch/de/internet/index.php

7 www.ssr-csa.ch

Key concerns for recent governmental strategy are improvements in the field of e-health[8] and e-government.[9] The FSO has also launched a network dealing with digital integration in Switzerland (OFCOM, 2007). The national Communication Commission has begun promoting fibre-to-the-home (FTTH) technology, which has yet to impact on access for enterprises and end-users (OFCOM, 2008).

Based on a national strategy (OFCOM, 2006), the Swiss government has launched a number of projects over the last few years, like Schools to the Net, which aims to install PCs in schools. However, this has been hampered by a lack of complementary training programmes for teachers (Ludwig, 2006).

Despite these and other initiatives, civil society actors raise concerns about open access, open standards, privacy and data protection, security and trust, child pornography, violence on mobile devices, internet literacy, intellectual property abuses and open licensing models (or the development of a legal framework for the public commons, such as Creative Commons licensing).

Some observers note a "lack of coordination at different levels" or "dispersion of efforts" in the government, especially given the federal political structure of the country. As suggested, coordination, political consensus and implementation at different levels, as well as across Switzerland's different linguistic areas, are often perceived as difficult, time consuming and ineffective. Compared with more centralistic neighbouring countries like France or Austria, Switzerland is traditionally familiar with splendid procedures of consultation in almost all fields of society. Reaching consensus among its different interest groups is a parameter of national politics and still considered a pillar of national identity – and once a decision is taken it is largely approved and broadly accepted.

For OFCOM, the WSIS process was a milestone in multilateral diplomacy. The Swiss delegates continue to promote the multi-stakeholder approach, and the continued participation of civil society and business in international organisations such as the International Telecommunication Union (ITU), the United Nations Educational, Scientific and Cultural Organization (UNESCO) and the World Intellectual Property Organisation (WIPO) (OFCOM, 2006).

Comunica-ch and other civil society actors recommend the improvement of monitoring structures dealing with the information society, and the creation of a national observatory made up of different stakeholders.

There are several multi-stakeholder initiatives from academia and business (such as the National Year of Informatics 2008) that promote a coherent implementation of the national strategy on the information society. There are also plans to create discussion forums like the Internet Governance Forum (IGF) on the national or regional levels to enhance cooperation among stakeholders and to foster common projects on emerging issues of the information society. The European Dialogue on Internet Governance (EuroDIG) can be a model for such efforts. ■

8 www.bakom.admin.ch/themen/infosociety/01689/index.html?lang=de

9 www.efd.admin.ch/dokumentation/grundlagenpapiere/01106/index.html?lang=de

References

Access For All Foundation: www.access-for-all.ch

Demunter, C. (2005) *Fracture numérique en Europe: Statistique en bref.* Brussels: Eurostat.

FSO (Federal Statistical Office) (2006) *Internetnutzung in den Haushalten der Schweiz, Ergebnisse der Erhebung 2004 und Indikatoren.* Neuchâtel: FSO.

FSO (2007) *Indikatoren zur Informationsgesellschaft Schweiz.* Neuchâtel: FSO.

FSO (2008) *Statistical Yearbook of Switzerland 2008.* Neuchâtel: FSO.

IGEM/Publica Data AG: www.publicadata.ch/index.cfm?page=3&lang=D

Ludwig, W. (2006) Die neue Strategie für eine Informationsgesellschaft Schweiz. *Medienheft*, 23 May. Available at: www.medienheft.ch/politik/bibliothek/p25_LudwigWolf.html

NET-Metrix-Base (2008) *Internetstudie NET-Metrix-Base 2008-1.* Zurich: NET-Metrix AG.

NZZ Online (2007a) Informatiker sucht das Land. *Neue Zürcher Zeitung Online*, 5 November. Available at: www.nzz.ch/nachrichten/zuerich/aktuell/informatiker_sucht_das_land_1.579712.html

NZZ Online (2007b) Digitaler Graben zwischen den Generationen. *Neue Zürcher Zeitung Online*, 17 December. Available at: www.nzz.ch/nachrichten/schweiz/digitaler_graben_zwischen_den_generationen_1.600087.html

OFCOM (Federal Office of Communication) (2006) Federal Council adopts revised strategy for an information society in Switzerland. Press release, 23 January. Available at: www.bakom.admin.ch/dokumentation/medieninformationen/00471/index.html?lang=en&msg-id=2252

OFCOM (2007) *e-Inclusion – Eine Informationsgesellschaft für alle.* Available at: www.uvek.admin.ch/dokumentation/00474/00492/index.html?lang=de&msg-id=15596

OFCOM (2008) Glasfasernetze bis in die Haushalte: konstruktive Diskussionen. Press release, 9 May. Available at: www.bakom.admin.ch/dokumentation/medieninformationen/00471/index.html?lang=de&msg-id=19243

SATW (Swiss Academy of Engineering Science): www.satw.ch

SSR (Schweizerischer Seniorenrat): www.ssr-csa.ch

UNCTAD (United Nations Conference on Trade and Development) (2006) *Digital Divide Report: ICT Diffusion Index 2005.* New York and Geneva: United Nations. Available at: www.unctad.org/en/docs/iteipc20065_en.pdf

WEMF/REMP: www.remp.ch/de/internet/index.php

TAJIKISTAN

Civil Internet Policy Initiative (CIPI)
Parvina Ibodova and Asomudin Atoev
www.cipi.tj

Introduction

The Republic of Tajikistan, located in Central Asia, is a landlocked country encompassing an area of 143,100 kilometres, stretching 700 kilometres from east to west and 350 kilometres from north to south. Tajikistan borders on the People's Republic of China, Afghanistan, Uzbekistan and Kyrgyzstan. South-eastern Tajikistan is only separated from Pakistan by a narrow strip of Afghan territory 15 to 65 kilometres wide. The terrain in the west of the country is hilly desert and semi-desert. To the east the elevation rises to form the highest mountain systems in Central Asia: the Tien Shan and the Pamirs.

Tajikistan is 93% mountainous with more than half of the country sitting at altitudes over 3,000 metres above sea level. Several well-known mountain peaks are over 7,000 metres, such as Ismoili Somoni Peak (formerly Communism Peak, renamed in 2000) at 7,495 metres, and Lenin Peak at 7,134 metres.

The Amy Darya and Syr Darya basins consist of about 1,000 rivers and temporary streams, which are part of the largest system in Central Asia. There are more than 2,000 lakes here, containing 44 cubic kilometres of water, including 20 cubic kilometres of fresh water.

Tajiks (who refer to themselves as Tojiks) make up the majority of the country's population. According to a 2000 census, the population of Tajikistan is more than 6,100,000. Of this 68.8% are Tajik, 24.9% Uzbek, 3% Russian, and 3.3% other nationalities. The official language is Tajik, and Russian is considered as a language of international relations.

The Tajikistani information and communications technology (ICT) market is considered one of the fastest growing and advanced in the region. Internet access technologies in the market include traditional dial-up, digital subscriber line (DSL), Wi-Fi and WiMAX, while mobile technologies include global system for mobile (GSM), third generation services (3G) and code division multiple access (CDMA). There are ten first level internet service providers (ISPs) and ten mobile telephony operators competing in the market. However, the applications of these technologies is poor.

The online population of TajNet (or the internet in Tajikistan) is about 500,000 (April 2008, Ministry of Transportation and Communications) and mobile telephony users stand at about three million (August 2008, Association of Mobile Operators). The capacity of land-line telephony, owned by Tajiktelecom, is over 300,000 users. This network is digitised and is mainly available in urban and suburban areas.

The main technology used to access the internet in Tajikistan is very small aperture terminal (VSAT) technology. Though this technology is considered one of the most expensive in the world, it is 24% to 30% cheaper than fibre-optic connectivity in Tajikistan. Due to its geographic isolation, Tajikistan is not along the main route of the only transnational fibre-optic communication line in the region, the Trans-Asia-Europe Fibre Optical Cable System (TAEFOS). Only two out of ten ISPs have connections to TAEFOS, via Uzbekistan and Kyrgyzstan. Fibre connectivity is mainly used for voice data. The upgrading of the land-line network to next generation network (NGN) is also taking place.[1]

Tajikistan's experience in the management of its country code top-level domain (ccTLD) is unique in the region. Originally .tj was registered in early 1997 by an ISP in the United States, and re-delegated in June 2003 to a local entity. Currently it is managed by the Information Technical Centre of the administration of the president of Tajikistan. The policy of .tj management is jointly developed by local internet stakeholders and the domain manager. It allows every ISP in the country to be a domain name registrar. As of September 2008 there were nine registrars of domain names.[2]

Human capacity and training

The first national official document focused on ICTs for human capacity building was the United Nations Development Programme's (UNDP) National Human Development Report for 2001-2002 (UNDP, 2002). The report was developed by local experts under the joint auspices of the government of Tajikistan and the UNDP, with financial support from the Open Society Institute (OSI) Tajikistan. It suggests that ICTs may work as an enabler of development if a "development dynamic" consisting of five elements – policy and legislation, human capacity, infrastructure, the private sector, content and applications – is in place.

One of the impacts of this initiative was the adoption of the State Strategy on ICT for Development, an e-strategy ratified by Presidential Decree 1174 on 5 November 2003. The e-strategy aims to narrow the social digital divide inside Tajikistan and to improve the ICT status of the country globally. One of the strategy's priorities is improving access to and the quality of the education system. To coordinate the e-strategy, an ICT Council has been established. This unites representatives of public sector and civil society institutions (private companies are represented via the latter) focused on the ICT market. However, the council has yet to begin its work.

1 www.tojikiston.com

2 www.nic.tj/get.htm

The academic community of Tajikistan consists of over 20 research institutes and over 30 universities. Most of these establishments are members of the Tajik Academic, Research and Educational Networks Association (TARENA).[3] In partnership with local and international civil society institutions (OSI Tajikistan, CIPI, CEENet) and international organisations (UNDP, NATO Security Through Science Programme), TARENA works to apply ICTs to the community's needs. At the same time there are a number of governmental programmes and international/local initiatives focused on the computerisation of secondary schools, e-government development, education management information systems, health management information systems, etc.

However, even after so many initiatives focused on both infrastructure and human capacity development, the main challenge has remained weak human capacity. Research on ICT penetration in state agencies in Tajikistan showed very high demand amongst civil servants for computer skills training (95% of respondents). It also showed a lack of data exchange via the local network, despite the fact that the quality of computer hardware available in state institutions is high and internal and external networking facilities are available. State authority bodies, ignorant of ICTs, make employees use outdated technologies or use a computer simply as a typewriter.

The research study, jointly conducted by the Presidential ICT Council and CIPI in 2007, also found that:

- There is a lack of policy on ICT implementation in the education field as well as other sectors.
- The academic community and secondary education system are focused on applying specific proprietary software applications, rather than technologies generally.
- Most of the internationally funded ICT projects are focused on proprietary software applications that cannot be adapted to local needs.
- Technology is considered a luxury, not a tool.
- The local community of developers is weak.

Socio-cultural factors

The value of TajNet, according to Metcalfe's law which states that the value of a network equals the square of the number of users, is the lowest in the region. TajNet is one of the few cybernets that are lacking social networks and an affordable national webmail service. It is quite common to meet civil servants and representatives of the academic community with email accounts from RuNet in Russia (e.g., mail.ru, inbox.ru, list.ru). On the one hand it suggests ignorance, and on the other illustrates that ICTs have remained a luxury for the majority of citizens and organisations.

Cyberspace offers an unprecedented opportunity for landlocked countries like Tajikistan. Considering its geographic location and historical and cultural heritage, Tajikistan has a unique position among former Soviet Central Asian and other Persian-speaking states of the region, like Afghanistan and Iran. Assuming it manages to develop TajNet properly, Tajikistan may become a cultural bridge in the region among those states.

Legal and regulatory framework

The state policy on the telecommunication industry is mainly regulated by the Main Department of Communications and Informatisation (MDCI), a branch of the Ministry of Transportation and Communications. The MDCI coordinates the activities of its two subordinate entities:

- The State Communications Inspectorate, which deals with technical issues in the ICT industry (standards, spectrum, certificates, etc.)
- The Communications Regulation Agency, which deals with licensing and other legal issues related to the ICT industry (licensing of services).

The Presidential ICT Council is coordinating the e-strategy implementation. It deals more with ICT policy development, unlike MDCI, which is focused on technical issues.

The different types of licences for service provision in the ICT industry can be divided into four categories:

- Telematics and data transfer (internet service licence)
- Voice over internet protocol (VoIP) telephony
- Mobile telephony services, including advanced mobile phone system (AMPS), GSM, CDMA, CDMA2000, 3G
- Fixed telephony services, i.e., public switched telephone network (PSTN) services.

According to ICT legislation, every Tajikistani legal or private entity, regardless of its legal status, is eligible to apply for a licence and to be a service provider. These licences are issued by the State Service on Supervision and Regulation in Communications and Informatisation under the Ministry of Transportation and Communications. The time it takes for an application to be considered cannot be more than one month.

The service also issues separate technical licences that are required for the import and installation of telecommunications equipment such as VSAT, Wi-Fi, WiMAX, etc., and licences for frequency spectrum allocated to run the equipment.

Some positive changes have resulted from an improvement in ICT legislation in the country. These include doubling the number of communications operators, facilitating the use of ICTs in almost all spheres of life, developing infrastructure, and the implementation of various industrial projects and informatisation programmes throughout the country. These changes have allowed the government to begin developing a coherent state policy on developing the information society to meet the information needs of the citizens.

At the same time there are challenges, including legal, economic and administrative ones.

3 www.tarena.tj/en

Action steps

Tajikistan's e-strategy is one of the main documents constituting the state's ICT policy. It has the potential to play a catalytic role in the ICT sector in the country. This is not only because it seriously considers ICTs an enabler of socioeconomic development in the country, but also because it creates the opportunity to promote the development of a transparent and competitive market by establishing the ICT Council under the president of Tajikistan. The most urgent step to be taken to make use of its advantages is to trigger the work of the council.

It is vital for the policy and legislative experience since independence to be researched and analysed, and for recommendations to be made to strengthen and improve the current legal context. This research needs to include an analysis of why intellectual property rights legislation does not currently exist. ■

References

CIPI (Civil Internet Policy Initiative) (2007) *Research on Information and Communication Technologies Penetration in the State Authority Agencies of the Republic of Tajikistan.* Dushanbe: CIPI. Available at: www.cipi.tj

Ershova, T. and Hohlov, Y. (2006) *Global Internet Policy Initiative Contribution to Information and Communication Technology Application for Development in Tajikistan: Case Study.* Dushanbe/ Moscow: GIPI.

Government of Tajikistan (2003) *State Strategy on Information and Communications Technologies for Development of the Republic of Tajikistan.* Available at: www.cipi.tj

Tajik Academic, Research and Educational Networks Association (TARENA): www.tarena.tj/en

.TJ Network Information Centre: www.nic.tj

UNDP (2002) *Tajikistan National Human Development Report 2001-2002: Information and Communications Technology for Development.* Dushanbe: UNDP. Available at: hdr.undp.org/en/ reports/nationalreports/europethecis/tajikistan/name,2927,en. html

TANZANIA

Tanzania Internet Service Providers Association (TISPA)
Suhail Sheriff
www.tispa.or.tz

Introduction

Tanganyika gained independence in 1961 from British rule, and formed a union with Zanzibar in 1964 to create Tanzania, a vast country covering 945,000 square kilometres with an estimated population of 40 million (CIA, 2008).

The first president, Julius Nyerere, led the country under socialist rule for 21 years until 1985.[1] However, his policies of socialism and collective farming have all but been reversed, and Tanzania has at present a capitalist-based economy. Even though a multiparty system was reintroduced in 1992 after 30 years of single-party rule (Baregu, 2004), the ruling party has retained power, placing three presidents in office after Nyerere.

The current president is Jakaya Kikwete, who was elected in 2005 with a margin of 80%. His stated focus was job creation, promising Tanzanian youth an additional one million jobs by the end of his term. He still enjoys overall support, although he is challenged by rampant institutionalised corruption, high rates of unemployment and continued political deadlock in Zanzibar, with renewed discussion and debate on the state of the union.

Tanzania has experienced steady economic growth over the past five years. In 2007, the gross domestic product (GDP) per capita was approximately TZS 550,000 (USD 475), up by 7.1% compared to 6.7% in 2006 (Government of Tanzania, 2008).

The fastest growing sectors were communications (19.8%), mining (14%), financial services (12%) and construction (9.7%) (Bank of Tanzania, 2008). However, the growth in the communications sector contributed only 2.3% to GDP (Government of Tanzania, 2008).

Tanzania had its first store-and-forward e-mail service in 1989, pioneered by the then Muhimbili University College of Health Sciences (MUCHS) in partnership with FidoNet[2] and GreenNet,[3] using low earth orbiting satellites. The first commercial full-fledged internet service was provided in 1996 by a company called CyberTwiga.

As the regulatory environment improved, more companies began to offer data connectivity services, resulting in rapid growth in the use of the internet. In 2005, the whole regulatory framework changed to a converged licensing framework, ending the exclusivity period for the incumbent telecoms operator. This licensing regime introduced a completely different approach for investors in that it was technology and service independent (*info*Dev/ITU, 2008), which allowed companies and institutions to get licences that were more appropriate in terms of services offered and regions covered. This effectively allowed fairer competition and eased restrictions on new entrants into the market. The framework has been hailed as a great achievement by both local and international stakeholders and a pioneering move within the region (Van Gorp & Maitland, 2007).

Access to the internet

By March 2008, the number of cellular users was 9.5 million, almost 10% of the population (TCRA, 2008), while internet users amounted to only 400,000, or about 1% of the population (ITU, 2008). However, the steady growth in the communications sector has been accompanied by small but commendable strides in internet access.

Formation of tzNIC

In 2008, the Tanzania Communications Regulatory Authority (TCRA) and the Tanzania Internet Service Providers Association (TISPA) collaboratively formed the Tanzania Network Information Centre (tzNIC), which has taken on the responsibility of .tz domain name management. Previously this name space was managed on a voluntary basis with certain institutions and people offering their assistance until such time as a formal institution was established. The formation of tzNIC will ensure the transparency, security and neutrality of the internet.

Figure 1: Communications sector growth rate

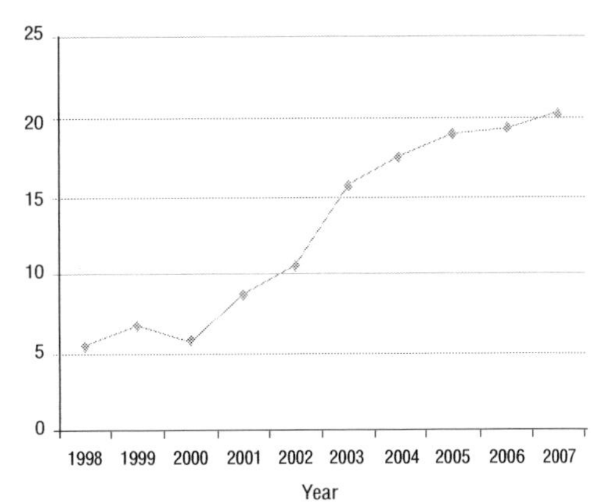

Source: **Budget Speech 2008**

1 en.wikipedia.org/wiki/Julius_Nyerere

2 www.fidonet.org

3 www.gn.apc.org

Proliferation of local internet exchange points (IXPs)

TISPA launched the Tanzania Internet Exchange (TIX) in 2003. This was the first initiative that attempted to interconnect different internet service providers (ISPs), in order to route traffic between them locally instead of over their independent satellite links, which was not only expensive but also inefficient. Upon launching, the exchange had only two ISP peers, but now it has over twenty peers, including commercial ISPs, telecommunication firms, non-commercial institutions and learning centres.

Based on the success of TIX, the TCRA has supported TISPA in the formation of the Arusha IXP, Mwanza IXP and Dodoma IXP. The building of these key infrastructure initiatives encourages the growth of the Tanzanian internet, facilitates the generation and sharing of local content, improves service for consumers, and helps to maintain the neutrality and independence of the internet.

Implementation of the East African Internet Exchange Point (EAIXP)

In extending the concept of "keeping local traffic local" to a regional perspective, the East African Regulatory, Postal and Telecommunications Organisation (EARPTO) has initiated the East African Internet Exchange Point (EAIXP) in an attempt to interconnect Tanzania, Kenya and Uganda. Successful peering has already started between Tanzania and Kenya. Although it is a satellite hop between the three East African countries, it still greatly increases the efficiency and lowers the cost of routing traffic from one country to another.

Creation of the Universal Communications Service Access Fund

Although growth in the ICT sector has been impressive, it still covers only 25% of the population (World Bank, 2006). The government has recognised the pattern in the penetration of communication services and has acted proactively by enacting the Universal Communications Service Access Act, passed by parliament in 2006. This act dictated the formation of a fund whose objectives are to "ensure the availability of communication services in rural and under-served areas," and "promote the participation of the private sector in the provision of communication services in rural and under-served areas." The fund will generate revenue and maintain its financial sustainability from a tax on communication services (Government of Tanzania, 2006).

With the increased availability of funds, commercial and non-commercial operators will be encouraged to venture into new geographic areas, reducing the percentage of the population who do not enjoy access to the internet. Although the creation of this fund has been delayed, the Ministry of Communication, Science and Technology has now revived the initiative, and the fund should be operational in the near future.

Preparations to host international fibre systems

Currently the East African coastline hosts no international fibre connectivity, routing all international voice and data traffic via satellite. This has been an obstacle for the greater development of the sector as prices remain comparatively expensive. In light of fibre systems landing in Tanzania, and assuming that any new fibre systems will be governed by an open-access policy that does not promote a monopoly or facilitate "price-fixing" practices, Tanzania can greatly benefit economically and strategically with the arrival of the various fibre projects at its shores.

The East African Marine System (TEAMS) is an initiative of the Kenyan government to build a 4,500-kilometre fibre-optic submarine system between Fujeira in the United Arab Emirates and Mombasa on the Kenyan coast. A separate spur of this cable is being planned to stretch from Mombasa to Dar es Salaam. The cable is owned by Etisalat (15%) and the Kenyan government (20%), while the rest is owned by private investors, including Safaricom, Telkom Kenya, Kenya Data Networks (KDN), Econet, Wananchi Telecom, Jamii Telkom, Access, Inhand, Flashcom, Equip and Uganda's Fibre Network.[4] This cable is expected to be complete by the second quarter of 2009.

The SEACOM cable is a private equity project owned by South African companies (50%), Industrial Promotion Services-Kenya, a unit of the Aga Khan Fund for Economic Development (25%), and the New York-based Herakles Telecom (25%) (SouthAfrica.info, 2007). It aims to link South Africa, Madagascar, Mozambique, Tanzania, Kenya, India and Europe. It is expected to be operational by June 2009 (SEACOM, 2008).

Finally, the Eastern Africa Submarine Cable System (EASSy) project, which has now been in discussion for some time and is at least a year behind schedule, aims to connect all countries along the East African coast from South Africa to Sudan. The project is supported in part by the World Bank and Development Bank of Southern Africa. It is expected to be operational by the second half of 2010.[5]

Establishing a national fibre backbone

The government, through the then Ministry of Communication and Transportation, commissioned a team in 2004 to "look into identifying infrastructure initiatives and to suggest the best ways to move forward" (MoID, 2004). The team looked at all the options and possibilities of building a converged national fibre backbone that can cater to national development goals, as well as allow Tanzania to excel as an information technology hub by offering terrestrial fibre connectivity to our neighbouring landlocked countries. Based on the recommendations of this study, a national fibre backbone technical plan has been drafted, aimed at connecting the existing fibre systems, as well as building new routes

4 en.wikipedia.org/wiki/Teams

5 en.wikipedia.org/wiki/EASSy_(cable_system)

and reaching most, if not all, of the 128 district capitals in Tanzania. The government is in advanced stages of securing a developmental soft loan from the Chinese government, and construction is set to start soon after.

Accessibility of technology

The total numbers of landline, cellular and internet customers do not fully address the issue of accessibility of ICTs. There are many factors that limit physical access to technology.

The biggest and most fundamental factor limiting access is affordability. In Tanzania, the cost of communication services remains comparatively higher than rates enjoyed in so-called developed markets. Table 1 provides a sampling of per-minute costs for mobile telephony.

Similarly, the average cost of internet access is also comparatively high. A home customer in urban Tanzania would pay a minimum of USD 35 for a shared 64 kilobits per second (kbps) link and a business may pay USD 400 for a dedicated 128 kbps link. In the rural areas, this expense may be higher due to the limited infrastructure to deliver internet access. A small office/home office (SOHO) user in Europe or North America may pay as little as USD 20 a month for a reliable broadband connection, getting a minimum speed of one megabit per second (Mbps).

Another factor is the geographic reach of technology and networks. In Tanzania, 75% of the population lives in low population density areas (Thomas, 2007).

The highest levels of technology penetration are enjoyed by cellular networks. At present, they cover 25% of the population (World Bank, 2006). These are impressive statistics, even though 75% of the population has yet to be reached. Healthy competition in the sector, as well as a favourable regulatory environment, have encouraged telecommunication companies to venture into isolated parts of the country, including areas that are not on the electricity grid. These networks are predominantly used for voice communication. Use of these networks for internet over general packet radio service (GPRS) is possible in most areas, but not commonly used. Third generation (3G) access is only available in a few of the major towns and cities.

Cellular companies have predominantly used global system for mobile (GSM) technology. There has not been the expected growth and use of code division multiple access (CDMA) 800 or CDMA 450 technologies. These technologies are more appropriate for rural areas in that they have a much wider footprint, reducing the cost of covering a specific area. Similarly, other communication technologies, such as licence-free as well as licensed frequency wireless, remain concentrated only in the major towns and cities in Tanzania.

The use of very small aperture terminal (VSAT) satellite technology for rural institutions is widespread. It has unlimited geographic reach, but remains an exclusive medium due to the capital and operational costs involved. However, this service is also beginning to be more affordable, as some communications companies have launched local satellite hubs and are able to offer more competitive pricing. This is an area that Tanzania can still capitalise on as there are few infrastructure barriers.

A third major factor affecting access to technology is the availability of electricity. Even if access is present in the form of cellular coverage or the possibility of using VSAT technology, the absence of power either means access is not possible, or that its costs are much higher as alternative arrangements of power need to be used.

Tanzania has 577 megawatts (MW) of installed power production capacity, the majority of which is hydropower. It also has 2,248 kilometres of 220-kilovolt (kV) power transmission lines and 1,400 kilometres of 132-kV lines running across the country. Despite this, only 6% of the population is actually connected to the national power grid (AREED, 2001).

Action steps

The various stakeholders in Tanzania, including the government, have made commendable achievements that have resulted in the proliferation of the ICT sector and the economy in general. Such activities should continue so that the rate of progress is maintained, if not accelerated.

However, there are some specific areas where the government, as a custodian of national policies, can play a more active role. While foreign direct investment is directly proportional to the economic growth of the country, especially when one considers GDP, it does not encourage the growth of the nation's capabilities in terms of developing human capital, encouraging local investment and maintaining wealth in circulation within the country. The government, while encouraging the growth of the sector, should simultaneously pay special attention to the growth of home-grown Tanzanian businesses.

The government should also take strides to create an enabling environment in terms of supporting the growth of infrastructure. This includes encouraging investment in communication infrastructure so that parallel networks are unnecessary, as their weight is borne by end-users in terms

Table 1: Sample of per-minute cost of mobile calls (September 2008) (in USD at the rate of TZS 1,150 = USD 1)

Network	BOL	Tigo	TTCL	Vodacom	Zain	Zantel
Within network	0.04	0.16	0.16	0.23	0.30	0.19
To other networks	0.13	0.26	0.20	0.35	0.30	0.22
Calling United States	0.17	0.52	0.34	0.61	0.61	0.57

Source: **Official company websites**

of higher usage pricing. The regulatory environment is ripe for segment-specific investment in the communication sector, rather than one investor needing to build their own infrastructure in order to deliver a service. However, more needs to be done to amplify the possibilities and invite direct investment in those areas.

Likewise, the ongoing activity for the establishment of the Universal Communications Services Access Fund should be sped up as a matter of urgency. Such a fund, which subsidises investment in areas that are less profitable from a business perspective, can go a long way towards minimising the digital divide.

Businesses also have a large part to play. Consumers have many choices now, and more than ever innovativeness will be paramount to new successful businesses. They should focus on offering value-added services, developing new markets that are unique and relevant, and offering alternative, appropriate and enabling technologies. Most of all, they should venture into offering content and content-driven services. The smaller ISPs should also create greater synergies and partnerships with other companies so that they may be able to compete more vigorously.

References

AREED (African Rural Energy Enterprise Development) (2001) *Tanzania Country Assessment 2001*. Available at: www.areed.org

Bank of Tanzania (2008) *Monetary Policy Statement, Governor, Bank of Tanzania, June 2008*. Available at: www.bot-tz.org/Publications/MonetaryPolicyStatements/2008_Jun_MPS.pdf

Baregu, M. (2004) Parliamentary Oversight of Defence and Security in Tanzania's Multiparty Parliament. In Le Roux, L. et al. (eds.), *Guarding the Guardians*. Pretoria: Institute for Security Studies. Available at: www.iss.co.za/index.php?link_id=21&slink_id=207&link_type=12&slink_type=12&tmpl_id=3

CIA (2008) *The World Factbook: Tanzania*. Available at: www.cia.gov/library/publications/the-world-factbook/geos/tz.html

Government of Tanzania (2006) Universal Communications Service Act of 2006.

Government of Tanzania (2008) Budget Speech. Presented by Minister for Finance and Economic Affairs Mustafa Mkulo to Parliament in June 2008. Available at: www.tanzania.go.tz/budgetspeech/2008/budgetspeech.pdf

*info*Dev/ITU (2008) Tanzania – The Converged Licensing Framework (Practice Note). *ICT Regulation Toolkit*. Available at: www.ictregulationtoolkit.org/en/PracticeNote.aspx?id=3128

ITU (International Telecommunication Union) (2008) Internet World Stats: Usage and Population Statistics. Available at: www.internetworldstats.com/africa.htm

MoID (Ministry of Infrastructure Development) (2004) Report on the Status of the National ICT Infrastructure Backbone, November 2004.

SEACOM (2008) SEACOM project update, 14 August. Available at: www.seacom.mu

SouthAfrica.info (2007) Seacom cable construction begins. *SouthAfrica.info*, 13 December. Available at: www.southafrica.info/business/economy/infrastructure/seacom-141107.htm

TCRA (Tanzania Communications Regulatory Authority) (2008) Telecommunication Statistics as at March 2008. Available at: www.tcra.go.tz/publications/telecom.html

Thomas, J. (2007) Population of Tanzania now 39 million. *IPP Media*, 14 November. Available at: www.ippmedia.com/ipp/guardian/2007/11/14/102444.html

Van Gorp, A. and Maitland, C. (2007) The Regulatory Design Problem Revisited: Tanzania's Pioneering Position in Africa. Paper submitted for the 35th Research Conference on Communication, Information and Internet Policy (TPRC), Arlington, USA, 28-30 September. Available at: web.si.umich.edu/tprc/papers/2007/711/VanGorpMaitland_TPRC07_TZ.pdf

World Bank (2006) ICT at a Glance: Tanzania. *Information and Communications for Development 2006: Global Trends and Policies*. Available at: www.worldbank.org/ic4d

UGANDA

Women of Uganda Network (WOUGNET) and Collaboration on International ICT Policy for East and Southern Africa (CIPESA)
Dorothy Okello and Wairagala Wakabi
www.wougnet.org; www.cipesa.org

Introduction

Uganda is a landlocked East African country which relies exclusively on satellite for international connectivity. With a low per capita income of USD 280, and high taxation on telecom services, it has only about six million mobile phone subscribers and 165,788 fixed lines. The regulator, the Uganda Communications Commission (UCC), has a universal service fund known as the Rural Communications Development Fund (RCDF), which has been used to set up phone booths, internet cafés, internet points of presence, information and communications technology (ICT) training centres, and websites for districts, among others. However, many parts of the country remain unserved, even though the country's teledensity has risen to 20%, from less than 12% in 2006.

The liberalisation of the telecom sector in Uganda came after the Communications Act of 1997, and saw the licensing of two national operators (MTN Uganda and Uganda Telecom), as well as a mobile operator (Celtel Uganda). The national operators had an exclusivity period that expired in 2005, and three more operators have since been licensed. One of these, Warid Telecom, started offering services in early 2008. HITS Telecom was expected to start offering services in the second half of 2008.

The liberalisation of the sector has created a very competitive environment and pushed prices to their lowest levels ever. Operators say that if the government were to reduce the taxation on mobile phone services from the current high of 30% – comprising 18% value added tax (VAT) and 12% excise duty – they would be able to make their services affordable to a greater number of Ugandans and expand their networks to some of the areas which are currently unserved. Some observers also believe that telephone services would become more affordable if the regulator were to implement effective oversight over interconnection rates.

The low level of access to the internet is attributed to high tariffs arising from the fact that connectivity is delivered through expensive satellite bandwidth. Only about 1.5% of Ugandans have access to the internet. And while 35% of universities have internet access, only 40% of this access is through broadband connectivity. Ultimately, access to ICTs, as well as their affordability, present some of the critical challenges facing Uganda as it seeks to enable more of its citizens to enter the information age.

Access and affordability challenges

Uganda is among those countries in Eastern and Southern Africa which are not connected to international fibre – primarily because the east coast of Africa does not yet have a link to international marine fibre-optic cable. According to figures from the Uganda Internet Service Providers Association (UISPA), satellite costs are currently USD 4,000-USD 5,000 per megabit per second (Mbps) of delivered access. Comparatively, countries that rely on fibre pay less than USD 100 per Mbps of access. Satellite technology does not only consign Ugandan users to high costs; it also constrains the kind of applications which can be used on the internet.

High internet costs

Figures from UCC show that while there has been strong growth in the number of internet service providers (ISPs) – more than 20 are currently licensed – subscriber numbers have not grown as fast. The number of fixed internet subscribers stands at less than 20,000, while the estimated users are close to two million. The slow growth is attributed to high start-up and usage fees, such as USD 99 for a dial-up 64 kilobits per second (Kbps) link for 20 hours per month; the high cost of computers; limited infrastructure, including fibre; low internet usage by government, schools, and health and agricultural institutions; low ICT literacy; a lack of local content on the internet; low income levels; and an electricity shortage in some parts of the country.[1]

Only a negligible proportion of Ugandan internet users access broadband. Indeed, dial-up is by far the most prevalent means of access for residential and small and medium enterprise (SME) subscribers, primarily due to its affordability, while dedicated leased lines and high-capacity digital subscriber lines (DSL) are primarily a preserve of non-governmental and corporate organisations. Very small aperture terminal (VSAT) or satellite-based access remains the most feasible means of access in remote locations. Wireless internet connectivity has slowly emerged as a popular alternative means of access in the country. A number of WiMAX networks are currently being rolled out, in addition to general packet radio service (GPRS) and code division multiple access (CDMA) platforms.

According to the UISPA, ISPs are looking at attracting greater volumes of subscribers by bringing down prices (I-Network, 2006). Since 2006 a collection of ISPs have been buying bandwidth in bulk, which means it lands in Uganda at a lower price. They have then been able to sell it to users at significantly lower costs.

Despite the high costs of connectivity, the regulator says there has been an increase in multimedia messaging (MMS) and short messaging (SMS) in the market, with over ten

1 Uganda Communications Commission (UCC): www.ucc.co.ug

content and value-added service providers in operation as of December 2007. The roll-out of third generation (3G) mobile started in 2007, and was expected to grow its subscriber base steadily through 2008. The last part of 2007 also witnessed a spurt in bandwidth capacity. Total international bandwidth increased to 344 Mbps (257.5 Mbps downlink and 86.9 Mbps uplink). There was also an increase in the deployment of wireless hotspots (using Wi-Fi or WiMAX). There are an estimated 30 hotspots in the country, 95% of which are in the Kampala metropolitan area (UCC, 2007).

Gunning for fibre

There is hope that by the end of 2009 the country will have built a national fibre network and linked to international fibre. Uganda is a signatory to the New Partnership for Africa's Development (NEPAD) protocol on development of open access fibre in Eastern and Southern Africa. It is also an active member in the consortium that is building the Eastern Africa Submarine Cable System (EASSy), one of the marine cables expected to start commercial operations in 2009.

Uganda Telecom and MTN Uganda have been among the longstanding promoters of EASSy, and through them Uganda is an active participant in the East African Backhaul System (EABS), which seeks to create a network of fibre from Mombasa on the Kenyan coast, through the capital Nairobi, and on to the Ugandan border town of Malaba. From here it flows to Kampala, then through to Rwanda, Burundi and Dar es Salaam on the Tanzanian coast. As part of the EABS, and the cooperation between Ugandan and regional companies in building fibre, MTN and Uganda Telecom are sharing fibre on segments of the system between the Kenyan and Rwandan borders.

Ugandan ICT Minister Dr. Ham Mulira has said that Uganda would welcome any marine cable that comes into operation. The thinking among government officials is that it would be advantageous to have access to multiple cable systems, as this would increase competition and result in lower prices and better quality of services. Uganda has completed phase one of its national data transmission backbone, which has linked a major part of the economic and administrative hub of the country. The second phase is supposed to be even more elaborate, following major routes and taking the cable to most of the important towns in the country. The ICT minister says the government will not rest until Uganda is fully connected to international submarine cables, which will reduce the cost of using the internet and turn Uganda's landlocked position from a competitive disadvantage to a competitive advantage (Government of Uganda, 2008).

Universal access fund

Uganda was one of the first countries in Africa to develop a policy on universal access to communications, covering ICTs (including telephony). The RCDF is one of the tools that has enabled the government to motivate and mobilise private sector investment into rural areas by offering subsidies and grants that act as investment incentives. The fund is the result of a 1% levy on operators' revenues. Through the provision of subsidies, the RCDF has supported the establishment of internet points of presence in twenty districts of Uganda, set up 54 district information portals, internet cafés in 55 districts, ICT training centres in 30 districts, 316 public pay phones, two internet connectivity institutions, and five telecentres.

However, RCDF managers say despite 80% of its initiatives being implemented in rural areas, Uganda's teledensity growth has mostly been happening in urban areas. Moreover, although RCDF support has facilitated the further spread of ICT facilities and services to less privileged areas and communities, women have benefited less compared to their male counterparts. The Rural Communications Development Policy (UCC, 2001) does not make specific consideration for gender issues. As such, the supported projects do not necessarily aim at addressing gender imbalances.

Basic infrastructure deficits

The lack of access to electricity and the high costs incurred by those who have access need to be addressed comprehensively if meaningful improvements in connectivity are to occur. Only about 6% of Ugandans are connected to the national electricity grid, with rural areas largely unconnected. The Ugandan telecom sector is also characterised by high operational costs: there is a shortage of supporting infrastructure, such as the road network, which is often in poor shape and covers only a small part of the country. In some areas, hilly terrain also pushes up operational costs, as do security issues. Add to that the lack of an infrastructure-sharing corporate culture and the costs really hit the roof. A common scenario is for up to three operators to erect masts in the same locality, or build parallel fibre-optic networks over hundreds of kilometres.

High taxation rates

Uganda's telephone sector is highly taxed. As mentioned, the country has a 12% excise duty on mobile phone services, in addition to the 18% VAT. In June 2006, it introduced a 5% duty on land-line phone services. The GSM Association (GSMA) says African nations such as Uganda will have to lower taxes on cellular operators and cut red tape to spur rapid penetration and help their economies expand faster. A study by the association said the ten markets with the highest taxes on mobile telephony worldwide were Turkey, Uganda, Brazil, Syria, Zambia, Tanzania, Argentina, Ecuador, Kenya and Ukraine. Fixed taxes paid at the time of subscription and tax charges paid after subscription by mobile users, in addition to traditional sales tax, variable taxes levied on mobile use like VAT, and taxes due on the importation and sale of mobile handsets, were found to be high in many African markets. In countries with high taxes – amounting to 25% to 30% of costs in Kenya, Uganda, Tanzania and Zambia – expansion of mobile phone services has been much slower than those with lower tariffs, such as Nigeria, Sudan, Egypt and South Africa (GSMA, 2006).

Uganda introduced excise duty on mobile phones in 2001. The national budget for the financial year 2008/2009 did not introduce any changes with respect to the excise duty. However, import duties have now been exempted for deep cycle batteries that are not sealed for use with solar equipment, computer printers and telecommunication equipment.

Action steps

There are a number of measures that could be adopted to promote greater and more equitable access to ICTs:

- The government should cut taxes on mobile phone services to make them more affordable.
- The government and the private sector need to redouble efforts and work more speedily to build fibre both nationally and at regional level.
- The government should step up interventions that offer infrastructure and services in rural and underserved areas, including through the RCDF.
- The government (in association with the private sector, civil society, universities and research institutions) needs to work on creating demand for ICTs by developing appropriate and affordable content and applications.
- Efforts must be undertaken to increase power supply and to reduce power tariffs.
- Universal access objectives, strategies and targets should specifically address gender equity issues as well as access for people with disabilities.

References

Fibre for Africa: www.fibreforafrica.net

Government of Uganda (2008) National Budget Speech, Financial Year 2008-2009, delivered 12 June.

GSMA (GSM Association) (2006) *Global Mobile Tax Review 2006-2007.* Available at: www.gsmworld.com/documents/tax/tax_report.pdf

I-Network (2006) *An Easy Guide to Internet Connectivity in Uganda.* Available at: www.i-network.or.ug/fixed-content/frontpage/introduction.html

UCC (Uganda Communications Commission) (2001) *Rural Communications Development Policy.* Kampala: UCC.

UCC (2007) *Status of the Communications Market December 2007.* Available at: www.ucc.co.ug/MarketReviewDecember2007.pdf

UWCI (Uganda Women's Caucus on ICT) (2007) *Assessment of the Rural Communications Development Fund (RCDF) from a Gender Perspective.* Kampala: WOUGNET.

Women of Uganda Network (WOUGNET): www.wougnet.org

URUGUAY

ObservaTIC (Faculty of Social Sciences, Universidad de la República)
Ana Laura Rivoir
www.observatic.edu.uy

Introduction

Since the early 20th century, Uruguay has been considered a developed country in the Latin American context. But this status has deteriorated over the last decades due to policies that have given priority to economic growth over a more comprehensive view of development. In this regard, the view that the market would solve the problem of access to information and communications technologies (ICTs) was prevalent.

ICT infrastructure and access are relatively good in Uruguay, thanks to a flat geography, and to the fact that half the population lives in the capital Montevideo. Uruguay has a state-owned company, the National Telecommunications Administration (ANTEL), which holds the monopoly on fixed-line telephony. As a public enterprise, ANTEL shows satisfactory performance as far as efficiency is concerned and has achieved high coverage for fixed digital telephony. The mobile sector has been liberalised and various companies coexist, offering mobile access to 80% of the population. This gives the country a good basis for connectivity.

However, the fact that the population outside of Montevideo is scattered all over the country has negatively affected access, as it increases infrastructure costs per user. A programme for connecting schools called CEIBAL (*Conectividad Educativa de Informática Básica para el Aprendizaje en Línea*), which is analysed in this report, is intended to broaden access to infrastructure with a wireless network running parallel to ANTEL's. While its focus is schools, this programme offers great promise for widespread social inclusion through ICTs.

ICT policies for development in Uruguay

Information and knowledge society (IKS) policies and initiatives in Latin America have been marred by a technocentric approach which focuses on improving access to infrastructure and technology. This is indispensable, but not enough: as we know, in order to contribute to development it is necessary to bear in mind what ICTs will be used for. Otherwise public funds that have been invested merely lead to the creation of new consumers (Finquelievich, 2003; Mística, 2003; Mansell, 2002; Rivoir, 2005).

Although there is an awareness of this in Uruguay, IKS policies have been fragmented. In 2000, there was the intention to create a committee focusing on the information society, and to implement a strategy. But this policy lacked continuity, and there are records of activities only until 2003, even though some programmes are still going on today. There are also community-driven initiatives, which, although they could be considered successful, are unlikely to become as wide-ranging and far-reaching as national policies need to be. Since 2005, however, with the arrival of the first left-leaning government in the history of the country, IKS policies have gained momentum and new strategies and organisations have been created, including CEIBAL (AGESIC, 2007).

CEIBAL

CEIBAL is the first programme in the world to grant a laptop to each child and teacher at state schools in a whole country. It is the result of the One Laptop per Child (OLPC)[1] initiative, the brainchild of the Massachusetts Institute of Technology. The XO, as the laptop is called, is specially designed to be used by children, and has been adapted to suit CEIBAL's needs. It allows schoolchildren to be connected to each other and to the internet, and the laptops are loaded with educational software.

The implementation of CEIBAL started in the middle of 2007, with a pilot project in a school in Cardal, a small village of 1,500 inhabitants. Currently, 50% of the country has been covered by the programme, which involves a huge deployment of resources – financial, institutional and human. It is scheduled to be implemented in Montevideo by the end of 2009.

The programme was an initiative of the president of Uruguay, Tabaré Vázquez, who announced it during his inauguration as a means of promoting social inclusion. But the government officials in charge have had to develop the strategy on the fly, while at the same time handling operational and administrative challenges, dealing with team-building, and coordinating existing activities, amongst other things.

Some preliminary conclusions can be drawn from this experience:

- It is important that the authorities had a vision of ICTs as a mechanism for social inclusion. It overcomes the linear and simplistic view prevailing among some segments of the population and its leaders, which holds that first we should satisfy basic needs and then provide access to technology. But children, and poor people in general, also have the right to access ICTs. Waiting for other development problems to be solved might mean that the time for "technology rights" never arrives.
- The government and, in particular, the president, run a risk when announcing these sorts of programmes when they are not an electoral promise, or part of the public

1 laptop.org/index.es.html

agenda or a social demand. Its characterisation as an initiative for social inclusion was important, as it is crucial for these actions to reduce inequalities. It aims to not only bridge the technological divide specifically, but also other existing divides, such as social, economic and cultural ones.

- The laptop was given to both schoolchildren and their teachers. This is an important element not provided for in the OLPC programme. It shows respect for the teachers, who can have access to a tool which not all of them are familiar with. Teachers are crucial in that they need to stimulate interest amongst the children. The importance of this role has been shown in a recent study on the experience in Cardal (ANTEL, 2007).
- The training of teachers has been an important consideration from the start and was put into action together with the distribution of laptops. However, it was difficult to train all teachers before the distribution of the laptops. This has generated much anxiety, insecurity and also discontent among teachers, with varying degrees of acceptance and use depending on individual teachers.
- The management of CEIBAL is the responsibility of an interdisciplinary committee with members from various institutions, which has allowed the input of different perspectives and dynamics. One of the strengths of the committee is that it is formed by educators, engineers and managers of the different state organisations involved. This boosts the initiative, and helps overcome obstacles more effectively, even if the process is more time consuming and not devoid of conflict.
- The fact that the programme has been developed without consulting its participants has turned out to be negative in terms of their involvement and commitment. There are also difficulties arising from the lack of a clear formulation of work strategies and methods. Teacher training and content, for example, have been developed along the way. But it is also doubtful that it could have been done in any other way. If proper public consultation processes were followed, involving teachers, politicians, technicians, professionals and public officials, the programme might never have got off the ground.

As several authors have pointed out, we need to stress the importance of the generation of e-content, which means paying attention to people's knowledge and capacity to use ICTs. People must be considered producers of information and knowledge, and not merely as consumers (Gómez et al., 2003; Mística, 2003; Camacho, 2001; Martínez, 2001). Others hold the view that for the democratisation of knowledge, social participation is necessary, not only in the design of policies, but of technology too (APC/ITeM, 2007; García Urea, 2007; Araya, 2003).

A factor that seems to be helping to surmount any difficulties that arise with the CEIBAL programme is the wide acceptance it has found in the population, above all among children. They have been visibly excited and enthusiastic about the novelty of using a laptop.

Taking advantage of the programme in a way that benefits the population more broadly is key. Because the children take the laptops home, communities can benefit. As a result, there have been various proposals (e.g., from the government, social organisations and the university) to encourage wider application of the programme. The most interesting and promising one is called the CEIBAL Support Network (RapCEIBAL),[2] which offers volunteer support that has contributed to its efficiency and smoothness, and encourages teachers and the population in general to take ownership of the plan.

Action steps

There is no doubt that CEIBAL will materially improve access to technology in Uruguay, and could form the basis for any initiative aiming at social inclusion through ICTs. Action should be taken to broaden the programme's opportunities for individuals, groups or communities.

However, several issues are important. In the first place, it is essential to stimulate the meaningful use of the technology, and go beyond mere access. It is therefore very important to offer useful content and services for both children and adults in order to improve their quality of life – satisfying needs, solving problems, and opening up opportunities. But to do this, a cultural change is necessary, so that we begin to see ourselves as producers and not just consumers of content.

In the second place, although access to information and knowledge through the internet is very important, it does not reflect the diversity of today's world – neither culturally nor linguistically. Through CEIBAL, children and teachers should be able to obtain and produce information about their society, its history, its culture, and in their own language. The production of this information should be stimulated and funded in various ways (e.g., by local industry, the academic community, or independent professionals). Some initiatives have been taken – for instance, development of digital content for the programme has been put out to tender – but there should be many more of them.

In the third place, more people should become involved in the programme, which is vast in scope. The state should continue to seek the cooperation of interested social actors and diverse stakeholders. There is still great potential to involve citizens, social organisations and various state institutions.

Finally, a central aspect of any policy is to monitor and evaluate it in a way that problems and obstacles can be overcome, or positive and successful processes strengthened. There is room to improve the monitoring and evaluation of CEIBAL.

To sum up, CEIBAL constitutes a major step towards social inclusion through ICTs. Its impact is unforeseeable, as there are no precedents of a similar policy. One thing is certain: it is crucial to include diverse perspectives and stakeholders in the programme. The results will depend on the course of future policy decisions. ■

2 rapceibal.blogspot.com

References

AGESIC (Agencia para el Desarrollo del Gobierno de Gestión Electrónica y la Sociedad de la Información y del Conocimiento) (2007) *Libro Verde de la SIC en Uruguay.* Montevideo: AGESIC. Available at: www.agesic.gub.uy

ANTEL (Administración Nacional de Telecomunicaciones) (2007) *Evaluación del Programa de Conectividad Educativa.* Montevideo: ANTEL.

Araya, R. (2003) *Comunidades y portales ciudadanos: ¿Para que? Reflexiones desde una visión social sobre Internet.* Available at: redistic.org/brecha/es/17_-_Rub%E9n_Araya.html

APC/ITeM (Association for Progressive Communications/Third World Institute) (2007) *Global Information Society Watch 2007.* Available at: www.globaliswatch.org/download

Camacho, K. (2001) *Internet: ¿una herramienta para el cambio social?* Mexico City: FLACSO.

CEIBAL: www.ceibal.edu.uy/portal/index.htm

Castells, M. (2000) *La era de la información: Economía, sociedad y cultura. Vol. I: La sociedad red.* Barcelona: Alianza Editorial.

Finquelievich, S. (2003) *Indicadores de la Sociedad de la Información en Educación, Ciencia, Cultura, Comunicación e Información, en América Latina y el Caribe.* RICYT/OCT. Available at: www.itu.int/dms_pub/itu-s/md/03/wsispc2/doc/S03-WSISPC2-DOC-0007!!MSW-S.doc

García Urea, S. (2007) *La Democratización Tecnológica y la Inclusión Social: Un Análisis desde lo Sociocultural.* Available at: www.analitica.com/premium/ediciones2007/4876591.asp

Gascó-Hernández, M., Equiza-Lopez, F. and Acevedo-Ruiz, M. (2007) *Information Communication Technologies and Human Development: Opportunities and Challenges.* IGI Publishing. Available at: www.igi-pub.com/books/additional.asp?id=6454&title=Preface&col=preface

Gómez, R., Delgadillo, K. and Stoll, K. (2003) *Telecentros... ¿Para qué? Lecciones sobre telecentros comunitarios en América Latina y el Caribe.* IDRC. Available at: www.idrc.ca/es/ev-11917-201-1-DO_TOPIC.html

Martínez, J. (2001) Internet y políticas públicas socialmente relevantes: ¿Por qué, cómo y en qué incidir? In Bonilla, M. and Cliche, G. (eds.), *Internet y Sociedad en América Latina y el Caribe.* FLACSO/IDRC.

Mansell, R. (2002) From Digital Divides to Digital Entitlements in Knowledge Societies. *Current Sociology,* 50(3), pp. 407-426. Available at: csi.sagepub.com/cgi/content/abstract/50/3/407

Mística (2003) Comunidad virtual trabajando la Internet con visión social. In RedISTIC, *Otro lado de la brecha: Perspectivas latinoamericanas y del Caribe ante la CMSI.* Caracas: RedISTIC. Available at: redistic.org/index.htm?body=proyectosj

One Laptop per Child: laptop.org/index.es.html

RapCEIBAL: rapCEIBAL.blogspot.com

Rivero, M. (2004) *State Role on ICTs promotion in developing countries: General patterns and the Uruguayan experience.* Working Papers, General Series No. 410. The Hague: Institute of Social Studies. Available at: ideas.repec.org/p/iss/wpaper/410.html

Rivoir, A. (2005) The Information and Knowledge Society in Latin America and the Caribbean: Different Approaches and their Implications for Policies. In Third World Institute, *Information Society for the South: Vision or Hallucination?* Montevideo: ITeM. Available at: www.choike.org/nuevo_eng/informes/3592.html

UZBEKISTAN

GIPI Uzbekistan
Imam Zaynuddin

Introduction

Over the last decade, Uzbekistan has made considerable progress in developing information and communications technology (ICT) infrastructure. A number of projects are being carried out in different areas, including those involving state institutions and agencies. Substantial work has also been done on legislation. There are currently a number of highly qualified ICT specialists in the country, and there is strong cooperation with international institutions in the field.

However, the country still lacks an adequate ICT policy to guide the development of ICTs. This is having a negative impact on citizens' rights. This report draws a picture of the ICT landscape in Uzbekistan regarding access to technology, and then goes on to suggest several issues that need to be attended to in order to address the gaps in the legislative and policy framework.

Access to technology

It is unfair to compare Uzbekistan with developed countries in terms of ICT development. However, comparisons to developing countries, especially those located in the region, show significant progress in the area. Uzbekistan is extensive (447,400 square kilometres), and has the largest population in Central Asia (about 28 million as of mid-2008). Its communication network is said to cover all of the cities, towns, and regional centres in the country, and 95% of rural settlements. The number of regular internet users exceeds two million.[1]

Uzbek official statistics report the following:

- During January through March this year (2008), ICT services earned USD 210 million (foreign direct investment in this period amounted to USD 41.6 million).
- As of 1 April 2008, the number of base phones equalled 1,818,000 units (7.04 per 100 inhabitants).
- 85% of telephone networks are digitalised.
- The number of internet service providers (ISPs) stood at 797.
- The estimated number of active internet users was about 2.133 million (78.8 per 1,000 inhabitants) compared to 1.7 million in 2007.
- All public offices are connected to the internet.
- Three Digital Signature Registration Centres (DSRC) were operational, one of which is privately owned. The reported number of signatures issued to date is 12,688.
- The general speed of international access was 362 megabits per second (Mbps).[2]

Table 1 illustrates the growth in internet services, in terms of both ISPs and public access points.

Mobile

The mobile sector's growth over the past year is impressive. The number of mobile subscribers as of June 2007 was 3.537 million, while one year later the number had increased to 8.316 million (over 30% of the total population). At the beginning of 1996 there were 3,804 mobile customers, and only one cellular operator in the country. During 1996 five new operators appeared. The growth in the number of operators pushed up the number of customers, which reached 21,555 by the end of 1998. The cost of services was also reduced considerably – from USD 105 per 100 minutes in 1995 to USD 20 by the end of 2000. In 1997 six operators were active on the market. They utilised the two most popular standards – digital advanced mobile phone system (D-AMPS), specifically the IS-136 standard, and the global system for mobile communications (GSM). In September 2001 Perfectum Mobile started its operations using the code division multiple access (CDMA) standard. This year the largest cellular operators were licensed to offer third generation (3G) services. Currently the cost of a one-minute call is on average only USD 0.02.[3]

National backbone

One of the vital questions when approaching the issue of ICT for development is the choice of technology. For developing countries, the problem is made more complicated by

1 www.infocom.uz

2 www.infocom.uz

3 www.infocom.uz

Table 1: Number of ISPs and public access points

	2000	2001	2002	2003	2004	2005	2006	2007	2008
Public access points	-	-	90	125	348	463	350	579	799
ISPs	32	44	135	263	416	539	430	693	797

a lack of capital to invest in the area. A solution to this is twofold. Either a country can subsidise ICT development from a national budget (which is indeed difficult because of the shortage of the money available) or attract foreign investment (which is also not easy, taking into account the unwillingness of the foreign private sector to enter risky markets, as is the case in Uzbekistan).

In Uzbekistan the Programme for Computerisation and Informatisation implements several projects in the area. The programme allocates funds from the state budget, and receives grants mainly from the Japanese and Chinese governments. One of its key tasks is to replace ordinary lines with fibre-optic lines across the entire country (over 3,500 kilometres). By doing this, it is connecting major centres in the country, and increasing capacity significantly. The anticipated length of fibre lines by the year 2010 will be 10,000 kilometres.[4]

Broadband technologies

In March 2005 Sharq Telecom first introduced asymmetric digital subscriber line (ADSL) technology to private customers. The service quickly became available to customers in most of Tashkent's districts. Over the next several months three more ISPs (Sarkor Telecom, Technoprosystem and Buzton Telecom) had joined the ADSL "club". ADSL services are available to customers in the majority of Uzbekistan's regions (at least for large cities). However, they are most popular in Tashkent, Samarkand, Bukhara and the Fergana valley. Voice over internet protocol (VoIP) services are also available in major towns.

In 2005 Sharq and Buzton began offering Wi-Fi services (ADSL2+), and a WiMAX pilot project was initiated by Cisco in 2006.

IP-exchange network

In 2004, the first – and so far the only – internet protocol (IP)-exchange network was introduced in the capital Tashkent. It is used by 20 major ISPs in the city, resulting in some 59,422 gigabits per second (Gbps) of traffic in 2007.

Domain names in .uz

The administrator of Uzbekistan's country code top-level domain (ccTLD), .uz, reports the number of domain names as 6,550 as of 22 April 2008.[5] Another source, Voydod,[6] reports 7,400 active domestic domains.

4 www.infocom.uz

5 www.cctld.uz/stat

6 voydod.uz

E-commerce

In 2006, the first electronic payment system for local services was introduced by PayNet, which initially established 300 points in the capital. Demand for the service was so high that within two years PayNet had extended its services to all major towns in the country, and is now focusing on rural areas. The total number of PayNet points is currently estimated at 10,000.[7]

By the end of 2007, the first online purchasing system was introduced in Uzbekistan by eKarmon, following the passing of legislation on electronic payments in 2005 and 2007. The growth in the number of online transactions is suggested by the growth in demand for digital signature registration.

Policy and legislative framework

The Uzbekistan government approved an ICT development programme for the period 2002-2010 in June 2002 (Government of Uzbekistan, 2003). Under the programme the following goals for internet connectivity have been laid down for 2010:

- Installing more than 45,000 internet access points
- Providing access to international networks of speeds greater than 512 Mbps
- Achieving an internet penetration rate of 11.9 for every 100 citizens
- Connecting 100% of all state institutions and 60% of rural administrations to the internet
- Extending ICT services to all cities and villages in Uzbekistan by 2010.

A national database that will collect laws and regulations, statistics, patent rights, and financial statements of listed companies, amongst other things, is planned. The programme also deals with training specialists in the ICT field.

However, while numerous laws and decrees deal with things like ICTs, e-commerce and media in Uzbekistan, a general policy on ICT development has not yet been developed. As a result, the legislation that does exist is uneven, and has a negative impact on citizens' communication rights (for instance, in the area of a citizen's right to receive information, to prevent the circulation of defamatory information, or to protect intellectual property). Moreover, with the growing impact of ICTs on economic life, the weak legislative framework not only slows down economic development but compels Uzbek users to sign up for services located outside the country.

7 www.infocom.uz

Table 2: Number of domains

	2003	2004	2005	Jun. 2006	Sep. 2007	Apr. 2008
No. of domains	700	2,800	2,704	2,800	3,940	6,550

Source: ru.infocom.uz/more.php?id=A2270_0_1_0_M

Action steps

Uzbekistan has a number of areas that require attention in order to secure citizen rights in the information society, such as:

- Liberalising state policy dealing with the internet, which includes securing open access to the internet for citizens, and ensuring the right to exchange information online.
- Getting government institutions online, and making state information available. This also refers to public libraries, schools, and other social and cultural entities.
- Defining the legal status of information uploaded onto the internet or circulated online.
- Preventing publicly harmful content from being uploaded or circulated online (in particular, the dissemination of defamatory and obscene material) and creating normative conditions for monitoring online activities in this regard.
- Creating effective copyright protection and protection of other exclusive intellectual property rights for material uploaded onto the internet.
- Protecting private data, including that accumulated by ISPs.
- Regulating e-commerce, including recognising the legal effect of transactions entered into online.

While establishing a legal framework for ICTs in Uzbekistan, it is important to consider similar laws adopted in other countries and the region to ensure legislative uniformity across borders where appropriate.

References

Government of Uzbekistan (2003) Statement of the Government Delegation of the Republic of Uzbekistan at the World Summit on the Information Society, Geneva. Available at: www.itu.int/wsis/geneva/coverage/statements/uzbekistan/uz.html

infoCOM.UZ: www.infocom.uz

Uzbekistan domain name registrar: www.cctld.uz

UZINFOCOM Computerization and IT Developing Center: www.uzinfocom.uz/en

Voydod: www.voydod.uz

ZAMBIA

Panos Southern Africa
Caesar Jere
www.panos.org.zm

Introduction

This report is an overview of information and communications technology (ICT) initiatives in Zambia. It examines ICT indicators in three key areas: telephony, broadcasting and computer technology. The author outlines achievements and challenges in ICT accessibility and participation. Emphasis is placed on the regulatory and policy frameworks and the infrastructural network – how they support or inhibit the participation of the majority of the people, especially in the outlying rural areas.

The report has been compiled mainly through the use of existing documents on policy and regulatory frameworks on ICTs in Zambia, online research, interviews with persons in key institutions in the ICT industry, newspaper reports and other relevant literature on ICTs in Zambia and globally. The author acknowledges the support he received from Panos Southern Africa and other concerned parties.

Country situation

Once known as Northern Rhodesia, Zambia attained independence from British colonial rule in 1964 and was ruled by President Kenneth Kaunda until 1996, when Frederick Chiluba assumed power in a multiparty election ending Kaunda's one-party rule. In 2001, Levy Mwanawasa ascended to power. He ruled for seven years until he died in August, 2008.

Since Mwanawasa took over power, Zambia appears to have been on a track of economic recovery following the mismanagement of the economy by the Kaunda and Chiluba regimes. The country's poor economic performance was also the result of a rise in world oil prices and falling copper prices, on which Zambia's economy depends. At independence, Zambia was a middle-income country, but by the 1990s it had become one of the poorest countries in the world. In 2006, however, the country managed to reduce the double-digit inflation that had been recorded since the late 1980s to a single digit of about 9%. Macroeconomic indicators appear to have stabilised, with an average economic growth of 5% to 6% in the last four years (Times of Zambia, 2007).

It can be assumed that Zambia's economy, which had been on the decline for many years, was unable to support the growth of many industries, including ICTs. However, bold steps were taken by the government from 2004 to enhance the ICT sector, including a reduction of duty on computer equipment, introduction of an ICT policy and a project to lay a fibre-optic backbone.

Notwithstanding, there are still many challenges that the ICT industry faces, among them the lack of an appropriate infrastructure to support the growth of the industry, and the absence of electricity, good roads and reliable communication equipment. These factors have hindered ICT accessibility, especially in rural areas where the majority of Zambians live. At the same time, the operational and licence fees charged by regulatory authorities to service providers are high. These tariffs have been passed on to the consumer, making access prohibitive to many people. These challenges need to be addressed to enhance ICT participation.

Policy context

Broadcasting and telecommunications policy reforms

Liberal market reforms were introduced in 1991 to stimulate the liberalisation and deregulation of various industries. This was in line with the ruling Movement for Multiparty Democracy (MMD) election manifesto of moving away from Kaunda's socialist policies. The broadcasting and telecommunications sectors were no exception (Kasoma, 1997).

This saw the enactment of the 1993 Zambia National Broadcasting Corporation (ZNBC) Licensing Regulations Act, the 1994 Telecommunications Act, and the 1994 Radio Communications Act. These legal instruments were designed to liberalise and deregulate the communications sector. Prior to this shift, ZNBC was a monopoly that was unchallenged. However, with the coming of liberal reforms, a number of radio and television stations emerged to challenge ZNBC's monopoly (Banda, 1998). The Telecommunications Act of 1994 established the Communications Authority of Zambia (CAZ) as the independent regulatory body to supervise and promote the provision of telecommunication services. Under this act, the authority is mandated to manage and administer the utilisation of radio frequency spectrum.

In 2002, the Independent Broadcasting Authority (IBA) Act and the ZNBC Amendment Act were passed. However, the implementation of both acts has been frustrated by a lack of political will, and the state has yet to submit names of prospective board members to parliament for ratification. The old ZNBC board members appointed by the government under the 1987 act continue to serve, effectively defying the provisions of the 2002 ZNBC Amendment Act. This compelled the media fraternity to take the state to court in an effort to force it to submit the recommended names of both the IBA and new ZNBC board members to parliament for endorsement.

Initially the media community won the case in December 2004 when the information and broadcasting minister was ordered by the court to send the names to parliament for ratification (Matibini, 2006). However, the government appealed against the ruling and the Supreme Court overturned it in March 2007 on grounds that "the minister could not be used as a rubber stamp or conveyor belt in the process of appointments of the two boards" (Musenge, 2007). Since then, there have been no serious efforts to implement the two boards, as the current set-up seems ideal for the state's political expediency: to control ZNBC as a political mouthpiece for the ruling party.

Impact of technological change

Convergence and digitalisation have brought together media platforms that were once isolated. For instance, content which was conventionally classified as falling under the realm of print media is now suited to mobile and audiovisual internet services, while broadcasters are increasingly making data services accessible through the TV set. In other words, "content has become *cross-media* or, as generally put, *multimedia*" (Arino & Ahlert, 2004).

Owing to these technological changes, policy and regulatory frameworks all over the world are under pressure to adopt structures that respond to technological convergence (Collins & Murroni, 1996; Levy, 2001; Golding & Murdock, 1999; Steemers, 1998). The Independent Communications Authority of South Africa (ICASA), which is a converged regulator of telecommunication and broadcasting, is a typical example in Africa (Taylor & Berger, 2006).

The Zambian IBA Act is a replica of the outdated IBA Act of 1993 of South Africa. There are suggestions that the act be repealed and be replaced by one that will consider converged regulation for all communication sectors (MCT, 2006).

ICT policy

Zambia's ICT policy was adopted in 2005 and subsequently launched in March 2007. The ICT policy framework suggests proposals to re-establish the regulatory framework of all communication sectors to recognise convergence of technologies through the enactment of an ICT Bill. The policy seeks, among other issues, to bridge the digital divide between Zambians living in urban and rural areas (MCT, 2006).

The policy envisages the transformation of Zambia into an economy based on information and knowledge, supported by the consistent development of and access to ICTs for all citizens by 2030. The policy informs the framework for Zambia's participation in the global economy. As it states: "At the national level, the importance of ICT in national development is demonstrated by the approval of the ICT Policy and the inclusion of ICT as a priority sector in the Fifth National Development Plan 2006-2010" (MCT, 2006, p. ii).

Access to ICTs

Technology change and broadcasting market influence

The advent of convergence has seen the upswing of a competitive communications market in Zambia, especially in the broadcasting and telecommunications sectors. Satellite broadcasting opened up in 1995 when MultiChoice South Africa entered the Zambian airwaves by transmitting analogue and digital satellite pay television for the first time in the country. For well-to-do Zambians, this was a point of departure from being permanently exposed to ZNBC to a situation where they could enjoy the many genres offered by the new satellite services.

The implication of this challenge was that ZNBC had to rethink its programming if it was to continue attracting an audience and advertisers on whom it depended for its survival. ZNBC radio reaches out to 80% of the country, while its single television channel is mostly limited to the main cities and towns, and has yet to reach most rural areas. Some rural communities have access to community radio, an alternative media platform, whose presence is increasing rapidly in the country.

ZNBC has also been challenged by other new entrants, such as the relatively affordable digital satellite pay TV service British Gateway Television (GTV), and My TV. GTV has been instrumental in bringing a competitive atmosphere to pay television, which was previously dominated by MultiChoice.

After three months of being operational in Zambia, GTV recorded 4,000 subscribers in December 2007 (Chitala, 2007). GTV offers different packages that can also be accessed by low-income groups. This has forced MultiChoice to introduce affordable family "bouquets". My TV, which became operational in 2006, had a subscriber base of 5,000 in January 2008 (Chitala, 2008). It has fewer channels than MultiChoice or GTV.

Rural access

Access to ICTs, particularly the internet and telephone services, is still at its lowest in the rural areas compared to urban areas. The lack of infrastructure such as electricity, telephone lines, communications equipment and road networks has made it difficult for rural communities to access the information economy. Less than 3% of rural areas in Zambia have access to electricity, yet about 70% of Zambians live in rural areas (Phiri & Chanda, 2008).

Most rural areas lack ICT outlets such as internet cafés and telecentres, which are concentrated in the urban areas. However, with the advent of mobile telephony, the situation appears to have improved in a number of areas, and communities are able to use mobile phones at public make-shift phone kiosks. Some people in rural communities now own mobile handsets, which have become cheaper compared to five years ago when an average set cost about USD 300 – the same now costing about USD 50.

Comparatively, urban areas have better infrastructure and more people have access to the internet and phone services.

Zamtel monopoly

The state-owned Zambia Telecommunications Company (Zamtel) is the sole provider of land-line telephony. Zamtel is also the only authorised company that provides an international gateway to MTN and Zain, the two mobile phone

Table 1: Mobile phone access			
Period	Subscribers	Per 100 inhabitants	Growth rate
1 March-31 March, 2008	2,653,203	22.66	6.9%
Source: Quarterly ICT Indicators (CAZ, 2008)			

Table 2: Public switched telephony network (PSTN) access			
Period	Subscribers	Per 100 inhabitants	Growth rate
1 January-31 March 2008	90,951	0.77	-0.91%
Source: Quarterly ICT Indicators (CAZ, 2008)			

Table 3: Internet access			
Period	Subscribers	Per 100 inhabitants	Growth rate
1 January-31 March, 2008	16,464	0.14	-2.17%
Source: Quarterly ICT Indicators (CAZ, 2008)			

service providers. However, MTN and Zain have expressed concern over high tariffs charged by Zamtel for using its gateway, the Mwembeshi satellite (Cho, 2007).

Additionally, Zamtel distorts competition by being both a fixed network and mobile phone operator: Cell-Z is its mobile arm, with automatic access to its own gateway. This was acknowledged by the Zambia Competition Commission in 2003 in its submission to the Select Committee on Transport and Communication: "The position of Zamtel means that it has the power to prevent, restrict or distort competitor access to this essential infrastructure which was built with public funds" (Cho, 2007). Zain and MTN have made appeals to allow them to use their own gateways, but this has drawn a negative response from the authorities (Mwale, 2008).

On the internet platform, which is generally open to competition, Zamtel's dominance as a fixed-line operator eliminates the level playing field. Since most of the internet services in Zambia are through dial-up connections using the fixed-line telephone network controlled by Zamtel, the company offers better access conditions to its own internet subsidiary than to competitors (Cho, 2007). As a result, it can be argued that Zamtel, representing the state, is a dominant player in the political economy of the communication landscape in Zambia (Golding & Murdock, 2000).

Nevertheless, despite Zamtel's market influence, its mobile and internet services still remain unattractive to most consumers. This could be attributed to a sloppy working culture and bureaucratic tendencies adopted from government (Zamtel is a former government department). Currently Zamtel has the lowest number of mobile subscribers, standing at 155,000 (Mwape, 2008). Zain, from the Middle East, which took over Celtel in July 2008, had the highest subscriber base of 1.3 million in January 2008 (Shacinda, 2007). MTN, a South African company, had a subscriber base of 110,000 in December 2006, which rose by 34% in March 2008.

Internet

There are many internet service providers (ISPs) in Zambia. However, the majority are corporate providers, and include key players such as Zamnet, Coppernet and Zamtel. While Zambia was among the pioneers of internet in sub-Saharan Africa outside South Africa in the early 1990s, this advantage has not been exploited (MCT, 2006).

Because internet cafés and telecentres are mainly concentrated in urban areas, this leaves the rural population with literally no access worth recording. The reason for this disparity is the lack of infrastructural growth to support ICT enhancement and accessibility in rural communities. Another factor is the high cost of operating licences (USD 40,000) charged by CAZ to ISPs. This amount is prohibitive to many Zambians who wish to invest in this service.

Fibre-optic access

In response to the imperative to bridge the digital divide between urban and rural areas, the government, through the state-owned Zamtel and the Zambia Electricity Supply Corporation (ZESCO), has embarked on an initiative to install a fibre-optic cable system across the country. This system will enable the transmission of various forms of electronic data over longer distances at higher speeds, essentially feeding into all forms of communication platforms: computers, television, radio, telephony and other related technologies (Mwale, 2008; Kanyungu, 2008). The fibre network will offer options for international connectivity and will link to the Eastern Africa Submarine Cable System (EASSy) project (Kanyungu, 2008).

Action steps

The ICT industry in Zambia is still struggling – especially owing to the fact that participation is still very low in the rural areas where 70% of Zambia's 10.1 million people reside. It is therefore critical to scale up rural ICT infrastructural support programmes, including electrification, building accessible roads, and rolling out communication equipment, in order to enhance the presence of ICTs in rural communities.

Additionally, regulatory practice that inhibits access to ICTs should be shed – for instance, Zamtel's gateway monopoly and the high licence costs for internet operators. This will genuinely liberalise the market and promote competition, ultimately passing the benefits of reduced costs of services on to consumers.

It is gratifying to note the remarkable efforts made by the government to promote ICT participation. The development of an ICT policy, the installation of the fibre backbone and introduction of ICT training in schools are typical examples. However, the support of the corporate world, non-governmental organisations, the donor community and the general public at large remains vital if ICT participation is to be enhanced in line with the objectives of the World Summit on the Information Society (WSIS).

References

Arino, M. and Ahlert, C. (2004) Beyond Broadcasting: The Digital Future of Public Service Broadcasting. *Prometheus*, 22(4), pp. 394-395.

Banda, F. 1998. Broadcasting in Zambia. In Opoku-Mensah, A. (ed.), *Up in the Air: The State of Broadcasting in Southern Africa.* Harare: Holdings.

Central Statistical Office: www.zamstats.gov.zm

Chitala, N. (2007) GTV subscriber base grows to 4,000. *Zambia Daily Mail*, 7 December, p. 4.

Chitala, N. (2008) My TV 'eyes' LuSE. *Zambia Daily Mail*, 24 January, p. 4.

Cho (2007) Zamtel's monopoly...why I oppose it. *Zambian Economist*, 22 July. Available at: zambian-economist.blogspot.com/2007/07/zamtels-monopolywhy-i-oppose-it.html

Collins, R. and Murroni, C. (1996) *New Media, New Policies.* Cambridge: Polity.

CAZ (Communications Authority of Zambia) (2008) Quarterly ICT Indicators. Available at: www.caz.zm

Golding, P. and Murdock, G. (2000) Culture, Communications and Political Economy. In Herman, E.S. and McChesney, R.W. (eds.), *The Global Media: The New Missionaries of Corporate Capitalism.* London: Creative Print & Design.

Government of Zambia (2002a) Independent Broadcasting Authority (IBA) Bill, Act 17 of 2002.

Government of Zambia (2002b) Zambia National Broadcasting Corporation (ZNBC) Amendment Bill, Act 20 of 2002.

Kanyungu, S. (2008) Zesco fibre project II to consume $30m. *Times of Zambia*, 11 April, p. 7.

Kasoma, F.P. (1997) Communication and Press Freedom in Zambia. In Eribo, F. and Jong-Ebot, W. (eds.), *Press Freedom and Communication in Africa.* Trenton: Africa World.

Levy, D. (2001) *Europe's Digital Revolution: Broadcasting Regulation, the EU and the Nation State.* London: Routledge.

Matibini, P. (2006) *The Struggle for Media Law Reforms in Zambia.* Ndola: Mission Press.

MCT (Ministry of Communications and Transport) (2006) National Information and Communication Technology Policy. Lusaka: Ministry of Communications and Transport. Available at: www.mct.gov.zm/pdf/ict.pdf

Ministry of Information and Broadcasting (1996, 1999) Policy Statements.

MTN Zambia: www.mtnzambia.co.zm/index

Musenge, L. (2007) Minister can veto IBA. *Zambia Daily Mail*, 16 March, p. 1.

Mwale, C. (2008) Bridging the digital divide through ICTs. *Zambia Daily Mail*, 16 January, p. 9.

Mwape, N. (2008) Zamtel optic fibre to improve network. *Zambia Daily Mail*, 6 August, p. 4.

Phiri, B. and Chanda, M. (2008) Zambia is not benefiting from mineral revenues, says Levy. *The Post*, 12 January, p. 4.

Shacinda, S. (2007) Celtel Zambia to list 20 pct shares, increase users. *Reuters*, 5 December. Available at: www.reuters.com/article/rbssTechMediaTelecomNews/idUSL0524275820071205

Steemers, J. (1998) *Changing Channels: The Prospects for Television in a Digital World.* Luton: University of Luton Press.

Taylor, A. and Berger, G. (2006) *Mixed Signals: The State of Broadcasting in Southern Africa.* Lusaka: Panos.

Times of Zambia (2007) Economic growth to benefit all – Levy. *Times of Zambia*, 23 October, p. 1.

Zain Zambia: www.zm.zain.com/en/get-connected/coverage

47863467R00113

Made in the USA
Charleston, SC
19 October 2015